THE BUSINESS OF CONSUMPTION

Studies in Social, Political, and Legal Philosophy
General Editor: James P. Sterba, University of Notre Dame

This series analyzes and evaluates critically the major political, social, and legal ideals, institutions, and practices of our time. The analysis may be historical or problem-centered; the evaluation may focus on theoretical underpinnings or practical implications. Among the recent titles in the series are:

Liberty for the Twenty-First Century: Contemporary Libertarian Thought
    Edited by Tibor R. Machan, Auburn University, and Douglas B. Rasmussen, St. John's University
In the Company of Others: Perspectives on Community, Family, and Culture
    Edited by Nancy E. Snow, Marquette University
Perfect Equality: John Stuart Mill on Well-Constituted Communities
    By Maria H. Morales, Florida State University
Citizenship in a Fragile World
    By Bernard P. Dauenhauer, University of Georgia
Critical Moral Liberalism: Theory and Practice
    By Jeffrey Reiman, American University
Nature as Subject: Human Obligation and Natural Community
    By Eric Katz, New Jersey Institute of Technology
Can Ethics Provide Answers? And Other Essays in Moral Philosophy
    By James Rachels, University of Alabama at Birmingham
Character and Culture
    By Lester H. Hunt, University of Wisconsin–Madison
Same Sex: Debating the Ethics, Science, and Culture of Homosexuality
    Edited by John Corvino, University of Texas at Austin
Approximate Justice: Studies in Non-Ideal Theory
    By George Sher, Rice University
Living in Integrity: A Global Ethic to Restore a Fragmented Earth
    By Laura Westra, University of Windsor
Necessary Good: Our Responsibilities to Meet Others' Needs
    Edited by Gillian Brock, University of Auckland, New Zealand
The Business of Consumption: Environmental Ethics and the Global Economy
    Edited by Laura Westra, University of Windsor, and Patricia H. Werhane, University of Virginia

THE BUSINESS OF CONSUMPTION

Environmental Ethics and the Global Economy

edited by
Laura Westra
and
Patricia H. Werhane

ROWMAN & LITTLEFIELD PUBLISHERS, INC.
Lanham • Boulder • New York • Oxford

ROWMAN & LITTLEFIELD PUBLISHERS, INC.

Published in the United States of America
by Rowman & Littlefield Publishers, Inc.
4720 Boston Way, Lanham, Maryland 20706

12 Hid's Copse Road
Cumnor Hill, Oxford OX2 9JJ, England

British Library Cataloguing in Publication Information Available

Library of Congress Cataloging-in-Publication Data

The business of consumption : environmental ethics and the global
    economy / edited by Laura Westra and Patricia H. Werhane.
        p.   cm. — (Studies in social, political, and legal
    philosophy)
    Includes bibliographical references and index.
    ISBN 0-8476-8668-X (cloth : alk. paper). — ISBN 0-8476-8669-8
    (pbk. : alk. paper)
    1. Environmental ethics.   2. Consumption (Economics)—Moral and
ethical aspects.   3. Economic development.   I. Westra, Laura.
II. Werhane, Patricia Hogue.   III. Series.
GE42.B88   1998
179'.1—dc21   98-10307
                                                        CIP

Printed in the United States of America

⊗ ™ The paper used in this publication meets the minimum requirements of
American National Standard for Information Sciences—Permanence of Paper
for Printed Library Materials, ANSI Z39.48–1984.

For my father, Pino Menassé, in memoriam

—*Laura Westra*

For my parents, in memoriam

—*Patricia Werhane*

Contents

Preface

Laura Westra

Our affluent northern lifestyle is based on a free enterprise system, emphasizing consumption. We depend on an ongoing proliferation of products and services, the presence of which defines, circumscribes, and supports our "good life." However, in recent times, we have begun to acknowledge the need to emphasize sustainability as well as economic growth and development. We have also accepted the fact that there are global dimensions to both and that justice requires that our "development" and its "sustainability" be viewed in the light of the consequences they engender beyond our own countries.

Further, it is not only those in developing countries who may be adversely affected because of our practices but also our own minority communities. One could object that the problems of justice, fairness, and their multinational dimensions are standard issues in business ethics and that corporations are increasingly aware of the need to consider ethics in order to help steer a clear path in their corporate activities to ensure that these are both politically correct and ethically unexceptional.

The articles in this volume do not address the question of how to avoid the Bhopals and the Chernobyls, the Sevesos and other terrible accidents. Our main concern is foundational. It is not about *how* to conduct business but about *whether* to continue to sustain an enterprise that is based on increased consumption. Not everyone agrees that this is a dangerous trend. Some suggest the possibility of "technological fixes" through substitutions, and many corporations in fact see their future gains as closely allied to the "greening" of their operations. Others, instead, argue that we should no longer speak of growth or even development, particularly in the Northwest, because even an average North

American lifestyle is completely unsustainable. Our ecological footprint appropriates many times the resources of others (particularly in developing countries) in order to support our lifestyle and preferences. Folke, Larsson, and Sweitzer, for instance, show that "to satisfy consumption of renewable resources, the 29 cities in the Baltic Sea region appropriate 'an area of ecosystems that is 200 times the total area of the cities themselves.' "[1]

Hence, many argue, the drive to development and increased productivity is unsustainable, as both sources and sinks are as finite as the earth in which they are placed. In fact, even the necessary economic expansion of poorer countries in the Southeast can only be envisaged, realistically, in the context of *reduced* consumption on our part. But our institutions and democratic laws support individual choices and preferences and often militate against restraints, or the promotion of a communitarian good at the expense of limits to our individual freedoms.

Predictably, environmental ethicists are often skeptical about the possibility of sustainable consumption, let alone sustainable development. In contrast, business ethicists may view the present environmental crisis as a new opportunity to modify, adapt, and find new ways to "green" their operations, while maintaining or even increasing their profits. The present collection of new essays views these questions from both the environmental and the business perspective. The issues here debated are at the forefront of international concerns about global legislation and regulation. We propose this group of readings as an introduction to help us frame the questions we must urgently address *now*, as individuals and global citizens.

Note

1. C. Folke, J. Larsson, and J. Sweitzer, "Renewable Resource Appropriation," *Getting Down to Earth* (Washington, D.C.: Island Press, 1996), 68.

Acknowledgments

Chapter 2, "The Need to Face Conflicts between Rich and Poor Nations to Solve Global Environmental Problems," copyright © 1998 Donald A. Brown.

Chapter 5, "Marketing, the Ethics of Consumption, and Less-Developed Countries, copyright © 1998 George G. Brenkert.

Chapter 6, "Reducing the Ecological Footprint of Consumption," appeared in an earlier form in *Towards the Goal of Sustainable Society: Policy Measures for Changing Consumption Patterns,* proceedings of a 1995 workshop at the Korean Environmental Tehcnology Institute. Copyright © 1991 William E. Rees; reprinted by permission of the author.

Chapter 8, "A Nonanthropocentric Environmental Evaluation of Technology for Public Policy: Why Norton's Approach Is Insufficient for Environmental Policy," appeared in an earlier form in *Journal of Social Philosophy.*

Chapter 10, "Environmental Sustainability: Eat Better and Kill Less," previously appeared in *Ethics of Consumption: The Good Life, Justice, and Global Stewardship,* ed. David A. Crocker and Toby Linden. Copyright © 1998 Rowman & Littlefield.

Chapter 12, "Scarcity or Abundance," previously appeared in *Scarcity or Abundance? A Debate on the Environment* by Norman Myers and Julian L. Simon. Copyright © 1994 Norman Myers, Julian Simon, and the Columbia University School of International and Public Affairs. Reprinted by permission of W. W. Norton & Company.

Chapter 13, "Holes in the Cornucopia," copyright © 1998 Ernest Partridge.

Chapter 14, "Do We Consume Too Much?" copyright © 1997 Mark Sagoff, as first published in *Atlantic Monthly.*

Chapter 15, "A Boat for Thoreau: A Discourse on Ecology, Ethics, and the Making of Things," copyright © 1998 William A. McDonough.

Chapter 18, "Shades of Green: Business, Ethics, and the Environment," copyright © 1998 R. Edward Freeman, Jessica Pierce, and Richard Dodd.

Special thanks to the Olsson Center for Applied Ethics at the Darden School for their financial support of the manuscript preparation and to Amanda Lee for her fine work in preparing and proofreading the manuscript.

Introduction

Environmental and Economic Sustainability

Patricia H. Werhane

The Academy Award-winning 1950 Japanese movie *Rashomon* depicts an incident involving an outlaw: a rape or seduction of a woman and a murder or suicide of her husband. A passerby, who is also the narrator, explains how the story is told to officials from four different perspectives: that of the outlaw, the woman, the husband, and himself. The four narratives agree that the outlaw, wandering through the forest, came upon the woman on a horse being led by her husband, tied up the husband and had sex with the woman in front of the bound husband, and that the husband was found dead. The narratives do not agree on how these events occurred or who killed the husband. The outlaw contends that consensual sex occurred between him and the wife, and he claims to have killed the husband. The wife depicts the sex as rape and claims that because of her disgrace, she killed her husband. The husband, through a medium, says that the sexual act began as rape and ended as consent, and that, in shame after being untied by the outlaw, he killed himself. The passerby's story agrees with the husband's account of the sex and the bandit's account of the murder of the husband. Interestingly, because the passerby is also the narrator of the film, recounting to friends the strange contradictory reportings of this event, we tend to believe his version. But what actually took place is never resolved.

I begin by stating a commonly held and, I believe, true assumption. All experience is framed and interpreted through sets of conceptual schemes or mental models that function on the individual, institutional, societal, and cross-cultural levels. We can neither experience an event nor present a story except through mental models. Still, depending on

1

which model or models is or are operative, interpretations of a situation or event by persons, groups, institutions, or societies may differ greatly from each other. Because conceptual schemes are learned and incomplete, we can also create, evaluate, and change our mental models.[1] Still, sometimes we become so embroiled in a particular set of mental models that shape our stories or narratives, whether or not of our own making, that we fail to compare a particular narrative with other accounts or evaluate its implications. Thus, the ways we present or re-present a story, the narrative we employ, and the conceptual framing of that story, affect its content, its moral analysis, and the subsequent evaluation.[2] Sometimes, narratives clash or contradict each other. Other times, when one narrative becomes dominant we appeal to that one for reinforcement of facts, even though it may have distorting effects. The result in either case is a Rashomon Effect.[3] Yet we seldom are aware of the "frame" or mental model at work or attempt to reframe the narratives we employ. If my thesis is not mistaken, it is important, morally important, to understand the constructive nature and limits of narratives so that we can have a clearer view of our stories about environmental sustainability, consumption, economic growth, and the role of business.

The essays in this collection frame at least three different narratives about consumption, economic development, population growth, and their effects on the ecosystem. As one can well predict, these narratives contradict each other in many respects, and since none of us is infallible, how each will play out in the future cannot be predicted with certainty. The first set of narratives is one most often reiterated by scientists, ecologists, and philosophers working in the field of environmental ethics. This narrative argues that the consumption and economic growth that have fueled the economies of the industrialized or highly developed countries (HDCs) are environmentally unsustainable, ecologically destructive, and unachievable in lesser developed countries (LDCs). Population growth, particularly in LDCs, and continuing poverty in those countries exacerbates ecological problems and spells disaster for the planet unless we change our consumption and growth patterns in the very near future.

In contrast, led by the economist Julian Simon, a second set of narratives argues that despite or because of economic development, the planet earth is not in dire straits. We are not running out of natural resources in any crucial sense, improved technology creates efficient and clean processes, and biotechnology increases food production every year. Indeed, opportunities abound to provide adequate food for increasing numbers of people and economic growth in lesser developed countries.

The third set of narratives takes a different approach. Failure to resolve the controversy between doomsayers and cornucopians is not a mandate to continue those arguments. Rather, those issues appear at least in part to be unresolvable, because we do not have all the data on the future of the planet. Instead, let us think of ways to take what appear to be two contrasting stories, that of economic growth and the other of environmental sustainability, and begin to create a new narrative, a narrative that sets out a model for sustainable economic development, that redefines consumption in terms of exchange, and that adapts William McDonough's edict, "waste equals food."

To examine these different narratives in more detail, let us begin with the word *consumption*. According to Webster's Dictionary, to consume is "to expend by use, use up, devour, destroy, [or] spend wastefully."[4] Thus when I consume I use up something; when I overconsume I use up more than I need, desire, or can assimilate, and I may use up resources that become unavailable to others. Herman Daly, in the article that begins this collection, defines consumption as "the disarrangement of matter." Consumption uses up value added by nature. Some three hundred years ago John Locke argued that labor increased the value of nature and gave it most of its worth. The value Locke was referring to was economic value. Oil in the ground is of no value for human well-being, no economic value; only oil that is drilled and refined has economic worth.[5] However, Daly argues, economic value is *not* added value to nature, and indeed, in most industrial settings labor and capital contributions use up resources and energy that are then lost to nature. Thus, while labor and capital produce increases in economic value, there is usually a net loss of *natural* capital. Since the ecosystem is finite, economic growth along with population increases and the accompanying increase in consumption are anti-ecological, and the value lost, unlike the value of labor and capital input, is not replaceable.

This picture of the irreplaceable damaging effects of consumption is reinforced by William Rees, who points out how consumption creates waste as well as depletes natural capital. Using the analogy of a footprint, Rees points out that industrialized countries (HDCs) such as the United States consume ten to twenty times as much as lesser developed countries (LDCs), thus creating a huge ecological footprint in nature. If all countries of the world consumed as much as the HDCs, Rees argues, we would require six planets the size of Earth to accommodate those consumption patterns. To achieve economic sustainability will require significant reduction in energy and resource consumption in HDCs, a reduction that cannot be achieved merely by increased efficiency or improvements in technology. Rather, this requires a change in lifestyle and thus a change in what we value as a human society.

Don Mayer tells an even more dismal story of overconsumption. Focusing on the United States economy, he argues that consumption and overconsumption are institutionalized activities in the U.S. political economy. Free markets encourage consumption, and the political system, based on property rights, commodifies rather than values nature for its own sake. U.S. politicians are preoccupied with economic growth as the salvation for present and future well-being. Preserving or cleaning up the environment is measured in terms of costs and benefits to humans, and environmental sustainability takes, at best, last place, after material consumption, economic growth, and wealth.

Worse, Mayer argues, LDCs are mimicking our lifestyle. According to George Brenkert, this is encouraged by global marketing strategies. Marketers everywhere tend to foster consumerism. They do this by strategies that identify happiness with what one owns, equate self-esteem with possessions and consumption, and promote the idea that the "good life" must be the American or Western materially affluent way of life. Global marketing by multinational companies undervalues cultural differences and indeed, may create false hopes for people in LDCs.

Joel Reichart's analysis of the tragedy of the commons through game theory demonstrates how truly difficult it is to change the way we regard the commons, given that many of us in HDCs have adopted an economic model for rationality as maximizing utilities often from a primarily self-interested perspective. To change that model, a model that encourages overgrazing and results in almost every case in the destruction of commons, would require linking rational self-interest and well-being to environmental health, minimally, the recognition that our survival and well-being depend on the health and regeneration of nature. Ideally, if we could imagine nature as a value in itself apart from its utility we would begin to reconceptualize how we think about the environment. But Reichart is not altogether certain that in the end we will change the ingrained model of rational self-interest and utility maximization so dramatically.

Both John Lemons and Donald Brown paint very bleak pictures of the environmental and developmental issues facing the planet in the next century. LDCs that have not had adequate opportunities for economic development argue that exploitation of their natural resources and economic growth are their only means to alleviate poverty. Like HDCs in the past, LDCs contend that they need an opportunity to develop and to enhance the economic well-being of their populations. At the same time, the cost of environmentally sustainable economic development is often outside the means of these countries. The result is exploitation of natural resources, pollution, deforestation, and environmental waste, results that have worldwide negative consequences on the ecosystem. If these problems are not dealt with, and dealt with quickly, we will find increased environmental degradation in LDCs, degradation that will be ecologically costly to all inhabitants of the planet. But if LDCs cannot take on the costs of environmentally sustainable economic development, who, then, *is* responsible for these costs? Who should help fund environmentally friendly projects that provide jobs and increase the well-being of these populations? Brown envisions the formation of global partnerships between HDCs and LDCs to deal with these problems; Lemons argues that since HDCs have benefited from an abundance of natural resources and had few restrictions on their use in the past, it is the responsibility of these countries to share most of the financial burden for ensuring ecologically sound development in LDCs.

If these thinkers are correct in their assessment of consumption and overconsumption, then redressing these problems is not merely a simple matter of more efficient uses of energy, cleaning up pollution, slowing our consumption rates, or helping LDCs improve their economies. Nor are drastic improvements in technology enough to counteract what these writers see as a doomsday scenario for future generations on this planet. Rather, we need to change the narrative—the story that extols economic growth, property rights, and consumption as the ideals for human happiness and well-being. That is, those of us in HDCs need to change our mental model by decoupling the notion of well-being from material wealth.

Laura Westra argues that because we share interests with nature, interests to survive and flourish, we need to create a new narrative. This narrative decenters human beings and places us within and as a part of nature where ecological integrity is the primary value and end for human action, and the ground for justifying economic and political activities. Ecological integrity should be the standard for technological development, consumption, environmental sustainability, and economic development throughout the world. This does not imply the end of economic well-being, private property, or free enterprise, but she calls for a revaluation of activities generated from free enterprise in terms of this standard of ecological integrity where an ecocentric point of view forms the moral ground.

Eric Freyfogle suggests that part of this new narrative should be a reunification of human beings with land and land health. If we rethink nature as the subject of our activities rather than as a commodity to be used up, we will begin to reidentify with nature, with land, and with the values exhibited by nature: health, regeneration, preservation, and conservation. Consumption then becomes limited by using the analogy of what the land can yield, and thus what we consume can be replaced, under the guidelines of conservation, reuse, and rejuvenation. Freyfogle goes further and suggests that we need to value local land health and thus local cultures. Economic development and trade agreements should be restricted by the presumption that local land health is of primary and intrinsic value. When a country is encouraged to give up grain production for an exportable commodity such as tobacco, for example, this violates local land health and the autonomy of that region to be self-sustaining.

One of the ways in which we consume is by eating. Robert Goodland, in a devastating critique of our eating habits, argues that the global food crisis is, in part, due to the dietary extravagances that value meat over grain, and tobacco and grains for alcohol over food for hungry people. Raising meat animals takes much more energy than raising grains, fruits, and vegetables, and Goodland argues that we need to radically revise our model of food consumption so that we are no longer wastefully producing food and overconsuming—that is, we need to eat sustainably.

In another effort to rethink our mental models about consumption, Rogene Buchholz and Sandra Rosenthal first set up the problem of consumption in very negative terms. They argue that we are using up our natural resources, that populations are growing, and that the planet cannot support every inhabitant in the lifestyle of HDCs. Green marketing, they argue, still encourages consumption, and sometimes we imagine that if we create a sustainable product we have solved environmental problems, even if we encourage increased consumption through marketing that product.

One of the philosophical bases of HDC consumption is an individualistic view of the self. Many of us in Northern countries have inherited the Enlightenment tradition such that we think of ourselves as autonomous individuals with rights to freely engage in activities that will preserve our rights to be independent and increase our well-being. If each of us has a right to survive and to work in order to survive, and if labor adds economic value to nature, we then think of nature as an object, and one of our most basic rights as the right to the property (i.e., nature) we improve with our labor. Consumerism perpetuates economic value as the most important human value, thus dividing us from nature and even, Buchholz and Rosenthal argue, dividing us from each other. This has led us to value ourselves and our things, and to think less about our social relationships and our interrelationships with nature. Buchholz and Rosenthal suggest that we need to rethink that model of autonomy. As organisms we are part of nature; as human beings we are part of a social system; we cannot exist apart from nature nor apart from society. Thus if we think of ourselves not as independent individuals but as relational selves that are part of nature and interconnected with each other in family, culture, religion, and other social relationships, we might begin to rethink ourselves as part of an organic system that is valuable and worth preserving and sustaining for its own sake as well as merely for ourselves. If we define happiness as being interconnected to each other and to nature, we will begin to think of economic development more creatively in terms that prioritize nature and societies as ends of human endeavors. We will also, then, begin to direct our interests to everyone on this planet, all of whom are related to us, including those who are less fortunate than ourselves.

These articles, together, tell a story. It is a story of economic and political exploitation, overconsumption, greed, shortsightedness, a story of economic development in HDCs that ignores environmental sustainability, a tale of continued poverty in LDCs, and of ecological doom. Many of these essays assume that development entails economic growth, that economic growth entails consumption of raw materials, that consumption entails environmental degradation (or, at best, more using up of raw materials), and all of this together adds up to ecological and planetary disaster, the solution of which will require drastic measures to reduce consumption and to revalue our priorities.

However, there is another set of stories about the environment, a set of stories told most clearly by the economist Julian Simon. In his article, "Holes in the Cornucopia," Ernest Partridge lays out Simon's argument, and asks, albeit rhetorically, "Why take Julian Simon seriously?" Simon argues that it is distribution of technology, human personal freedom or the lack thereof, the scarcity of brain power, and the availability of capital, not consumption or the scarcity of natural resources, that are at issue. Simon contends that "[h]uman beings create more than they use, on average. It had to be so, or we would be an extinct species."[6] As we appear to be using up a certain natural resource, we replace that use with another resource. As we pollute, so too we learn new techniques to clean up and even improve the environment. Increases in population also provide increases in human brain power, an increase that will, in turn, deal more effectively with problems normally associated with population explosions. Simon appeals to the historical progress of humankind for his belief that we are in a cornucopian world that will only get better, and he treats nature as an "inert . . . warehouse of resources" that we manipulate for our own ends. Value is identified with economic value, and natural resources are valuable just when they are useful. Our task is to manage nature and continue to devise creative technologies that replace energy sources, increase land productivity, and even find uses for what we presently call waste. Thus human ingenuity, if allowed to exercise freely, will continue to find creative solutions to alleged environmental concerns and increasingly expand economic value throughout the globe.

In a detailed critique of Simon's theses, Partridge argues that Simon has created a worldview, a mental model, that, while attractive, presupposes that it is correct despite evidence to the contrary. Like the concept of perfect markets, a construct that has no analog in the real economic world, Simon has created a construct of the natural world that similarly has no actual analog. This *a priori ontology*, as Partridge labels it, can be called into question by evidence of ozone depletion, global warming, biological degradation, and species extinction, phenomena that are not replaceable nor able to be regenerated by any technology or human cleverness. Partridge concludes that Simon has created a paradigm that has little to do with what a number of scientists are warning us about—environmental degradation, population explosion, and overconsumption.

Interestingly, however, Simon's model is not without its advocates. Mark Sagoff, in his piece "Do We Consume Too Much?" appears at least in part to agree with Simon that, despite the fact that industrialized nations are increasing their consumption rates, the results are not disastrous or not disastrous in ways commonly believed. Reserves of nonrenewable raw materials have actually increased, and new technologies continue to help us learn how to conserve and substitute for them. World food production has expanded, food has become less expensive, and advances in biotechnology increase food production every year. We are moving, albeit slowly, to using solar energy, and we are becoming much more efficient in uses of present energy sources. Finally, Sagoff argues, it is not true that the North consumes at the expense of the South. Rather, we tend to find substitutes for what the South has to offer on the world market. The poverty that exists in the South accounts for much of the world's environmental degradation, deforestation, and pollution; thus, improving those economies would help world ecology.

Having made this positive prognosis for the future of the ecosystem, Sagoff then creates another story of why, nevertheless, we consume too much. We consume too much, he argues, because the distribution of wealth skews economic well-being to the high consuming countries. Agreeing with George Brenkert, Sagoff contends that the Northern model of consumption is often copied in other markets, leading to a global uniformity that destroys local culture and diversity. Moreover, the pursuit of materialism disengages us from other values, in particular the value of human relationships, as Buchholz and Rosenthal also argue, and the value of nature as an end in itself. Consumption often leads to a loss of appreciation for nature for its own sake. When nature becomes a commodity we no longer think of ourselves as part of nature, and its aesthetic beauty is no longer loved or appreciated for its own sake. "Overconsumption challenges our deepest conceptions of how we should live in relation to the natural world," Sagoff concludes. Overconsumption brings into question our deeply held moral attachment to nature and appreciation for the diversity of natural species and the ecosystem, because consumption becomes the end, not merely a means, for human happiness.

We have before us, in this collection, a number of narratives about consumption, the environment, and the ecosystem. Some of the narratives portray a doomsayer perspective; others are more positive. These narratives contradict each other, and the questions each raises are, at least in part, unresolvable, given our present knowledge. However, none of the narratives in parts 1, 2, and 3 of this collection, with the exception of Julian Simon's arguments, have much of a positive nature to say about the role of business. Free enterprise in general, and business in particular, are portrayed as the purveyors of consumption, the salespersons of overconsumption, the trumpeters of materialism as an end, a value, or an ideal for humans to strive for.

The fourth section of the book presents a different set of narratives. Without affirming Julian Simon's point of view or denying that we are in ecological deep trouble on this planet, the articles in this section tell another kind of story. Andrea Larson points out that in the marketplace the focus is often on production, not on consumption. Businesses produce for consumption, but rarely do they think about the consumption and waste dimensions of production. Moreover, as Don Mayer also points out, economic growth is thought to be a positive indicator of political and economic worth. The result, Larson argues, is that we are consuming our planet, our habitat, and our means for survival. In other words, we are literally consuming ourselves.

However, there is another marketplace concept that might be useful in helping to reframe economic growth in more environmentally sustainable terms. In the marketplace we talk about exchange: economic exchanges, or trades, of some goods for others, of goods for services, of services for other services, and so on. Not all market exchanges are fair exchanges, and we would consider an exchange fair if each party received what she or he thought was appropriate for what they had given, and if others would judge that exchange to be fair given that particular economic situation, other possible alternatives, and the scarcity of goods, services, or capital. Now what would happen if, when discussing environmental issues and environmental sustainability, we told a story of exchange instead of consumption? Marketplace exchanges are all just that—trades or exchanges. What if we rethought consumption in terms of exchange, so that the notion of "using up" was no longer a viable moral option. So if, for example, I need clean water for a pulp mill, I must either exchange that by creating some other equally irreplaceable good or repurify the water I use. Similarly, if I insist on using oil, I must exchange or replace it. But if I cannot replace it with oil (and I cannot, because it takes thousands of generations to make more oil), then I must recycle it or find another commodity—perhaps solar energy that *is* replaceable.

When one consumes, one often creates waste, the stuff that is left over or allegedly useless after consumption. But what if we told a different story about waste? In his article, "A Boat for Thoreau," William McDonough challenges us to rethink our story about environmental sustainability and waste. If we continue to think in terms of continuous improvement, for example, more efficient waste disposal, cleaning up what we have degraded, or reducing polluting effects, we set goals. But as soon as we have achieved one milestone, say, reducing emissions by 60 percent, in that process we then create a new milestone—reducing the remaining emissions by 60 percent and so on. McDonough challenges us to abandon this project and instead to think in terms of zero emissions, zero pollution, and zero waste. His edict, "waste equals food" is meant to challenge us to design industries, products, and services that are completely self-contained, reusable or recyclable, and regenerating. McDonough is not asking us to restrict free enterprise or trade. Rather, he challenges us to rethink our enterprises using a new framework or model. Rather than alter our patterns of consumption or reduce our consumption, McDonough is proposing that we achieve zero consumption, zero "using up," and that we, instead, exchange. A fair exchange under this model would be a self-contained and self-generating trade in which there were no leftovers, no waste, and no external side effects. A morally exemplary exchange would be one in which the design or production process actually improved the environment.

McDonough's model and the story he tells are not as utopian or idealistic as they may appear. One of the problems with environmental challenges to business is that business does not always hear those challenges, as Westra points out in her essay. However, Andrea Larson and Michael Gorman et al., along with McDonough, each give illustrations of companies that have adapted McDonough's principles or other environmentally sustainable frameworks like the Natural Step. McDonough describes the Swiss company, Rohner, where the effluent water that leaves that plant is cleaner than the intake water, intake water that has met the very stringent Swiss environmental requirements. Larson describes IKEA, the furniture manufacturer that uses only lumber from new, replantable forests and engages in that reforestation as well, and Ecover, the Belgian company that makes completely compostable, indeed, eatable washing products in a totally self-sustaining factory.

These activities do not occur merely in small companies. Recently, DesignTex, a division of Steelcase, one of the largest manufacturers of office furniture in the world, with Rohner developed a compostable fabric, a development process described by McDonough. According to McDonough, a division of Interface, Guilford of Maine, is developing recyclable carpeting. In Chattanooga, Tennessee, DuPont took the lead in cleaning up industry and making that city more ecologically viable.

All but one of the companies described by McDonough, Larson, and Gorman are for-profit operations. The exception is a company described by Gorman, Mehalik, Sonenshein, and Warren: SELF, the Solar Electric Light Fund. However, SELF will soon become a for-profit organization, because its founder, Neville Williams, thinks that privatization will bring in much-needed capital to expand his project to electrify rural communities in LDCs. SELF is an interesting company not merely because it is attempting to electrify rural communities in China with photovoltaics, a form of solar energy. It is developing this project through a Western notion of private property. SELF has a policy of not giving away its photovoltaic units. This is because, it argues, if people have to pay something, even a small amount, for this service, they will value it more. So SELF has set up complex long-term lending schemes so that poor rural people can afford electricity and own their own units as well.

These illustrations, and there are others, point to the fact that environmental sustainability is no longer some weird idea of obscure academics. Environmentally sustainable business is not only possible, but it gives companies a competitive advantage, and it offers them opportunities in global markets that do not degrade or exploit LDCs. Companies like SELF illustrate how economic development is possible that does not uproot indigenous cultures, use up natural resources, or harm the ecosystem, while at the same time continuing the free enterprise principle of economic viability. These articles in part 4 challenge the equation that economic development encourages overconsumption and destroys the ecosystem. They encourage us to create a new equation that redefines consumption as exchange, and overconsumption as adding more back than just replacement value. Economic development means getting a competitive advantage and that in turn is equated with design, goods, and services that turn waste into products and function on the principle of exchange. If this is a viable model, then economic development of LDCs is not an impossibility and, in fact, offers global companies new ways to be creative, more efficient, and ecologically acceptable. If these companies become the model of what can be done by free enterprise, there is hope for future generations on this planet.

Near the end of the film *Rashomon* the narrator of the tale, the passerby, laments the lack of trust in society that results because we can never agree or get at truth. But perhaps he is asking the wrong question. The mental models we use and the narratives in which we embed our lives and our activities frame our expectations and what we take to be knowledge and truth. In coming into contact with others' narratives one should not depend on a single point of view as presented in their stories. Yet, we can never reach certainty or The Truth. Given this uncertainty, in particular, the uncertainty about the future of the planet, R. Edward Freeman, Jessica Pierce, and Richard Dodd argue that we should accept Pascal's Wager.[7] Since we do not have conclusive evidence about the future of the planet, we should not gamble our children's future on the possibility that wasting natural resources, continued environmental degradation, and overconsumption will *not* have adverse effects on future generations or the ecosystem. If we lose the wager, we will become extinct.

Accepting Pascal's Wager does not imply, however, that we should adopt a doomsayer scenario that argues for the halting of economic development, and in fact, there is scant evidence so far that HDCs will do that. Rather, we need to try to develop new narratives that take into account the contrasts and contradictions of the well-worn stories that we tend to repeat. The so-called classic narratives, or mind-sets proclaiming that only public policies will curb the excesses of business, that environmental quality should be measured only in terms of costs and benefits, that the environment is not a concern of business, that we need a set of international policies that restrain economic growth, or that most businesses merely "greenwash," using green public relations campaigns to hide their excesses, are narrow mental models. These mind-sets belie how limiting and ineffective regulations can be, they assume all business is "bad," and they do not tell the whole story about what some businesses do. The stories of the doomsayers and the prognoses of the cornucopians, too, need to be revisited or they will become clichéd prototypes. While we cannot arrive at The Truth, we can at least approximate sets of well-grounded beliefs, distinguish them from myth and fantasy, and more importantly try to formulate new narratives that more adequately take into account what we know and challenge us to overcome the dilemmas posed in the older stories. Otherwise we will find ourselves in *Rashomon*'s postmodern world where neither Julian Simon's exhortations nor those of Herman Daly will be taken seriously, and then, indeed, we will have chosen a poor wager.

Notes

1. Donald Davidson, "On the Very Idea of a Conceptual Scheme," *Proceedings and Addresses of the American Philosophical Association* 47 (1973): 5–20; Peter Senge, *The Fifth Discipline* (New York: Doubleday, 1990).

2. Tod Chambers, "From an Ethicist's Point of View: The Literary Nature of Ethical Inquiry," *Hastings Center Report* 26 (1996): 25–33.

3. Patricia H. Werhane, "Moral Imagination and Management Decision-Making," *Ruffin Lecture Series Special Issue: Business Ethics Quarterly* 8 (1998), forthcoming.

4. *Webster's School & Office Dictionary* (New York: Random House, 1995), 96.

5. John Locke, *Second Treatise on Government 1689;* reprint (Indianapolis: Hackett Publishing Company, 1980).

6. Norman Myers and Julian L. Simon, *Scarcity or Abundance?* (New York: Norton, 1994), 197; reprinted in the selection in chapter 12 in this volume.

7. Blaise Pascal was a seventeenth-century French mathematician and philosopher who argued that we do not know whether or not God exists, but we should gamble on the fact that God does exist. This is a better wager, since if God exists and we acknowledge that, we will be granted eternal life. If God does not exist, it does not matter anyway.

Part One

The Problem with Consumption

1

Consumption: The Economics of Value Added and the Ethics of Value Distributed

Herman E. Daly

Introduction

The total of resource consumption (throughput), by which the economic subsystem lives off the containing ecosystem, is limited—because the ecosystem that both supplies the throughput and absorbs its waste products is itself limited. The earth-ecosystem is finite, nonexpanding, materially closed, and while open to the flow of solar energy, that flow is also nonexpanding and finite. Historically these limits were not generally binding, because the subsystem was small relative to the total system. The world was "empty." But now it is "full," and the limits are more and more binding—not necessarily like brick walls, but more like stretched rubber bands.

John Stuart Mill (1857) foresaw the problem of moving from an empty to a full world and stated it clearly:

> Nor is there much satisfaction in contemplating the world with nothing left to the spontaneous activity of nature; with every rood of land brought into cultivation, which is capable of growing food for human beings; every flowery waste or natural pasture plowed up, all quadrupeds or birds which are not domesticated for man's use exterminated as his rivals for food, every hedgerow or superfluous tree rooted out, and scarcely a place left where a wild shrub or flower could grow without being eradicated as a weed in the name of improved agriculture. If the earth must lose that great portion of its pleasantness which it owes to things that the unlimited increase of wealth and population would extirpate from it, for the mere pur-

pose of enabling it to support a larger, but not a happier or better population, I sincerely hope, for the sake of posterity, that they will be content to be stationary, long before necessity compels them to it.[1]

The total flow of resource consumption is the product of population times per capita consumption. Many people have for a long time urged the wisdom of limiting population growth—few have recognized the need to limit consumption growth. In the face of so much poverty in the world it seems "immoral" to some to even talk about limiting consumption. But populations of cars, buildings, TVs, refrigerators, livestock, and yes, even of trees, fish, wolves, and giant pandas, all have in common with the population of human bodies that they take up space and require a throughput for their production, maintenance, and disposal. Nevertheless, some think the solution to human population growth lies in increasing the growth of populations of all the commodities whose services we consume. The "demographic transition" will automatically stop population growth only if per capita consumption grows fast enough. Arguing that one term of a product will stop growing if only the other term grows faster is not very reassuring if it is the product of the two terms that is limited. Will the average Indian's consumption have to rise to that of the average Swede before Indian fertility falls to the Swedish level? Can the eroding and crowded country of India support that many cars, power plants, buildings, and so on?

Never fear, the same people who brought you the demographic transition are now bringing you the Information Reformation, a.k.a. the "dematerialized economy." McDonald's will introduce the "infoburger," consisting of a thick patty of information between two slices of silicon, thin as communion wafers so as to emphasize the symbolic and spiritual nature of consumption. We can also dematerialize human beings by breeding smaller people—after all, if we were half the size there could be twice as many of us—indeed we would have to dematerialize people if we were to subsist on the dematerialized GNP! We can certainly eat lower on the food chain, but we cannot eat recipes. The Information Reformation, like the demographic transition before it, expands a germ of truth into a whale of a fantasy.

While all countries must worry about both population and per capita consumption, it is evident that the South needs to focus more on population, and the North more on per capita consumption. This fact will likely play a major role in all North-South treaties and discussions. Why should the South control its population if the resources saved thereby are merely gobbled up by Northern overconsumption? Why should the North control its overconsumption if the saved resources will merely allow a larger number of poor people to subsist at the same level of misery? Without for a minute minimizing the necessity of population control, it is nevertheless incumbent on the North to get serious about consumption control. Toward this end, a reconsideration of the meaning of consumption is offered below.

Consumption and Value Added

When we speak of consumption, what is it that we think of as being consumed? Alfred Marshall reminded us of the laws of conservation of matter/energy and the consequent impossibility of consuming the material building blocks of commodities:

> Man cannot create material things—his efforts and sacrifices result in changing the form or arrangement of matter to adapt it better for the satisfaction of his wants—as his production of material products is really nothing more than a rearrangement of matter which gives it new utilities, so his consumption of them is nothing more than a disarrangement of matter which destroys its utilities.[2]

What we destroy or consume in consumption is the improbable arrangement of those building blocks, arrangements that give utility for humans, arrangements that were, according to Marshall, made by humans for human purposes. This utility added to matter/energy by human action is not production in the sense of creation of matter/energy, which is just as impossible as destruction by consumption. Useful structure is added to matter/energy (natural resource flows) by the agency of labor and capital stocks. The value of this useful structure imparted by labor and capital is what economists call "value added." This value added is what is "consumed," that is, used up in consumption. New value needs to be added again by the agency of labor and capital before it can be consumed again. That to which value is being added is the flow of natural resources, conceived ultimately as the indestructible building blocks of nature. The value consumed by humans is, in this view, no greater than the value added by humans—consumption plus savings equals national income—which in turn is equal to the sum of all value added. In the standard economist's vision we consume only that value which we added in the first place. And then we add it again, and consume it again, and so on. This vision is formalized in the famous diagram of the isolated circular flow of value between firms (production) and households (consumption), found in the initial pages of every economics textbook.

For all the focus on value added one would think that there would be some discussion of *that to which value is being added*. But modern econo-mists say no more about it than Marshall. It is just "matter," and its properties are not very interesting. In fact, they are becoming ever less interesting to economists as science uncovers their basic uniformity. As Barnett and Morse put it: "Advances in fundamental science have made it possible to take advantage of the uniformity of matter/energy—a uni-formity that makes it feasible, without preassignable limit, to escape the quantitative constraints imposed by the character of the earth's crust."[3]

That to which value is being added are merely homogeneous, inde-structible building blocks—atoms in the original sense—of which there is no conceivable scarcity. That to which value is added is therefore inert, undifferentiated, interchangeable, and superabundant—very dull stuff indeed, compared to the value-adding agents of labor with all its human capacities, and capital that embodies the marvels of human knowledge. It is not surprising that value added is the centerpiece of economic accounting, and that the presumably passive stuff to which value is added has received minimal attention.[4]

Consumption and Physical Transformation

The vision sketched above, that of Marshall, of Barnett and Morse, and of all textbooks founded on the circular flow of value added, is entirely consistent with the first law of thermodynamics. Matter/energy is not produced or consumed, only transformed. But this vision embodies an astonishing oversight—it completely ignores the second law of thermo-dynamics.[5] Matter is arranged in production, disarranged in consump-tion, rearranged in production, and so on. The second law tells us that all this rearranging and recycling of material building blocks takes en-ergy, that energy itself is not recycled, and that on each cycle some of the material building blocks are dissipated beyond recall. It remains true that we do not consume matter/energy, but we do consume (irrevocably use up) the *capacity to rearrange* matter/energy. Contrary to the implica-tion of Barnett and Morse, matter/energy is not at all uniform in the quality most relevant to economics—namely, its capacity to receive and hold the rearrangements dictated by human purpose, the capacity to receive the imprint of human knowledge, the capacity to embody value added. The capacity of matter/energy to embody value added is not uniform, and it wears out and must be replenished. It is not totally pas-sive. If the economic system is to keep going it cannot be an isolated circular flow. It must be an open system, receiving matter and energy from outside to make up for that which is dissipated to the outside. What is outside? The environment. What is the environment? It is a complex ecosystem that is finite, nonexpanding and materially closed, while open to a nonexpanding flow of solar energy.

Seeing the economy as an open subsystem forces us to realize that consumption is not only disarrangement within the subsystem but involves disarrangements in the rest of the system, the environment. Taking matter/energy from the larger system, adding value to it, using up the added value, and returning the waste clearly alters the environment. The matter/energy we return is not the same as the matter/energy we take in. If it were, we could simply use it again and again in a closed circular flow. Common observation tells us, and the entropy law confirms, that waste matter/energy is qualitatively different from raw materials. Low-entropy matter/energy comes in, high-entropy matter/energy goes out, just as in an organism's metabolism. We irrevocably use up not only the value we added by rearrangement, but also the pre-existing arrangement originally imparted by nature, as well as the very energetic capacity to further arrange, also provided by nature. We not only consume the value we add to matter, *but also the value that was added by nature before we imported it into the economic subsystem*, and that was necessary for it to be considered a resource in the first place. Capacity to rearrange used up within the subsystem can be restored by importing low-entropy matter/energy from the larger system and exporting high-entropy matter/energy back to it. But the rates of import and export, determined largely by the scale of the subsystem, must be consistent with the complex workings of the parent system, the ecosystem. The scale of the subsystem matters.

From this perspective value is still being added to resources by the agents of labor and capital. But that to which value is added are not inert, indifferent, uniform building blocks or atoms. Value is added to that matter/energy which is most capable of receiving and embodying the value being added to it. That receptivity might be thought of as "value added by nature." Carbon atoms scattered in the atmosphere can receive value added only with the enormous expenditure of energy and other materials. Carbon atoms structured in a tree can be rearranged much more easily. Concentrated copper ore can hold value added; atoms of copper at average crustal abundance cannot. Energy concentrated in a lump of coal can help us add value to matter; energy at equilibrium temperature in the ocean or atmosphere cannot. The more work done by nature, the more concentrated and receptive the resource is to having value added to it, the less capital and labor will have to be expended in rearranging it to better suit our purposes. If all value added is the result of labor and capital, then the total value that they jointly added should be distributed between them. But if nature also adds value, then there is a source other than labor and capital that has no obvious claimant in distribution. Who should get it? The ethical principle that value should go to whoever added it is no longer suffi-cient, unless nature is personified and somehow considered a claimant.

From a utility or demand perspective value added by nature ought to be valued equally with value added by labor and capital. But from the supply or cost side it is not, because value added by humans has a real cost of disutility of labor and an opportunity cost of both labor and capital use. We tend to treat natural value added as a subsidy, a free gift of nature. The greater the natural subsidy, the less the cost of labor and capital (value added) needed for further arrangement. The less the humanly added value, the lower the price, and the more rapid the use. Oil from East Texas was a much greater net energy subsidy from nature to the economy than is offshore Alaskan oil. But its price was much lower precisely because it required less value added by labor and capital. The larger the natural subsidy, the less we value it, and the less attention we pay to the ethical issue of how to distribute nature's value added.

Thanks in part to this natural subsidy the economy has grown relative to the total ecosystem to such an extent that the basic pattern of scarcity has changed. It used to be that adding value was limited by the supply of agents of transformation, labor, and capital. Now, value added is lim-ited more by the availability of resources subsidized by nature to the point that they can receive value added. Mere knowledge means nothing to the economy until it becomes incarnate in physical structures. Low-entropy matter/energy is the restricted gate through which knowledge is incorporated in matter and becomes manmade capital. No low-en-tropy matter/energy, no capital—regardless of knowledge. Of course, new knowledge may include discovery of new low-entropy resources, and new methods of transforming them to better serve human needs. New knowledge may also discover new limits, and new impossibility theo-rems.

The physical growth of the subsystem is the transformation of natural capital into manmade capital. A tree is cut and turned into a table. We gain the service of the table; we lose the service of the tree. In a relatively empty world (small economic subsystem, ecosystem relatively empty of human beings and their artifacts) the service lost from fewer trees was nil, and the service gained from more tables was significant. In today's relatively full world fewer trees mean loss of significant services, and more tables are not so important if most households already have several tables, as in much of the world they do. Of course continued population growth will keep the demand for tables up, and we will incur ever greater sacrifices of natural services by cutting more and more trees, as long as population keeps growing. The size or scale of the economic subsystem is best thought of as per capita consumption times population (which of course is the same as total consumption). The point is that there is both a cost and a benefit to increasing the scale of the subsystem (total consumption). The benefit is economic services gained (more tables); the cost is ecosystem services sacrificed (fewer trees to sequester CO_2, provide wildlife habitat, erosion control, local cooling, etc.). As scale increases, marginal costs tend to rise; marginal benefits tend to fall. Equality of marginal costs and benefits defines the optimal scale, beyond which further growth would be anti-economic.

As we come to an optimal or mature scale, production is no longer for growth but for maintenance. A mature economy, like a mature ecosystem, shifts from a regime of growth efficiency (maximize P/B, or production per unit of biomass stock) to a regime of maintenance efficiency (maximize the reciprocal, B/P, or the amount of biomass stock maintained per unit of new production). Production is the maintenance cost of the stock and should be minimized. As K. Boulding argued almost fifty years ago,

> Any discovery which renders consumption less necessary to the pursuit of living is as much an economic gain as a discovery which improves our skills of production. Production—by which we mean the exact opposite of consumption, namely the creation of valuable things—is only necessary in order to replace the stock pile into which consumption continually gnaws.[6]

Consumption and Welfare

The theoretical existence of an optimal scale of the economic subsystem is clear in principle. What remain vague are the measures of the value of services, especially of natural capital but also of manmade capital. But if economic policy is anything it is the art of dialectically reasoning with vague quantities in the support of prudent actions. We can have reasons for believing that an optimum scale exists, and that we are either above it or below it, without knowing exactly where it is. For policy purposes a judgment about which side of the optimum we are on is what is critical. Reasons are offered below for believing that we (both the United States and the world as a whole) have overshot the optimal scale—that is, that the marginal benefits of growth are less than commonly thought; that the marginal costs are greater than commonly thought; and that the marginal costs are on the whole greater than the marginal benefits.

Welfare is not a function of consumption flows, but of capital stocks. We cannot ride to town on the maintenance costs, the depletion and replacement flow of an automobile, but only in a complete automobile,

a member of the current stock of automobiles. Once again Boulding got
it right fifty years ago:

> I shall argue that it is the capital stock from which we derive satisfactions,
> not from the additions to it (production) or the subtractions from it (con-
> sumption): that consumption, far from being a desideratum, is a deplor-
> able property of the capital stock which necessitates the equally deplorable
> activities of production: and that the objective of economic policy should
> not be to maximize consumption or production, but rather to minimize it,
> i.e., to enable us to maintain our capital stock with as little consumption or
> production as possible.[7]

Our empirical measures of the value of natural capital services (enjoyed or sacrificed) are virtually nonexistent. Even the concept barely
exists in standard economic theory because the natural functions of
source and sink have been considered free goods, as was reasonable
when the world was relatively empty. But now the world is relatively full.
Also, contrary to what many think, we have only piecemeal measures of
the value of services of manmade capital. Our national income accounts
overwhelmingly measure throughput, not service of capital stock. Furthermore, the throughput is valued by market prices that are based on
marginal utility and consequently omit consumer surplus, by far the
larger part of welfare. Also, diminishing marginal utility is ignored—a
dollar used to satisfy basic needs counts the same as a dollar used to
satisfy velleities. Yet diminishing marginal utility is the keystone of economic theory. National income has many well-known defects as an index
of welfare—it adds up the utilities of different people, which is not allowed in standard economic theory; ignores the value of leisure, of
household work, of working conditions, of security, and so on. The
point is that even if we were able to construct accounts for valuing natural capital services that were *as good as* our accounts for valuing manmade capital services, we still would not have accomplished much
because the latter has itself only been done to a very limited extent. And
it is universally acknowledged that it is much harder to evaluate natural
capital than manmade capital.

The quest for empirical measures always requires some sacrifice of
conceptual purity, but so many sacrifices have been made in standard
national income accounting that the number no longer bears any relationship to welfare. Indeed, what is worse, welfare was not even the concept that the statisticians were, for the most part, aiming to approximate.
Politicians made that interpretation after the fact, and economists acqui-
esced in it because it enhanced their political importance. It is better to
reason via correct welfare-related concepts to the theoretical existence

of an optimal scale, and then figure out by dead reckoning from the North Star and familiar landmarks which side of the optimum we are on, than to rely on a statistical compass whose needle we know is not magnetized.

What then are our common sense, dead reckoning judgments about whether we are at, below, or above the optimal scale? I suggest we are beyond the optimal scale. To show that we have exceeded the optimum it is *not* necessary to show that growth is physically impossible, nor that it has catastrophic costs, nor that it would have negative or zero marginal benefit, even if free. It is only necessary to show that marginal costs are greater than marginal benefits. It is quite logical and reasonable to argue that on the whole, up to the present time, the total benefits of growth have been greater than the total costs, and yet to hold that growth should cease because at the margin costs have now begun to outweigh benefits. Economists, of all people, surely understand this! They apply this logic to the micro level every day. Why it is not applied at the macro level has never been explained.[8]

What "dead reckoning judgments" can we make about the marginal benefits of growth in manmade capital? (Note that benefits from qualitative *development* are not in question, just those from quantitative *growth*.) For rich, full countries the marginal utility of extra growth is surely low. Great sums of money have to be spent on advertising to cajole people into buying more. As we have become goods-rich we have become time-poor. In rich countries people die more from stress and overconsumption than from starvation. Relative, rather than absolute, income seems to be the main determinant of self-evaluated welfare, and growth is powerless to increase everyone's relative income. The effect of aggregate growth on welfare in rich countries is therefore largely self-canceling.

What about the poor? An increase in wealth from subsistence to middle-class comforts surely increases welfare, if all other things are equal. Should these high marginal utility uses by the poor be paid for by cutting low marginal utility luxury consumption of the rich, or by converting more natural capital into manmade capital? The rich favor the latter, and perhaps the poor do also because they want to emulate the rich, and because they doubt the political likelihood of redistribution or imposed limits to the takeover of natural capital. Inequality is converted into pressure for growth.

However, the growth that often results from the pressure of inequality usually does not go to the poor. Consider for a moment what, exactly, is growing in a growth economy. It is the reinvested surplus that grows in the first instance. Who controls the surplus? Not the poor. They get only the trickle down from growth, and their relative position is more likely to worsen than to improve as a result of growth. This is especially so in light of the far more rapid rate of population growth of the poor than of the rich (due to greater natural increase and frequently to greater immigration as well). A large and growing supply of labor will keep wages from ever rising and thereby also keep profits up.

What are the marginal costs of further growth? How serious are the ecosystem services lost as a result of transformation of more natural into manmade capital? Here one can recite the by-now-familiar litany of CO_2 buildup, biodiversity loss, stratospheric ozone depletion, acid rain, top-soil depletion, aquifer depletion, chemical pollution—in sum, an overall reduction of the capacity of the earth to support life. Loss of natural capital is not deducted from GNP in calculating NNP. Only the value added in the process of transforming the natural capital into manmade capital is counted. A large part of our GNP is regrettably necessary defensive expenditure that we are forced to make to protect ourselves from the unwanted side effects of increasing production and consumption—for example, extra health care resulting from tobacco and alcohol consumption, chemical and radioactive poisoning, cleanup costs of oil spills, longer commuting times, and so on. Defensive expenditures should be subtracted as an intermediate cost of the goods whose production or consumption imposed these regrettably necessary activities. But instead we add them, and politicians, along with their academic magicians and media jesters, rejoice in the improvement.

Add to these considerations the corrosive effects of economic growth on community and on moral standards. Capital and labor mobility rip communities apart in the name of growth. Furthermore, an economy that must grow must also sell. It is easier to sell in a community with low standards—if anything goes, then nearly anything will sell, no matter how tawdry or shoddy. Common prudence is now referred to negatively as "sales resistance." We have plenty of landmarks to suggest that the marginal costs of growth are very high. Even a dead reckoning comparison of the low marginal benefits with the high marginal costs should be enough to convince us that it is time to redirect our economy away from growth and toward development.[9] As a North Star, we may occasionally check our course by the principle that if we are reducing the long-run capacity of earth to support life, then we have overshot the optimum.

Conclusion

Consumption is the disarrangement of matter, the using up of value added that inevitably occurs when we use goods. We consume not only value added by human agents of labor and capital, but also value previously added by nature. We are consuming value added, converting raw materials into waste, depleting and polluting, faster than nature can absorb the pollutants and regenerate the resources. Consumption, that is the transformation of natural capital into manmade capital and then ultimately into waste, leads to the basic question of what is the optimal extent of this transformation. What is the optimal scale of the economic subsystem, the scale beyond which further conversion of natural into manmade capital costs us more (in terms of natural capital services lost) than it benefits us (in terms of manmade capital services gained). Growing beyond the optimum is by definition anti-economic. Currently growth is anti-economic, as indicated by our dead reckoning considerations about marginal costs and benefits of growth. The future path of progress therefore is not growth, but development. Individual nations, not the globe, will control consumption by limiting both population and per capita consumption. Different national strategies for limiting consumption cannot coexist in an integrated world economy dominated by free trade, free capital mobility, and free migration. The use of tariffs and a general backing away from global integration toward relative self-sufficiency will likely be necessary.[10]

What are the consequences of the issues here discussed for North/South cooperation in economic development and in sharing the global economic pie? Consider two views.

(a) The traditional value-added view of income would lead one to reject the very notion of a global pie of income to be divided justly or unjustly among nations. There is no global pie—there are only a lot of separate national tarts that some statistician has stupidly aggregated into an abstract pie. The separate tarts are the products of value added by the labor and capital of the nations that produced them, and nothing more. If nation A is asked to share some of its large tart with nation B who baked a small tart, the appeal should be made to nation A's generosity, and not to any notion of distributive justice, much less exploitation.

If you believe that all value comes from labor and capital, and that nature contributes only a material substratum that is nondestructible and superabundant, and hence valueless, then this is a quite reasonable view. Is your country poor? Well, just add more value by your own labor and capital. You already have your own labor, and you can accumulate your own capital, or borrow it at interest from abroad. There are no limits from nature. Stop whining and get busy—and shut up about this imaginary pie. This view is common among neoclassical economists. And given its presuppositions it is reasonable. In fact it is a corollary to John Locke's justification of private property—to claim something as one's property requires that one has mixed one's labor with the materials of which it is made and added value to it.

(b) The alternative view of the ecological economist, that nature too adds value, also rejects the imaginary global pie. But it looks more carefully at the tarts that different peoples have baked. Is the tart really only the product of the cook's labor and the kitchen's capital that alone add value to random, substitutable, and superabundant atoms? Certainly not. To bake a tart you need more than just atoms—you need flour, sugar, butter, and apples. Before that you need wheat, sugar cane, milk, and apple trees. And before that you need gene pools for wheat, sugar cane, cows, and apples, with some minimal degree of diversity, and soil whose fertility is maintained by all sorts of worms, microbes, and minerals, and sunlight without too much ultraviolet, and rainfall that is not too acidic, and catchment areas to keep that rain from eroding topsoil, and predictable seasonal temperatures regulated by the mix of gases in the atmosphere, and so on. In other words, we need nature or "natural capital" and the flow of natural resources and natural services that it renders—a whole lot more than indestructible building blocks! Our dowry of natural capital is more or less given and is not the product of human labor and capital. Parts of that dowry are highly systemic and indivisible among nations. And the part that is divisible was divided by natural, not economic, processes.

This distinction is why I want to shift attention from traditional value added to "that to which value is added." While one may argue that value added by labor and capital rightly belongs to the laborer and the capitalist (let them fight over how to divide it), one cannot distribute nature's value added so easily, especially the systemic life support services of global natural capital that transcend national boundaries. In this latter sense there really is a global pie, and the demands for justice regarding its division and stewardship cannot be subsumed under the traditional notion that value belongs to whoever added it. Nature's value added was not added by labor or capital—it is a gift. To whom was it given?

Notes

1. John Stuart Mill, *Principles of Political Economy* (London: John W. Parker, 1857).

2. Alfred Marshall, *Principles of Economics* (New York: Macmillan, 1961), 63–64.

3. Harold Barnett and Chandler Morse, *Scarcity and Growth* (Baltimore: Johns Hopkins University Press, 1963).

4. H. Daly and J. Cobb, *For the Common Good* (Boston: Beacon Press, 1994), chap. 10.

5. E. P. Odum, "The Strategy of Ecosystem Development," *Science* (April 1969): 262–70.

6. Kenneth Boulding, "The Consumption Concept in Economic Theory," *American Economic Review* (May 1945): 2.

7. Kenneth Boulding, "Income or Welfare? *Review of Economic Studies* 17 (1949): 79.

8. Reasoning in terms of broad aggregates has its limitations. Converting natural into manmade capital embraces both the extravagant conversion of tropical hardwoods into toothpicks, and the frugal conversion of pine trees into shelters for the homeless. The point is not that all conversions of natural into manmade capital simultaneously cease being worthwhile, but rather that ever fewer remain worthwhile as growth continues.

9. Statistical evidence, beyond "dead reckoning," that we have reached this point in the United States is provided by the Index of Sustainable Economic Welfare, which since the early 1980s has declined slightly even as GNP has continued to increase. See appendix in Daly and Cobb, *For the Common Good*; see also Clifford W. Cobb and John B. Cobb Jr., *The Green National Product: A Proposed Index of Sustainable Economic Welfare* (Lanham, Md.: University Press of America, 1994), and Manfred Max-Neef, "Economic Growth and Quality of Life: A Threshold Hypothesis," *Ecological Economics* 15 (1995): 115–18.

10. Daly and Cobb, *For the Common Good*, chap. 11.

2

The Need to Face Conflicts between Rich and Poor Nations to Solve Global Environmental Problems

Donald A. Brown

The Emergence of Conflicts between Rich and Poor Nations

In twenty years in the front trenches of environmental battles, I had grown to expect that the relentless power of money would continue to distort public debate about environmental issues. Time and time again, money not only influenced outcomes but also defined which and how environmental issues were debated in public forums. Yet, for the most part, environmental controversies had on the surface centered around scientific questions such as whether a proposed incinerator was safe. Although battles over these scientific questions were fueled by economic interests, how economic forces structured and controlled these fights was usually hidden in the public debate.

Recently, in the United States the social and economic dimensions of environmental problems have slowly begun to move from background to foreground. In a growing number of cases, the U.S. government was being asked to consider whether minorities and the poor are unfairly shouldering risks from incinerators or other polluting sources. Yet, for the most part, environmental controversies in the United States were still centered on such scientific matters as whether a proposed regulation was based on "good science."

At the international level, conflicts between rich and poor countries have become the transcendent issues blocking progress. Purely economic questions such as disagreements between rich and poor nations over who should pay for environmental protection have become the most visible disputes in international fora.

As a member of the U.S. delegation to the UN Commission on Sustainable Development, I had just been briefed at the U.S. Mission by the State Department on the day's controversies likely to confront the United States. On this cold March day in 1996, almost sixty nations would once again debate how much money the developed countries should give to poor nations to move the world on the path toward sustainable development. The poor nations would strenuously argue that if the richer countries wanted to advance the goals of sustainable development adopted at the Earth Summit in Rio de Janeiro in 1992, the rich countries would have to help the poor countries financially. The poor countries would also argue that because the rich countries caused much of the global pollution problems threatening the world, the richer countries had greater responsibilities to cut back on unsustainable consumption patterns.

These two issues raised by the poor nations, that is, the call for more development assistance and the differentiated responsibilities of the richer countries to reduce pollution, had become the intractable barriers that most frequently prevented progress in the four years since the Earth Summit. The entire world seemed to agree about the need to change the destructive development models threatening the planet and the quality of life for future generations. Yet, conflicts between rich and poor were the major obstacles on the road to a more sustainable future.

In a relatively short time, many international leaders throughout the world have accepted the concept of sustainable development as a way of reconciling potential conflicts between environmental protection and human development goals.

Although the concept of sustainable development had been used in some international circles for at least fifteen years, most commentators point to a report prepared for the United Nations by the World Commission on Environment and Development in 1987 for pushing the concept of sustainable development to center stage in international affairs. This report, entitled *Our Common Future*, received extraordinary international attention because it concluded that rapid deterioration of the global environment was threatening life on earth and that decisive political action was needed to ensure human survival. *Our Common Future* identified several environmental trends that threaten "to radically alter the planet, and many species upon it, including the human species."[1] Environmental deterioration identified in the report included (1) rapid loss of productive dry land that was being transformed into desert; (2) rapid loss of forests; (3) global warming caused by increases in greenhouse gases; (4) loss of the atmosphere's protective ozone shield due to industrial gases, and (5) the pollution of surface and ground water.

The scientific evidence of growing environmental degradation relied upon in *Our Common Future* was of even greater concern because Earth's environment was exhibiting stresses at a current population of approximately 5.5 billion people. These visible signs of deterioration became even more ominous when one considered the rapid growth in population expected for our planet in the twenty-first century. Because population may grow beyond ten billion people by the end of the next century, *Our Common Future* concluded that urgent and decisive political action was necessary to prevent widespread environmental destruction.

Until very recently, the problems of environmental degradation and poverty were viewed as unrelated. Of equal historical significance as its environmental conclusions, *Our Common Future* also focused world attention on the futility of separating economic development problems from environmental issues. The report explained how some forms of development eroded the environmental resources upon which they must be based, and how environmental degradation undermines economic development. For instance, development that can't afford to pay for treatment of sewage creates water pollution, and polluted water limits future development options. In addition, in many developing countries, in the absence of help from the developed world, rapid depletion of natural resources is the only hope of eradicating poverty. Thus, the report concluded, "poverty is a major cause and effect of global environmental problems."[2] That is, there is no hope of solving the global environmental problems unless the international community works rapidly to resolve problems of human development throughout the world. Thus, for the first time in human history, the international community was forced to see problems of poverty, population growth, industrial and social development, depletion of natural resources, and destruction of the environment as closely interrelated problems.

To solve the twin problems of environmental degradation and development, *Our Common Future* called for a world political transformation that supported "sustainable development" throughout the world. Sustainable development was defined as development that meets the needs of the present without compromising the ability of future generations to meet their needs. *Our Common Future*, because of its identification of the interrelationship between environmental destruction and poverty, put sustainable development on the front burner throughout the world.

In December 1989, the General Assembly of the United Nations, in reaction to the problems identified by *Our Common Future*, called for an unprecedented international meeting—a meeting of all the nations of the earth. The United Nations Conference on Environment and Development in June 1992, known as the Earth Summit, was held in Rio de Janeiro in response to *Our Common Future.* One hundred and ten heads of state assembled at the Earth Summit, more than at any other previous international conference.

Five documents were signed in Rio that will be implemented in the years ahead and that will keep sustainable development in the center of international affairs. They are: (1) The Treaty on Climate Change; (2) The Treaty on Biodiversity; (3) The Convention on Forest Principles; (4) The Rio Declaration; and (5) Agenda 21.

Although it did not receive as much publicity in the United States and some parts of the world as the Treaties on Climate Change and Biodiversity, Agenda 21 was viewed by many as the most significant of all the Earth Summit agreements. This document is an 800-page blueprint for international action in the twenty-first century. It contains forty chapters focused on solving the twin problems of environmental protection and sustainable development.

Agenda 21 is the international communities' response to the issues raised by *Our Common Future.* It called for the governments to adopt not only new environmental programs but to commit to significant economic, social, and international institutional reforms.

Agenda 21 is arguably the most important of the Rio documents from the standpoint of its potential to change unsustainable behavior because it is the first international agreement that creates international expectations that nations integrate environmental, economic, and social planning. Agenda 21 also creates norms about the responsibilities of the rich nations to poor ones. The purpose of Agenda 21 is nothing less than the transformation of human life on earth so as to make it harmonious with nonhuman life and environmental constraints.

Agenda 21 is premised on the notion that sustainable development is not an option but that it is an urgent requirement. The preamble to Agenda 21 demonstrates the strong sense of urgency that was motivation for the authors. The preamble states: "Humanity stands at a defining moment in history. We are confronted with a perpetuation of disparities between and within nations, worsening poverty, hunger, ill health and illiteracy, and the continuing deterioration of ecosystems on which we depend for our well being."[3]

Underlying Agenda 21 is the notion that the human community can either (1) continue present policies that both increase poverty and disparities between rich and poor and destroy ecosystems; or, (2) can change course. To change course, the governments of the world must integrate environmental, economic, and social programs in a new, historically unprecedented global partnership between the developed and the developing world.

Financing Sustainable Development

To follow up on the implementation of Agenda 21, the United Nations created the United Nations Commission on Sustainable Development (CSD). Chapter 33 of Agenda 21 is very controversial because it calls for the developed countries to contribute 0.7 percent of GNP for direct assistance aid to the developing world. Since the Earth Summit, direct assistance had actually fallen rather than approaching the 0.7 percent target.

Since Rio, the United States had fallen to last place in direct assistance among the developed countries aid as a percentage of GNP. Several other large northern countries had also failed to make progress toward the finance target. The United States had taken the position in Rio that it would have been unfair for the United States to agree to 0.7 percent of GNP because its economy was so much larger than any other nation and it was in first place among all nations in total dollars given for direct assistance. Therefore, the United States announced in Rio that it was not agreeing to the 0.7 percent target.

A March 1996 meeting of the CSD illustrates what is at issue. On that day, the United States no longer could argue that it was the largest donor in terms of total dollars. Japan, Germany, and France had eclipsed it in total foreign assistance. Because of the United States' poor track record on chapter 33, the U.S. delegation began the day with a sense of foreboding. During the morning briefing a member of the State Department predicted this would be "a day for the rest of the world to poke their fingers in the eye of Uncle Sam."

Later that morning, the discussion on financing sustainable development began with the European Union representative reaffirming the commitment of the European Union to the 0.7 percent target. The Italian ambassador, speaking on behalf of the European Union, stated that although not all European Union members had met the 0.7 percent target, some had exceeded it, and the European Union still was committed to this goal. The European Union believed that this target was still necessary to put the world on a sustainable footing. Several Scandinavian governments followed stating that they intended to exceed the 0.7 percent goal.

The Scandinavians were followed by the Colombian representative who spoke on behalf of the UN Group of 77 (G-77) and China. G-77 is a coalition of governments that includes some of the poorest countries. In the UN, the richer countries are generally referred to as the North while the poorer countries are referred to as the South. This is so even though some of the poorest countries are in the Northern Hemisphere and Australia, a wealthy country, is in the Southern Hemisphere.

The Colombian representative complained bitterly that several of the Northern nations had failed to live up to promises made in Rio. She acknowledged that although a few Northern governments should be congratulated for their generosity, in general, assistance from the North had actually declined since Rio. Her tone was a mixture of cynicism and disappointment.

The South had always argued that the North would use emerging global environmental problems as an excuse to freeze the South in place economically. To bring the South into the sustainable development tent, those Northerners pushing for a new sustainable development model understood that the South would seek assistance from the North. The centerpiece of incentives given to the South by the North was the 0.7 percent of GNP target for direct assistance aid.

Since Rio, the South consistently blamed the North for lack of progress in moving further down the path to a sustainable world. The South saw the North's failure to take the 0.7 percent target seriously as the major stumbling block to implementing Agenda 21.

Shortly after the Colombian representative spoke on behalf of G-77, the U.S. representative asked to speak. It was a dramatic moment. Almost without exception, diplomats in the UN speak with unusual poise and politeness. The U.S. State Department personnel usually meet or exceed these high standards of international diplomatic discourse. Yet, the U.S. representative was quite nervous as he began to speak.

As he spoke, the U.S. representative held a text that he usually read verbatim in similar circumstances. A verbatim reading was called for at this time because of the importance of accurately articulating a carefully crafted government position on the issues under discussion in opening remarks. As he spoke, the U.S. representative alternately read from the text and ad-libbed. The ad-libbing seemed to be a defensive reaction based on the need to explain a U.S. position that was at such odds with those that had preceded it.

Quite unusually, the U.S. representative dispensed with opening UN rituals requiring that the first time each country speaks it congratulates the chairman for being elected to chair the session. From the very beginning the U.S. representative plunged into a defense of the U.S. position. "Mr. Chairman," began the U.S. representative, "some people have to live in the real world." This statement was not in the U.S. written position that was handed out after the presentation. The U.S. representative then argued that because political support for increased direct assistance did not exist in the United States and in much of the North, the South should look for development assistance not in direct assistance from Northern governments but in the dramatically increasing flows of private sector investments. "The developing world should pursue structural adjustment strategies to take advantage of great increases in private sector investments since Rio," said the U.S. representative. There will be no free lunch, implied the U.S. representative, and the developing world should face the hard facts, take the bitter medicine of structural adjustment, and compete for private sector capital in a competitive global economy. Because private sector investment was outstripping public sector investment, the South should look to business investment to fuel lagging economies.

Structural adjustment is a term that first appeared in the early 1980s as new conditions began to be imposed on national development loans issued by the World Bank and the International Monetary Fund (IMF). Development strategists in the investment banks began to create structural adjustment conditions after the oil shocks of the 1970s and the worldwide recession of the early 1980s. Initially the South weathered these international economic crises by borrowing heavily, but it soon became apparent that the large debt load of the South was threatening Northern financial institutions. As a result, the Northern development banks began to condition loans on implementation of structural adjustment reforms.[4]

Structural adjustment is an umbrella term for a variety of macroeconomic policies designed to increase economic growth in a borrowing nation. Under the banner of structural adjustment, nations have been required to promise to implement monetary policy, reduce inefficient subsidies, decrease safety net benefits, divest government holdings, liberalize trade, and implement other export-oriented growth strategies. By 1992, the World Bank had financed whole or in part 267 macroeconomic or sectoral investment programs in seventy-five countries. A 1992 World Bank review of its adjustment programs concluded that the adjustment programs improved the status of the poor in the long run, but that short-term dislocations for some groups were high.[5]

From the beginning of their use by the development banks, structural adjustment programs have been very controversial. Supporters of structural adjustment policies saw them as necessary steps to lead the poorest countries out of poverty. According to proponents of structural adjustment programs, they lead to lower inflation rates, increased savings, lower budget deficits, improved trade balances, higher economic growth rates, employment creation, and poverty reduction.[6] According to one commentator, "For many governments and development agencies, it is a forgone conclusion that expanding economic growth through an outward oriented development strategy remains the only viable option for seeking better living conditions for citizens of developing countries."[7]

Critics see the following problems with structural adjustment policies:

(1) Increased economic activity triggered by structural adjustment policies without strong environmental protection laws often worsens environmental impacts.

(2) Low-income countries that make exports of commodities the centerpiece of their development strategy make themselves vulnerable to international commodity policies, interest rates, and conditions for which they have no control.

(3) Structural adjustment policies often increase the wealth of those individuals who control resources while worsening the income of already poor sectors.

(4) To the extent that structural adjustment policies reduce social safety nets, they make already vulnerable people more exposed to economic dislocations.[8]

In the 1980s a storm of controversy arose about the negative impacts on the environment created by the World Bank's loans. The bank was charged with issuing loans for projects that greatly harmed the environment and at the same time demanding that recipient countries agree to make structural adjustments that created additional adverse environmental and social impacts. As a result, the World Bank and other international development banks began to perform analyses to determine adverse impacts of loans and associated structural adjustment programs. The World Bank has also attempted to avoid the most adverse impacts of structural adjustment programs. Recent studies have concluded that structural adjustment programs can create both positive and negative environmental impacts.[9] Adverse environmental impacts include:

(1) In agricultural economies such as Mali and Cameroon, structural adjustment programs can create incentives to produce environmentally damaging crops and motivate subsistence farmers to increase agricultural activities that cause increased deforestation and soil erosion;

(2) In extractive economies such as Tanzania, Jamaica, and Venezuela, structural adjustment programs can bring widespread environmental degradation caused by increased environmentally unsound mining and forestry;

(3) In industrial societies such as Mexico or Thailand, structural adjustment programs that increase production in the absence of a strong environmental law framework can increase environmental degradation;

(4) Structural adjustment programs that include fiscal constraints on government spending may weaken a nation's ability to manage its natural resources and reduce funds available for monitoring, enforcement, standard setting, and extension services to the poor;

(5) Programs that remove subsidies for certain fuels can increase the use of more environmentally damaging fuels;

(6) Because the costs of many structural adjustment programs fall more

heavily on the poor, poverty-induced environmental degradation, including pollution from sewage and deforestation may increase.[10]

Despite these problems, the U.S. representative took the position that each Southern nation should rely on structural adjustment programs as the cornerstone of its efforts to attract private sector investment. Perhaps because he was ad-libbing, the U.S. representative failed to stress an important element of the U.S. position. The written U.S. position acknowledged that for private sector investment to work in bringing about sustainable development, each country needed to enact environmental laws that would assure that development was sustainable. That is, without strong environmental laws, economic growth triggered by business investment would likely be environmentally destructive. For example, although Thailand has experienced great economic growth in the past few years, the development has been environmentally damaging.

The U.S. position on financing sustainable development in the developing world was based upon the observation that private sector investment in the developing countries had increased dramatically since the end of the cold war. Much more money was now available from business investment than had ever been available from direct government assistance. As a result, parts of the world that were very poor just a few decade ago were experiencing dramatic increases in economic growth because of business investment. Examples abound of such economic transformations in the Pacific Rim. This growth was attributable to globalization of the economy, the implementation of trade reforms, and private sector investment. Yet where this growth has occurred has usually been environmentally disastrous.

Although the U.S. position recognized the need for environmental laws to keep development from its environmentally destructive propensities, the U.S. position ignored two practical problems that work against the creation of environmental laws in poorer countries.

The first was that in a competitive global market, there is great pressure to avoid costs created by strong environmental laws. One of the things that attracts foreign investment to poorer countries is the absence of regulatory programs that increase costs of production. Therefore, any country that enacted tough environmental laws would put itself in an uncompetitive position. In the United States, states failed to pass environmental laws that would impose costs on that state's industry. Not until minimum federal laws were passed did states develop modern regulatory regimes. In a similar fashion, it is not likely that poorer nations will want to penalize local businesses until there is greater harmonization of standards.

The second problem with the assumption that poorer countries will protect the environment by passing environmental laws is that costs of creating modern environmental regulatory programs are often prohibitive. Most countries in the South have neither the technical expertise nor the money to create effective environmental regulatory bodies. Environmental monitoring and enforcement is very expensive. For example, it costs as much as one thousand dollars to analyze one water sample for toxic substances. Ironically, the very people who advocate reliance on private sector investment often advocate structural adjustment programs that reduce government spending. There is an obvious conflict between a poor county's need to reduce government spending to attract foreign investment and any desire to create adequately funded environmental programs.

When the U.S. representative finished his presentation, several other nations reacted quite strongly. The German representative immediately reacted by emphatically stating that the U.S. position that direct government assistance was not necessary was wrong. Many of the poorest countries would not attract significant private sector investment even though others would, said the German representative. Several Southern nations repeated charges about the failure of the North to live up to the commitments made in Rio.

The final document coming out of the 1996 CSD did not resolve the continuing tensions between North and South on financing sustainable development in the South. It stated that financing sustainable development was an unresolved issue and that nations should consider alternatives for financing sustainable development. All seem to agree that not much has happened since Rio except that the North has not lived up to the target contained in chapter 33 of Agenda 21.

Sustainable Consumption Patterns

During the same week in which the CSD discussed financing sustainable development patterns, the CSD also considered progress made in reducing unsustainable production and consumption patterns. This is the second issue that continues to generate considerable animosity among rich and poor nations in CSD discussions.

Chapter 4 of Agenda 21 asserts that a major cause of global environmental deterioration is unsustainable production and consumption by developed countries. Chapter 4 states:

> While poverty results in certain kinds of environmental stress, the major cause of the continued deterioration of the global environment is the un-

sustainable pattern of consumption and production, particularly in industrialized countries, which is a matter of grave concern, aggravating poverty and imbalances.

Special attention should be paid to the demand for natural resources generated by unsustainable consumption and to efficient use of those resources consistent with the goal of minimizing resource depletion and reducing pollution. Although consumption patterns are very high in certain parts of the world, the basic consumer needs of a large section of humanity are not being met. This results in excessive demands and unsustainable lifestyles among the richer segments, which place immense stress on the environment. The poorer segments, meanwhile, are unable to meet food, health care, shelter, and educational needs. Changing consumption patterns will require a multipronged strategy focusing on demand, meeting the basic needs of the poor, and reducing wastage and use of finite resources in the production process.[11]

Therefore, Agenda 21 recognizes that the pollution loading of global ecosystems comes disproportionately from the high-consuming societies. For instance, Northern nations are discharging much higher levels of greenhouse gases and other air pollutants than the Southern countries on both a per capita and a total pounds basis. Northern countries also consume proportionally high levels of renewable and nonrenewable resources compared to those in the South. For instance, one-fifth of the world's population consumes 70 percent of all the energy, 80 percent of the wood products, and 75 percent of all metals.[12] Because of this disproportion, Agenda 21 calls on developed countries to take the lead in researching and moving toward sustainable resource use.

Several commentators have argued that because many of the global environmental problems such as the greenhouse effect have been caused largely by the developed nations, following the otherwise generally accepted principle that the polluter should pay, the Northern countries have duties to assume burdens of preventing future environmental damage, assist the developed world in moving toward sustainable development, or compensate the Southern countries for past damage.[13] Moreover, if global environmental problems are to be solved by new technologies, the poor nations cannot rely on expensive technology to solve environmental problems because they are already struggling to survive. Therefore, increases in technology costs mean the poor lose unless the richer nations accept responsibility for the pollution that they have created.[14]

Many economists from Western countries argue that the solution to global environmental problems lies in making sure that all human activities are forced to "internalize" full environmental costs. However, full costs are high when people are poor and low when the ability to pay is high. Therefore, development can only be sustainable when equity is made the leading edge.[15] Thus, an important question that must be paid attention to in implementation of Agenda 21 is "Who pays for environmental protection?"[16]

Moreover, consumer lifestyles in the developed world demand new, convenient, disposable goods with more and more consumers to respond to ever-increasing purchasing compulsion.[17] There is a vast gulf between the "wants" of most of the developed world and the "needs" of those in the developing world.[18] For these reasons, some argue that the developed world must both modify its consumptive behavior and assist the developing world in moving toward sustainable development.

Therefore the global environmental threats that influenced the development of Agenda 21 raise unprecedented issues of international distributive justice. Along this line one commentator argues that the international order has been dramatically transformed by Earth Summit developments, that is, Earth Summit documents have added to the list of recognized universal rights two new ones. They are: (1) the right to an equitable international order and (2) the right to an environment with health and dignity.[19]

The biggest fight in the CSD on unsustainable production and consumption during March 1996 came over the attempt of the South to insert in the document on Agenda 21, chapter 4, at various places language that recognizes that nations have "common but differentiated responsibility." Although this language was agreed to by the North in the Rio Declaration at the Earth Summit, every time the South attempted to have it inserted in documents relating to implementation of Agenda 21, the North resisted.

The United States and other Northern nations point to pollution prevention programs as their response to Agenda 21's call for moving away from unsustainable production and consumption practices. Pollution prevention programs seek to minimize pollution by redesigning industrial processes or installing treatment technologies that reduce pollution loadings. Many northern nations have developed pollution prevention programs that have significant potential to reduce pollution loading from some industrial activities. The United Nations Environment Program has also instituted a clean technology program that assists nations and industries in implementing pollution prevention programs.

Because pollution prevention programs are voluntary, investment in pollution prevention technology is most often made when the use of the technology will result in savings in resource or treatment costs in the industrial process. Therefore, the pollution prevention approach to unsustainable production has greatest potential to work most effectively when an economic analysis demonstrates an eventual return on investment in applying the technology. Proponents of pollution prevention programs see great hope in reducing pollution where "win-win" scenarios can be demonstrated. Pollution prevention technologies will work only in "win-lose" scenarios where governments mandate their application or where financing comes from government. Moreover, some environmental production-related problems are not likely to be solved by pollution prevention strategies. For instance, energy demand continues to rise worldwide despite potential savings in energy efficiency; problems of land-use-caused habitat destruction are not solvable by pollution prevention strategies; and forest product demand is also not likely to be greatly reduced by pollution prevention strategies.

Several NGOs and a few European nations argued at the CSD meeting that most pollution prevention programs are successful only in implementing "win-win" solutions, and that for "win-lose" problems such as energy and land use, additional efforts that go beyond unfolding pollution prevention programs are needed. Several NGOs argued that pollution prevention programs should be viewed as tools for obtaining targets designed to constrain consumption.

Several NGOs backed by a few Nordic countries introduced the ideas of "ecological space" and "ecological footprints," concepts that are nonstarters for the United States and many Northern nations. These ideas focus on the need for each society to consider the total space needed to sustain each society's resource use. Therefore, to understand the ecological footprint of New York City, one calculates the agricultural area needed to supply food to New York, the forest area needed to supply wood, the watershed area needed to supply water, the mining area needed to supply coal for electrical power, and so on. Each nation should limit its consumption to a proportionate share of the area of the earth available for specific uses. Needless to say, the concept of ecological footprint is an idea whose time has not yet come among the northern nations. Northern nations resist any limits on consumption and stress pollution programs related to production.

Although pollution prevention programs can be understood to be at least partial solutions by the North to problems of unsustainable production in the North, little has been proposed by the North under the banner of reducing unsustainable consumption. The North usually takes the position that a country should not have to worry about environmental problems created outside of its borders in the production of a commodity that is eventually imported to that country. The solution to an environmental problem caused in the production of a product that is exported to another country must be found in the country where the product is produced. That country should adopt environmental laws to prevent damage from the production of the commodity. The importing nation should not be concerned with another nation's environmental laws. When products are exported from the South it is the producing nation's responsibility to adopt environmentally protective legislation.

Yet, as we have seen in the discussion of financing sustainable development, above, to assume that a Southern nation will develop a strong environmental law regime is to overlook certain practical problems. These include, first, that any Southern nation passing a strong environmental law will put itself in a weakened competitive position. Second, many Southern nations don't have the funds to implement effective environmental law programs. It is therefore unlikely that the South will develop adequate environmental protection laws without assistance from the North.

At the end of the CSD debate on unsustainable production and consumption patterns, not much had been decided. The United States fought off the attempt of the South to focus on consumption, while the North argued that production changes should be the primary approach to implement reform in this area. The final decision deferred any action on sustainable production and consumption issues until later CSD meetings.

Conclusion

The CSD meeting illustrates how struggles between North and South were the biggest barrier in moving the world to solve the twin problems of environment and development. The South continued to see emerging global environmental problems as largely the responsibility of the North. Accordingly the South was unwilling to make commitments to reduce the South's growing share of these problems. The North saw this unwillingness as irresponsible. The South continued to see poverty as its most important priority. The South believed that poverty, not industrialization, was the cause of most of the serious environmental problems in the South including soil erosion, deforestation, desertification, and water polluted by sewage.

The North was concerned primarily with growing global environmental problems such as climate change, stratospheric ozone loss, and loss of biodiversity but was unwilling to take steps to reverse economic disparities between rich and poor nations or take meaningful steps to finance sustainable development in the South. The North eschewed more direct assistance to finance sustainable development in the South for two reasons. First, the North argued that it had its own financial problems caused by the globalization of the economy. Second, it argued that private sector investment was creating significant growth in the South, which was now competing with the North in an increasingly interconnected global market. The North seemed to assume that the South could protect the environment by passing environmental laws like those that existed in the North. This position assumed that northern environmental laws could serve as a model for the South. Such a position ignored the unresolved problems and limits of northern environmental laws created by politically powerful economic interests in northern countries.

Notes

1. World Commission on Environment and Development (WCED), *Our Common Future* (New York: Oxford University Press, 1987).

2. WCED, *Common Future.*

3. United Nations, *Agenda 21* (Rio de Janeiro: Report of the United Nations Conference on Environment and Development, 1992).

4. D. Reed, "An Instrument of Global Economic Policy," in *Structural Adjustment, the Environment, and Sustainable Development,* ed. D. Reed (New York: Earthscan Publications, 1996), 1–21.

5. Reed, "Global Economic Policy."

6. D. Reed, Introduction to *Structural Adjustment, the Environment, and Sustainable Development,* ixx–xxv.

7. Reed, "Global Economic Policy," 1–21.

8. Reed, "Global Economic Policy," Introduction, and "Conclusions: Short-Term Environmental Impacts of Structural Adjustment Programs," in *Structural Adjustment, the Environment, and Sustainable Development,* 299–333.

9. Reed, "Conclusions," 299–333.

10. Reed, "Conclusions," 299–333.

11. United Nations, *Agenda 21.*

12. Reed, "Global Economic Policy."

13. D. A. Brown, "The Role of Ethics in Sustainable Development and Environmental Protection," in *Sustainable Development: Science, Ethics, and Public Policy,* ed. J. Lemons and D. A. Brown (Dordrecht: Kluwer, 1995).

14. R. C. Heridia, "The Ethical Implications of Global Change: A Third World Perspective," in *Proceedings on Ethical Dimensions of the United Nations Program on Environment and Development, Agenda 21,* ed. D. A. Brown (Harrisburg, PA: Earth Ethics Research Group, 1994), 121–28.

15. Heridia, "Ethical Implications," 121–28.

16. R. Paden, "Free Trade and Sustainable Development, The Moral Basis of Agenda 21 and its Problems," *Proceedings on Ethical Dimensions of the United Nations Program on Environment and Development, Agenda 21,* 235–46.

17. J. F. Quinn, J. F. and J. A. Petrick, "Agenda 21 and Responsible Land Use Planning and Management: Legal, Scientific and Ethical Implications of Modernist, Post-Modernist and Universalist Environmental Philosophies," *Pro-*

ceedings on Ethical Dimensions of the United Nations Program on Environment and Development, Agenda 21, 247–66.

18. L. Westra, "Ecosystem Integrity and Agenda 21 Science, Sustainability and Public Policy," *Proceedings On Ethical Dimensions of the United Nations Program on Environment and Development, Agenda 21*, 382–92.

19. H. Rolston III, "Environmental Protection and the International World Order: Ethics after the Earth Summit," *Proceedings on Ethical Dimensions of the United Nations Program on Environment and Development, Agenda 21*, 267–84.

3

"The Tragedy of the Commons" Revisited: A Game Theoretic Analysis of Consumption

Joel E. Reichart

Introduction

Most environmental problems facing the world can ultimately be traced to the consumptive activities of humankind. The broad definition of consumption as used in this essay is that expressed by ecological economist Herman Daly, who writes that, "Consumption is the transformation of natural capital into manmade capital and ultimately to waste."[1] In other words, consumption is the appropriation and use of natural resources for the production of goods and services that primarily benefit human beings. By this definition, consumption occurs at both the front and back end of the production process. For example, a small coal-burning power plant consumes at the front end of the production process by appropriating natural capital (coal) for use in generating electricity, and consumes at the back end by appropriating natural capital (breathable air or clean water) through the expulsion of waste material. Back-end consumption is assumed here to be consumption of "common" resources. These are resources, such as air, fresh water, and the like, which are owned by no one in particular and thus are owned in common by all.

Given that all living beings must in some way consume natural resources to survive, consumption, in itself, is unproblematic. Rather, it is the manner in which natural resources are consumed by human beings that is the source of concern for the environment. For example, one can object as to whether the expulsion of waste by the small power plant above can genuinely be considered a destructive consumptive activity for two reasons. Certainly there are other arguments that can be made but these two suffice in making the point. First, the environment is enormous and can dissipate and assimilate waste material over time, hence the resources consumed will be largely untainted due to the size and regenerative abilities of biological systems, that is, the atmosphere and oceans are very large and can remove waste, thus the air is still fresh and the water clean. Second, since there are hundreds of such plants in existence and thousands of other nonrelated factories and individuals producing similar waste materials, the emissions of one small power plant add proportionately little to the volume of waste material already existing in the environment as a whole. Hence, for this one plant at least, the use of resources is so small that essentially no measurable harm is done, particularly in light of the fact that a great deal of benefit is obtained for the plant and its stakeholders vis-à-vis the amount of harm caused.

To the first objection, it is unquestionably true that natural processes like decomposition have the ability to convert much waste material into environmentally benign alternative forms. Even plutonium will eventually decay and become harmless, given enough millennia. The concern of the environmentalist is that the sheer volume of consumption and material composition of waste discharged into the environment is such that biological systems at some point cannot regenerate by converting all of the waste to benign forms at the same rate at which waste is added. Once this point, frequently referred to as "carrying capacity" or the "level of demand [that a biological system] can sustain," is reached, any further demand reduces the ability of the biological system to regenerate back to full capacity.[2] Therefore, unless consumers as a whole reduce their consumption, the result is a systematic, unsustainable buildup of waste material (pollutants) that effectively reduces the availability of usable common resources and inevitably leads to their degradation and destruction. Since human and other living beings depend on the common resources in question for survival, the destruction of the commons ultimately leads to the destruction of all living beings.

The second objection is much more difficult to answer. Assuming the carrying capacity has been reached, any additional demand above and beyond the carrying capacity of a biological system, however small, adds to the waste buildup regardless of its direct and countable impact. Therefore it makes intuitive sense for all consumers to set limits on their consumption as a whole because in the long run all benefit from the mutual cooperation of multilateral restraint. However, it is also rational for the individual to consume more than his or her fair share (whatever that may be) because, in the absence of some mechanism to enforce individual restraint, the benefits accrued can far outweigh the costs imposed. Therein lies the crux of one problem with the nature of human consumption. For it makes perfect sense for the individual or corporate consumer to continue to unsustainably exhaust resources, even if every consumer realizes that it is also in their interest as members of a community to restrain their consumption.

This is the result of what Garrett Hardin has referred to as "the tragedy of the commons."[3] To better understand the rationale underlying this destructive consumer behavior, it is fruitful to explore the nature of the consumptive decisions by reexamining Hardin's argument in detail. Specifically, the tragedy of the commons is analyzed below and reinterpreted using the fundamental precepts of game theory and the Prisoner's Dilemma. It is shown that a proposed rational solution, namely the "symmetry argument," to the tragedy is fundamentally flawed and that, to my knowledge, no rational solution exists that is applicable to real world commons problems. Finally, I demonstrate the mechanism whereby political, economic, and moral solutions, while not actually providing solutions to the Prisoner's Dilemma, resolve the tragedy by reframing the game being played. Hardin writes, "Therein is the tragedy. Each man is locked into a system that compels him to increase his herd without limit—in a world that is limited. Ruin is the destination toward which all men rush, each pursuing his own best interest in a society that believes in the freedom of the commons. Freedom in a commons brings ruin to all."[4]

The Prisoner's Dilemma

The tragedy of the commons is a problem of independent decision making that can be further simplified and modeled in accord with game theory. Game theory, which can be considered a subset of so-called rational choice theory, is the study of strategic decision making between two or more people.[5] For each strategic interaction analyzed, there exists a group of players, each of which has a set of possible strategies or choices available that, when chosen, will bring about a given state of the world, or payoff. In addition, each player has a preference ranking over the strategic alternatives and the choice of one strategic element affects the choices made by the other players.

The games analyzed can include two (two-person) or more (n-person) players.[6] In addition, games can have either a fixed payoff (zero-sum), where the total payoff divided between players remains constant so one's loss is another's gain, or a variable payoff (non-zero-sum), where the strategies chosen affect the total payoff divided between players. Finally, the games can be either cooperative or noncooperative.

In cooperative games, it is assumed that the players can openly communicate and make binding agreements before the game is played and thus coordinate their respective strategies. Here it has been claimed that, since an explicit means of enforcement is lacking in many cooperative models, much argumentative force is lost.[7] Noncooperative games consider the point of view of the rational individual acting in isolation. Any coordinating agreements made must be enforced through the game itself, thus the problem, often assumed away in cooperative games, of being able to make credible, binding commitments becomes clear.

There are a large variety of games that are analyzed by theorists but the game that has had the greatest impact by far, and is the most applicable for our purposes, is the Prisoner's Dilemma.[8] The Prisoner's Dilemma is a two-person, non-zero-sum, noncooperative game in which the paradoxical ramification of commons logic is made explicit; namely, that if participants in the game follow the rational course of action, the course of action chosen will prove to be to their collective detriment. The strategic form of the Prisoner's Dilemma is represented in the following two-by-two matrix (*fig. 3.1*).

The story of the Prisoner's Dilemma involves two prisoners who have jointly committed a crime and have been apprehended by the authorities. The numbers within each quadrant of the *fig. 3.1* matrix represent the possible years in jail faced by each prisoner. The top right number in each quadrant corresponds to Prisoner A and the lower left to Prisoner B. The authorities have enough evidence to convict both prisoners of a lesser charge that carries with it the one-year sentence, as shown in

FIGURE 3.1
Prisoner's Dilemma

Prisoner A

		Not Confess	Confess
Prisoner B	**Not Confess**	1 1	0 10
	Confess	10 0	5 5

the upper left-hand quadrant. However, in order to convict the prisoners of the greater offense, they need to obtain a confession from one or both.

To obtain a dual confession, the authorities question the prisoners separately and hold them in separate cells where they cannot communicate with each other. Each prisoner when questioned is told that enough evidence exists to convict both of the lesser charge where they will each receive one year. However, should one prisoner confess to the greater crime, the other will receive ten years while the confessor will go free. Should they both confess, each will receive the intermediate five-year sentence.

When the moment of truth for each prisoner arrives, they will both reason in the following way: "If the other prisoner confesses it is better for me to also confess because to do otherwise will result in me paying the ultimate price and being imprisoned for ten years as opposed to five. Likewise, if the other does not confess then it is still better for me to confess because then I will go free and avoid a one-year prison sentence. Therefore I should confess to the greater crime." Since both prisoners face symmetrical situations, the end result is that both will confess and be sentenced to five years. This is the rational solution to the dilemma because, in the absence of an enforceable agreement, the actions of one prisoner cannot be controlled or otherwise influenced by the other, thus confession is the rational choice.

Game Theoretic Interpretation of the Commons

The applicability of the Prisoner's Dilemma to the tragedy of the commons becomes clear when we substitute herdsmen for prisoners and change the prison sentences to reflect their ordinal utilities. The utilities represent the herdsmen's rankings of the strategic alternatives present within the structure of the game. The new "Commons Dilemma" is shown in *fig. 3.2.*[9]

The Commons Dilemma version of this game involves two herdsmen using one common pasture.[10] The herdsmen can choose to either cooperate with each other and preserve the health and integrity of the common by maintaining their herds at a steady state, or they may defect on their cooperation by increasing their herds. Each herdsman will view the choices available and the ordinal preference rankings, 4 being best, in the subsequent manner. In the best of all cases, either herdsman will prefer to defect and increase his herd while the other herdsman cooperates and maintains a steady state. He will thereby receive all of the benefits of increased grazing on the common while sharing only a fraction

FIGURE 3.2
Commons Dilemma

Herdsman A

		Cooperate	Defect
Herdsman B	Cooperate	3	4
		3	1
	Defect	1	2
		4	2

of the costs. Next, the herdsman will prefer that both parties cooperate and maintain their herds at a steady state. This is followed by the case where both herdsmen defect and add cattle. Finally, the herdsman's least preferred alternative is to cooperate while the other defects and continues to add cattle, thus absorbing some of the cost while receiving no benefits. Therefore, both herdsmen are faced with the following symmetrical ranking of the payoffs:

$$(4, 1), (3, 3), (2, 2), (1, 4)$$

If Herdsman A assumes that Herdsman B will cooperate then the rational choice would be for A to defect and thereby achieve the highest possible utility; (4, 1) vs. (3, 3). Conversely, if A assumes that B will defect on the bargain and add cattle to his herd, then the rational choice for A is also to defect, else A would achieve the worst result; (1, 4) vs. (2, 2). Either way, the rational choice for A is to defect. Since B is faced with identical payoffs, he will reason similarly. The net result is that both herdsmen defect and cattle are added by both; thus, the payoff to both is (2, 2).

In the parlance of game theory, the "defect" choice is a dominant strategy. The usual prescription for most game theorists is that, whenever a dominant strategy exists, that is to say a strategy that provides payoffs at least as good as any other available strategy, it is the rational choice. When two players in a game play their dominant strategies and can do no better, they have reached equilibrium. Games like the Commons Dilemma are characterized as paradoxical because "if both players make the rational choice . . . both lose."[11] Given an instrumental definition of rationality, both players are rational because they have followed the precepts of game theory and have chosen their dominant strategy, yet both players lose because there exists a cooperative surplus, (3, 3) vs. (2, 2), that could be harvested by them if they could only find some way to cooperate and maintain their herds, and therefore the commons, at a steady state. When extrapolated to real-world environmental problems, the Commons and Prisoner's Dilemmas can be renamed to reflect the problem under consideration, becoming the "Polluter's Dilemma,"[12] the "Fisheries Dilemma," the "Ozone Depletion Dilemma," and so on.

Here it might possibly be argued that the Prisoner's Dilemma is inappropriate for modeling these problems because it is inordinately abstract or simplified. Real world problems are much too complex and involve far too many actors to admit of a two-person model, so one might be better served exploring other, more realistic alternatives. The short answer to this objection is that, though it may be the case for some that a two-person game seems too abstract and simplified, we do indeed find the logical structure of the Prisoner's Dilemma in effect wherever it is possible to free-ride on the cooperative effort of many people. The "Free-Rider Dilemma" therefore can be considered an n-person Prisoner's Dilemma. The tragic element of free-riding, as in the tragedy of the commons, is that if few people do it there is little problem, but, if *everyone* does it, the cooperative effort collapses.

The term *free-ride* refers to a public transportation system where the potential user is on her honor to pay for her use of the system. Catching a subway train late at night when no one else is around is a suitable example. The user can either pay for the subway ride, and thus contribute toward his fair share of the public system's upkeep, or, since there is no one else around and he cannot be caught, he can elect to ride the train without paying, hence the term *free-ride*.[13] One person free-riding could not cause much harm to the subway system. But if everyone does it, the system might eventually collapse due to the disparity between revenue and costs.

The possibility of free-riding in general exists whenever goods are available for consumption without adequate control mechanisms in place to ensure equitable payment, or compliance with a distributive scheme, as appears to be the case for the various Commons Dilemmas mentioned above. Other, more mundane, free-rider dilemmas found in everyday life would be whether to pay for public television programs, whether to leave a note on an unattended car that you have somehow damaged, or the temptation to under-report income taxes. In addition, the logic of free-riding is nearly identical to that of the two-person game. Free-riding is the best case since one can enjoy the good without contributing to its provision. Second best is enjoying the good while contributing one's share along with all other users. Third best is doing without the good. And the worst case is having everyone else free-ride on one's own contribution. If everyone else pays, then it is in the potential user's interest to free-ride because she is made better off by saving the cost of the public good. Likewise, if everyone else is not paying for their use of the public good, then, rationally, she should also free-ride or else pay for a good that will soon be unavailable.

It may be that the preceding discussion is a bit misguided because some, or maybe most, users of the public good prefer to have the good available regardless of others' contributions to the common resource. Thus the ranking of the third and worst outcomes would alternate. The result can be illustrated by the infamous, if somewhat dangerous, 1950s youth game known as "chicken," where two cars speed toward a head-on collision and the first driver to veer away to avoid the accident is said to "chicken out." The strategic form of this game for our herdsmen, dubbed "Environmental Chicken,"[14] is shown in *fig. 3.3.*[15]

Notice that in Environmental Chicken neither herdsman possesses a dominant strategy. When each herdsman defects the other should cooperate, and when one cooperates the other should defect. This arrangement occurs when the failure to provide a public good is worse than when others free-ride on one's contribution. Ozone depletion may be more accurately characterized in this way as well as many local environmental issues where the individual actors are few. In Environmental Chicken, as opposed to the Commons Dilemma, it may be individually rational to cooperate to avoid the worst payoff, or conventions can arise under certain conditions regulating the herdsmen's strategies.[16]

FIGURE 3.3
Environmental Chicken

Herdsman A

		Cooperate	Defect
Herdsman B	Cooperate	3 / 3	4 / 2
	Defect	2 / 4	1 / 1

Robert Goodin argues that this is a limited case for most commons problems, because "the case for the Environmental Chicken model must rest on an extreme claim about the efficacy of a single man's (sic) [commons preserving] efforts."[17] For the herdsman, unilateral cooperation only makes sense if it has some advantage over unilateral consumption; namely, preserving the commons. If the commons is going to deteriorate regardless of one's individual effort, then the Commons Dilemma model is more suitable. It is for this reason, according to Goodin, that only at the international level is Environmental Chicken appropriate as a model. For only at this level are the actors large and few enough to make positive unilateral impact on the environment. However, I would also argue that the local, micro level also seems appropriate for the same reasons. Locally, one or two firms or individuals may have the ability to make a difference between a clean and a dirty local environment. So unilateral restraint might also be rational in regard to local, small-scale environmental issues.

Are There Any Rational or Technical Solutions to the Tragedy?

At this point the reader may be wondering if there is any rational solution to the Commons Dilemma. Why do the herdsmen continue to make such poor decisions in the face of the possible benefits of cooperation? Can they not see that their inability to cooperate and preserve the commons is not in their interests? Furthermore, why is it not rational to perceive the tragic results of defection and rationally cooperate? And, since one aspect of the problem seems to be the limitation of the commons itself, why not look for solutions that simply act to increase the commons, thereby eliminating the problem altogether? In this section we explore the efficacy of some posited rational solutions to the Prisoner's Dilemma and elaborate on Hardin's argument regarding technical solutions.

Some theorists attempt to resolve the Prisoner's Dilemma by appealing to the rationality of the players and in so doing rely on so-called "symmetry" arguments to achieve the cooperative outcome. Symmetry arguments can broadly be defined as arguments whereby rational players are shown to cooperate with others in games where the payoff structure for both players is identical. The general idea is that cooperation can be achieved because one may be playing the game with one's equally rational, or similarly disposed, counterpart and the rational choice is to cooperate.[18]

To illustrate, consider the following symmetry argument, which posits an even stronger relation between two players in a Prisoner's Dilemma.

Assume that the players are exact copies of each other, or doppelgang-ers, and are thus perfectly identical in their dispositions. Each player when faced with the decision will realize that he is playing against his doppelganger, who will reason identically and, it is argued, end up mak-ing the same choice as he. They will both reason that if one defects (cooperates) the other will do likewise. Therefore, given the consistency of each players' intimate knowledge of the other's decision making, they will be faced with only the diagonal outcomes, (2, 2) and (3, 3), of which the rational choice is to cooperate.

But why are the off-diagonal outcomes (1, 4), (4, 1) simply ruled out from the outset? Since the Prisoner's Dilemma is considered a noncoop-erative game in which the two players' choices are causally independent, either the symmetry argument seems to violate this independence clause, or the game being played is merely a "mirror choice" game with the payoffs shown in *fig. 3.4.*

Notice that the decision is identical for both players. Many game theo-rists would reject *fig. 3.4* as a misrepresentation of the Prisoner's Di-lemma for it does not necessarily follow that both individuals will always make the same choice.[19] It could very well happen that one of the players errs in their reasoning and makes a choice that leads to an off-diagonal outcome. The point is that, although the players may *believe* that the same choice will be made, the independence of their actions in the game does not lead the players to *necessarily* make the same choice. In addition, it is common during this phase for a player to evaluate the various alternatives available through the use of subjunctive conditionals by asking one's self questions like, "If I cooperate then there is great likelihood that the other player will cooperate also. But what would hap-pen if I did not cooperate? Will I not increase my payoff since the other player's decision is independent of mine?" Since the doppelganger will reason and deliberate in the same manner, we cannot determine the

FIGURE 3.4
Doppelgangers

A & B

	2
	2
	3
	3

final choice of the players with any degree of certainty. There appears to be no reason to rule out this type of deliberation and, therefore, no reason to rule out the possibility that the noncooperative solution is achieved, even in the unlikely event that a player is interacting with an identical partner.

Furthermore, if we assert that only the (2, 2) and (3, 3) outcomes are epistemically possible for the doppelgangers,[20] i.e., relative to and consistent with what the doppelgangers know about the game and each other, it may still be the case that *causally* possible outcomes are valid. The heart of the dilemma is that a rational solution must meet the condition that it be causally necessary that the players make the same choice while simultaneously satisfying the condition that each player's choice be causally independent, a daunting challenge indeed. Thus, symmetry arguments seem to ultimately fail in the attempt at achieving the cooperative solution based on the individual rationality of the players.

Another possible argument for achieving the cooperative solution appeals to the characteristics of real world Commons Dilemmas. The game as discussed thus far is limited in that it is played only once. Actual Commons Dilemmas are "iterated," that is, they are played many times, maybe even indefinitely. Notable experiments involving iterated games have demonstrated that the so-called tit-for-tat strategy, in which the decision rule is to initially cooperate then reciprocate in kind to the other player's cooperation or defection, is collectively stable and outperforms many other strategies.[21] Since real world dilemmas are more akin to the iterated game, modeling the tragedy of the commons in terms of the one-shot game may be a bit disingenuous.

It is true that the real world Commons Dilemmas might be more appropriately represented as iterated games. However, iterated two-person games appeal to the long-term rational self-interest of the players to achieve the cooperative solution. If the argument presented above is correct, defection in these same dilemmas is characterized as free-riding, and no amount of iteration will reduce the temptation to defect. In other words, the payoff in iterated two-person games may change to favor cooperation when one looks forward to future gain. Conversely, in a Free-Rider Dilemma the payoffs might never change because one is actually playing with no one in particular. The costs of defection are not borne by a particular other, but are instead externalized to all individuals who use the commons. Therefore, the temptation to free-ride remains an option, regardless of the number of plays.

Finally, there is the question whether technical solutions to the Commons Dilemma are feasible. Hardin defines a "technical solution" as "one that requires a change only in the techniques of the natural sciences, demanding little or nothing in the way of change in human values or ideas of morality."[22] The tragedy of the commons is a dilemma for which there is no technical solution, according to Hardin.

A devotee of technical solutions might deny that the tragedy of the commons even exists. Human ingenuity leads to scientific advances in commons management, which in turn can lead to an ever-expanding commons capable of supporting the needs of ever-expanding consumer demand. Arguments for the potency of technical solutions are perhaps exemplified by economist Julian Simon who calls into question many of the pressing issues forwarded by environmentalists.[23] On the issue of overpopulation, for example, Simon points to various statistics regarding human economic and social well-being that have improved in tandem with population growth. Per capita Gross Domestic Product, Gross National Product, life expectancy, infant mortality, levels of education, and so on have all improved as the world has become more populated. By denying limits to growth, Simon effectively denies the existence of the tragedy. Simon writes, "I believe that the population restrictionists' hand-wringing view leads to despair and resignation. My 'side's' view leads to hope and progress, in the reasonable expectation that the energetic efforts of humankind will prevail in the future—as they have in the past—to increase worldwide our numbers, our health, our wealth, and our opportunities."[24]

The primary concern with arguments such as Simon's is that they seem to defy logic. The implied argument is that the commons, human population in this case, can continue to grow indefinitely without concern for the limits of carrying capacity. In fact, there apparently is no such thing as carrying capacity in Simon's view. It may very well be the case that human ingenuity could, at least temporarily, abate the environmentalists' concern. But, if we agree with economist Herman Daly, among others, that "the earth will not tolerate the doubling of even one grain of wheat 64 times," then surely the earth will not tolerate an equally exponential growth in human beings.[25] This is not to argue that advances in technology are not important for the goal of stabilizing or ensuring the health and integrity of the commons.[26] This is merely a warning against, and denial of, a blind faith view of the benefits and hopeful salvation of human technological ingenuity in the face of apparent mathematical certainty.

Politico-Economic Solutions: Changing the Game

Having found no solution to the Commons Dilemma that appeals to the rationality of the individual players within the structure of the game, it is tempting to conclude that no solution exists. And this may in fact be a truism. Yet there are solutions that, though they do not resolve the dilemma within its strategic parameters, warrant discussion nonetheless.

One obvious method of resolving the Commons Dilemma that is briefly mentioned by Hardin is through privatization.[27] Privatization involves removing the commons from the public sphere entirely in an effort to remove the incentive to destroy it. This can be accomplished through the actual selling of the property, or through the issuing of some form of permit that temporarily allocates the right to use the property. Unfortunately, many of the commons found in real life will admit of no privatization system. How does one privatize the air we breathe, the ozone layer, or the world's fisheries?

There is also no little concern that privatization of common property may have little effect on its ultimate destruction.[28] A case in point is modern agriculture, which favors absentee ownership in the hands of the few. In rural communities, according to Wendell Berry, this has led to increasing communal disruption as small-scale farmers are forced to remove themselves from the land.[29] The result of this disruption is the continued degradation of the environment as those who are most motivated to protect its health and integrity, local owners, are removed. This is not to claim that absentee owners are "bad guys" or uncaring people in any way. Yet their stake in the local communities and environments where they do business is naturally reduced for their absenteeism. Therefore it is a dubious conclusion that privatization, though it may work in some instances, is *the* solution to the tragedy.

A critical problem facing the players in a Commons Dilemma is coordinating their individual strategies because, assuming that a credible commitment could be made by both players to abide by a coordinative scheme, the players could then enjoy the long-term fruits of the cooperative surplus. A coordination problem exists "whenever it is rational for *all* agents involved to prefer joint to independent decision-making" (author's emphasis).[30] A coordination of strategies would involve some sort of coordinative scheme, accompanied by a formal enforcement mechanism to ensure compliance.

The coordinative scheme would necessarily be of a scale suitable to preserve the commons by curtailing consumption across cities, states, and even countries. Such a large, macro scale is requisite for the scheme because the Commons Dilemma "presents itself in only marginally different terms to sub-units of government."[31] Cities face a Commons Dilemma when deciding whether to pass more demanding environmental regulations that may have the effect of driving industry to cities with less strict, and less costly, regulations. States face much the same problem and, in the age of the multinational corporation, countries face a Commons Dilemma much like the small-scale problem facing the two herds-men. Therefore, the coordination of strategies, and subsequent reduction in consumption necessary to preserve the commons and avert the tragedy, must stem from global politicoeconomic coordination and control.

The economic strategies found in the literature are plentiful, the most promising of which involve harnessing market mechanisms. "Green fees," tradable emission permits, throughput taxation, and improved resource accounting are some of the more prevalent strategies suggested.[32] The effect of economic strategies on the Commons Dilemma is to provide incentives that make rational defection less attractive. In addition, some form of coordination and control mechanisms must be instituted to ensure compliance. The form of mechanism instituted is dependent upon the geographic scope of the problem. For example, local pollution prevention mechanisms may vary between cities based on local needs, while fisheries depletion or ozone depletion would need coordinated global initiatives to be effective. In either case, the strategies implemented require coordination and control in an effort to prevent free-ridership.

The implementation of coordination and control mechanisms to enforce economic strategies does not solve the Commons Dilemma, however. What coordinative enforcement mechanisms essentially do in game theoretic terms is change the payoff structure of the game. Recall that the ability to create an enforceable agreement between players is what separates noncooperative from cooperative games.[33] One strategy for contending with prisoner's dilemmas is to convert them from noncooperative games to cooperative ones, such as the Assurance Game in *fig. 3.5.*

In the Assurance Game, both herdsmen might prefer to cooperate with each other and do their part in safeguarding the commons. It is best for one to cooperate providing the other does not defect and force the worst outcome. All that the herdsmen need to achieve the cooperative solution is some form of "assurance" that the other will likewise cooperate, hence this is deemed an "assurance problem."[34] Assurance, the motivation to believe that the other will cooperate in Commons Dilemmas in this case, is provided by economic incentives combined with their successful enforcement.

As should be clear, in assurance problems, social cooperation is much easier to achieve and the likelihood of harmonizing individual rationality with an optimal social state is vastly improved. In effect, the herdsmen will now assign significant *disutility* to nonperformance and their problems of commitment can be resolved. A similar line of argument applies to solutions that rely on a person's feelings of guilt, human decency,

FIGURE 3.5
Assurance Game

Herdsman A

		Cooperate	Defect
Herdsman B	Cooperate	4 4	3 1
	Defect	1 3	2 2

and the like to resolve the Prisoner's Dilemma.[35] The players are no longer in a Prisoner's Dilemma but are instead in a situation that merely "looks like" one.[36]

Some of the more comprehensive environmental proposals recognize the destructive nature of free-riding on the commons and present solutions that correspond to the above analysis. For example, the global implementation phase of Laura Westra's "Principle of Integrity" requires the setting aside of pristine wilderness areas as yet undamaged by the consumptive activity of humankind for the purpose of maintaining strong-form integrity, or I_a.[37] Buffer zones, in which only the most environmentally benign production is allowed, would then be established around these areas in an effort to maintain I_a in pristine areas, and weak-form integrity, I_b, within the buffer zones. In addition, the productive activities in urban centers would be such that I_a and I_b are not compromised. For example, in urban centers, the Principle of Integrity would prohibit the manufacture and release of toxic and ozone-destroying chemicals, nuclear waste, pesticides, and so on, presumably through the use of either market mechanisms or various regulations and prohibitions. Finally, to insure compliance with the tenets of her theory, Westra posits that something like an environmental United Nations could possibly be created to oversee the world's consumptive activities. This global political organization would be empowered to intervene when necessary, thus enforcing the market and regulatory measures implemented.

Here we can see that a fully implemented Principle of Integrity would furnish the requisite motivating incentives that transform Commons Dilemmas to Assurance Games and provide the control necessary to resolve the assurance problem. Thus the tragedy of the commons can be averted. However, some might argue that an enforcement scheme such as Westra's would be highly coercive, and thus politically unpalatable or, at worst, impossible to realistically implement. If it is true, as I believe it is, that the overconsumption of the commons is ruinous to life on earth, then some form of coercive control appears to be called for. Whether the necessary control mechanism should optimally be in the form of a single governing body with global reach, or possibly another form such as a multilateral agreement between and within nations, is a subject for future discussion. Yet unilateral coercion during the implementation of any control mechanism may ultimately subvert the scheme proposed, regardless of the good intentions of its adherents.

All social arrangements that shift incentives are coercive to some degree as they involve the infringement of personal liberty. It is the nature of such coercion that may be questionable. Hardin argues that the only agreeable coercion is "mutual coercion, mutually agreed upon."[38] For our purposes, he means that any cooperative effort producing commons-preserving, politicoeconomic incentives and control mechanisms must, at least, be supported by a majority of the individuals that it affects.

For environmental commons, freedom to consume the commons at will means freedom to bring universal ruin to all. The implementation of mutually agreeable, mutually coercive politicoeconomic coordination and control mechanisms would preserve the commons and have a similar effect on individual freedom. Individuals agreeing to abide by a coercive, commons-preserving, politicoeconomic scheme are free to pursue their own goals, secure in the knowledge that life-sustaining ecological systems are less likely to be destroyed.

Conclusion: A Question of Values

To summarize the argument presented thus far, the tragedy of the commons underscores one major problem of human consumption as it relates to many current environmental concerns, namely, that the usage of common natural resources, upon which human (and much nonhuman) life depends for its very existence, beyond their carrying capacity is a logical outcome of the strategic interaction among users of those resources. To better understand the intricacies of applicable strategic interaction, the fundamental concepts of game theory were outlined along with the structure and underlying logic of the Prisoner's Dilemma. The tragedy of the commons was reinterpreted in game theoretic terms and the paradoxical ramification of the Commons Dilemma was made clear . . . if the players in the game follow the rational choice, they both lose. Even if one objects that the Commons Dilemma model is oversimplified or too abstract to allow a realistic comparison to real world problems, the logical structure of the decision being made was shown to exist in the form of free-riding whenever public goods, like common resources, are available for consumption.

Three proposed solutions to the Commons Dilemma were explored and found lacking in some respect. It was argued that privatization and politicoeconomic measures resolve the dilemma by, respectively, enclosing the commons and changing the structure of the game. A critical problem facing the players is coordinating their individual strategies. This is accomplished, it was argued, by creating incentives to cooperate through the implementation of economic strategies that, in essence, change the payoffs of the Commons Dilemma to represent a cooperative game. In addition, a coordination and control mechanism must also be implemented to assure the players of mutual cooperation by enforcing compliance with the preferred economic strategies. The mechanism must necessarily be of suitable geographic scope and, since many Commons Dilemmas are of global proportions, effective enforcement implies that some form of global politicoeconomic coordination and control is requisite. Given that all such coordination and control would be coercive, the only acceptable and realistic politicoeconomic scheme would be one that was mutually agreed to by, at least, a majority of those affected.

The major hurdle in implementing such a scheme, particularly on a global scale, would obviously be obtaining the requisite consent. If a change in human values and ideas of morality are needed to resolve the tragedy of the commons, then why, one might ask, have they not been mentioned as possible solutions to the Commons Dilemma? One reason is that game theory is the study of rational, strategic decision making and, in general, claims to make no moral claims.[39] That game theory may in fact be supporting a misguided sense of morality is a major criticism.[40] Where individual values and morals do play a part, however, is in establishing the payoffs of individuals playing a game. It is not difficult to imagine a player in a Commons Dilemma that, for whatever ethical reason, would refuse under most circumstances to defect. The player basically assigns significant *disutility* to defection and, like the effect of emotions or enforceable agreements, is in a game that merely appears to be a Commons Dilemma.

However, if we are searching for a notion of values or morality that can act as a catalyst in achieving collective consent to a politicoeconomic coordination and control scheme, then a radical reconceptualization of how the commons is collectively valued might provide a solution. This reconceptualization of value would understand the commons, and thereby recognize value in nonhuman nature, apart from the instrumental benefits accrued to human beings. The growing discipline of environmental ethics is continuing to evolve in response to this challenge. For example, environmental philosopher Holmes Rolston III argues convincingly that there is a multitude of values existing in nonhuman nature, in addition to anthropocentric values, and they ought to be acknowledged and respected.[41]

To accumulate the collective will necessary for a majority consent to a politicoeconomic scheme, however, a growing number of human beings will need, at the very least, to recognize that their personal well-being depends intimately and completely on the health and integrity of the commons, both now and in the future. In addition, those same individuals will need to realize that it is not just some nameless group of herdsmen that suffer from being trapped in the logic of the Commons Dilemma. Indeed, it is every human being that is playing the paradoxical and destructive game. We are all caught in a Commons Dilemma, on a global scale, with global cumulative ramifications, every day of our lives.

Notes

1. Quoted in Neva R. Goodwin, "Overview Essay," in *The Consumer Society*, ed. N. R. Goodwin, F. Ackerman, and D. Kiron (Washington, D.C.: Island Press, 1997), 2.

2. Lester R. Brown, Christopher Flavin, and Sandra Postel, *Saving the Planet: How to Shape an Environmentally Sustainable Global Economy* (New York: W. W. Norton, 1991), 74.

3. Garrett Hardin, "The Tragedy of the Commons," *Science* 162, no. 3858, reprinted in C. Pierce and D. VanDeVeer, *People, Penguins and Plastic Trees*, 2d ed. (Belmont, Calif.: Wadsworth Publishing Company, 1995).

4. Ibid., 332–33.

5. For an introduction to rational choice and game theory, see *Rational Choice*, ed. Jon Elster (New York: New York University Press, 1986). See John Von Neumann and Oskar Morgenstern, *Theory of Games and Economic Behavior* (Princeton: Princeton University Press, 1944), and Duncan R. Luce and Howard Riaffa, *Games and Decisions* (New York: John Wiley, 1957), for the fundamentals of game theory.

6. For our purposes, we are concerned mainly with two-person games as a representative model of the tragedy of the commons. N-person games have an advantage in that they could be said to more accurately model the real world, and some relevant aspects of them are briefly discussed below. However, the complexity of the bargaining models would carry the analysis beyond the scope of this essay without adding much to the argument. See John C. Harsanyi, *Rational Behavior and Bargaining Equilibrium in Games and Social Situations* (New York: Cambridge University Press, 1977); Luce and Riaffa, *Games and Decisions*; Von

Neumann and Morgenstern, *A Theory of Games*; and William Thomson and Terje Lensberg, *Axiomatic Theory of Bargaining with a Variable Number of Agents* (New York: Cambridge University Press, 1989), for discussions of n-person bargaining games.

7. John C. Harsanyi and Reinhart Selton, *A General Theory of Equilibrium Selection* (Cambridge: MIT Press, 1988).

8. See Luce and Riaffa, *Games and Decisions*, 94–102; Daniel M. Hausman and Michael S. McPherson, *Economic Analysis and Moral Philosophy* (Cambridge: Cambridge University Press, 1996), chap. 13; and other game theory references in this essay. For a fascinating historical study of the development of game theory, see William Poundstone, *Prisoner's Dilemma: John Von Neumann, Game Theory and the Puzzle of the Bomb* (New York: Anchor Books [Doubleday], 1992).

9. The terms Prisoner's Dilemma and Commons Dilemma are used interchangeably throughout the remainder of this essay.

10. See Robert E. Goodin, *The Politics of Rational Man* (New York: John Wiley, 1976), chap. 15.

11. Anatole Rapoport, "Escape from Paradox," *Scientific American* 217 (1967): 51.

12. Goodin, *Politics of Rational Man*.

13. See James M. Buchanan, *The Demand and Supply of Public Goods* (Chicago: Rand McNally, 1968), chap. 5, and Garrett Cullity, "Moral Free Riding," *Philosophy and Public Affairs* 24, no. 1 (Winter 1995): 3–34.

14. Goodin, *Politics of Rational Man*.

15. Here I am following Goodin, *Politics of Rational Man*.

16. Robert Sugden, *The Economics of Rights, Co-operation and Welfare* (New York: Basil Blackwell, 1986).

17. Goodin, *Politics of Rational Man*, 167.

18. See Anatole Rapaport, *Two-Person Game Theory* (Ann Arbor: University of Michigan Press, 1966); Lawrence H. Davis, "Prisoners, Paradox and Rationality," in *Paradoxes of Rationality and Cooperation: Prisoner's Dilemma and Newcomb's Problem*, ed. R. Campbell and L. Snowden (Vancouver: University of British Columbia Press, 1985); and David Gauthier, *Morals by Agreement* (Oxford: Oxford University Press, 1986).

19. Cristina Bicchieti and Mitchell S. Green, "Symmetry Arguments for Cooperation in the Prisoners' Dilemma," in *Contemporary Action Theory: The Philosophical Logic of Social Action* (Boston: Kluwer, 1997), and R. K. Campbell, "The Prisoner's Dilemma and the Symmetry Argument for Cooperation," *Analysis* 49: 60–65.

20. Davis, "Prisoners, Paradox and Rationality."

21. Robert Axelrod, *The Evolution of Cooperation* (New York: Basic Books, 1984).

22. Hardin, "The Tragedy of the Commons," 330.

23. Norman Myers and Julian L. Simon, *Scarcity or Abundance: A Debate on the Environment* (New York: W. W. Norton, 1994).

24. Myers and Simon, *Scarcity or Abundance*, 34.

25. Herman E. Daly, "Sustainable Growth: An Impossibility Theorem," in *Val-*

uing the Earth: Economics, Ecology, Ethics, ed. H. Daly and K. N. Townsend (Cambridge: MIT Press, 1993), 268.

26. Joel E. Reichart and Patricia H. Werhane, "Sustainable Development and Economic Growth," in *Perspectives on Ecological Integrity*, ed. Laura Westra and John Lemons (Boston: Kluwer, 1995).

27. See Hardin, "The Tragedy of the Commons."

28. Malcolm Gillis, "Economics, Ecology, and Ethics: Mending the Broken Circle for Tropical Forests," in *Economics, Ecology and Ethics: Mending the Broken Circle*, ed. F. H. Bormann and S. R. Kellert (New Haven: Yale University Press, 1991).

29. Wendell Berry, *The Unsettling of America: Culture and Agriculture* (San Francisco: Sierra Club Books, 1977).

30. Goodin, *Politics of Rational Man*, 27.

31. Goodin, *Politics of Rational Man*, 168.

32. David Malin Roodman, "Harnessing the Market for the Environment," in *State of the World 1996*, ed. L. Stark (New York: W. W. Norton, 1996); Gillis, "Economics, Ecology and Ethics"; William A. Butler, "Incentives for Conservation," in *Economics, Ecology and Ethics: Mending the Broken Circle*, ed. F. H. Bormann and S. R. Kellert (New Haven: Yale University Press, 1991); Herman E. Daly and John B. Cobb, *For the Common Good: Redirecting the Economy Toward Community, the Environment, and a Sustainable Future* (Boston: Beacon Press, 1994).

33. James D. Morrow, *Game Theory for Political Scientists* (Princeton: Princeton University Press, 1994).

34. Amartya K. Sen, "Isolation, Assurance and the Social Rate of Discount," *Quarterly Journal of Economics* 81 (1967): 112–24.

35. Robert H. Frank, *Passions Within Reason* (New York: W. W. Norton, 1988).

36. John C. Harsanyi, "Advances in Understanding Rational Behavior," in *Rationality in Action: Contemporary Approaches*, ed. P. K. Moser (Cambridge: Cambridge University Press, 1990).

37. Laura Westra, *An Environmental Proposal for Ethics: The Principle of Integrity* (Lanham, MD: Rowman and Littlefield, 1994), part 2. The ecological and philosophical details of Westra's Principle of Integrity are not discussed here, for to give Westra's argument suitable attention would require significantly more space and might detract from the present discussion. See Westra, *Environmental Proposal*; and *Perspectives on Ecological Integrity*, ed. Laura Westra and John Lemons (Boston: Kluwer, 1995), for a more detailed accounting of the Principle of Integrity and its ramifications.

38. Hardin, "Tragedy of the Commons," 336.

39. Of note here is that solutions have been forwarded that approach the Prisoner's Dilemma from sophisticated utilitarian perspective in Russell Hardin, Collective Action (Baltimore: Johns Hopkins University Press, 1988), and Kantian perspective in Thomas C. Schelling, *Micromotives and Macrobehavior* (New York: W. W. Norton, 1978).

40. Robert Salomon, *Ethics and Excellence* (New York: Oxford University Press, 1993).

41. Holmes Rolston III, *Conserving Natural Value* (New York: Columbia University Press, 1994).

4

Institutionalizing Overconsumption

Don Mayer

The consumer-driven economy of the United States is based on a constellation of concepts about ourselves, God, growth, wealth, and the world we live in. These conceptions deny the relevance of God or spiritual life to business activities. Nature is primarily to be used for human benefit, and anything that cannot be counted or measured in monetary terms has limited or marginal "utility." Earth is valued for its resources, which are assumed to be both infinite and inexhaustible. Even if not, we have faith that human ingenuity will find suitable substitutes for any shortages and technological "fixes" for serious degradation of our natural environment. The consumer-driven economy presumes that nations and corporations must grow in order to "progress" and assumes that the "rational economic person" will strive to amass as much material wealth and experience as much pleasure as possible. "You only go around once in life," the Schlitz beer commercial used to implore, "So go for all the gusto you can!"

These beliefs encourage overconsumption as a way of life, for they posit a world of boundless freedom without natural limits or moral restraints on human action. Electing freedom to disobey God's limits, mankind exits the Garden of Eden and enters a world where nature is to be conquered rather than accepted or embraced. The roots of our alienation from nature are deep; not surprisingly, then, the institutional engines of overconsumption are many and varied. They include the "free market economy" as presently practiced in the United States and the "free trade" regimes of the General Agreement on Tariffs and Trade (GATT). The institutional supports for overconsumption also include laws that protect the rights of "free speech" as exercised by large corporations in lobbying, advertising, and contributing to political parties and candidates. Such supports include the U.S. political system generally, political parties, the U.S. judicial system, the media, and administrative agencies. In the course of this article, various laws, domestic and international, will be examined as part of national and global legal structures, along with international institutions that—unwittingly or not—promote overconsumption.

Overconsumption, like any general phenomenon, is multifaceted and eludes precise definition. As a working definition, I suggest that overconsumption occurs where (1) people (individually or collectively) make consumption an end in itself, rather than a means to some higher human purpose, where (2) economic/legal systems fail to follow free market principles, or where (3) the economic/legal system fails to adequately recognize and account for future costs, the interests of future generations, or finite limits to the use of natural resources as "capital." We will look first at overconsumption in its first aspect, where consumption has become an end in itself.

Creating Want: Corporate Capitalism and the Dream Merchants

One recent book reassures us that *God Wants You To Be Rich*.[1] In fact, the illusions created by the corporate dream merchants have become the new religion, as William Leach has shown in his 1993 book, *Land of Desire: Merchants, Power, and the Rise of a New American Culture*. In feeding the dreams and desires of material salvation here and now, corporations have deliberately created "the consumer," an ideal marketing target who rejects tradition, focuses on immediate gratification, and is steeped in desire for all things new. Paul Wachtel claims that "having more and newer things each year has become not just something we want but something we need. The idea of more, of ever increasing wealth, has become the center of our identity and our security, and we are caught by it as an addict by his drugs."[2]

The institutionalized aspects of this addiction will be hard to break, indeed. When environmentalists claim that we need to reduce consumption, business and the consumer both recoil. The U.S. economy was not always built on consumer demand, but consumer demand now accounts for two-thirds of U.S. economic activity. U.S. consumers are so well-conditioned to satisfying needs through things that any suggestion to cut back is met with "intense anxiety, depression, rage, and even panic."[3] In part this is because the average American is exposed to hundreds of advertisements each day, and the process begins at an early age. Even if the specific product is not remembered, the overall message is: there is a product to meet your every need, if only you will buy it. As Alan Durning has noted,

> People actually remember few ads. Yet commercials have an effect nonetheless. Even if they fail to sell a particular product, they sell consumerism itself by ceaselessly reiterating the idea that there is a product to solve each of life's problems, indeed that existence would be satisfying and complete if only we bought the right things. Advertisers thus cultivate needs by hitching their wares to the infinite yearnings of the human soul.[4]

As Kanner and Gomes point out, "large-scale advertising is one of the main factors in American society that creates and maintains a peculiar form of narcissism ideally suited to consumerism. As such, it creates artificial needs within people that directly conflict with their capacity to form a satisfying and sustainable relationship with the natural world."[5]

The irrational nature of this addictive consumption leads a majority of Americans to focus on ourselves to the exclusion of community. Even as the Gross Domestic Product (GDP) continues to rise, there is strong evidence of declining social welfare in the United States[6] and large holes in the "moral fabric" of U.S. society. The popular desire to consume and possess more and more is also at the root of increasing social inequities throughout the world. Tom Athanasiou, in *Divided Planet: The Ecology of Rich and Poor*, uses data from demographer Paul Bairoch to contrast the relative wealth of developed and less developed countries from 1750 to the 1980s. From 1750, when living standards in "the North" were not notably higher than those in the "South,"

> the "average citizen" of the capitalist world grew to be eight times richer than one in the noncapitalist world, and contrary to all the tales told by friends of "progress," this "improvement" has not always been by virtue of the North's technological and cultural innovations. The less-flattering and, according to Robert Heilbroner, "more important" side of the story, "was the drainage of wealth from the underdeveloped Periphery to the developed Center—a capitalist version of the much-older imperialist exploitation of the weak by the strong."[7]

Many have expressed disenchantment with overconsumption in the North, both for its negative effects on the South and for its failure to bring social progress in the North. Still, the path of "growth and progress" through consumption remains the principal agenda of consumers, corporations, and the government.

As Robert Samuelson notes in *The Good Life and Its Discontents*, "the central ambition of postwar society has been to create ever expanding prosperity at home and abroad . . . because prosperity has seemed to be the path to higher goals."[8] Those goals originally included the end to poverty, crime, slums, and racial conflict, but as the 1960s and 1970s ended the failure to meet such goals was evident. The 1970s and 1980s were, increasingly, a time of retrenchment from social progress, a time of self-help psychology, leveraged buyouts, and the celebration of wealth for the sake of wealth. The hippies and yippies of the 1960s gave way to the yuppies of the 1980s. During those two decades the country retained its belief in greater material wealth but largely gave up hopes of achieving any end to poverty, crime, or racial strife.

Samuelson also notes the initial postwar vision of America and the world: global prosperity would contain communism, spread democracy, and solidify U.S. global leadership. The United States democracy would be the most admired and our economy would be the wealthiest. Several postwar institutions were established to keep the peace and establish commercial prosperity, including the World Bank, the IMF, the United Nations, and the General Agreement on Tariffs and Trade (GATT). The UN would keep the peace, the World Bank would work to bring new nations into the international trading system, and free trade through GATT would reduce the likelihood of trade wars and, thus, reduce the likelihood of military conflict. In all of this, the United States was a leader, and in our postwar conception of the American Dream, we professed the belief that other nations could develop in the same way. Yet in over fifty years since World War II, "development" and free trade have not brought economic or social well-being to many of the "developing" nations, and much of the blame can be placed squarely on industrialized nations—particularly the United States—that continue to command the lion's share of the world's resources for themselves.

In sum, consumption has become an end in itself, rather than a means to individual enlightenment or happiness, or as a means to social justice, either domestically or globally. And as the consumption habit becomes an end in itself, our own deeper needs become obscured.

"Free Markets" in the Age of Corporate Capitalism

Along with the irrational addiction to more and more, we practice a kind of collective blindness. While many in the United States pay frequent lip service to the "free market," our public and private institutions often disregard its most basic precepts. At least four aspects of current corporate capitalism are not true to free market theory and result in various forms of overconsumption. First, the current system fails to discourage monopolies and ever-greater concentrations of capital. Second, the system will generally reward a business that imposes costs on others by generating negative externalities. Third, reliable factual information is not easily available to consumers. Fourth, government and business have become inexorably intertwined, with massive subsidies tilting the free market playing field toward some highly consumptive economic activities and away from other less consumptive activities. Overall, systematic pressures on corporate executives to enhance the bottom line are matched by governmental efforts to assure annual increases in the Gross Domestic Product (GDP), yet both sets of measurement are unreliable indices of social improvement.

Confusing Bigger with Better: Monopolies and Well-Being

In the ideal market envisioned by economists, there are few barriers to entry and considerable competition among sellers. Monopoly power is power to break the market. Conversely, it is competition—the existence of many alternatives for both buyer and seller—that keeps profits at normal levels and properly allocates resources. Yet the largest corporations now dictate the direction of global business. Nearly 70 percent of world trade is controlled by just 500 corporations, and one percent of all multinationals own half the total stock of foreign direct investment. Moreover, joint ventures and strategic alliances are emerging among those large companies to make global markets "more rational" (that is, more predictable and less "cutthroat" for the corporations in such alliances). In short, a few multinational corporations (MNCs) are consolidating their hold on the global economy. Giving MNCs this kind of control over the global economy will have unpredictable repercussions for local economies and the environment. While a more "rational" market might in theory restrain excessive consumption of natural resources, many large corporations—either directly or through intermediaries— are using their clout by creating barriers to entry, stifling local, sustainable economies, and racing to liquidate finite resources.

Partial-Cost Pricing: The Rising Tide of Externalities

In the ideal market economy the price of a product as reflected by the demands of buyers and sellers in a free market would represent the best possible allocation of resources. But in reality, many economic exchanges create "spillover effects" or "externalities" that impose costs on people who are not parties to the transaction. The number and gravity of these "externalities" has risen remarkably in the second part of this century. They include not only localized externalities (for example, toxic substances from industrial manufacturing that leach into public water supplies) but also pervasive externalities (such as acid rain, ozone depletion, or CO_2 buildup).

This problem is accelerated by MNCs operating globally. In effect, local markets are no longer local; those responsible for environmental degradation or unsustainable forms of economic activity do not actually witness the harms done, and need not worry about accountability—they can take their profits, cut their losses, and move on to the next investment. As Paul Hawken puts it: "Money thus acts as a self-propelled force, ostensibly in the hands of institutions and fiduciaries but, practically speaking, in the control of a well-programmed calculus that constantly reevaluates where it can find the greatest return, in the form of currencies, interest, or equity, or a combination of the three."[9]

Hawken notes that if the Penan tribespeople of Sarawak experience the utter devastation of their culture and way of life at the hands of logging companies contracted to the Mitsubishi Corporation, nothing happens to Mitsubishi's shares on the Nikkei exchange. "Mitsubishi's bonds are not discounted for cultural annihilation."[10] In short, there is overconsumption, not because free market economic theory is misguided, but because the pervasiveness of negative externalities means that price does not give consumers or corporations the feedback necessary either to optimally allocate resources or to consider the moral consequences of particular production or consumption decisions.

Information or Disinformation? Corporate Free Speech for a "World Without Limits"

AT&T—Bringing You a World Without Limits
(advertising slogan for the 1996 Summer Olympics)

The basic building block of modern economic theory is the rationally self-interested actor maximizing his consumer preferences in a free market context. The rational buyer needs information about the price of a product, its qualities, who produced it, and what kinds of warranties are part of the bargain. For a seller, only limited information is required: the credit-worthiness of the buyer. At present, such information is generally available to the seller. It is the buyer whose information is far more limited, and at times that information is deliberately obscured by marketing tactics. Where large corporations compete with each other for "shelf space" and largely control what is sold and where, it is difficult for the average consumer to have access to local products or to know much more about nationally distributed products than their price or general appearance. In products marketed globally, the General Agreement on Tariffs and Trade (GATT) does not permit nations to mandate disclosure of information about a product's origins, other than its country of origin. Under GATT as well, nations cannot impose penalties or taxes for imported goods that have been produced under desperate labor conditions or produced at a cost to another country's environmental health.[11]

Other than price, what the consumer "knows" or desires is crafted by corporate image-makers. Creating the culture of desire was not an overnight event. According to William Leach, much of the story of big business in America is the story of how the giants of the late nineteenth and early twentieth centuries took a land of spiritually oriented, frugal folk and "created a material culture of self-indulgence."

> Business became skilled in using colors, glass, and light to create exciting images of a this-world paradise conveyed by elegant models and fashion shows. Museums offered displays depicting the excitement of the new culture. Gradually, the individual was surrounded by messages reinforcing the culture of desire. Advertisements, department store show windows, electric signs, fashion shows, the sumptuous environments of leading hotels, and billboards all conveyed artfully crafted images of the good life. Credit programs made it seem effortless to buy that life.[12]

Advertising gained considerable momentum after World War II, especially with the advent of television. The average American adult sees about 21,000 commercial messages a year; the largest one hundred corporations in the United States pay for about 75 percent of commercial television time and about half the public television time. With advertising for a thirty-second segment in prime time costing over $200,000 on network television, only the largest corporations can afford it.

In giving commercial speech constitutional protection, we are not just giving consumers information about price, quality, maker, and warranties. We are systematically stimulating the addictive, irrational impulse to feed a spiritual emptiness with more and more "goods." To say that commercial speech merely allows buyers and sellers to exchange information in a free market transaction seems naive, if not downright disingenuous. By the end of this century, the "culture" of television largely replaced community and family life, cultural pursuits, and reading. Coupled with big corporations' ability to influence the legal environment of business, corporate "freedom of speech" encourages a consumer-driven economy, with consumers perennially in pursuit of this year's hottest toy.

The Government/Corporate Nexus

Because of their size and central role in the economy, America's core corporations came to identify themselves, and be identified by Americans and others around the world, with the American economy as a whole. They were the champions of the national economy; their successes were its successes. They *were* the American economy.

                                    Robert Reich, *The Work of Nations*[13]

The government-business partnership in the United States is by now well institutionalized. The Department of Commerce was created for and has worked on behalf of U.S. business since Herbert Hoover's time and continues to do so under President Clinton. The military-industrial complex that seemed dangerous to outgoing President Dwight Eisenhower has consumed a large share of the U.S. budget and has helped spawn advances in the computer and aviation industries, among others. Government research grants to universities have aided U.S. "competitiveness." Government supports large agribusiness while corporate welfare makes far greater claims on public monies than all the "nonworking welfare mothers" combined. Political contributions from large corporations with vested interests in government largesse have become more and more evident,[14] and the free market as realized in the United States gives some players a distinct advantage over others.

In terms of overconsumption, some governmental choices have been fateful indeed. In both home construction and automobiles, the government has provided considerable largesse since World War II, making possible the vast suburban areas that the free market, unaided, would not have created.[15] Prior to World War II, people in urban areas tended to live within walking distance of schools, retail establishments, and churches, or within walking distance of streetcars. Streetcar lines moved people efficiently without public subsidies. While Henry Ford and his competitors "churned out more than a million new vehicles a year," politicians and developers found common interest in advancing auto use. Realtors and developers often dominated city planning boards (and still do); tire makers and members of the building trades saw fortunes to be made in "development," but the streetcar development promoted only a limited number of corridors within a few minutes' walk of the trolley lines. The automobile could "fill in the blanks" between streetcar corridors, then develop spaces far beyond city limits.[16]

In 1916, the Federal Road Act contributed $75 million to improve post roads, and the Federal Road Act of 1921 sought to improve 200,000 miles of state highways and link them up to form a national network. At the same time, streetcar companies received little government support, and city governments required many companies to stick with nickel fares and continue operating unprofitable routes. Starting in the 1930s, National City Lines, a company backed by General Motors, Standard Oil, Phillips Petroleum, Firestone Tire and Rubber, Mack Truck, and other auto interests, "systematically bought up and closed down more than 100 electric trolley lines in 45 cities across the country,"[17] with GM using its financial strength to buy up streetcar lines, scrap the tracks, and convert the routes for buses. By the time that GM's activities were reviewed in 1974 by the Senate Subcommittee on Antitrust and Monopoly, GM defended its actions as having given mass transportation a "new lease on life." By now, of course, only the poorest segments of the population ride city buses; everyone else is out on the freeways.

GM's work spanned the Depression and World War II. During that time, the housing industry had been devastated. To jump start the housing construction business, the Roosevelt administration created the Federal Housing Administration (FHA), which guaranteed bank loans, allowed 10 percent down payments, and stretched mortgage terms from ten to thirty years. But the kinds of houses that would qualify for an FHA guaranteed mortgage were typically new ones, built outside of the inner cities. In the 1930s, new suburbs were a short drive from the city, and gas was cheap. Inside the cities, entire neighborhoods became "redlined," and the process of urban decay accelerated. At the end of World War II, Congress added another program of easy mortgages for veterans, who could qualify for suburban housing with no down payment. Developers like William Levitt could mass produce "50 houses a day in the potato fields of central Long Island," and under new federal income tax rules, mortgage interest payments became deductible expenses.

Meanwhile, easy credit terms released pent-up demand for automobiles, and by the mid-1950s, suburban expansion ran headlong into the limits of existing highway infrastructure. Rather than stop the expanding economy (for the auto and housing industries *were* the economy), the national network of interstate highways was conceived. In 1956, Congress approved the Interstate Highway Act, which called for 44,000 miles of new toll-free expressways. The federal government would pay 90 percent and the states 10 percent. The 1956 legislation also subsidized the widening of local feeder roads to the interstate system, further facilitating suburban sprawl. At the time, it was the largest public works project in the history of the world. The political justification was that these expressways would help move military equipment during national emergencies and ease evacuation of cities during nuclear attack.

Most readers already know the rest of the story: suburban development was facilitated by cheap gas and better highways, and the American Dream of a house, yard, and picket fence was realized by more and more people in the middle class. The more spread out people became, the greater was demand for asphalt and cement for roads, bridges, and parking lots, as well as new water and sewer lines. Individual homes, spread out from the core of commercial services, would need their own washing machines, lawnmowers, telephones, television sets, air conditioners, and swimming pools.[18] The expansion of consumer goods spawned by suburban life was good for the economy, and the widespread enjoyment of these commodities came to represent "the world's highest standard of living" and "the American Way of Life."

Not only is the auto industry heavily subsidized by public expenditures on roads, but the social costs of the automobile are not included in either the sticker price or the price of gas. Social costs—notoriously difficult to measure but real nonetheless—include health-threatening smog and further additions to carbon dioxide buildup. Air conditioners in cars are the single largest source of CFCs that destroy stratospheric ozone. Motor vehicles account for nearly 20 percent of all carbon dioxide emissions worldwide (with the richer nations having 81 percent of all cars even though having only 13 percent of the population). More easily measurable social costs include public road building and maintenance costs, traffic police, courts, accidents, and insurance, all of which contribute to the GDP but not, on the whole, to social well-being. In addition, there are considerable costs in maintaining a high degree of military preparedness to fight a local or regional conflict. In the Persian Gulf, the United States went to war against Saddam Hussein for several reasons, but continued U.S. access to oil was a primary concern. There are also the social costs of time lost in traffic jams and commuting; a person who commutes an hour a day each way spends a month each year in his or her car,[19] time not spent with family or involved in community life.

In sum, the price of gasoline is political, not economic. It is driven by all sorts of decisions, not just the invisible hand of a free market with numerous buyers and sellers setting optimal prices. Norman Myers of Oxford University uses work by Durning to calculate that if the total social cost of gasoline used by trucks and autos were included in the price of gasoline, U.S. motorists would pay almost ten dollars a gallon.[20] Paying less for gas than for bottled water only assures that we continue to overconsume in our use of motor vehicles.

Measuring Quantity Rather than Quality

When a small oil company drains an oil well in Texas, it gets a generous depletion allowance on its taxes, in recognition of the loss. Yet the very same drainage shows up as a gain to the nation in the GDP. When the United States fishes its cod population down to remnants, this appears on the national books as an economic boom—until the fisheries collapse. As . . . Herman Daly puts it, the current national accounting system treats the earth as a business in liquidation.[21]

Much of the economic activity created by the rise of the automobile in American life is economically measurable and appears positive. Jobs are created, money changes hands, economic activity is stimulated. The GDP purports to measure the health or overall progress of the economy by measuring the total market value of all goods and services produced in the United States in a given year. But, as noted above, the GDP will count as positive the monetary activity generated by a three-car collision, including body shop repairs, lawyer's fees, police activities, wrecker services, and ambulance and hospital charges, as well as ongoing physical therapy.

For overconsumption, the basic problem is that GDP does not measure the value inherent in our natural environment. It does not measure any kind of natural resource, such as a pure aquifer, old-growth forest, or an undammed watershed until that resource is "tapped." When, and only when, *people* find a way to exploit resources are they counted in GDP, even though "untapped" they all have an important value for ongoing ecosystems and perform a service just by being left alone. As David Suzuki notes, "a standing forest provides numerous ecological 'services' such as inhibition of erosion, landslides, fires, and floods while cleansing the air, modulating climate and weather, supporting wildlife, and maintaining genetic diversity."[22]

GDP also fails to account for social and environmental costs arising from economic activities. For example, the wreck of the Exxon *Valdez* (carrying its cargo of crude oil for refining into motor fuels) created a rise in the GDP. Finally, as Clive Ponting has pointed out, "In the long term the notion of GNP takes no account of the fundamental question of whether its level at any one time, let alone continual growth in the future, is in fact desirable or sustainable."[23] In sum, our "free market" economic system allows monopolies, negative externalities, disinformation, and subsidies, thus encouraging inefficiencies, waste, and misallocation of resources. We do not legally, systematically enforce the discipline of the economically idealized free market. Corporations continue to follow their own logic, which is the accumulation of ever-greater concentrations of capital, while governments continue to play favorites.

Economics Reconsidered: The Earth as Finite Resource

The third form of overconsumption is related to "consumption as an end in itself" and to free market fundamentals, but it deserves separate identification. Even if we avoided free market failures such as subsidies, monopolies, negative externalities, and lack of information to consumers, current neoclassical economic theory assumes that the earth's resources may properly be treated as capital—a set of assets to be tapped as a source of profit. As Ponting notes, "Trees, wildlife, minerals, water and soil are treated as commodities to be sold or developed. More important, their price is simply the cost of extracting them and turning them into marketable commodities. . . . Yet this view overlooks the basic truth that the resources of the earth are not just *scarce*, they are *finite*."[24]

Consider the draw-down of a major aquifer such as the Ogallala Aquifer under the Great Plains. The ongoing, massive draw-down on this aquifer generates no observable externalities (no obvious hurts or injuries are inflicted on humans), there are no significant barriers to entry for competitors (lots of large farms are pumping from the aquifer simultaneously, and farms are being bought and sold on a routine basis), and consumers and producers are all well aware that the bounty cannot last forever. The market is functioning perfectly, but there is still overconsumption. How so? Because a nonrenewable resource is being rapidly depleted with no rational expectation that a substitute resource can be found and utilized. The market system of neoclassical economics, even in theory, invariably chooses present consumption as rational, even where there is no realistic prospect of finding a substitute resource.

There are, of course, denials from some quarters that future resource deficits pose any serious problem for business or society. Most of these denials opine that wealth is created by the application of human intelligence to the world, and that abundance is our birthright. Technology and human ingenuity, it is said, will find a way. That may be, but if we extrapolate from the past, it seems clear enough that the dominant patterns of wealth creation have relied on abundant natural resources. Adam Smith wrote *Wealth of Nations* during the period of colonial expansion, and while it is true that in a free market system producers had every incentive to be thrifty as well as innovative, the cost of acquiring control over abundant natural resources has been, by historical standards, relatively cheap. This explains, at least in part, why classical economics (as well as corporate and national accounting systems) does not recognize the finite boundaries of earth's natural resources.

Democracy and Corporate Capitalism

This section of the article surveys several key institutions in the U.S. political/legal system and how they relate to the overconsumptive economic system described above.

Legislation in the Age of Corporate Capitalism

Corporate interests (considerably more than labor unions or other interest groups) have effectively captured the legislation process. Prior to the 1970s, business interests were represented by lobbying organizations with fairly straightforward names such as the U.S. Chamber of Commerce or the American Petroleum Institute. Now, however, corporations speak out through a variety of forms, not only in advertising, but in public-interest speeches sponsored by groups like Consumer Alert (fighting government regulations on product safety), Keep America Beautiful (fighting bottle bills and other mandatory recycling legislation) or the Safe Energy Coalition (promoting nuclear power).[25] They exist to convince members of the public that the corporate interest is *their* interest, and their efforts are often combined with front groups that give legislators the appearance of a groundswell of "grassroots" public opinion.

There are now over 170,000 public relations employees engaged in manipulating news and public opinion, rapidly outnumbering actual news reporters. Many such specialists in "corporate communications" have organized citizen letter-writing campaigns on behalf of corporate interests and have provided paid operatives to pose as "housewives" to present corporate views at public meetings. David Korten cites a Columbia Journalism Review study that found that more than half of the *Wall Street Journal*'s news stories are based solely on press releases. "The distinction between advertising space and news space," writes Korten, "grows less distinct with each passing day."[26]

Political Parties

Third parties in the United States are consistently marginalized by the two major parties, and across the possible spectrum of opinion and action, voters are given little basic choice. In the 1996 elections, Libertarian, Green, and Natural Law parties were given scant attention by the media and were not given full participation in the presidential debates. In some key electoral states, voters could choose the Green Party's presidential candidate only by write-in vote. Campaigns for national office are increasingly expensive and now require constant fund-raising by presidential aspirants and congressional candidates; it is almost unthinkable that anyone could be elected to Congress from a third party; the Perot and Forbes presidential campaigns suggest that "outsiders" are visible to the public only when they make massive personal expenditures on media advertising. Because of the high cost of gaining visibility with the public, both parties have been pursuing moneyed interests to finance their campaigns.

As a result, each party has become largely captive of corporate interests and is required to pursue the major contributors that can put the party's message into the media and out to the public. Thus, the Democratic party under Bill Clinton has moved toward a centrist position that pays close attention to Wall Street and uses diplomatic leverage to bene-fit U.S. companies competing for international business. The Clinton Administration bailed out the Mexican government during the peso de-valuation to settle global investors' fears and championed both NAFTA and the World Trade Organization (WTO). With political parties depen-dent upon cash contributions from the well-endowed, public policy can only tend toward the interests of those same contributors. Neither politi-cal party will push for significant change in the consumption status quo; Clinton's proposed BTU tax early in his first term is a good example of a policy geared to taxing consumption that was dead on arrival on Capi-tol Hill. As political analyst Kevin Phillips notes, there is little difference between the parties in their approach to soft money, and this explains "why the Clinton Administration has so little courage on so many fronts. . . . The parties are so thickly intertwined with this stuff, the only thing they agree on . . . is getting money."[27]

Courts and the U.S. Litigation System

Certain scholars and social critics have argued that replacing legisla-tion/regulation with property rights in a common law regime would remedy most environmental problems faster and more efficiently than current "command and control" regulations. But plaintiffs generally do not have the resources to fight polluting corporations on equal terms. If a company pollutes, not all plaintiffs will actually sue (some distrust of lawyers is evident here), and an even smaller percentage will win. This is largely because better-financed defendants can afford to delay the day of reckoning at trial—usually through a prolonged discovery process—and exhaust the financial resources of plaintiffs.[28] Against smaller corpo-rations, plaintiffs may not recover because the defendant has gone bankrupt, or because the defendant has limited assets upon which to levy execution of judgment.

As well, many deserving cases would be of little or no interest to most attorneys. In common law causes of action (negligence, nuisance, tres-pass), attorney's fees are the responsibility of each party. Unless the case potentially generates a large recovery against a defendant, attorneys will not be interested in taking the case on a contingent fee basis. Whether the case is small or large, the nature of negative environmental external-ities is such that expert witness opinions would ordinarily be needed to establish the causal link between defendant's conduct and harm to the plaintiff. For plaintiffs this will be neither simple nor cheap. Often, there are multiple sources of pollution, and demonstrating the precise source of the pollution becomes more difficult; several defendants may be involved, and each is likely to point to others as the principal culprit. Time lag is also a problem, since companies come and go in a particular watershed or region, and proving which of several successive companies in a particular location has caused the harmful health effects is no simple matter. Moreover, there is usually scientific uncertainty about the effects of a particular substance on human health and experts hired by well-endowed defendants can undermine a plaintiff's case.

The Mass Media in a Postmodern Age

The mass media have some inherent biases or inclinations that are neither liberal nor conservative and that ill serve the public. In reporting political campaigns, or specific issues, the won/lost column is likely to be what readers/listeners get, rather than in-depth analysis. Truth, per se, is no longer fashionable in postmodern society. It is the debate itself that gets covered. In the media's attention to an issue of, say, global warming or ozone depletion, the contrarian critics tend to get respect, even though their opinions have been subsidized by those responsible for the problem. This is because a contrary opinion "makes it a horse race," and because the media believes that if it reports various or diverse viewpoints, the public will be able to sort it all out in the end.

Perhaps so, but the public is often at a loss as to what information they can trust and what is disinformation. A constant exposure to "maybe this, but maybe also that" in matters of earth's preservation is an invitation to utter disbelief of anything, or the deconstruction of other people's motives. By simply "reporting" what people say, the media retreats behind a mask of objectivity, which in reality takes no moral courage or responsibility and allows the public to retain a false sense of sophisticated, postmodern skepticism. An informed public is vital to democracy; a public awash in images, sales pitches, and competing concepts and ideas inevitably becomes politically anemic.

Domestic Laws and Policies that Promote Overconsumption

Constitutionally, legislatively, and administratively, significant laws and policies push overconsumption, not always intending to do so but having that effect nonetheless. Let us start with the Constitution.

First Amendment of the Constitution

"Freedom of speech and the press" under the First Amendment allows corporate interests to overstimulate demand beyond a rational extent and to lobby legislators to a disproportionate extent. The First Amendment prohibition of the establishment of religion also makes it more difficult (if not impossible) for a sectarian state to emerge with laws that fully reflect religious values. Yet the United States was "settled" primarily by those having Christian beliefs and early laws did reflect those beliefs. Sunday closing laws (or blue laws) were once the norm. Families spent the day together at home or at church, not at the shopping malls. Sunday was—not long ago—considered sacrosanct, a day of relief from commercialism. In countries with less separation between church and state, materialism and consumerism are often more restrained. In Islamic countries, for example, the Shari'a (sacred law) forbids the charging of interest. In the United States, a significant amount of overconsumption is encouraged by the retailer's ability to finance a consumer's purchase at fairly high interest rates.

Fifth Amendment of the Constitution

There is a growing movement to make property rights the most fundamental right of citizenship, and the most important guaranty in the Bill of Rights. The government's "interference" with property rights for the purpose of preserving habitat for endangered species survives by the most slender of political threads. The takings clause of the fifth amendment has already been construed by the Supreme Court to require public compensation for regulatory takings. In *Lucas v. South Carolina Coastal Commission*,[29] the Court required South Carolina to pay a house builder (Lucas) the value of his land when the Coastal Management Act was interpreted by state officials to deny him a building permit on his oceanfront property. South Carolina's attempt to preserve the dune system of its Atlantic coastline as an aesthetic and ecological barrier was limited by the Supreme Court's decision that would require the state to make full payment to the landowner for restricting his private "right" to destroy a set of sand dunes that provided a public good.

A few states have also adopted takings legislation, and a proposal for federal takings legislation would require government payment to landowners where, for example, enforcement of the Endangered Species Act or the Clean Water Act prevented the owner from realizing the "full economic value" of his property. In effect, these laws would require the public to pay for diminished property values whenever the public determines that certain uses of private property generate negative externalities. The onus is thus on government to pay for prevention of public harm, rather than on private property owners to prevent public harms in the first place. As a result, conservation or sustainable uses would be sacrificed to well-entrenched notions of property rights and "freedom."

Cost-Benefit Analysis in Government Regulations

It seems like moral common sense to say that our actions should produce no harm to others and, preferably, do some good. Requiring that government actions produce more good than harm seems to partake of this bedrock common sense. Presidents Reagan and Bush, and Vice President Quayle, all endorsed and pursued such a requirement for government regulation. It also formed part of the GOP's 1994 "Contract with America." Such a requirement also fits nicely with a certain mental outlook: that costs (debits incurred) and benefits (credits to be enjoyed) can be reasonably well measured and compared with one another.

In practice, however, and particularly with regard to environmental issues, cost/benefit analysis proves to be problematic. Bill Shaw and Art Wolfe have pointed out that cost-benefit analysis cannot set priorities among competing "goods."[30] The greatest good for the greatest number invites us to choose between alternatives but does not tell us which goals or purposes are best. Nothing in "the greatest good for the greatest number" tells us that cleaning up the environment or "sustainable development" is a good idea, goal, or purpose. They also note that cost-benefit analysis cannot provide a single scale against which many types of choices can be measured. What, for example, are the benefits of health from a cleaner environment as weighed against decreased income for all? Without a common scale, we are forced to measure different kinds of goods and bads, certain kinds of costs weighed against certain other kinds of benefits. In brief, we must compare apples to oranges.

Finally, cost-benefit analysis almost always devalues future interests and the future. Denis Hayes sardonically suggests that if we had a cheap, clean, inexhaustible source of energy that we could use without any harmful side effects for ten thousand years we would begin doing so with a vengeance, even if we knew that after ten thousand years the world would blow up. He's probably right when he says we would all be "scrambling for a piece of the action."[31] The example is absurd but makes the point: to both economists and the average person, a million detriments (if placed far enough into the future) will never diminish our enthusiasm for a single benefit we can enjoy right now. To this extent, at least, economics is well-rooted in human nature.

Corporate interests continue to work for "cost/benefit analysis" requirements in legislation and regulatory rulings; these requirements place the burden on regulators to show that their proposed regulation is justified. Those affected by any proposed regulation will be readily armed with seemingly precise figures as to the negative impact (cost) of the proposal; but the benefits for human health and safety will tend to

be diffused over time and space, real enough but not nearly so immediate or compelling. A system that requires "objective" cost/benefit analysis is already skewed toward those that can demonstrate specific present
or near-future costs, and against those that speak on behalf of future
generations or long-term but more diffuse social benefits.

Corporate Law

The law governing corporations has traditionally been the province
of state governments. Historically, corporations were only granted
charters for public purposes. Over time, however, state corporate law
granted charters to "for profit" corporations and gradually enabled corporations to avoid any societal obligations or responsibilities.[32] Rather
than being accountable by law to the public, corporations are now only
accountable to their stockholders. This has given birth to the general
view often attributed to Milton Friedman that the only ethical duty a
corporation owes is to increase the profits of its shareholders. Yet the
fact that the law now allows corporations to pursue profit without responsibility to the very society that gives them birth and maintains them
does not imply that they *should* have no moral duties to society, or that
society cannot insist on accountability. Others have written formidably
and at length about the consequences of failing to link corporate rights
with greater corporate accountability.[33]

One major systemic failure involves the unique pressures that publicly
held corporations experience in a new world order where capital is king.
Most state corporate laws require that directors and officers of a corporation act as "fiduciaries" for shareholders: their primary responsibility is
to safeguard the investments of the company's stockholders. In a publicly held company, stockholders may freely transfer their shares and
often feel compelled to do so if their portfolio is not "growing" sufficiently in value. Any shareholder who wants the corporation to maximize the value of his/her shares will often propose actions that are
driven by short-term, profit maximizing strategies rather than long-term,
sustainable paths.

David Harris's *The Last Stand* [34] illustrates how, under existing rules of
the game, a publicly held company can barely resist the dynamic of hungry capital. Pacific Lumber was dedicated to sustainably cutting its natural capital, the last stand of virgin redwood on the continent. Charles
Hurwitz made a hostile takeover bid for the company and succeeded
largely because the laws allowed it. His aim, like Gordon Gekko's in the
movie *Wall Street*, was to seize another company by force and realize
short-term returns by quickly selling off irreplaceable assets. The accounts of this takeover by Harris show us that a socially responsible busi-

ness will, under present rules of the game, be swimming against the capital tide. Maxxam's "use" of Pacific Lumber's natural capital illustrates the pressures that Wall Street can bring to bear on Main Street. The only way this pressure could have been resisted in the long run would have been for Pacific Lumber to have remained closely held.

Tax Policies and Societal Overconsumption

In general, tax policy in the United States has not rewarded conservation and investment and has, on the contrary, tended to stimulate consumer borrowing and spending. In addition, tax policies give corporations greater latitude in terms of free speech and the ability to get a tax write–off for harming others. A corporation's advertising expenses are deductible, its lobbying expenses are deductible, and its litigation or arbitration expenses are deductible. A company that pollutes an aquifer can deduct all litigation expenses. For individuals, there are no such deals; if you want to contribute to a political candidate, your personal contribution is not deductible, and if you have legal expenses trying to fight a civil complaint or criminal prosecution, there is no tax deduction.

Tax policies also subsidize the housing industry. It is generally considered good news for the U.S. economy when housing starts and home sales are up. The home mortgage interest deduction in the Internal Revenue Code is a key subsidy for the housing market. The construction industry, banks, realtors, and a variety of other interests believe that repealing the mortgage interest deduction would "kill the home building industry" and be "unfair to the middle class." Yet the interest deduction has no cap, and as such encourages homeowners to take on very large mortgage interest burdens. Until recently, this incentive combined with the code's deferring recognition of capital gains on the sale of a home provided that each subsequent home cost more than the last. The typical strategy for post–WW II homeowners was to buy a "starter" home and buy more and more expensive homes (often, more than they needed) until at last, after age fifty-five, they could take advantage of the one-time nonrecognition of real estate capital gain.

International Laws and Institutions that Promote Overconsumption

For developing countries, an overall pattern has emerged in this century. The political institutions of colonialism have given way, but in their place, different forms of Northern control of Southern economies have emerged. Communist and socialist regimes (and efforts at land reform) have receded in most parts of the developing world. Confiscation of private property through expropriation and nationalization were concerns for companies in the 1960s and 1970s, but by the 1990s it was hard to find developing nations with strong regulatory restrictions. From the late 1950s to the early 1980s, many developing countries' legal regimes were hostile to or wary of foreign direct investment, but currency and commodity crises softened their defiant stances. Mexico, Chile, and Brazil all illustrate this pattern, where foreign direct investment is now welcomed, with far fewer restrictions than in the past. Consumption of natural resources and the creation of a consumer-driven economy is the implicit (if not the explicit) goal of these new legal/political developments. Moreover, these developments coincide with the rise in power and influence of multinational corporations relative to sovereign nation-states, who find themselves increasingly less powerful in setting terms of trade.

The path for development blazed by "first world" nations is often imitated by developing nations and is encouraged by international institutions such as the International Monetary Fund (IMF) and the World Bank. After nearly fifty years of Bretton Woods institutions—of which the IMF and World Bank are a key part—the so-called developing world finds itself further and further in debt. The widely celebrated success of several Asian economies, at least until their collapse in 1997, has been accompanied by substantial liquidation of natural assets and resources. In most developing nations, subsistence agriculture has given way—at the insistence of international banking and corporate institutions—to monoculture crop exports that have not enriched the exporting nations nor served the interests of sustainable development. There is still, in large measure, a neocolonial regime in effect, where the poorer countries provide cheap natural resources—and, more recently, cheap labor—to serve the needs/pleasures of the developed states and their people. In effect, these key institutions have not served the developing nations so much as they have assisted the already developed nations to continue their overconsumptive ways.[35]

A few years ago, the GATT secretariat acknowledged that relaxed or less stringent environmental regulation is a legitimate "comparative advantage" for developing nations. "Developed" nations cannot restrict entry of products based on environmentally unsustainable production or processing methods. The net effect of this is to encourage foreign direct investment in countries where economic activity is relatively unregulated, and negative "externalities" abound. GATT rules and the WTO would also limit a country's ability to require information about a product's origin and method of production as a nontariff "trade barrier." The net effect of this is to prevent consumers from choosing *not* to buy a given item because it is produced in a way that is unsustainable or environmentally harmful.

Conclusion

In *Land of Desire,* William Leach confers the status of a new religion on the beliefs and attitudes that characterize the U.S. consumer culture. Multinational corporations now seek to pitch the same dream of secular salvation to a global market,[36] promoting consumption of all things new (and Western) as the shining path to freedom and personal fulfillment. The current regime of "free trade," which coincides with diminished regulatory powers of nation-states,[37] sets the stage for the ultimate binge of global overconsumption. In the "new world order" after the fall of communism, "development" outside the industrialized nations appears to be following the standard model; this entails rapid draw-down of natural capital and environmental degradation, with progress measured in growth in economic activity without regard to social costs or limits on natural resources, with scant regard for future generations, and with control of resources largely in the hands of multinational corporations and distant investors rather than local citizens.

Curbing overconsumption and moving toward more sustainable economies does not require that we disavow capitalism or free markets and may even require that we take free market principles more seriously. But it will also require a renunciation of the basic tenets of what amounts to a false religion of salvation through material overconsumption. Given the number of institutions that directly or indirectly promote overconsumption, overly optimistic prognoses about the future would sound a false note. Nonetheless, with sufficient clarity about what is at stake, the United States and other industrialized nations could affirmatively lead by taking free market principles more seriously in regulating monopoly power, negative externalities, and in mediating the market by providing as a public service reliable information about products, their origins, and production processes.

Within the United States public financing of political campaigns will be essential. Liberated from politics dominated by money, state governments could require corporate accountability and the federal government could measure social progress rather than gross levels of economic activity. Information technologies could begin to deliver more reliable information about products and their means of production. Taxes could be restructured to tax consumption to a greater extent than income or value added activities. On the international level, the GATT could be renegotiated to refuse a temporary comparative advantage to nations bent on overconsuming natural resources or rapidly degrading their environments. The GATT could allow reasonable, nonprotectionist tariff discrimination against goods that are harvested or produced unsustainably. Under pressure, the World Bank might forever renounce development projects that drive out sustainable economies in favor of economies that serve the needs of international capital.

In total, the kinds of measures needed to deinstitutionalize overconsumption are a large and daunting package. The political will for such changes could come from ecological collapse, but reforms born of an acute environmental or natural resource crisis may be neither rational nor systematic. Preferably, socially and environmentally minded citizens can find common cause and the wisdom to work together. Ecocentrism may be essential in rejecting the culture of desire, yet even a homocentrist outlook can mandate significant restraints on consumption, and many useful reforms can proceed from a more honest implementation of free market principles.

But it also seems clear that neoclassical free market principles cannot, by themselves, fundamentally alter our collective outlook or, in turn, public policy. The agenda for change, from overconsumption to more rational consumption, also requires a rejection of the pursuit of happiness through ever-increasing material consumption. And it seems unlikely that we can reject the insistent messages of the corporate dream merchants unless we come to a more holistic relationship with the natural world, one that does not require our dominance of nature so much as our acceptance and a sense of permanence on this island home.

Notes

1. Paul Zane Pilzer, *God Wants You To Be Rich: The Theology of Economics* (New York: Simon and Schuster, 1995).

2. Paul Wachtel, *The Poverty of Affluence: A Psychological Portrait of the American Way of Life* (Philadelphia: New Society, 1989).

3. Allen D. Kanner and Mary E. Gomes, "The All Consuming Self," in *Ecopsychology: Restoring the Earth, Healing the Mind*, ed. T. Roszak, M. Gomes, and A. Kanner, (San Francisco: Sierra Club Books, 1995), 79.

4. Alan Durning, *How Much Is Enough? The Consumer Society and the Future of the Earth* (New York: Norton, 1992), 119.

5. Kanner and Gomes, *"The All Consuming Self,"* 81.

6. Nick Ravo, "Index of Social Well-Being Is at the Lowest in 25 Years," *New York Times*, 14 October 1996, 14 (A).

7. Tom Athanasiou, *Divided Planet: The Ecology of Rich and Poor* (Toronto:

Little, Brown, 1996), 53–54, citing Paul Bairoch in Robert Heilbroner, *Twenty-First Century Capitalism* (New York: Norton, 1993), 55–56.

8. Robert Samuelson, *The Good Life and Its Discontents* (New York: Random House, 1995), 5.

9. Paul Hawken, *The Ecology of Commerce* (New York: HarperCollins, 1993), 93.

10. Hawken, *Ecology of Commerce*, 95.

11. See generally Don Mayer and David Hoch, "International Environmental Protection and the GATT: The Tuna/Dolphin Controversy," *American Business Law Journal 31* (1992): 187–244.

12. William Leach, *Land of Desire: Merchants, Power, and the Rise of a New American Culture* (Random House, New York, 1993), Vintage Edition, 1994, 150–51.

13. Robert Reich, *The Work of Nations: Preparing Ourselves for 21st Century Capitalism* (New York: Vintage Books, 1992), 47.

14. Vicki Kemper and Deborah Lutterbeck, "The Country Club," in *Common Cause* (Spring/Summer 1996): 16–35. The article names corporate names and also amounts. While heavy union and other "special interest" contributions are also noted, the top ten donors to both the GOP and the Democratic Party were corporations, with Phillip Morris and Archer Daniels Midland Co. leading the list.

15. See generally, James Howard Kunstler, *The Geography of Nowhere: The Rise and Decline of America's Man-Made Landscape* (New York: Simon and Schuster, Touchstone Edition, 1994).

16. Kunstler, *Geography of Nowhere*, 89.

17. Steve Nadis and James J. MacKenzie, *Car Trouble* (Boston: Beacon Press, 1993), 5.

18. See Kunstler, *Geography of Nowhere*, 107–8.

19. A worker who commutes five days a week over forty–eight weeks would spend 480 hours a year in his car (not including time spent cleaning or maintaining his car); that amounts to thirty sixteen-hour days.

20. Norman Myers, "Consumption in Relation to Population, Environment, and Development," working paper, July 1996, citing Alan Durning, *This Place on Earth: Home and the Practice of Permanence* (Seattle: Sasquatch Books, 1996).

21. Clifford Cobb, Ted Halstead, and Jonathan Rowe, "If the GDP Is Up, Why Is America Down?" *Atlantic Monthly* (October 1995): 66.

22. David Suzuki, *A Time to Change* (Toronto: Stoddart Publishing, 1994), 122.

23. Clive Ponting, *A Green History of the World* (New York: Penguin Books, 1991), 157.

24. Ponting, *Green History*, 155–56.

25. David Korten, *When Corporations Rule the World* (West Hartford: Kumarian, 1995), 143.

26. Korten, *When Corporations Rule*, 146.

27. Phillips is quoted by Kemper and Lutterbeck in "The Country Club," 35.

28. See generally, Ralph Nader and Wesley J. Smith, *No Contest: Corporate Lawyers and the Perversion of Justice in America* (New York: Random House, 1996). See also Jonathan Harr, *A Civil Action* (New York: Random House, 1995).

29. *Supreme Court Reports* 112 (St. Paul, MN: West Publishing Co., 1992), 2886.

30. Bill Shaw and Art Wolfe, *The Structure of the Legal Environment: Law, Ethics, and Business* (Boston: PWS Kent, 1991), 274–75.

31. Denis Hayes, "Earth Day 1990: Threshold of the Green Decade," *World Policy Journal* 7, no. 2 (Spring 1990): 293–94.

32. Jonathan Rowe, "Reinventing the Corporation," *Washington Monthly*, May/June 1992, 17.

33. See generally Korten, *When Corporations Rule;* Nader and Smith, *No Contest;* and Hawken, *Ecology of Commerce*, all cited above. See also Ralph Estes, *Tyranny of the Bottom Line: Why Corporations Make Good People Do Bad Things* (San Francisco: Berrett-Koehler, 1996).

34. David Harris, *The Last Stand* (San Francisco: Sierra Club Books, 1996).

35. See generally Bruce Rich, *Mortgaging the Earth: The World Bank, Environmental Impoverishment, and the Crisis of Development* (Boston: Beacon Press, 1994).

36. See generally Richard J. Barnet and John Cavanagh, *Global Dreams: Imperial Corporations and the New World Order* (New York: Simon and Schuster, 1994).

37. See generally Kenichi Ohmae, *The Borderless World* (New York: Free Press, 1990) and *The End of the Nation State* (New York: Free Press, 1995).

5

Marketing, the Ethics of Consumption, and Less-Developed Countries

George G. Brenkert

Introduction

Several centuries ago large numbers of western Europeans fanned out into the "new world" to serve as missionaries on behalf of the true way of life. They were to use subtle, as well as vicious, means to persuade, cajole, and coerce those they encountered to adopt the "true religion." To them, it was clear what their responsibilities were, viz., to convert the heathen to enlightened views and thereby to win salvation for them. They were little concerned with the culture of these heathens, except insofar as it impeded their own efforts to bring them a superior culture.[1]

Centuries later large numbers of western Europeans and North Americans have also fanned out as modern missionaries, of a sort, on behalf of a very different way of life. They too have sought to persuade, cajole, and even coerce people and societies in the less developed world to adopt their views on commerce and marketing, on economic development and the consumer society. Some of them, at least, also claim a sense of responsibility for bringing to the less developed world skills, techniques, and capital by which they might improve their lives and develop their societies.

However, the moral responsibilities of these modern missionaries are much less clear than at least some marketers think. In general, the moral responsibilities of marketers (and business) are discussed within the contexts of such issues as bribery, corruption, gift-giving, entertainment, market freedom, and international human rights. Only infrequently are the responsibilities of marketers to the cultures of the societies in which they operate noted. There are exceptions. For example, Laczniak and

Murphy claim that "these influences [of international marketers] on local cultures, institutions, religions, and ways of life must . . . be carefully assessed."[2] And DeGeorge affirms as one of his ten moral guidelines that "to the extent that local culture does not violate ethical norms, multinationals should respect the local culture and work with and not against it."[3] However, though these authors recognize that marketers should be concerned about their effects on other cultures and that they should respect those cultures, these claims and their implications for the moral responsibilities of marketers remain largely unexplored.

This chapter ventures into this territory by exploring the responsibilities of marketers toward the peoples and cultures of less developed countries (LDCs) as they engage in activities that promote forms of economic development within those societies that alter their culture(s). In particular, I examine this issue with regard to the efforts of marketers to foster consumer societies in LDCs and thereby to promote a higher level and extent of consumption. The implications of my argument are not limited, it will be obvious, to the responsibilities of marketers to less-developed countries. Instead, they extend to the wider issues of the transfer of the marketing practices of one society to another society when the use of such practices is to promote consumer societies in the mode of their own society and culture.

Marketing, Consumer Societies, and the Ethics of Consumption

To examine the moral responsibilities of marketers toward LDCs when their activities foster a consumer culture in those societies, I must first say something about the concepts of a consumer society and of contemporary western marketing.[4] By marketing I refer most frequently to advertising and other promotional components of marketing. However, other components of marketing such as product development, marketing research, and forms of distribution are also relevant to this discussion.[5] The concepts and techniques of these aspects of marketing variously involve a number of values and metaphysical assumptions that not all societies or cultures presently hold.[6] In short, promotion is not a neutral activity but comes value-laden and metaphysically charged.

Among the values that marketing assumes are the affirmative role of consumption rather than abstention in life; the link of consumption with happiness, acceptance, and status; the importance of individual freedom as the lack of restraint; and the needlessness of denial and the acceptability of "instant" gratification. Other values include self-interested behavior on behalf of individual wants and needs, the acquisitive nature of humans, the importance of promoting one's products to consumers, and the inappropriateness of blatant deception, fraud, or physical coercion in marketing relations. Finally, marketers are out to promote change. Growth is essential to their approach.[7] Accordingly, whether it is Calvin Klein ads using provocatively posed teenagers, Virginia Slims appeals to young women, or MasterCard efforts to encourage buying on credit, marketers have pressed upon social conventions and boundaries, customs, and traditions to expand the audience of those who might buy their products.

More metaphysically, marketing has tended to encourage the identification of people with what they possess. Marketers (and the consumer society they promote) view people as consumers. Thorelli, for example, comments that "all human beings are consumers."[8] Of course, in one sense this is correct. All humans do consume; they eat, drink, use clothing, and so forth. However, to be a consumer is different from being a person who consumes. To be a consumer is to be a person for whom one's identification is (more or less) closely bound up with what one owns or consumes within a certain set of values and assumptions (noted below). Some marketers put this very strongly. They argue that a person's sense of self comes from what that person possesses. Belk, for example, maintains that "we are what we have and . . . this may be the most basic and powerful fact of consumer behavior."[9] However, this is hardly a view that many cultures have countenanced. Indeed, in some societies, it is only through the renunciation of one's material possessions that one can become what one truly is. For example, Hinduism has traditionally distinguished four life stages (student, householder, anchorite, and *samnyasin*) that lead from one's youthful instruction by a guru to one's final attempt to seek spiritual liberation and release from worldly limitations. The standard representation of this final stage of human life is that of a person who turns into a "homeless beggar-medicant, with no fixed place to lay one's head, no regular road, no goal, no belongings."[10] Only in this manner can one attain self-knowledge.

Consequently, comments such as those of Thorelli and Belk expose marketing's very modern, Western (if not American) concept of what it is to be a human, one in which one's identity or sense of oneself is bound up with one's consumption and possessions. They also reveal how action in accord with marketing's values and assumptions is, in effect, action that aims (wittingly or unwittingly) at creating a consumer society.

Finally, the preceding view of the self underlies not simply marketers' view of individuals but, according to Moravcsik, has also worked its way into some Western moral theories. Such theories might be taken to constitute the underlying "moral theory" of much of Western marketing. On such a view,

> life is just a stretch of time, to be filled with certain things and to be kept clean of others (the valuable and the immoral respectively). This view is in harmony with the consumer conception of the self (e.g., as a satisfaction-seeking mechanism) that reaches its climax with the development of industrial societies. The candidates for the "fillings" are the sorts of things that one can HAVE, POSSESS, or CONSUME (pleasure, satisfaction, happiness, goods, etc.), rather than BE.[11]

Drawing upon the preceding brief discussion, we may characterize a consumer society in terms of what might be called its "ethics of consumption."[12]

a. Products are for individual satisfaction. They are to be acquired, exchanged, and disposed of to the extent they meet this criterion. More satisfaction is better than less satisfaction; present or "immediate" satisfaction is superior to delayed or future satisfaction.

b. There is a positive connection between consumerism and self-esteem.[13] Indeed, a person's identity tends to be bound up with the products he or she owns and uses. Thus, the consumption of goods and services is at least in part identified with human happiness and welfare.

c. Individuals have a right to choose freely among all the various products produced. Accordingly, the free market plays a central role in the ethics of consumption. This implies restricted government intervention.

d. Material success is emphasized as a dominant goal in a consumer society.[14]

e. Products are acquired by the exchange of money. Their price captures their interchangeability. Consumers need have little knowledge of how or where the objects they consume are produced.

f. The world is a collection of resources whose primary value lies in their use for consumption purposes according to the preceding precepts.

The connection between this ethics of consumption and modern, Western marketing should be clear.[15] Accordingly, the implications of applying Western marketing practices in LDCs are of considerable importance since they introduce not simply the resulting products, skills, knowledge and techniques, but also the preceding values, norms, and assumptions. They are the "hidden" dimensions of what LDCs accept. Thus, marketing in LDCs tends to portray an image of "the good life" as bound up with the consumption of products. This is not inconsequential since, as William Leach has commented, "[w]hoever has the power to project a vision of the good life and make it prevail has the most decisive power of all."[16] Accordingly, assuming that marketers have, or seek to have, some influence in LDCs through the introduction of their marketing practices, an influence that may modify those societies and their cultures, what moral responsibilities do marketers have for the changes they might effect?[17]

The Contradictory Positions of Business Ethicists

If we turn to contemporary philosophical business ethicists, very little, rather disappointingly, is said about the morality of economic development, their implications for the creation of consumer societies within LDCs, or, indeed, about the role of consumption in the good life.[18] Marketers are told to respect local cultures, at least insofar as they do not violate human rights.[19] What is meant by "respect of the culture" is left largely unexplored or unexamined. Indeed, there seems little awareness that marketers might be challenging the local culture through their very activities. Thus, though DeGeorge urges marketers to respect local cultures, he also maintains that Western business people do not have to give up their way of doing things.[20]

Philosophical business ethicists tend to be ethical universalists, though of a restricted sort.[21] They are prepared to apply various basic moral values, principles, or rights to all people. But they are also willing to leave some "moral space" for cultural variances that do not affect such basic norms. Thus, they have proposed two-dimensional analyses of the ethics of international business. One level is that of universal norms, rights, and values. The second level is the local moral space within which individual cultures might adopt moral measures for their own societies, which other societies might reject, for example, nepotism (the hiring of one's family members or friends into jobs, rather than impersonally and objectively considering only the person's job-related characteristics).[22]

We need, however, a three-dimensional analysis of international business ethics. This third dimension takes into account the effect of Western marketing and business activities on the culture of the society in which they take place. It focuses on how the activities of Western marketers might actually be challenging that moral space in more subtle ways than has caught the attention of philosophical business ethicists. This cultural setting plays an extremely important role in people's lives and is the context within which moral values and norms operate. To change this situation invariably ends up changing the local moral values and norms by which people live. Accordingly, philosophical business ethicists may be said to advocate contradictory policies. They urge that marketers should respect the local culture(s) of LDCs, but they also (unwittingly) permit them to engage in measures that undercut those cultures.

Philosophical business ethicists, however, are not the only ones who take contradictory positions. Though marketers have examined the effects of marketing on economic development, their concern has been primarily one of describing changes that are going on and advocating the use of marketing techniques to foster such economic development. When marketing business ethicists, in contrast to philosophical business ethicists, consider the effects of marketers on LDCs, they tend to be ethical relativists.[23] They advocate that marketers should behave in other countries as the people in those countries behave. But, once again, the very activities in which Western marketers engage are not neutral, value-free activities. Instead, they bring with them a train of assumptions and values that may undermine the values and assumptions of the cultures in which they carry on their activities. For example, they urge individual concern for one's needs and goals, but this may undercut the joint family system of other countries such as India in which "the needs and well being of the individual is a responsibility of the system."[24] Likewise, Western organizational forms tend to be contractual, individualistic, and lacking the commitment between members and the system that has characterized organizations in LDCs. Furthermore, these Western organizational forms require personal characteristics of autonomy, self-assertion, and goal-centeredness, which contrast, for example, with "the psycho-cultural realities of Indian managers," which is to be "committed to systems and people rather than goals and tasks, [to] constructively channelise [their] dependence rather than be autonomous, and cope functionally with [their] ambivalence rather than polarise it."[25] Malhotra claims that the upshot of Indian managers working within such Western-style organizations has been an erosion of trust and alienation.[26] In short, the assumptions and values of Western marketing activities may conflict with various cultural and ethical values of LDCs apart from any of the standard questions of bribery, corruption, gifts, intellectual property and so on. Finally, other marketing activities bring with them a view of the good life and moral assumptions about the attainment of that good life that may be incompatible with various elements of the cultures of LDCs, for example, that looking to personal gain or satisfaction is acceptable, rather than the search for fulfillment without attachment to worldly goods that India's *Bhagavad Gita* urges.[27] Chakraborty, director of the Management Center for Human Values in Calcutta, claims that this latter view of human action is part of the Indian ethos. He refers to it as "a theory of work (*nishkam karma*) which requires work without concentration on reward."[28]

Thus, though marketing business ethicists hold that marketers should behave in other countries as do the people in those countries, the very marketing activities they advocate are often at odds with the cultural bases of the people in those countries. Accordingly, they too (at least unwittingly) take contradictory positions.

Part of the problem here is that marketing business ethicists tend to assume that they may distinguish two realms: the economic and the moral. Thus, they maintain, as noted above, that marketers ought to act in accord with the morals of the society in which they are active. Accordingly, marketers should be allowed to engage in gift giving, minor bribery, and the like as the local culture's morality prescribes. However, when it comes to economics, marketing business ethicists have thought that marketers can proceed apace because these activities do not raise moral issues. But this is an undefended and, I suggest, an unwarranted separation. Moral values inhabit both realms.[29]

How, then, are we to get to the bottom of these problems and identify what (if any) moral responsibilities marketers have to the culture(s) of LDCs?

Criticisms of Marketing in LDCs

Four points of clarification regarding the criticism of marketing efforts to promote economic development and consumer societies in LDCs will be helpful at the outset. First, it is clear that marketers have often provided positive benefits to LDCs: they have brought higher standards of quality for products produced, reduced infant mortality rates, improved yields of crops, distributed those yields more efficiently, and so on. These beneficial results should not be denied. It is also obvious that, in general, people in LDCs both need and want greater goods and services than they presently have.[30] There is little to be said for a primitivist approach to LDCs that would defend realizing in such societies some past, idealized condition of "natural" humanity. We must also be wary of paternalistic efforts that have the effect of not sharing important material goods, services, and resources with people in LDCs because it would be "better" for them. In raising the question of the responsibilities of marketers to less-developed countries and their cultures, my point is not to deny the importance of increased consumption and economic development for such countries, but to speak of the nature of that increased consumption, and thereby its relation to the cultures of LDCs.[31] Instead, my concern is with the *form* that development takes, and, in particular, the implications that arise for the culture(s) of LDCs when that development takes the form of a consumer culture.[32] In particular, my concern is that marketing to LDCs transforms their cultures, and that this transformation, when it takes the form of a Western-style consumer society, is morally questionable. It is here that I believe marketers must look more closely at their responsibilities.

Second, the objection against such marketing activities cannot simply be that they cause change or alteration in the unique cultures of LDCs. Cultures are dynamic features of a society. Some changes are desirable; others are not. In either case, change is inevitable. Marketers do not necessarily show disrespect for such cultures by participating in the changes they undergo. Further, marketers need not hold that all aspects of a culture are beyond moral criticism or may not be legitimate candidates for the changes they might bring. Though I cannot defend the view here, marketers may hold that there are certain international basic moral norms according to which cultures may be found morally lacking. For example, Donaldson has argued that such basic international moral norms include the rights to physical security, fair trial, subsistence, and minimal education.[33] Rather than delineating these norms, I focus on the situation of LDCs whose cultures accord with international basic moral norms, but which differ from Western consumer cultures.[34]

Third, I assume that the culture of a society is something that may be worthy of respect, for its own intrinsic value. The culture of each society represents the efforts of humans to create themselves as humans. As such, culture is the form in which the members of a society have given meaning and definition to their lives. Through one's culture one is provided with a sense of place, identity, connectedness, and tradition.[35] The disappearance or alteration, then, of a culture due to external forces is potentially an important loss for humanity. Whether or not it is a loss will depend upon the nature of the changes and how they are brought about. Further, it is through culture that the achievement of the self-creation of humans is transmitted to succeeding generations.[36] Thus, cultures also have instrumental value. Accordingly, the role that marketers play in cultural changes should be a matter of concern to everyone. And respect of the cultures of LDCs should be a matter of concern for marketers.

Finally, I assume that such respect includes (at least) the following four conditions: (a) *Understanding.* Marketers understand the cultures with which they are dealing and which their activities may affect. One cannot respect someone or a culture if one is unaware of the basic values and assumptions of that person or culture. (b) *Nondisruption.* Respect also requires that marketers do not undertake actions that would block or hinder culturally significant values or goals, as determined by that society. They do not seek to degrade or undercut these values and goals. (c) *Consideration.* Marketers give moral weight to the values of the culture in their own decisions. That is, the cultural values of an LDC are affirmatively included in marketing decisions. Conversely, marketers do not engage in actions that lead to modification of these values toward impossible or highly unrealistic ends without the culturally relevant determination of the culture's own members. (d) *Moral bounds.* Finally, for such respect to be compatible with morality it must occur within certain broad moral limits. Thus, for example, one does not show moral respect for a person or culture when one accedes to actions that violate basic international moral norms.

Our question, then, should focus on those marketing activities that may impinge upon and undercut the values of distinct cultures, for these affect the self-understanding and definition of people in the other society in ways that fail to show them respect. There are a number of objections that have been raised to the role that marketers have hitherto played.

At the outset, we may consider the criticism that marketing has brought about a homogenization of people and cultures. Marketing to LDCs is said to reduce their cultures and people to variations on a very few themes determined by profit-seeking corporations. The products and services they consume are transformed into nondistinct, abstracted goods. With this comes the homogenization of values across cultures. What defines a particular culture as unique is modified, molded, or made compatible with other cultures in a way that reduces them to a common denominator. Leach comments that "businesspeople and advertisers boast of their ability, through telecommunications, to 'homogenize' tastes throughout the world and to encourage everybody to desire the same goods and services."[37] And Korten charges that "[p]resent-day corporations have no reservations about reshaping the values of whole societies to create a homogenized culture of indulgence conducive to spurring consumption expenditures and advancing corporate political interests."[38]

The problem with such objections is that, through the generalized form they take, they fail to distinguish between different forms of homogenization, as well as blur a distinction between the moral and the aesthetic.[39] Surely not all homogenization between societies is undesirable. It depends upon the forms it takes. Thousands of years ago, common signals and ways of measuring weight between the traders of different societies was desirable, since it could prevent misunderstanding and violent conflict. More recently, it is plausible to think that common standards for steel girders, pipes, air traffic controls, and various commodities and services may be very desirable and leave the cultures of societies relatively untouched. Further, the prior differentiation of products such as radios, steel girders, and automobiles may not necessarily have meant those distinct products were of higher quality.

Instead, only that homogenization is morally undesirable that undercuts the cultural identification of LDCs, insofar as they accord with basic international moral norms. In short, the most interesting objection relates to the impact of marketing activities on the moral identity of cultures, rather than simply the homogenization (or differentiation) of products. It is here that a moral objection might be raised. There may also be other forms of homogenization (say, of products) that offend the aesthetic tastes of people and to which they object. These too should be considered by marketers. However, they raise a different question than the one presently under consideration.

One of the principal ways in which marketers may homogenize the cultural identity of LDCs is through fostering within them a consumer society, that is, a society in which an ethics of consumption prevails. When these cultures are altered such that people come to see themselves as consumers whose wants and needs require Western-style products and levels of consumption, the value of their own culture wanes. Thus, the real problem arises when marketers engage in marketing that fosters a consumer society, that is, forms and levels of consumption not sustainable (or even attainable) within those societies and not valued by their indigenous culture. For example, Western marketers have sought to alter the frugality of Indian customers by encouraging them to throw away used goods. They have met resistance in this.[40] Should they transform this aspect of Indian culture, given the scarcity of resources, their culture will be altered in ways that bring negative consequences of various sorts both for individuals and for society.

More generally, the relevant criticism is against that form of marketing that emphasizes the primary values of a consumer society, values that include efficiency, growth, and profit, to the exclusion of concern for those values and assumptions that uniquely define each society. This form of marketing ends up creating products and forms of consumption that import lifestyles to LDCs that level down morally important differences between societies and cultures. If one is concerned primarily about quantity of goods, low price, and economic efficiency, then one should be satisfied with these events. However, we should also be concerned that something important is being stripped away from society and its members. In effect, this approach to marketing does not take seriously the people or the cultures it modifies. Instead, it treats the cultures of such societies and individuals simply as means or vehicles, which may be used, or must be overcome, to promote the economic ends of marketers.

This criticism is similar to one that Rawls and others have made of utilitarianism. The criticism is that utilitarianism cares only about the maximization of utilities, while whose utilities are maximized is a matter of indifference. This, it has been said, denies, or at least neglects, the differences that make us who we are. Thus, Rawls and others have said that utilitarianism fails to take people seriously. Whether this criticism can be sustained against all forms of utilitarianism is not at issue here. What is at issue is that when marketers focus on the creation of more efficient channels of distribution, quantities of consumer goods, and so on (all of which are important) but neglect the effects of their activities in creating a consumer society and consequently the effect on the local culture, they become susceptible to the criticism that some have brought against utilitarianism.

A second important criticism of marketers when they foster a consumer society in LDCs is that they are promoting a form of society and a set of aspirations that people in LDCs will not be able to fulfill. "It is certain," G. A. Cohen has noted, "that we cannot achieve Western-style goods and services for humanity as a whole, nor even sustain them for as large a minority as has enjoyed them, by drawing on the fuels and materials that we have hitherto used to provide them."[41] If this is correct, then besides their products, services, values, and metaphysical assumptions, marketers are also fostering a set of frustrations. Such global marketing is "spreading global dreams of the good life based on spending and consuming, a window but not a door for the vast majority of people who lack money or credit to buy much of anything."[42] "It is giving poor people 'dreams which cannot be fulfilled. It can create social tensions.' "[43]

The objection to this marketing implication stems from the respect owed the culture of other people and societies. Such respect would entail promoting forms of economic development within it that are attainable, as well as sustainable. The arguments concerning both notions are, of course, long and controversial. But if one seeks to promote a way of life or activity that the agent or society cannot achieve or live up to—and (perhaps) should not seek to live up to—then questions may justifiedly be raised about the respect that one shows for that agent or society. Accordingly, reports that marketers view the frugality of the people in India as an important cultural hurdle to be overcome should be both striking and disturbing.[44] Whether it be razors, cigarette lighters, or old saris used as sanitary napkins, Jordan relates that Indians reuse, refill, and recycle. In a time when many are urging that greater measures be taken to promote sustainable business practices in all parts of the world, marketing in India seeks to modify, or overturn, this facet of Indian culture. The preceding objection suggests that marketing that was properly attuned to the cultural values of Indians would seek to work with this cultural trait, rather than undermine it.

Third, some make even stronger charges against the impact of marketing on LDCs. Petras condemns the export of "cultural forms most conducive to depoliticizing and trivializing everyday existence. The images of individual mobility, the 'self-made persons', the emphasis on 'self-centered existence' (mass produced and distributed by the US mass media industry) now have become major instruments in dominating the third world."[45] Galbraith made a similar criticism regarding the influence of marketing on public and private values in developed nations years ago.[46] It is not surprising that this charge is now brought against Western marketing in the LDCs. Thus, the effort to expand personal consumption and greater economic productivity is an effort whose success has long been questioned in Western countries.[47] The point here is not to affirm or deny these contentions themselves, but to indicate that they too suggest that marketers have moral responsibilities to ascertain what the effects of their activities are on those distinctions crucial to social and cultural life. Since their activities may contribute to these effects, marketers cannot simply market their products without taking such considerations into account. Particularly crucial here is the focus of marketers on consumption activities, rather than on the importance of other values, such as work and the meaning of work in life. In contrast, "all religious traditions place primacy of importance on work over consumption. It is only the liberal tradition of the West that has reversed the ordering and given pride of place to consumption over work."[48]

Similarly, John Lachs speaks of a "Consumer's Fallacy," which is "the claim that we do not even begin to *live* until we have the right or approved kind of food bought in a good store, fashionable clothing, and a cave as good as our neighbor's. . . . We *live* when we have as many of these and other goods as our fortune will allow or our stratagems create."[49] At the basis of this fallacy "is the supposition that a man is what he has: that happiness is a function of the goods we possess and the things we consume."[50] This supposition is, he insists, a fallacy as manifested by the unhappiness and dissatisfaction of the many who pursue it. Instead, he argues, "the cure for human dissatisfaction is not by concentrating on increasing our possessions, nor again by concentrating on combating the natural urge to have, but by relegating possession and consumption to their rightful and limited place in a comprehensive scheme of human values."[51] To the extent, then, that marketers promote consumer societies and "the Consumer's Fallacy" in LDCs they undercut important traditional cultural sources of meaningfulness, while offering forms of meaning in consumption that have proven to be of questionable value in the Western countries.

If the preceding objections are acceptable, it follows that marketers do indeed have moral responsibilities to market products to LDCs in a manner that is not only appropriate to their cultural, economic, and social situation, but which also meet other demands on behalf of the integrity of their culture(s). Accordingly, greater attention needs to be given to this responsibility than it has previously received.

Implications for Marketers

A number of implications appear to follow from the preceding. To begin with, many marketers have, quite understandably, attacked the inefficient distribution systems in LDCs. Kotler complains that such distribution is fragmented and inefficient, resulting in higher final prices to consumers.[52] Similarly, Zikmund and d'Amico note complaints that have been raised about the inefficiency in the channels of distribution even in non-Western, though developed, nations such as Japan. One of the reasons for this inefficiency, they note, is "tradition-bound commitments and long-standing relationships among distributors."[53] However, given the preceding considerations, marketers ought not simply look to criteria of efficiency. Longer channels of distribution may include other values that are important for the particular culture. For example, longer distribution channels may preserve other values such as customers being known by the businesses with which they deal. In addition to maintaining personal relationships, individuals may, in this way, gain better information about the products and services they purchase. Further, if we do not assume that traditions or customs have either no worth in themselves or have only negative value, then the fact that "tradition-bound commitments" give rise to inefficiencies does not imply that those commitments ought to be simply overturned to promote greater efficiency. On the other hand, shorter channels of distribution are not value-neutral either. They tend to require larger stores, which have other implications, for example, their customers must have means of transportation (often individual cars) and the stores require large parking lots, both of which can have negative environmental impacts. In short, respect for another culture entails recognizing that forms of production and distribution that marketers consider to be inefficient or to have less value than other forms of operation may fulfill important cultural values, goals, and assumptions. Changes in these practices must be considered within this cultural context.

Second, respect for the cultures of LDCs would mean not insisting on entry to their markets, or threatening to impose sanctions (or advocating that their government do so) if that society did not agree to permit such entry for reasons that pertained to protection of their own cultural values. Respect would also involve not standing in the way of those societies attempting to adopt measures that protect their culture, even if this had negative consequences for one's own marketing programs. Obviously this does not imply that one could not inform the government or its leaders that there were these negative impacts. But such information is one thing; threats and sanctions are another. The former is compatible with respect, the latter is not.

Suppose, however, that an LDC demanded access to the markets of the developed nation but did not permit return access. Suppose even further that access of the LDC's merchants did not negatively affect the developed country's culture, but the activities of marketers of the developed country might harm the culture of the LDC. Now, if a society's culture is something of intrinsic value and deserves protection and respect, then demands that a society open itself up to the marketing activities of developed nations cannot be viewed simply on the basis of higher levels of products, economic growth, and freedom as the lack of constraint. There is another variable that needs to be mixed into the equation and given weight in any final determinations. This cultural variable has a rightful place in the ethical balance. It may also justifiedly require that marketing in a society may only be conducted in ways or forms that protect its local culture. On the other hand, if an LDC seeks to take part in a world economy then it also has responsibilities of seeking forms of economic interchange that not only protect its own culture but are also fair to all participants. The global market is not a one-way street.

Third, marketers require an account of the compatibility (or incompatibility) of their activities with the culture of the societies in which they are active. This involves identifying the essentials of that culture and attempting to anticipate the consequences their activities will have on them. In a discussion of marketing in India, Jordan has noted that "traditional family bonds inhibit Western marketers' access: Yuppies, deferring to their elders, don't make household-purchasing decisions."[54] The preceding discussion implies, at the least, that attempts to change purchasing decisions in India in ways that circumvent and destroy these traditional family bonds are matters for moral consideration by marketers. They are not matters of indifference to be determined simply on the basis of the efficiency or quantity of goods sold. The reasons may be both intrinsic (due to the inherent value of such relations) and extrinsic (due to the effects that their elimination might cause). For example, Chakraborty worries about the disintegrating effects of marketing on the Indian family and local communities. He observes that such effects

will be especially detrimental in countries like India where the local community has often served as an informal social-welfare system. In the vacuum created by the disappearance of this system, due to the disintegration of the local community, people will inevitably turn to the state for the help they require. The demands which this will put on the state will in all likelihood be insupportable and will promote further political fractionalization and social turmoil.[55]

Thus, concern for the cultural implications of marketing activities may help to head off various problems that are otherwise avoidable. The cultures of LDCs are constituted by a web of values, norms, interrelationships, and patterns of dependencies that the introduction of marketing practices may disrupt without providing adequate replacements. Another example is that as a result of the imposition of

the exchange centered marketing concept in LDCs . . . systems of need satisfaction which historically emerged in these societies, for example, reciprocity systems in the Urubamba Valley in Peru, and redistribution/shared labor systems in Anatolia, disappear from the scene. If recognized at all, they are treated as impediments for the development of market exchange systems, as primitive practices to be broken, rather than as alternative need satisfaction systems. Growth of market exchange, not satisfaction of human/social needs, becomes the foremost objective for scholars and policy makers who employ these approaches.[56]

It might be objected that this is just a failure of marketing's own precept, the marketing concept, which urges marketers to determine the needs and wants of the people and satisfy them. In this case, it might be said, marketers have not followed their own directives. However, though the marketing concept speaks of satisfying people's wants and needs, it advises such efforts because of their positive effect on profits. But this approach to people's wants and needs subordinates them to profit-making considerations. Consequently, marketers in LDCs have often allowed the determinations of profit to dominate other considerations regarding the local culture and the effects of their actions on that culture. Thus, marketing in these contexts has led to results such as those just noted. Accordingly, the introduction of modern marketing techniques and the creation, thereby, of a consumer culture has transformed some relations within LDCs with little consideration for collateral and background implications for people outside the market exchange system. Recognition of marketers' responsibility for the cultural effects of their actions would help avoid such consequences.

Fourth, how are marketers to know which aspects of a culture it might be acceptable to change and which not? There are two aspects of this question. Some of the preceding objections suggest that there are certain forms of marketing that are questionable in themselves because of their nature and implications. Thus, to instill an ethics of consumption that cannot be fulfilled in the same manner as presently in Western countries raises questions of justice and respect. This is particularly the case if Western countries are not prepared to alter their consumption patterns to accommodate greater consumption levels of LDCs. There is hypocrisy in such behavior as well.

On the other hand, it is not simply up to marketers to make these decisions by themselves in other cases. It must be a "decision" of the society involved. Obviously, this is not a simple matter. This is where procedural matters enter in. The mere economic power that some marketers have, over and against local marketers and certain cultural forms of life, may tilt the balance against local values and assumptions. Dholakia notes, for example, that emphasis on the marketing of brand name products may homogenize consumer tastes by eliminating traditional products that may be more closely linked with the local or national culture:

> brand proliferation increases choice at the brand level but frequently reduces choice at the product/category level. While this creates larger markets and homogeneity in consumer tastes, it also reduces diversity. This is further exacerbated because the products/categories that are eliminated are frequently traditional, low capital and/or energy intensive and ecologically more compatible.[57]

However, more generally the problem of the commons arises here, since culture is not simply an individual, but a public or common, good. Perhaps this is why it has slipped through the fingers of philosophical and marketing ethicists. Popular demands in any number of different segments might not be terribly significant in themselves regarding the culture of the society. However, collectively they may have a significant effect. Similarly, the actions of this or that marketer may not in themselves be terribly significant, just as the pollution from any single manufacturing plant might not degrade the environment. However, once again, collectively their effects may be very significant. Accordingly, marketers ought not simply consider the individual effects of their actions as if they were unrelated to some larger set of consequences. They must also consider the role that their individual effects have within the collective consequences occasioned by all marketers.

It is at this point that marketers and public policy persons must work together.[58] In the past decade we have seen in Iran and, more recently, Turkey and India, cases in which those promoting Western-style consumer societies did not sufficiently take into account clashes of Western values and assumptions with the cultures of the society where they were introduced. It is not plausible to say that individual marketers are to blame for such societal and cultural upheavals. However, given the preceding arguments, it is also implausible to say that they do not share any of the responsibility. Surely Meffert is correct when he contends that "it cannot be recommended to uncritically transfer living and consumer styles from the industrial countries to the developing countries."[59] The responsibilities of marketers in this regard deserve greater attention. Laczniak and Murphy suggest that when a host community or culture brings pressures to bear upon a business organization that are opposed to the organization's core values, it should consider suspending its marketing activities in that society.[60] Conversely, they might also suggest that when the values an organization fosters, through its products and activities, are opposed to the core values of another culture, they should consider not doing business in that society, or modifying their products and activities to make them compatible with that culture.

Conclusion

Almost one hundred fifty years ago, that great critic of the capitalist system, Karl Marx, charged that

> [t]he bourgeoisie, by the rapid improvement of all instruments of production, by the immensely facilitated means of communication, draws all, even the most barbarian, nations into civilization. The cheap prices of its commodities are the heavy artillery with which it batters down all Chinese walls, with which it forces the barbarians' intensely obstinate hatred of foreigners to capitulate. It compels all nations, on pain of extinction, to adopt the bourgeois mode of production; it compels them to introduce what it calls civilization into their midst; i.e. to become bourgeois themselves. In one word, it creates a world after its own image.[61]

Though many of Marx's criticisms have been mistaken, in light of the globalization of the world economy, this one has proven to have considerable substance. However, whereas Marx appears to have shared Mill's views on customs and traditions and hoped that the extension of bourgeois forms of production would lead to a world society of abundant productivity, we should question the desirability of a world within which the cultures of different societies are homogenized into similar forms of an ethics of consumption.

Movement toward a global homogenized society characterized by the ethics of consumption is fostered, perhaps, by frequent and unreflective talk about the creation of "a global village" with a "borderless economy."[62] Since villages tend to have the same customs and values, we ought to consider whether such talk might not actually be threatening to the maintenance of distinct but morally valuable cultures around the world. Rarely when people use these phrases do they reflect on what the moral effects will be on the many distinct cultures presently existing. In contrast, the argument of this essay has been that marketers in LDCs (or other countries for that matter) cannot approach their task as simply that of creating customers so as to foster higher levels of consumption without any regard for the implications of those higher levels of consumption on the society and culture within which those customers live. To do so is to reenact the role of European missionaries hundreds of years ago. The danger and the difficulty for marketers is that in marketing their goods to receptive people (due in part to their ads, promotions, etc.) they may be working to eliminate or modify something (viz., their culture) of importance and value, thereby creating problems and frustrations in the people of that society, while all the while seeming to be satisfying customer wants. D. H. Smith comments that "[w]ithout strong cultural identity, economic development can lead to simple consumerism."[63] By protecting the cultural identity of LDCs, marketers could help contribute to a solution of the above problems. This would still give those who market in these countries tremendous room to do business. But it would demand that they more closely consider their aims and responsibilities when they do business in less developed countries.

Notes

I am indebted to Iain Clelland, Michael Davis, Richard DeGeorge, Donald Mayer, and Pat Werhane for helpful comments on earlier versions of this essay.

1. In the case of native North Americans, they were viewed by many as not having any culture at all. Cf. Michael K. Green, "Images of Native Americans in Advertising: Some Moral Issues," *Journal of Business Ethics* 12 (1993), 155–62.

2. Gene R. Laczniak and Patrick E. Murphy, *Ethical Marketing Decisions: The Higher Road* (Upper Saddle, NJ: Prentice-Hall, 1993), 228. But according to what standards? If Korten is to be believed, then there are problems with "these influences" undercutting the culture, its members, etc. Cf. David Korten, *When Corporations Rule the World* (West Hartford: Kumarian, 1995).

3. Richard T. DeGeorge, *Competing with Integrity in International Business* (New York: Oxford University Press, 1993), 52.

4. I will speak of marketing only in the business context—not in the broader senses it has been given such as in "social marketing," where marketing techniques are used for purposes of advancing various social, educational, political, or religious purposes.

5. Fullerton's comment is relevant: "Operationally, Modern Western Mar-

keting can be defined as the vigorous cultivation of existing markets and equally vigorous efforts to open up new ones through insistent promotion, frequent introduction of new products, careful study of market demand, and ongoing efforts to control and coordinate distribution channels. Existing channels may be bypassed in the quest for larger markets" (Robert A. Fullerton, "Modern Western Marketing as a Historical Phenomenon: Theory and Illustration," in *Historical Perspectives in Marketing*, ed. Terence Nevett and Ronald A. Fullerton [Lexington: Lexington Books, 1988], 73–74). Accordingly, marketing is understood here in a broad sense. It would include, for example, decisions over whether to introduce products and techniques requiring high or low levels of technology.

6. Such marketing is clearly bound up with capitalism. Fullerton claims that "it is capitalism which provides the central value of Modern Western marketing" (Fullerton, *Historical Perspectives*, 74). To the extent, then, that capitalism reaches into less developed nations through marketing, this essay is also on capitalism and less–developed countries. However, the effects of capitalism in LDCs might be felt in other ways than through marketing, for example, through various financial and banking policies, theories of accounting, management, and so on. This essay does not consider these issues but, instead, focuses on ethical questions marketers face with regard to LDCs. Nevertheless, this essay has clear implications for these other areas of capitalism.

7. Fullerton, *Historical Perspectives*, 73.

8. Hans B. Thorelli. "Consumer Policy for the Third World," *Journal of Consumer Policy* 3 (1981): 201.

9. Russell W. Belk, "Possessions and the Extended Self," *Journal of Consumer Research* 15 (1988): 160.

10. Heinrich Zimmer, *Philosophies of India* (Cleveland: World Publishing Co., 1951), 159.

11. Julius M. E. Moravcsik, "On What We Aim at and How We Live," in *The Greeks and the Good Life*, ed. David J. Depew (Fullerton: California State University Press, 1980), 229.

12. It should be noted that this "ethics of consumption" is stated universally, i.e., without restriction to Western or American society. Such a universal statement is also a characteristic of this ethics. This is why it is taken to apply to all human societies.

13. Cf. Gregory P. Stone, "Comments on 'Careers and Consumer Behavior,' " in *Consumer Behavior* 2 (New York: New York University Press, 1995), 25.

14. Ernest Zahn, "The Consumer Society: Unstinted Praise and Growing Criticism," in *Human Behavior in Economic Affairs*, ed. Burkhard Strumpel, James N. Morgan, and Ernest Zahn, (San Francisco: Jossey-Bass Inc. 1972), 443.

15. Perhaps, for some, the ethnocentric nature of this consumer society is less clear due to the influence of logical positivism and neoclassical economic theory in marketing. These factors have isolated the treatment of the issues of consumption and development from social, moral, and historical contexts while seeking universally applicable laws. Cf. A. Fuat Firat, Erodoğan Kumcu, and Mehmet Karafakioğlu, "The Interface between Marketing and Development:

Problems and Prospects," in *Marketing and Development: Toward Broader Dimensions*, ed. Erodoğan Kumcu and A. Fuat Firat (Greenwich, CT: JAI Press, 1988), 327–29.

16. William Leach, *Land of Desire: Merchants, Power and the Rise of a New American Culture* (New York: Pantheon Books, 1993), xiii.

17. I assume that marketers have had an influence in LDCs through the introduction of their marketing practices. If this is false, or if marketers cannot have any such influences, then discussion of their moral responsibilities for those influences is, obviously, unnecessary. It is not necessary for me to hold, however, that marketers create new basic wants or needs in people in LDCs. It is sufficient, for my present purposes, that they are able to create or foster desires in people for consumer goods that fulfill prior (basic) wants and needs but do so in ways that undercut the cultural identity those individuals share.

18. I distinguish here between philosophical business ethicists, such as DeGeorge, Donaldson, and Velasquez, and marketing business ethicists, such as Robin, Reidenbach, Laczniak, and Murphy. Though members of both groups may call themselves simply "business ethicists," their different backgrounds (philosophy or theology and marketing) tend to have a significant effect on their views of business ethics. Rather than simply refer to the former group as business ethicists, thereby denying that title to those in marketing who "do" business ethics, I prefer the present distinction.

19. This, of course, raises significant problems regarding women, children, and others. However, I do not discuss these problems.

20. DeGeorge, *Competing With Integrity*, 106.

21. Cf. Norman E. Bowie and Ronald F. Duska, *Business Ethics* (Englewood Cliffs, NJ: Prentice-Hall, Inc., 1990). Richard T. DeGeorge, *Competing with Integrity*; Thomas Donaldson, *The Ethics of International Business* (New York: Oxford University Press, 1989); Patricia H. Werhane, *Persons, Rights and Corporations*, (Englewood Cliffs, NJ: Prentice-Hall, Inc., 1985).

22. Cf. Donaldson, *The Ethics of International Business*.

23. Cf. Donald P. Robin and R. Eric Reidenbach, "Searching for a Place to Stand: Toward a Workable Ethical Philosophy for Marketing," *Journal of Public Policy & Marketing* 12, no. 1 (1993): 97–105; Gene R. Laczniak and Patrick E. Murphy, "International Marketing Ethics," *Bridges* 2 (1990): 155–77.

24. Ashok Malhotra, "Value Erosion and Managerial Alienation in Indian Organisations," *BusinessIndia* (Jan. 14–27, 1985): 79.

25. Malhotra, "Value Erosion," 79.

26. Malhotra, "Value Erosion," 81.

27. P. L. Tandon, "The Propertyless Manager: Culture and Ethics in India," in *Corporate Ethics*, ed. T. A. Mathias (New Delhi: Allied Publishers, 1994), 4.

28. Darryl Reed, "Business Ethics in an Indian Setting," *Business Ethics: A European Review* 4, no. 4 (1995): 164.

29. This might be cited as an example of what has been called "the separation thesis." In fact, I suggest that there are two separation theses. One is the view that economics or business does not involve moral values or issues; it is morally neutral in itself. Ethics or morality is a separate area or field. The second separa-

tion thesis is that the morals of business differ from the morals of everyday life. The former thesis is what Ed Freeman has recently discussed. Cf. Edward R. Freeman, "The Politics of Stakeholder Theory: Some Future Directions,*" Business Ethics Quarterly* 4, no. 4 (1994): 409–22. The latter is a view I have discussed. Cf. George G. Brenkert, "The Environment, the Moralist, the Corporation and Its Culture," *Business Ethics Quarterly* 5, no. 4 (1995): 675–98.

30. Still, we should remember that there are many very wealthy people in LDCs. Not everyone in an LDC requires greater goods and services.

31. From the fact that certain countries have been designated "less developed" it does not follow that their cultures are less developed as well.

32. The argument of this essay does not assume that there is a single, unified culture that all people, without exception, adhere to in each country. There may be subcultures within any society. In addition, people within each country will variously adhere to different cultural strands within their country. Thus, for instance, there are clear cultural differences in India between Tamil Nadu and Uttar Pradesh. Still, there are similarities that unite these areas of India and distinguish them from New York and Georgia in the United States. Marketers, this chapter urges, must be sensitive to cultural differences on both levels.

33. Donaldson, *International Business*, 81.

34. Or at least we may assume that they correspond with these international basic norms approximately as well as do Western consumer societies. In short, I do not want to consider the case where marketers might have these kinds of justifications to bring change in the cultures of LDCs.

35. Cf. Michael K. Green, "Images of Native Americans in Advertising: Some Moral Issues,*" Journal of Business Ethics* 12 (1993): 158.

36. Cf. Green, "Native Americans," 156.

37. Leach, *Land of Desire*, 384.

38. Korten, *Corporations Rule*, 150.

39. I do not claim that moral and aesthetic issues are wholly separable. Only that they are distinguishable.

40. I assume that such frugality among Indians is not simply their response to economic necessity. Scarcity may have played a role thousands of years ago in this value having a place within their cultural values. But it is also part of their culture, just as it used to be part of Western and American values. I assume, for example, that Benjamin Franklin advocated his prudent and frugal ways not simply because they were imposed by economic scarcity. Rather he viewed these as part of the construction of a moral person.

41. G. A. Cohen, *Self-Ownership, Freedom, and Equality* (Cambridge: Cambridge University Press, 1993), 9.

42. Richard J. Barnet and John Cavanagh, "The Sound of Money," *Sojourners* 23, no. 1 (1994): 14.

43. Barnet and Cavanagh, "Sound of Money," 14.

44. Miriam Jordan, "Marketing Gurus Say: In India, Think Cheap, Lose the Cold Cereal," *Wall Street Journal*, 11 Oct. 1996, 9 (A).

45. James Petras, "Cultural Imperialism in Late 20th Century," *Economics and Political Weekly*, 6 Aug. 1994: 2072.

46. John Kenneth Galbraith, *The Affluent Society*, 2d ed., rev. (Boston: Houghton Mifflin, 1969).

47. The implications of my argument for marketing within Western nations where a consumer society already exists are left unexplored in this essay. This is a topic for another work.

48. Raymond Benton Jr., "Work, Consumption, and the Joyless Consumer," in *Philosophical and Radical Thought in Marketing*, ed. A. Fuat Firat, Nikhilesh Dholakia, and Richard P. Bagozzis (Lexington, MA: Lexington Books, 1987), 241.

49. John Lachs, "To Have and To Be," *The Personalist* 45 (1964): 7.

50. Lachs, "To Have," 8.

51. Lachs, "To Have," 9.

52. Phillip Kotler, "The Potential Contributions of Marketing Thinking to Economic Development," *Research in Marketing*, Supplement 4, *Marketing and Development: Toward Broader Dimensions* (Greenwich, CT: JAI Press, 1988), 10.

53. William G. Zikmund and Michael d'Amico, *Effective Marketing: Creating and Keeping Customers* (Minneapolis: West Publishing Co., 1995), 314.

54. Jordan, "Marketing Gurus," 9 (A).

55. Reed, "Business Ethics," 165.

56. Firat et al., "Problems and Prospects," 331.

57. Ruby Roy Dholakia, "Consumer Issues in Development: Consumer Behavior in the Third World," in *The Role of Marketing in Development*, ed. Erodoğan Kumcu, A. Fuat Firat, Mehmet Karafakioğlu, Muhittin Karabulut and Mehmet Oluc (Muncie, IN: Ball State University Publications, 1986), 18.

58. Cf. Ruby Roy Dholakia, Mohammed Sharif, and Labdhi Bhandari, "Consumption in the Third World: Challenges for Marketing and Development" in *Marketing and Development: Toward Broader Dimensions*, ed. Erodoğan Kumcu and A. Fuat Firat (Greenwich, CT: JAI Press, 1988).

59. Heribert Meffert, "Developing Countries: Role of Marketing," *Marketing and Management Digest* 9, no. 6 (1976): 49.

60. Gene R. Laczniak and Patrick E. Murphy, *Ethical Marketing Decisions: The Higher Road* (Upper Saddle River, NJ: Prentice-Hall, Inc., 1993), 166.

61. Karl Marx, "Manifesto of the Communist Party," in *The Marx-Engels Reader*, ed. Robert C. Tucker (New York: W. W. Norton, 1972), 339.

62. Cf. Akio Morita, "Toward a New World Economic Order," *Atlantic Monthly* (June 1993): 92.

63. Dean Howard Smith, "The Issue of Compatibility between Cultural Integrity and Economic Development among Native American Tribes," *American Indian Culture and Research Journal* 18, no. 2 (1994): 199.

6

Reducing the Ecological Footprint of Consumption

William E. Rees

Introduction: Defining a Historic Turning Point

In 1986 a team of ecologists led by Peter Vitousek showed that human beings directly or indirectly appropriate almost 40 percent of net terrestrial photosynthesis to their own use.[1] More recent work suggests that the world fish catch now represents 35 percent of net primary production in shallow coastal areas and over the continental shelves. These areas, only 9 percent of the marine environment, account for 96 percent of the global ocean fishery.[2] To ecologists these are startling figures that warrant clear-eyed reappraisal of the growing impact of the human economy on the ecosphere—Vitousek et al. is one of the most frequently cited papers in the recent biological literature. Such data show that humanity's harvest of nature is already approaching half of the available output at a time when the prevailing international development model anticipates a five- to tenfold increase in world economic activity by the time the human population stabilizes (at about ten billion) toward the middle of the next century.

Vitosek et al.'s findings did not go entirely unremarked in other circles. Using this and related evidence, Robert Goodland of the World Bank made the case that growth in the energy and material *throughput* of the world economy cannot be sustained.[3] Similarly Herman Daly, then a senior economist with the World Bank, argued that this new reality marks "an historical turning point in economic development" that should force a social transition from "empty-world to full-world economics."[4] However, despite the alarm expressed by ecologists, ecological economists, and other scientists concerned about the biophysical di-

113

mensions of sustainability, the apparent convergence of the economy with the ecosphere has had virtually no impact on mainstream thinking and the prevailing international development model. The purpose of this essay, therefore, is twofold. First, I show that, if anything, Vitousek et al. underestimated the present scale of human intervention in the ecosphere. I use a new technique, ecological footprint analysis, to show that the total "load" of the human enterprise already exceeds the carrying capacity of the Earth. This reality requires a more urgent corrective response by the global community to the issue of overconsumption than any suggested to date. Second, I review some of the policy directions being explored by informed researchers to address the problem. This analysis suggests that so far the world has treated sustainability mainly as a technical problem. We have therefore largely ignored sociocultural solutions and failed to explore development policy options that may provide great additional leverage in reconciling humanity with "the environment."

The Human Ecological Footprint[5]

As implied above, a fundamental question for *ecological* sustainability is whether supplies of so-called "natural capital" (natural resource stocks) will be adequate to meet anticipated demand into the next century.[6] This is a question of human carrying capacity, a critical issue to ecologists but one that has historically been rejected by economists as irrelevant to human beings.

Carrying capacity is usually defined as the largest population of a given species that can live in a defined area without permanently damaging the ecosystem(s) that sustain it (i.e., without destroying its habitat). Most conventional economists argue that the limits implied by this concept do not apply to humans. Since local resource shortages can be relieved by technology (through substitution or efficiency gains) and by trade, regional population or economic growth should not be constrained by local resource scarcities.

However, if we invert the standard carrying capacity ratio we have a powerful way both to address the fundamental question posed above and to overturn the objections of economists. Rather than asking what population or level of economic activity a particular region can support sustainably, the carrying capacity question becomes: How large an area of productive land is needed to sustain a defined population indefinitely, *wherever on Earth that land is located?*[7]

Since most forms of "natural income" (resource and service flows from nature) are produced by terrestrial ecosystems and associated water bodies,[8] it should be possible to estimate the area of land and water required to produce sustainably the quantity of many resources and ecological services used by a defined population at a given level of technology. The sum of such calculations for all significant categories of consumption would give us a conservative area-based estimate of the natural capital requirements for that population. We call this area the population's ecological footprint. The "ecological footprint" is therefore defined as *the area of productive land and water (ecosystems) required on a continuous basis to produce the resources consumed and to assimilate the wastes produced by a defined population, wherever on Earth that land is located.* Ecological footprint analysis enables us to compare the natural capital requirements of any subject population with available supply.[9]

Implications for Urban Land Use Planning

Eco-footprint analysis shows clearly that the large populations and high per capita energy and material consumption rates of modern cities have dramatically transformed the relationships between human settlements and the land/water ecosystems that sustain them. Most importantly, the above data suggest that the idea of a "sustainable city" per se has little meaning—more than 99 percent of the natural capital upon which typical modern cities depend for survival lies outside their own boundaries and therefore beyond their direct political control. Thus, conventional urban land use planning may result in more compact and efficient cities and can enhance local amenities, but this contributes only to local livability, not to sustainability. Urban sustainability is ultimately governed by land and resource management practices in the rural hinterland. Put another way, it seems that in an increasingly urbanized world it would be wise to consider the global hinterland as an integral functional component of the global urban system. Perhaps, for ecological security, the land use planning areas for individual cities should be redefined to include as much of the supportive rural land base as possible.[10] For example, the "sustainability" of the Greater Vancouver–Lower Fraser Valley region of British Columbia is dependent on imports of ecologically significant goods and services whose production requires an area elsewhere on Earth vastly larger than the internal area of the region itself. This means, in effect, that however healthy the region's economy appears to be in monetary terms, the Vancouver region is running a massive ecological deficit with the rest of Canada and the world.

The Global Context

This situation is typical of so-called "industrialized" (or high-income) regions and even entire countries. To support their current consumption levels, many industrialized countries run an ecological deficit an order of magnitude or more larger than the sustainable natural income generated by the ecologically productive land within their political territories (table 6.1; marine areas not included). The last two columns of table 6.1 represent low estimates of these *per capita* deficits. Even if their land were twice as productive as the world average, European countries would still run a deficit more than three times larger than domestic natural income.

These data throw new light on current world development models. For example, Japan and the Netherlands both boast positive trade and

TABLE 6.1
The Ecological Deficits of Industrialized Countries

Country	Ecologically Productive Land (in hectares)	Population (1995)	Ecologically Productive Land per capita (in hectares)	National Ecological Deficit per capita (in hectares)	(in percentage available)
	a	*b*	*c = a/b*	*d=Ftprint - c*	*e = d/c*
Countries with 2-3 ha Footprints				*assuming a 2 hectare Footprint*	
Japan	30,417,000	125,000,000	0.24	1.76	730
S. Korea	8,716,000	45,000,000	0.19	1.81	952
Countries with 3-4 ha Footprints				*assuming a 3 hectare Footprint*	
Austria	6,740,000	7,900,000	0.85	2.15	253
Belgium	1,987,000	10,000,000	0.20	2.80	1,400
Britain	20,360,000	58,000,000	0.35	2.65	757
Denmark	3,270,000	5,200,000	0.62	2.38	384
France	45,385,000	57,800,000	0.78	2.22	284
Germany	27,734,000	81,300,000	0.34	2.66	782
Netherlands	2,300,000	15,500,000	0.15	2.85	1,900
Switzerland	3,073,000	7,000,000	0.44	2.56	582
				assuming a 3.74 hectare Footprint	
Australia	575,993,000	17,900,000	32.18	(28.44)	(760)
Countries with 4-5 ha Footprints				*assuming Can 4.3 and US 5.1 hectare Footprint*	
Canada	434,477,000	28,500,000	15.24	(10.94)	(254)
United States	725,643,000	258,000,000	2.81	2.29	81

Source: Revised from M. Wackernagel and W. Rees, *Our Ecological Footprint: Reducing Human Impact on the Earth* (Philadelphia and Gabriola Island, BC: New Society Publishers, 1995–96). For more comprehensive estimates see M. Wackernagel et al., *Ecological Footprints of Nations: Report to the Earth Council* (Costa Rica, 1997) (contact: Dr. Mathis Wackernagel, Centro de Estudios Para la Sustentabilidad, Universidad Anáhuac de Zalapa, Apdo. Postal 653, 91000 Xalapa, Ver., Mexico. Footprints estimated from studies by Ingo Neumann from Trier University, Germany; Dieter Zürcher from Infras Consulting, Switzerland; Rod Simpson, Katherine Gaschk, and Shannon Rutherford of Griffiths University, Australia; and our own analysis using World Resources Institute (1992) data.

Note: Ecologically productive land means cropland, permanent pasture, forests, and woodlands as compiled by the World Resources Institute (1992). Semi-arid grasslands, deserts, ice fields, etc., are not included.

current account balances measured in monetary terms and their populations are among the most prosperous on Earth. Densely populated yet relatively resource (natural capital) poor, these countries are regarded as stellar economic successes and held up as models for emulation by the developing world. Ecological footprint analysis, however, tells a different story. It shows that Japan has a 2.5 hectare/capita and the Netherlands a 3.3 hectare/capita ecological footprint, which give these countries national ecological footprints about ten and twenty-one times larger than their respective domestic productive land bases. Each is running a large eco-deficit and accumulating a nonrepayable debt with the rest of the world.

The marked contrast between the physical and monetary accounts of national economies raises difficult developmental questions in a world whose principal strategy for sustainability is economic growth. Global sustainability cannot be (ecological) deficit-financed; simple physics dictates that not all countries or regions can be net importers of biophysical capacity. Ecological footprint analysis shows that *there is simply not enough natural capital on the planet to sustain present international development trends using prevailing technology.* Indeed, to support even the present world population sustainably at North American ecological standards would require two to three additional "phantom" planets like Earth. How should this reality be reflected in national and global strategies for ecologically sustainable socioeconomic development?

The Factor-10 Economy

There is no getting around the fact that material consumption is at the heart of the sustainability crisis—the aggregate ecological footprint of humanity is already larger than the Earth.[11] The ecological challenge for sustainability, therefore, is how to accommodate both rising material expectations and a near doubling of population over the next fifty years while actually *reducing* total throughput.

Barring disaster, most analysts agree that this can be achieved in two ways: through an absolute reduction in average material standards of living or through a massive increase in material and energy efficiency (or some combination). The increasingly ubiquitous cultural values implied by consumerism render the first approach politically unfeasible in developed countries,[12] and it would quite justifiably be rejected outright by the impoverished quarter of the world's population living mostly in developing countries. Indeed, many economists insist that global sustainability is achievable only through large increases in the consumption of goods and services in both the poor and rich countries.

The bad news, then, is that growth is seen as the only politically and economically viable means to alleviate poverty and inequity both within countries and between rich and poor countries. The good news is that many advocates of this approach have at last accepted the fact of limits to *material* growth. A consensus is emerging that the needed increase in consumption would be sustainable only if there is a corresponding reduction in the material and energy intensity of goods and services.[13]

Numerous researchers and organizations are therefore exploring the policy implications of reducing the energy/material throughput of so-called advanced economies. Conscious of the need for growth, particularly in the developing world, they conclude that the material intensity of consumption in industrial countries should be reduced by a factor of up to ten to accommodate it.[14] Since markets do not reflect ecological reality, governments must create the necessary policy incentives to ensure that as consumption rises, the material and energy content of that consumption falls apace. Achieving a "factor-10" economy will require major changes in industrial strategy, fiscal and taxation policy, and consumer-corporate relations. However, if managed properly, the net effect of this transformation should be not only less consumption and waste but also more jobs and increased regional self-reliance.

Ecology and Fiscal Reform: Taxing Our Way to Sustainability

It is an economic axiom that underpricing leads to overuse. Much of the sustainability crisis derives from the fact that today's prices do not reflect the resource depletion or pollution damage costs of economic goods and services. Ecological and economic sustainability requires the restructuring of economic incentives and taxation policy to encourage material and energy conservation and to increase the demand for labor. This can best be achieved by replacing present subsidies by a system of resource use and depletion taxes, and marketable quotas offset by corresponding reductions in other taxes, particularly on labor.[15] By raising prices closer to the full social cost of goods and services, taxes on energy and resources create an incentive for industry to minimize material throughput; meanwhile, lower labor costs (further) increase workers' comparative advantage over capital.

On Taxes and Quotas

Resource depletion taxes would be easier to implement than quotas but do have a major weakness if applied in the trial-and-error manner of traditional pollution levies. Determining the magnitude of the levy needed to achieve the desired reduction in consumption (or pollution) is an imprecise art. Taxes set either too high or too low will not achieve the desired conservation objective and the resultant misallocation of expenditures by both industry and consumers is economically inefficient. Moreover, the demand curve may shift upward in response to changing tastes, rising incomes, reduced choice, and other exogenous factors, thereby defeating any initial gains and requiring potentially costly adjustments to the tax regime. In short, both the environmental and economic impacts of environmental taxes are inherently uncertain. This is not an argument against resource taxation but rather a plea for sound deliberation and planning of ecological fiscal reform. Von Weizsäcker argues for a "gradualist" approach in which the initial levies on targeted goods and services would "increase predictably [at, say, 5 percent per year] over a very long time-scale, e.g. over 40 years, in order to encourage the private sector [etc.] . . . to invest in long-term solutions for sustainable development."[16]

Quotas have an important advantage over taxes in that they limit aggregate throughput to a definite pre-determined amount. When resource use must be reduced by a known amount, or when only a fixed quantity of some public resource is to be made available for consumption—a common characteristic of "natural income"—a quota may be preferred over a conventional tax. A marketable quota system allows government to set the total "harvest" directly while the market sets the price (for example, by competitive bidding for use rights by resource companies). As Daly emphasizes, "it is quantity that affects the ecosystem, not price, and therefore it is ecologically safer to let errors and unexpected shifts in demand result in price fluctuations rather than quantity fluctuations."[17]

Taxing Consumption, Not Labor

Ecological tax reform is ultimately likely to produce more economic gains than losses. Income, value added, and similar taxes increase the upward pressure on wages and salaries. This reinforces an already undesirable incentive for industry to replace labor with energy and machinery which, in turn, increases resource use, unemployment, and pressure on the environment. Resource taxes/quotas can reverse the incentives, helping to reduce consumption and to stimulate employment by enabling payroll tax reductions.[18] An analysis of just eight "green taxes" for the United States, covering such items as carbon emissions ($US 100/ton) and groundwater depletion ($US 50/acre-foot), suggested that these levies alone could raise $US 130 billion, allowing a reduction of 30 percent in personal income taxes.[19]

Reducing income and other taxes in proportion to resource taxes would make the latter revenue neutral, so ecological tax reform would not necessarily increase the average fiscal burden on taxpayers. Nor (unlike regulation or add-on pollution charges) would it jeopardize international competitiveness.[20] On the contrary, those countries that act first to develop new energy- and material-efficient technologies and processes will gain the upper hand in marketing these products and services in a global market of enormous potential demand. Note that economies that retained or increased energy prices after the OPEC oil price shock of the 1970s have subsequently generally fared better than those that kept domestic energy prices low.[21]

There are additional advantages at the other end of the consumption stream. Because they reduce throughput, resource use and depletion levies may be as effective at reducing pollution as are comparable existing pollution charges. Moreover, as a part of fundamental tax reform, ecological taxes can be fifty or even one hundred times greater than the special environmental charges presently set in some jurisdictions. This may be both necessary and sufficient to bring about the rapid and fundamental restructuring of the economy required for sustainability.

As noted, ecological taxes should be increased gradually over a period of several decades to maintain a constant, predictable, and manageable pressure for innovation on industry. Increasing the initial tax on the most damaging input factors such as fossil fuels by 5 percent per year would double the tax cost in fourteen years. With indirect labor cost falling simultaneously, "It should gradually become more profitable to lay off kilowatt hours and barrels of oil than to lay off people."[22]

Material Conservation Means More Jobs . . .

Ecological tax reform will also confirm the central role of reuse, repair, reconditioning, and recycling in an optimal utilization economy. The cost advantages of product-life extension activities will make them a substitute for "the transformation and service activities of extractive industries and base material production and thus a replacement of large-scale, energy- and capital-intensive units by smaller-scale, labour- and skill-intensive, independent, locally integrated work units."[23]

Recycling is already an important source of employment. Estimates suggest that as early as 1988, solid waste disposal in the United States may have been employing 43,000 people. (This at a rate of one job for every 465 tons of waste handled, or only 10 percent of the 200 million tons of municipal solid waste generated each year. Increasing the recycling rate to 75 percent could yield 375,000 jobs.)[24] However, recycling is not nearly as environmentally effective or economically efficient as reuse, repair, and remanufacturing. Reconditioning a car to make it last a second ten years, for example, requires 42 percent less energy and 56 percent more labor than manufacturing a new car.[25]

. . . and a New Lease on (Product) Life

Thinking sustainable development may lead to new methods of manufacturing and could transform the relationship between producers and consumers. For example, in today's consumer society technological upgrading can often be achieved only through complete product replacement. Product life can therefore be enhanced "by designing inter-compatible systems with distinct functional modules, separating, for instance, structural elements (a car chassis), skin elements (bodywork), wear and tear components (engine), and control components."[26] These structural modules can be replaced with new or (preferably) remanufactured units as required, without discarding other modules still in good working order.

Such new production methods lead to other forms of commercial innovation. In general, the profitability of commercial enterprises must be decoupled from the throughput of goods. This has already started in the energy sector, where the profitability of many utilities is shifting from the sale of energy commodities to the provision of energy services. Conservation enables the same level of the service—and the same price—with much reduced energy consumption. In the case of washing machines, for example, perfect "end-of-pipe" recycling of the appliance can reduce resource consumption and waste volume by a respectable 90 percent; however, selling clothes-cleaning services instead of washing machines can reduce resource consumption and waste per wash cycle by a factor of 40![27] With such large gains in efficiency possible on such everyday services, the "factor-10" economy does not seem such a formidable goal.

As profitability shifts from the selling of things to the selling of services, it will also change the relationships between producers and consumers, including patterns of ownership, throughout the economy. For many consumer durables, operational leasing will replace the outright sale of goods as the basis of exchange and corporate profitability. This will significantly alter the prevailing consumer-producer dynamic. Lease arrangements give greater leverage to consumers confronted with poor quality products and services and should motivate top performance from producers since people can walk away from faulty equipment they don't own. This in turn should reinforce the shift to modular construction of many durable goods, which enhances the ease of continuous maintenance and upgrading. In such a service-oriented economy, successful "producers" will enjoy the benefit of lifelong customer loyalty in exchange for the burden of ensuring long-life product dependability.[28]

Without Tax Reform, Efficiency Can Reduce Sustainability

Many analysts, including some economists and environmentalists, believe that advances in technological (energy and material) efficiency alone is a panacea for the global ecological crisis. They assume that efficiency gains automatically lead to reduced consumption and less waste. As logical as this might seem, decreasing the input:output ratio for goods and services does not necessarily result in reduced resource use.[29] On the contrary, technological efficiency can actually lead to increased net consumption.

This should be no surprise. Jevons argued over a hundred years ago that "it is a confusion of ideas to suppose that the economical use of fuel is equivalent to diminished consumption. The very contrary is the truth."[30] He observed that total coal consumption by relatively inefficient machines was low because the high rate of fuel consumption made them uneconomical for most uses. By contrast, "the reduction of the consumption of coal, per ton of iron, to less than one-third of its former amount, was followed, in Scotland, by a tenfold increase in total consumption, between the years 1830 and 1863, not to speak of the indirect effect of cheap iron in accelerating other coal-consuming branches of industry."[31]

Many mechanisms work to produce such counterintuitive results, including the price and income effects of technological savings. Improved exploration technology, or energy or material efficiency (i.e., lower costs), may enable firms to raise wages, increase dividends, or lower prices, which may lead to increased net consumption by workers, shareholders, or customers, respectively. Similarly, technology-induced savings by individuals are usually redirected to alternative forms of consumption, canceling some or all of the initial gain. As Hannon points out, "the [environmentally conscious] traveler who [switches] from urban bus to bicycle would save energy and (and dollars) at the rate of 51,000 Btu per dollar. If he were not careful to spend his dollar savings on an item of personal consumption which had an energy intensity greater than 51,000 Btu per dollar then his shift to bicycle would have been in vain."[32] These income and price effects are summarized as the "rebound effect" by economists.[33]

Partially as a result of the rebound effect, "continuing growth . . . will eventually overwhelm gains from efficiency, causing total resource use (and the corresponding environmental damage) to rise." U.S. data show that despite the increasing fuel efficiency of cars, aggregate fuel consumption is up.[34] Similarly, the *Ecologist* observes that although energy intensity (joules/$GNP) improved by 23 percent in OECD countries between 1973 and 1987, total annual energy consumption by these countries increased by 15 percent between 1975 and 1989.[35]

Ironically then, thanks to unfettered efficiency, the ecological footprint of the consumer economy may expand rather than contract. To be effective in reducing ecological impacts, efficiency savings must be captured by governments, preferably for investment in essential natural capital (and in social capital—see below). Ecological taxes increase the motivation for innovation but, as importantly, preempt much of the savings for the common good. In a globally interlinked economy, the question is: Can we afford cost-saving energy efficiency? The answer is "yes" only if efficiency gains are taxed away or otherwise removed from further consumption-driven circulation.

An Alternative Approach: Investing in Social Capital

The "Factor-10" efficiency revolution is based on the assumption that economic growth everywhere is essential for sustainability. It also requires unbridled optimism in technological innovation. It is therefore a predictable response from the industrial scientific or expansionist paradigm that prevails in international development circles today.

The problem is that technological fixes address neither the growth ethic nor the fundamental cultural values (e.g., consumerism as a way of life) that have produced the ecological crisis and that lie at the heart of the mainstream paradigm. Arguably, by focusing exclusively on potential efficiency gains, policy makers may overlook other potentially effective paths to ecologically sustainable socioeconomic development. One such option is to consider the efficacy of investing in social capital.[36] If building up our stocks of social capital can substitute for the perceived need to accumulate manufactured capital, then *large reductions in society's ecological footprint may be possible even without technological efficiency gains.*

Welfare and Income

There are at least two lines of evidence that encourage exploration of the social dimensions of sustainability. The first is revealed in the interesting relationship between income (consumption) and well-being. Available data show that life expectancy initially rises rapidly with per capita income but then levels off and is virtually flat between $10,000 and $25,000. It appears that 90 percent or more of the gain in life expectancy is "purchased" by the time income reaches $7,000–$8,000 per annum.[37] Similar relationships hold for related health and social indicators.

Seven to eight thousand dollars is only one third to one half of the per capita income of the world's wealthier countries. It seems clear, therefore, that quite substantial reductions in consumption by people in these countries might well be possible before there would be any significant deterioration in population health or individual welfare as measured by standard "objective" indicators. We should also note that various studies show that subjective "happiness" or well-being is not correlated with income in the upper income range and may even deteriorate. Indeed, people's perception of their own social and health status seems more a factor of relative social position than of absolute material wealth.

This last point is particularly significant in light of the worsening income distribution produced by our present growth-bound development trajectory. In the early 1960s, the top 20 percent of income earners took home thirty times the income of the bottom 20 percent. By the early 1990s, this ratio had doubled to 60:1 and a billion people still lived in abject poverty.[38]

These data pose a serious challenge to conventional assumptions about the social need for continuous economic growth. They suggest that a healthy and sustainable society may, in fact, be possible at relatively modest income levels even without any dramatic restructuring of society or social relationships. They also show that growth alone is not effectively addressing poverty. At the very least, the residents of high-income countries should start to ask themselves just what the prize is for victory in the (inter)national growth stakes. What is the point of the present furious competition to achieve an ever-expanding GDP if the already rich feel no better off, the chronically poor remain chronically poor, and the entire exercise threatens to undermine the ecosphere, decreasing security for all?

The Case of Kerala

The second argument for investing in social capital can be found in the state of Kerala, India. With an annual income per capita of only $US 350, Kerala has achieved a life expectancy of seventy-two years (the norm for states earning $5,000 or more per capita), a fertility rate of less than two, and a high-school enrollment rate for females of 93 percent. According to Alexander, "extraordinary efficiencies in the use of the earth's resources characterize the high life quality behavior of the 29 million citizens of Kerala."[39] Similarly, Ratcliffe claims that Kerala refutes "the common thesis that high levels of social development cannot be achieved in the absence of high rates of economic growth. . . . Indeed, the Kerala experience demonstrates that high levels of social development—evaluated in terms of such quality of life measures as mortality rates and levels of life expectancy, education and literacy, and political participation—are consequences of public policies and strategies based not on economic growth considerations but, instead, on equity considerations."[40]

The point here is not to suggest that Kerala, with its unique political and cultural history, is a model for others to follow in detail. Rather it is simply to emphasize that every society and culture is in part a social construction, not entirely a product of natural laws. In short, *there is nothing sanctified about our high-throughput industrial culture.* Kerala shows that a high quality of life with minimal impact on the earth is possible through the accumulation of social rather than manufactured capital. As such it is a hopeful example that other people in other cultures—possibly even in the global village as a whole—may also be able to organize in ways that distribute nature's limited bounty more equitably. There is no intrinsic reason why we cannot learn to live sustainably in a low throughput economic steady state.

Policy Implications

Empirical evidence suggests that the economy has already exceeded carrying capacity, yet we seem more determined than ever to address the problems of sustainability and persistent poverty through a new round of material growth.[41] This is a potentially dangerous path that depends on two false assumptions: that GDP growth alone will reduce inequity, and that technological efficiency gains alone can succeed in reducing the human ecological footprint on the earth (even as the demand for goods and services rises by as much as tenfold).

At the same time there is clear evidence that meaningful social relationships and supportive community infrastructure may be more effective than technology in reducing the demand for energy and material. Policy makers would therefore be well advised to consider the "soft" alternative toward sustainability. Some relevant questions include:

- How can the state facilitate the shift in personal and social values implicit in a more caring society?
- What circumstances facilitate the development of sharing and mutual aid as a mode of life even in the face of material scarcity?
- What kinds of formal and informal social relationships enhance people's sense of self-worth and personal security?
- Which of these personal relationships and community qualities re-

duce the compulsion to consume and accumulate private capital? In other words, what forms of social capital can substitute for manufactured capital?

- What sorts of policies would facilitate the development of these forms of social capital?

So far material industrial society has avoided such questions in the production-consumption debate. However, addressing these issues would contribute not only to ecological sustainability but also to filling the spiritual void and general social malaise that increasingly seems to plague high-income, high-consumption societies.

A Final Caution: Consumption and the Knowledge-Based Economy

It is frequently asserted in discussions of sustainability that moving to a knowledge-driven or service-oriented economy will increasingly decouple the economy from the environment. Many people believe that information and service-based economies are inherently more ecologically benign than manufacturing economies and therefore will have smaller ecological footprints. This is a misperception. Keep in mind that this appealing argument is rooted in the belief that the appropriate economic niche for the most advanced of the developed countries in a globally restructured economy is as purveyors of high-priced technology, of so-called "intellectual capital," the unpolluting products of the mind. However, the whole point is to ensure that postindustrial societies remain at the upper end of global income distribution. Indeed, if these countries do manage to make the shift so that most of their citizens earn their livings in computer software, engineering services, or similar high-tech industries, their incomes may well remain among the highest in the world and even increase: but then, so will their per capita consumption.

The point is that it is not how one earns a living, but rather how much and what one consumes, that determines one's personal ecological footprint. For example, if North Americans continue to build large houses with three-car garages and five bathrooms, well-stocked with all the big-ticket consumer appliances and electronic gadgetry that their high incomes command, then their average contribution to ecological destruction may well increase, not decline, as their economies become increasingly knowledge-based. In fact, the negative impact per unit consumption may be worse than at present. The migration of manufacturing to the developing world where environmental standards may be lower or unenforced is no victory for the global commons. An automobile or microwave oven manufactured in China, using steel made and electricity generated in inefficient and poorly regulated plants burning high-sulphur coal, is a much "dirtier" product than the comparable item made in Windsor or Detroit. The air immediately over Northern cities might seem cleaner, but the world's atmosphere is much the worse for wear.

We also hear the argument that with increasing income, consumption shifts to less material-intense products and activities such as dining out or the performing arts. Certainly spending $100 at a restaurant or the opera has less direct ecological impact than a similar payment toward that microwave oven. However, expenditures on many services and luxury entertainment don't increase in proportion to income until basic material needs and many nonessential material wants have first been taken care of. We often drive to the opera in a large expensive car.

Moreover, there is the multiplier effect. The expansion of the service and the entertainment sectors supports increasing numbers of people who also enjoy material lives. While the majority of these people live little differently from the rest of us, and there are famous examples of starving artists, those inhabiting the upper income strata of the modern sports and entertainment industries are hardly noted for material self-denial.

Notes

1. P. Vitousek, P. Ehrlich, A. Ehrlich, and P. Matson, "Human Appropriation of the Products of Photosynthesis," *BioScience* 36 (1986): 368–74.

2. D. Pauly and V. Christensen, "Primary Production Required to Sustain Global Fisheries," *Nature* 374 (1995): 255–57.

3. R. Goodland, "The Case that the World Has Reached Limits," in *Environmentally Sustainable Economic Development: Building on Brundtland*, ed. R. Goodland, H. Daly, S. El Serafy, and B. Von Droste (Paris: UNESCO, 1991).

4. H. Daly, "From Empty World Economics to Full World Economics: Recognizing an Historic Turning Point in Economic Development," in *Environmentally Sustainable Economic Development*, ed. R. Goodland et al.

5. Abstracted and revised from W. Rees, "More Jobs, Less Damage: A Framework for Sustainability, Growth and Employment," *Alternatives* 21, no. 4 (1995): 24–30; W. Rees, "Revisiting Carrying Capacity: Area-based Indicators of Sustainability," *Population and Environment* 17, no. 3 (1996): 195–215.

6. Rees, "Revisiting Carrying Capacity."

7. W. Rees, "Ecological Footprints and Appropriated Carrying Capacity: What Urban Economics Leaves Out," *Environment and Urbanization* 4, no. 2 (1992): 120–30; Rees, "Revisiting Carrying Capacity"; W. Rees and M. Wackernagel, "Ecological Footprints and Appropriated Carrying Capacity: Measuring the Natural Capital Requirements of the Human Economy," in *Investing in Natu-*

ral Capital: The Ecological Economics Approach to Sustainability, ed. A. M. Jansson, M. Hammer, C. Folke, and R. Costanza (Washington, D.C.: Island Press, 1994); M. Wackernagel and W. Rees, *Our Ecological Footprint: Reducing Human Impact on the Earth*, (Philadelphia, PA, and Gabriola Island, BC: New Society Publishers, 1995–96).

8. Exceptions include services provided by the ozone layer and the hydrologic cycle, both of which are purely physical forms of natural capital.

9. Details of the method, calculation procedure, and numerous examples can be found in Rees and Wackernagel, "Ecological Footprints"; Rees, "Revisiting Carrying Capacity"; Wackernagel and Rees, *Our Ecological Footprint*.

10. W. Rees, "Urban Ecosystems: The Human Dimension," *Urban Ecosystems* 1 (1997): 63–75; W. Rees, "Is 'Sustainable City' an Oxymoron?" *Local Environment* (in press).

11. This section is abstracted and revised from W. Rees, "More Jobs, Less Damage," 24–30.

12. A major ecological catastrophe might change the political climate. This is the paradigm-shift-by-disaster scenario.

13. See D. Pearce, *Sustainable Consumption through Economic Instruments*, paper prepared for the Government of Norway Symposium on Sustainable Consumption, Oslo, 19–20 January 1994.

14. F. Schmid-Bleek, "MIPS–A Universal Ecological Measure," *Fresenius Environmental Bulletin* 1 (1993): 306–11; *Fresenius Environmental Bulletin* 2, no. 8 (1993); P. Ekins and M. Jacobs, "Are Environmental Sustainability and Economic Growth Compatible?" in *Energy-Environment-Economy Modelling Discussion Paper No. 7* (Cambridge, UK: Department of Applied Economics, University of Cambridge, 1994); J. Young and A. Sachs, *The Next Efficiency Revolution: Creating a Sustainable Materials Economy*, Worldwatch Paper 121 (Washington, D.C.: Worldwatch Institute, 1994); BCSD, *Getting Eco-Efficient: Report of the First Antwerp Eco-Efficiency Workshop* (Geneva: Business Council for Sustainable Development, November 1993); RMNO, *Sustainable Resource Management and Resource Use: Policy Questions and Research Needs*, Publication No. 97 (Rijswijk, the Netherlands: Advisory Council for Research on Nature and Environment, 1994); RMNO, *Toward Environmental Performance Indicators Based on the Notion of Environmental Space, Publication No. 96* (Rijswijk, the Netherlands: Advisory Council for Research on Nature and Environment, 1994).

15. Since steep depletion taxes will increase the prices of goods and services, the burden will fall disproportionately on lower income brackets. To compensate, income taxes would have to be reduced more for the poor than for the rich. Consideration may have to be given to financing a negative income tax or other offsetting scheme from depletion tax revenues for the bottom end of the income distribution. L. Brown, C. Flaven, and S. Postel, *Saving the Planet: How to Shape an Environmentally Sustainable Global Economy* (Washington, D.C.: Worldwatch Institute, 1991).

16. E. U. Von Weizsäcker, *Earth Politics* (London: Zed Books, 1994), chap. 11: "Ecological Tax Reform."

17. H. Daly, "The Steady-State Economy: Toward a Political Economy of Bio-

physical Equilibrium and Moral Growth," in *Economics, Ecology, Ethics: Essays Toward a Steady-State Economy*, ed. H. Daly (San Francisco: W H. Freeman, 1980).

18. Pearce, *Sustainable Consumption*; CEC, *Growth, Competitiveness, Employment: The Challenges and the Ways Forward into the 21ˢᵗ Century* (Brussels: Commission of the European Communities, 1993); see also C. Flaven and N. Lenssen, *Beyond the Petroleum Age: Designing a Solar Economy*, Worldwatch Paper 100 (Washington, D.C.: Worldwatch Institute, 1990).

19. Brown, Flaven, and Postel, *Saving the Planet*.

20. Von Weizsäcker, *Earth Politics*, chap. 11.

21. Rechsteiner, cited in Von Weizsäcker, *Earth Politics*, chap. 11.

22. Von Weizsäcker, *Earth Politics*, 134.

23. W. Stahel and T. Jackson, "Optimal Utilization and Durability," in *Clean Production Strategies*, ed. T. Jackson (London: Lewis Publishers, 1993), 270.

24. From data cited in M. Renner, *Jobs in a Sustainable Economy*, Worldwatch Paper 104 (Washington, D.C.: Worldwatch Institute, 1991).

25. Stahel and Jackson, "Optimal Utilization," 270.

26. Stahel and Jackson, "Optimal Utilization," 276.

27. W. Stahel, *Langlebigkeith und Materialrecycling—Strategien zur Vermeidung von Abfällen im Bereich der Produkte* (Essen: Vulken Verlag, 1991).

28. Stahel and Jackson, "Optimal Utilization," 287–90.

29. This section is abstracted in part from M. Wackernagel and W. Rees, *Perceptual and Structural Barriers to Investing in Natural Capital*, paper presented to the Second Meeting of the International Society for Ecological Economics (Investing in Natural Capital), Stockholm, 3–6 August 1992 (Vancouver: UBS School of Community and Regional Planning, 1992).

30. W. Jevons, *The Coal Question*, reprint of the 3d edition (New York: Augustus M. Kelley, 1865).

31. Jevons, *Coal Question*.

32. B. Hannon, "Energy Conservation and the Consumer," *Science* 189 (1975): 95–102.

33. M. Jaccard, *Does the Rebound Effect Offset the Electricity Savings of Powersmart? Discussion Paper for BC Hydro* (Vancouver: BC Hydro, 1991).

34. L. Brown, S. Postel, and C. Flavin, "From Growth to Sustainable Development," in *Environmentally Sustainable Economic Development*, ed. R. Goodland et al.

35. "Whose Common Future?" *Ecologist* 22 (1992): 4.

36. Social capital usually refers to networks of interpersonal relationships and mutual support at the community level. In the present context, it includes publicly supported social infrastructure such as public health services, public education, and so on.

37. World Bank, *World Development Report 1993: Investing in Health* (New York: Oxford University Press, 1993), fig. 1.9. Figures in "international dollars" based on purchasing power.

38. UNDP, Human Development Report (New York: Oxford University Press [for United Nations Development Program], 1994).

39. W. Alexander, *Humans Sharing the Bounty of the Earth: Hopeful Lessons From*

Kerala, paper prepared for the International Congress on Kerala Studies, Kerala, India, 27–29 August 1994; see also W. Alexander, *The Kerala Phenomenon: Throughput, Information and Life Quality Lifestyle Choices for the 21ˢᵗ Century,* paper prepared for the International Systems Dynamics Society Meetings, Cambridge, Mass., 22–26 July 1996.

40. J. Ratcliffe, "Social Justice and the Demographic Transition: Lessons from India's Kerala State," *International Journal of Health Services* 8 (1978): 140.

41. This often seems like a convenient way to avoid addressing inequity through policies to redistribute wealth.

7

Who Should Bear the Burdens of Risk and Proof in Changing Consumption Patterns?

John Lemons

During the 1992 United Nations Conference on Environment and Development (UNCED) held in Rio de Janeiro, the question of changing consumption patterns to promote sustainable development and environmental protection was a contentious issue.[1] Major recommendations of UNCED to change unsustainable consumption patterns to sustainable ones were promulgated in chapter 4 of Agenda 21. The basis for action included: (1) recognition that poverty and environmental degradation are closely interrelated; (2) recognition that high and unsustainable patterns of consumption and production, particularly in industrialized countries, are a matter of grave concern; (3) measures to be undertaken at the international level for the protection of the environment must take into account the current imbalances in the global patterns of consumption and production; (4) changing consumption patterns will require a strategy focusing on demand, meeting the basic needs of the poor, and reducing wastage in the use of finite resources; and (5) a reorientation of existing production and consumption patterns that have developed in industrial societies and that in turn are emulated in much of the world.

Examples of recommended activities include: (1) adopting an international approach to achieving sustainable consumption patterns, wherein developed countries should take the lead in achieving sustainable consumption patterns and developing countries should seek to achieve sustainable consumption patterns in their development process; (2) undertaking research on consumption, wherein countries should assess the relationship between production and consumption and the environment; (3) developing new concepts of sustainable economic growth and prosperity that allow higher standards of living that are more in harmony with the earth's carrying capacity; (4) encouraging greater efficiency in the use of energy and resources; and (5) reinforcing values that support sustainable consumption.

In this essay, I discuss what I believe are two difficulties that need to be overcome in order to implement UNCED's actions and recommendations to change patterns of consumption. The first has to do with why scientific and legal burdens of proof hinder implementing changing consumption patterns and why the placement of the burdens carries with it implicit ethical implications that often are not known or understood by either the public or decision makers. The second has to do with why industrial countries should assume some responsibility for bearing the burden of risk imposed by changing consumption patterns—a responsibility that for the most part they have failed to assume.

Burden of Proof Requirements

Chapter 35 of Agenda 21 focuses on recommendations to improve the use of science in sustainable development, including changing patterns of consumption. Four program areas are identified: (1) strengthening the scientific basis for sustainable management; (2) enhancing scientific understanding; (3) improving long-term scientific assessment; and (4) building scientific capacity and capability. The chapter recommends that one role of the sciences should be to provide information to better enable formulation and selection of environment and development policies in the decision-making process. In order to fulfill this requirement, it will be essential to enhance scientific understanding, improve long-term scientific assessments, strengthen scientific capacities in all countries, and ensure that the sciences are responsive to emerging needs.

Understanding and solving environmental and human health problems stemming from consumption patterns requires application of the best scientific knowledge available. Many sources of information used by scientists and managers focus on what is known about methods, techniques, models, and data that might be helpful in solving the problems, although limitations of knowledge or scientific uncertainty sometimes is discussed as well. However, as the problems have become more complex it is questionable whether or to what extent our scientific knowledge is adequate to inform management decisions with reasonable certainty.

Assessment of Scientific Uncertainty

Consumption patterns pose many problems, some of which have to do with concerns about the depletion of resources, problems of solid, toxic, and hazardous waste disposal, and the environmental and human health consequences of obtaining and using the resources we consume. Recent studies by collaborators on scientific uncertainty and environmental problem-solving focused on these types of problems and yielded the following assessment.[2]

First, the extreme variability of the world outside of laboratory settings limits our ability to improve predictions of ecosystem-scale responses to human-induced environmental perturbations stemming from patterns of consumption. Except for a few cases such as global warming and marine fisheries where underlying mechanisms are understood poorly, additional studies likely will not increase our ability to predict the consequences of human consumption activities upon the environment.

Second, the state of science for monitoring and predicting sustainability status and trends in managing important production ecosystems in agriculture, forestry, fisheries, and grazing lands indicates that they are self-controlled insofar as they may evolve in a nondeterministic manner toward increasing adaptability to environmental change and that adaptability is maximized when the system has evolved to the verge of chaos. This implies that sustainability is inherently uncertain and even its probability is uncertain.

Complicating problems of understanding and maintaining sustainable ecosystems is the problem of natural variation, wherein any perturbations in natural ecosystems due to the activities of humans are often masked by the natural changes in the attributes measured. Accordingly, it may not be possible to achieve a 95 percent confidence level that generally is regarded as an essential scientific standard. Consequently, the usual means of dealing with uncertainty through decision theory and models may not work in such a near-chaos situation.

Third, scientists are unable to make reasonably accurate predictions of future climate, yet without such predictions, the consequences of climate change and the societal responses and alternative choices of action cannot be assessed fully. Yet it is known that there is a substantial risk of climate change and that the consequences will affect countries and regions, as well as future generations, differently. Thus, from the scientific understanding of the problem of climate change, including the problem of uncertainty, flows the ethical problems of: (1) whether to take action to mitigate the problem despite the uncertainties, or whether to delay action until more information is obtained; and (2) how to distribute risks and burdens both spatially and temporally. In addition, while

Agenda 21 recommends the use of cost-benefit analysis and other forms of economic valuation and methods to assess the consequences of climate change, it must be recognized that such analyses and methods are value-laden and do not sufficiently take into account how costs and benefits are distributed, including across generations. Further, they do not adequately take into account the protection of nonhuman nature. Thus, their application should be viewed as an ethical problem requiring analysis and resolution, lest decisions be based on economics alone and not on ethical reasoning.

Fourth, one of the most scientifically, technologically, and politically complex and controversial issues confronting the United States during the past several decades is how and where to dispose of high-level nuclear waste generated by both the production and consumption of fissile material. An analysis of the use of science in the decision to characterize Yucca Mountain, Nevada, as the United States' only high-level nuclear waste repository and the capabilities of science to yield reasonably certain information about future repository performance suggest that both short-term and long-term uncertainties regarding the adequacy of Yucca Mountain likely will remain pervasive and that existing regulatory standards might have to be changed in order for the site to be judged acceptable.

Fifth, using case studies focusing on the ocean dumping of sewage sludge, acid precipitation, estuarine eutrophication, and pesticides such as tributyltin, the successes and failures of science to influence environmental policy were assessed. The assessment included the extent to which monitoring approaches and field studies: (1) can detect subtle or actual effects in unequivocal terms; (2) are likely to detect ecosystem effects prior to the effects being no longer subtle; (3) can link in situ effects with specific causes or pollutants; and (4) can provide a sufficient basis to explain fully the large-scale changes noted in fish or plankton populations, fish disease occurrences, or reduced oxygen conditions. These findings suggest that only one of the four case studies can be considered to be a clear success.

Sixth, the developing field of ecotoxicology or environmental toxicology is the offspring of mammalian toxicology in which extrapolations were made from surrogate species to humans. During the past two decades, this field has grown in response to the increased production of harmful compounds. However, this approach is laden with uncertainties because each species differs physiologically from other species. In addition, the field has developed further as a "bottom-up" approach in which extrapolations are made from single species to ecosystems. Both ecological and statistical uncertainties are associated with this approach as illustrated by assumptions about the shape of the distribution of tolerance to a toxicant, and the ability to extrapolate information on laboratory species and conditions to field species and conditions and to the conditions of communities and ecosystems.

Seventh, water resources management and scientific uncertainties were analyzed to determine how water resources management encompasses both quantitative and qualitative considerations of surface and groundwater systems, including pollution prevention and control, the need for remediation, and the use of natural assimilation capacities. Because many industrial and public works development projects can cause changes in both flow and quality parameters, it is important to understand the various components of water resources management in view of uncertainties related to measurement techniques, data, modeling, and decision making. However, often the uncertainties are so great as to preclude decision making based upon reasonably certain scientific information.

Eighth, the problem of resolving uncertainty in marine fisheries management was investigated by analyzing how uncertainty in the decision-making process for marine fisheries has developed by focusing on critical periods of fisheries management. This historical analysis of environmental change in marine fisheries demonstrates the evolution of scientific paradigms over time and how humans have constructed knowledge to satisfy their needs and wants within certain political and economic systems. These constructions of knowledge have provided us, in part, with what we know scientifically about resources as well as what we do not know. One conclusion of this study was that it is impossible for us to understand where we are or where we are heading in terms of resource use unless we know where we have been.

Ninth, environmental problems are complex, and the environmental sciences are limited in their ability to predict with reasonable certainty future impacts of actions. This situation makes it difficult for the party with the burden of proof to sustain that burden if challenged by others who assert that the burden of proof has not been met. For example, scientists are very skilled in exposing technical weaknesses in an adversary's position when the adversary has the burden of proof. As a result, a governmental agency is often troubled about what decisions to make when its knowledge is likely to be viewed as inadequate but when it is under pressure to take action as, for example, in recent decisions allowing for harvesting of timber in the Northwest United States at the expense of the Spotted Owl.

Given the imprecise nature of the environmental sciences and their lack of predictive ability, scientific and technical experts within government agencies are reluctant to take strong regulatory action on controversial issues out of fear they will alienate politicians and higher level administrators of mission-oriented agencies. Scientific experts also are trained to be very conservative when positing cause and effect relationships between, say, actions and environmental impacts; they do not act quickly if reasonable uncertainty exists about such relationships. In this manner, they avoid being discredited by their peers if an original position is later discredited by subsequent scientific research.

The consequence of placement of the burden of proof is that those advocating environmental protection must demonstrate with reasonable certainty that human health, species, or ecosystems are threatened, the causes of the threats, and that recommended solutions have a reasonable chance of success. However, placement of this burden of proof often imposes a requirement for a level of environmental knowledge that may not be possible to meet. Consequently, if precautionary principles are to be applied to environmental protection measures, the burden of proof may have to be shifted so that those proposing to take significant activities that potentially threaten environmental harm would have to demonstrate that adverse impacts from such activities are not likely.

Finally, four types of uncertainty of special relevance to environmental decision making have been analyzed: (1) framing uncertainty, (2) modeling uncertainty, (3) statistical uncertainty, and (4) decision-theoretic uncertainty. One of the most important issues raised by the first type of uncertainty is how to frame problems of uncertainty, such as whether one should use a two-valued epistemic logic or a three-valued epistemic logic. In other words, what are the consequences of framing the solutions to particular problems in terms of two solution options or three options? Often, environmental impact assessors assume that a two-valued epistemic logic, according to which a particular solution is acceptable or unacceptable, is an adequate way to frame a particular problem. However, in other situations problem-solvers frame their solution options in terms of a three-valued epistemic logic with a particular solution being acceptable, unacceptable, or lacking adequate data to judge acceptability one way or the other. In numerous cases of controversial environmental decision making, such as siting hazardous and nuclear waste facilities, decision makers and scientists have framed problems in terms of an inadequate two-valued logic. In ignoring the three-valued epistemic logic, they have thereby made logically fallacious appeals to ignorance and ignore reasons why a three-valued epistemic logic might be more suitable for an ethically based public policy.

Consequences of Uncertainty

The consequence of the uncertainties summarized above is fivefold.[3] First, when scientists do not provide an explicit and rigorous treatment of scientific uncertainty in their treatment of specific problems, environmental decision makers and managers often accept scientific analyses of environmental problems as being more factual than is warranted. Such acceptance can bias the outcomes of procedures used to make decisions, such as risk assessment and economic cost-benefit calculations. Further, this bias often is not apparent to many environmental decision makers, resource or agency managers, or the general public unless they are aware of the sources of the uncertainties and their implications.

Second, most environmental laws and regulations place the burden of proof for demonstrating human health or environmental harm on governmental regulatory agencies or others wishing to demonstrate harm from development or technological activities. For example, in the United States, many environmental actions are governed by the U.S. Supreme Court decision in *Daubert v. United States*.[4] Under *Daubert*, evidence that establishes a reasonable basis for concern about harm but does not conclusively establish causation is not admissible in court. A failure to meet the burden of proof requirements under *Daubert* means that status quo activities and practices that might be causing environmental harm likely will continue.

The standard used to meet the burden of proof test often is the normal standard of scientific proof, such as a 95 percent confidence level or an equivalent criterion. This standard has been adopted by members of the scientific community in order to minimize type I error and therefore reduce speculation in the interpretation of scientific data (a type I error is to conclude an effect when none exists). When this standard is adopted as a basis for environmental decisions the scientific uncertainty that pervades most environmental problems means that the burden of proof usually is not met, despite the fact that some information might indicate the existence of environmental or human health harm.

Third, the absence of a more complete understanding of scientific uncertainty means that decision makers and managers will not have adequate information to guide them in terms of whether or to what extent decisions should reflect a precautionary approach. What needs to be recognized is that when decisions to protect the environment or human health are delayed in order to obtain more reasonable scientific certainty, this is tantamount to a decision to continue with status quo behaviors and activities that either are or might be causing harm. In order to avoid this situation, public policy makers and decision makers must therefore seek ways to deal with scientific uncertainty in a more effective manner in order to avoid continued harm to the environment and human health.

Fourth, scientific uncertainty complicates the understanding of the relationships between scientific and political levels of problem-solving, which are seldom clearly separable because interactive influences are characteristic. An environmental problem may have a scientific answer, but the ultimate solution for human society is political and is expressed as policy.

Multidisciplinary teams are usually needed to define and propose solutions for large and complex environmental problems, such as changing consumption patterns. Because there may be alternative assessments and answers to an environmental problem, policy solutions may require a choice involving nonscientific considerations. To the extent that the science solution is uncertain or disputed, the latitude of the policy maker to act or postpone action is broadened.

Intermediate between the scientific and political levels of problem-solving is the policy analyst who may, or may not, be conversant with science and scientists. Even at the highest levels of scientific opinion and advice, as in the United States' Presidential Office of Science and Technology Policy, proposed science-based problem solutions must compete with other considerations such as the financial, economic, military, bureaucratic, and ideological. Uncertainty in problem-solving may occur at all levels or stages in the process. Because of the other-than-scientific considerations, an environmental policy solution can seldom be finalized at the level of scientific research only. If, as is usually the case, the problem solution must occur at the policy level, the process of policy analysis between scientific findings and policy decisions is likely to be critical for the applied solution.

At this stage, unwarranted certainty and misconception of the actual problem can lead to ineffective policy solutions. Worse, it may lead to unforeseen and unwanted consequences. The so-called paradigmatic or ideational context in which a problem is perceived influences and may determine the way in which the problem is defined. For example, is the problem of consumption too little or too much of something, inadequate distribution, inadequate waste disposal methods, or too many people? Unexamined assumptions about a problem may lead to different answers based upon spurious certainty in the validity of the problem as defined. Consequently, environmental problem-solving requires careful examination of underlying assumptions and a recognition that a specious certainty about a perceived problem, especially one shaped by cultural and political biases, may be a greater threat to the problem solution than is scientific uncertainty.

Fifth, scientific uncertainty complicates the problems of trying to achieve a solution to problems of consumption patterns based upon ethical reasoning. On a priori grounds, uncertainty can be used as a basis for concluding that there are no theoretical grounds for obligations to, for example, the future, if information is so speculative that it is considered to be unreliable. On a posterior grounds, uncertainty can be said to preclude taking into account obligations that might be said to exist on theoretical grounds if the information is so speculative that we cannot determine the consequences of our actions.

Ethical Guidelines under Conditions of Uncertainty

Kristin Shrader-Frechette[5] analyzes the reasons why there should be an ethical preference for minimizing type II error in environmental issues and why the burden of proof for demonstration of no adverse environmental harm from development or human activities should be placed upon those calling for such development or activities. (A type II error is to conclude that there is an effect when there is none. Under most situations, minimizing type II error increases the chance of making a type I error.) She bases her conclusion on: (1) minimizing the chance of not rejecting false null hypotheses with important public policy consequences is reasonable on the grounds of protecting the present and future public; (2) the proponents of development or activities that potentially threaten environmental resources typically receive more benefits from the development or activities than do members of the public and, consequently, minimizing type II error would result in a more equal distribution of benefits and risks; (3) natural resources typically need more risk protection than do promoters of development or human activities because the advocates for protection usually have fewer financial and scientific resources than developers or promoters of activities that potentially can harm the resources; (4) the public ought to have rights to protection against decisions that could impose incompensable damages to natural resources; (5) public sovereignty justifies letting the public decide the fate of development and human activities that potentially threaten natural resources; and (6) minimizing type II error would allow enhanced protection of nonhuman species that typically receive inadequate consideration in decision making based upon cost-benefit methods. Consequently, following Shrader-Frechette's reasoning, the scientific and legal burdens of proof would need to be altered to allow for the use of indicators' change and impacts.

Burden of Risk Approaches

In addition to the ethical issues pertaining to the placement of the burden of proof insofar as patterns of consumption and scientific uncertainty are concerned, there are numerous other ethical issues that need to be explored, including global environmental justice, duties to future generations, duties to nonhumans, and the ethics of using cost-benefit analysis for decision making, to name a few. Obviously, space limitations preclude a discussion of many of these issues.

During UNCED, many of the industrialized countries (particularly the United States) were reluctant to assume any responsibility for the impact of their comparatively high levels of consumption on the environment or to assume risk imposed from changing consumption patterns. This reluctance stemmed from a wish to avoid having to make any reparations in the form of aid or assistance for past actions, as well as from the fact that assuming some historic responsibility would be tantamount to assuming responsibility for present impacts from consumption, which on the whole has increased on a per capita basis due to the combined effect of rising affluence and changing technology. In the remainder of this essay, I focus on some of the ethical implications of the stance by industrialized countries not to assume responsibility for ameliorating the impacts of their comparatively high historic and present levels of consumption. I adopt a perspective that I believe reflects concerns of developing nations and that deals with: (1) the burden of risk and the price of change, (2) equity-based ecological development, (3) intergenerational responsibility, (4) environmental and financial debt, and (5) environmental rights and ecological duties.

There are two obvious approaches that can be taken to deal with consumption patterns. One approach is to continue with status quo patterns of consumption. One reason for this approach would be because the more affluent and powerful countries disavow any responsibility for the problems. Another reason is that we should continue with the status quo while we continue to collect additional information and data with the goal of reducing scientific uncertainty so that decisions can be more sound and less speculative; this reason is consistent with existing scientific and legal burden of proof norms. This approach generally is favored by those who benefit from the status quo and who wish to avoid unnecessary costs of changing patterns of consumption if subsequent data or information do not demonstrate a need for change.

The second approach would implement changes to consumption patterns based upon reasonable indicators of change as opposed to those said to be reasonably certain in the traditional scientific sense. This approach would be based upon the knowledge that present consumption patterns have the capacity to adversely affect environmental and human health and that they disproportionately affect the poorer people and nations. It also would reflect the idea that affluent nations have a responsibility to incur substantial costs of changing consumption patterns because of their historical contributions to the problem, as well as on the view that a response to consumption patterns ought to favor people who are least able to cope with the adverse consequences. It also is based on the view that if we wait for more scientific data before adopting effective measures to change the patterns, then we are not reducing the risk of present patterns of consumption and its consequences, but rather we are increasing it. The longer we delay implementation of more effective patterns, the more difficult it will be to reduce risk or ameliorate adverse consequences of consumption at some future date.

Parenthetically, I might add that it seems curious that some would want scientific certainty to be established before taking actions to mitigate problems of consumption patterns, while at the same time certainty is never demanded of economic policy interventions, even though these are based on statistical probabilities. But then too often such interventions are dictated by the market and by political preferences rather than ethically derived from commitments to members of the global community.

Obviously, different responses to consumption patterns will affect groups of people differently. Ethically speaking, the essential question regarding the management of risks from consumption patterns is: How should the risks and costs of changing patterns of consumption be distributed between different groups of people or nations?

The Burden of Risk and the Price of Change

Agenda 21 makes many recommendations concerning the application of cost-benefit methods as a means to provide information needed for making decisions about problems such as consumption patterns. Despite the fact that one of the recommendations calls for improvements in cost-benefit analysis, both methodological and informational uncertainties make a cost-benefit analysis of the risks involved in many patterns of consumption inadequate and unfeasible. Further, from an ethical standpoint the use of cost-benefit analysis is questionable because it is tantamount to basing decisions (in large part) on economic calculations and political priorities.[6] One result is that decisions about the distribution of risks and costs typically is dependent on the bargaining power of the parties involved and usually ends up with the weakest bearing the burden of risk and the poorest paying the price of change.

Alternatively, an ethical approach to problems of consumption patterns would seem to require that patterns of consumption be distributed equitably and that risks be minimized and redistributed equitably, including their costs. This implies that the poor ought to be able to increase their consumption to meet basic needs and to improve their quality of life to acceptable levels, while for the more affluent changes in their consumption patterns will mean a reduction or at least a restriction of some preferential wants.

With respect to increasing the quality of life for the poor, an ethical solution to problems of consumption patterns implies an increase in productivity so that an acceptable quality of life can be achieved. But if this is to be done in a manner consistent with principles of sustainability, such as avoiding the externalization of costs, then consumption products and patterns must be based on environmentally friendly technologies. However, most developing nations do not have the resources to develop or implement these technologies on their own, or those necessary to buy them from the developed nations. For the more affluent countries, concerns about changes in production technology have to do with decreasing waste while at the same time expanding employment and other benefits. While newer forms of technology are being developed, their transfer to poorer nations still remains a much-disputed and problematic area.

Globally speaking, changing consumption patterns will very much depend upon how such problems are resolved. In my opinion, an approach based upon economic and political preferences will only postpone and accentuate whatever risks might be imposed by consumption patterns, because those who benefit from the status quo will be reluctant to make changes—and it is the beneficiaries themselves who are the more affluent and politically powerful. I do not have a good solution for this problem, but what seems to be required really is a structural adjustment on a global scale, not only of the economic structures of our societies, which might affect the developing nations more, but more particularly in our lifestyles as well, and this concerns the more developed nations most urgently. Such an adjustment would change the manner and the kind of the goods and services that are provided, and it would be based upon the realization that ecological productivity differs from productivity in the economic sense, because the economic utilization of resources through extraction under certain conditions undermines and destroys vital ecological processes, leading to heavy but hidden diseconomies.[7]

Equity-Based Ecological Development

Agenda 21 recommendations reflect the widely held view that equity is integral to achieving sustainability.[8] These recommendations reflect the understanding that conditions of poverty and environmental degradation are inexorably linked. For instance, development that can't afford to pay for treatment of sewage creates water pollution, and polluted water limits future development options. Further, in many developing countries, in the absence of assistance from developed nations, rapid depletion of natural resources is the only prospect for eradicating poverty.

With respect to equity-based sustainable development, one question is: Do present technological and other capabilities exist on a worldwide basis to alleviate conditions of poverty significantly for many people? If they do, then it would seem that this ought to be done even if some changes in consumption patterns in affluent nations would be required, because it is ethically unacceptable that concerns for humans be displaced by an inequitable distribution of the consumptive products of this world. In other words, it is not right to forego the alleviation of poverty because of the preferences of affluent nations for present patterns of consumption. Further, if changing patterns of consumption were imposed on the developing nations at the cost of their sustainable development, then this means that those nations would remain impoverished in order to sustain the more affluent nations. This situation, were it to occur, would be based more on political and economic power than on an ethical response to the problem.

Consequently, ecological-based equity very well might require a reduction of the gap between the rich and the poor both intranationally and internationally. If this reduction is to be done within the carrying capacity of the earth, then further problems arise. If the poor of the developing nations aspire to reach the same consumption levels of the developed nations, then this cannot be accomplished within the earth's potential carrying capacity as we know it, in spite of any technological advances or institutional changes we may realistically hope for. To be sure, it seems improbable to narrow this gap solely by reducing the consumption of the rich, though this would surely be fairer than restraining the development of the poor.

Accordingly, a more equitable redistribution of consumption and production between developed and developing nations, in a manner that will allow both to become sustainable, seems warranted. But just as sustainable development must meet the ecological necessity of containing itself within the carrying capacity of the earth, it also must meet the ethical imperative of equity among nations. Consequently, international bargains or cooperative arrangements between the rich and poor nations for a more stable and sustainable world seem to be called for.

A beginning for such a bargain with regard to some consumption problems, say, greenhouse gas emissions, would be to consider quotas based on a per capita basis and not on an aggregated national one. This would be an equitable way of fixing the responsibility for change on the polluters, who must pay the price for it. National emission quotas would then be fixed not in terms of present levels of pollution but in terms of population size (which needs to be limited) on a per capita calculation, not an aggregated nationwide one.[9] Those countries not using their quotas could then trade them in with those unable or unwilling to limit themselves to theirs. While greenhouse gas emission must be reduced in the long term, in the short term such trade-offs could be used for a transfer of technology and resources that would lead to a more equitable development now and a more sustainable one later. Moreover, such transactions would be a matter of trade and not aid, because the latter would make for a less equal exchange between industrialized and nonindustrialized countries. Until such unequal and unfair exchange between rich and poor peoples, nations, and regions, both intranationally and internationally, is remedied, there seems little possibility of sustainable, let alone regenerative, development on the global scale we so urgently need.

Intergenerational Responsibility

Philosophers are divided on the exact nature of responsibilities to future generations, with views ranging between the extremes of no obligations to the future, to obligations to the future that are equal to those of the present, to obligations to the future but wherein the future is discounted relative to the present.[10] The view that present generations have responsibility or obligation to future generations is gaining more widespread acceptance and is, of course, reflected in many recommendations contained in Agenda 21. If we can say that at least some responsibility exists to the future, can we not also say that some responsibility exists for the past, one that would entail addressing the adverse consequences of past actions that still affect us and that we have benefited from? In other words, is it right that we accept the benefits left to us and not make remuneration for the harm they might have done to others?

A public policy principle now gaining acceptance is that "the polluter pays," and this concept is recommended in Agenda 21. If the polluter pays for the pollution caused in the present by consumption, who should pay for the pollution caused in the past and that still affects us now? While present people may not be guilty of causing past pollution, should they accept the advantages obtained from such past actions without making remuneration for them? Would not this be like someone keeping stolen property even though that person actually may not have been guilty of the theft? And if, as we know, prior generations in some countries, because of their unecological development, have in the past borrowed from our common future (e.g., emitting large quantities of greenhouse gases into the atmosphere such that future levels and, hence, developmental options have to be curtailed in order to mitigate problems of climate change), should their descendants now refuse to remunerate in the present those who are being affected adversely by this? Consequently, if present members of industrialized nations enjoy and accept a certain amount of affluence because of past development that has led to harmful levels of pollution or a decline of natural resources, thereby threatening other people spatially and temporally, should they not also be responsible for mitigating the harm caused by such development and affluence that they have accepted?

The issue of whether industrialized countries ought to accept responsibility for past consumption patterns is of great concern when put into the context of both improvements in the quality of life and the sheer number of people in some countries. For example, a certain alarm has been expressed at the rapid industrialization of some developing countries in Asia. If every Chinese person or household has a refrigerator, what will happen to the ozone layer, especially if the Chinese continue to use older refrigeration technology? But when there were two cars in many Americans' garages—often both gas guzzlers adding carbon to the greenhouse effect—few if any governmental leaders acknowledged the role of American technology and consumption in contributing to global problems such as climate change, much less took steps to mitigate the problem. Obviously, concern for unecological development in Asia only can become legitimate by an equal concern for the unecological effects of development in other countries, not excluding their prodigal past.

It would seem that a community cannot be built unless and until people come to terms with their past. Unless past actions are redeemed, at least in the sense of remunerating those who have suffered or will suffer because of advantages accrued to present people due to unecological past actions, it is unlikely that a sustainable future will be created. Only when a global community transcends both space and time will a prospect exist that the global ecological crisis will be dealt with effectively.

Environmental and Financial Debt

Chapters 33 and 34 of Agenda 21 deal respectively with financial resources and mechanisms to promote sustainable development and environmental protection and with issues relating to the transfer of environmentally sound technology. The transfer of more appropriate technology to help solve the problems of consumption patterns, of course, is dependent upon the developing nations' acquisition of necessary financial resources. Chapter 33 identifies multilateral development banks and funds, specialized agencies and other United Nations agencies and international organizations, multilateral institutions for

capacity-building and technical cooperation, bilateral assistance programs, private funding, investment, innovative financing, and debt relief
as the primary sources and means of financial support for implementing
Agenda 21 recommendations. Interestingly, during the Agenda 21 de-
liberations, the head of the World Bank stated that the bulk of developing countries' investment needs for environmental purposes must come
from savings that they achieve through improved economic policies,
from private sector sources, and from improved trade, although some
recognition was given to the need for increased aid from developed to
developing nations.[11]

Many developing countries have significant financial debts to other
governments or world lending institutions, and many are selling off natural resources with little environmental regulation in order to raise income to finance their debt burden.[12] Financial borrowing mortgages the
future of the next generation of a group by making them debtors to the
creditors of this one. National financial debts are not written off if a
government fails or a generation passes. The debtor pays, or the debt-
or's children, for such financial debts are inherited. The debt burden is
forced onto the next generation by international financial agencies. The
agencies often justify this by the need to support the international global
economic order, which they claim would collapse without such accountability. International financial bodies may reschedule payments or make
structural adjustments, but there is no reprieve from such debt—there
is no free lunch.

Financial borrowing, then, is living beyond one's financial means, but
there is an ecological parallel. There is an ecological borrowing, which
involves living beyond the limits of one's ecological resources—that is,
utilizing natural resources at a rate that exceeds their rate of regeneration, externalizing costs, polluting the global commons, and incurring
a debt with nature that future generations will have to pay for. This
situation is tantamount to a Faustian bargain between humanity and
nature that leaves little possibility of appealing for debt relief, reschedul-
ing, or default.[13]

If a financial debt is to be taken seriously, as it is by lending governments and international agencies (in other words, the debtor must pay),
then why should environmental debts not be taken just as seriously (in
other words, the polluter must pay)? If there is no such thing as an
economically free lunch for anyone, why is it that there seems to be an
ecologically free dinner for some? Why should not structural adjustments be made for past polluters to help them undo the damage done
by the pollution they have caused and thus repay the environmental
debt that they owe to the global community, especially the poor, who
suffer most from such environmental degradation? Repayment of envi-

ronmental debts by the rich is unlikely to the extent that decisions are based on political and economic power as opposed to ethical reasoning, because the poor of this world have little bargaining power in the international political arena and economic markets.

One way of paying an environmental debt would be the transfer of technology and resources to the less developed countries from the more developed ones responsible for past pollution. This could be a feasible way of reversing the transfer of assets from the less developed to the industrialized countries, as is happening at present and which perpetuates the debt crisis. This could also help the less developed countries to bypass the polluting first stage in the industrialization process, which the present industrialized countries went through, to environmentally cleaner and ecologically more friendly technologies. Such a transfer of technology, then, is not a matter of aid with all of its political implications but rather a matter of right, of ethical demands, and of ecological urgency. To this extent, the resource transfers could be interpreted as polluters' dues made toward repayment of environmental debts. International agencies could cost the environmental debts of the industrialized countries and suggest how they could be written off against the financial debts of the less developed countries. International agencies have been established to deal with the financial debts of less developed countries. If the global community takes the ecological crisis seriously, then international bodies should be established to deal with the environmental debts of developed nations as well. The creation of such international bodies also would seem to parallel the globalization of the world's economy. If there is to be a single global financial community with greater interdependence, this must in turn call for a single global ecological community with correspondingly greater reciprocity as well.

Environmental Rights and Ecological Duties

I would suggest that the issues raised so far call for the development of a new social contract, not just to enforce legal conventions between nations but also to foster a global community for the global environmental crisis and guarantee further environmental rights for individual persons and local communities. In other words, action is needed not only at the international and national levels but also at the local community level. For the only sound way of building an effective global community is with a bottom-up process, although this may need some top-down facilitation. Of course, this suggestion is hardly new.[14] Accordingly, nations should derive some of their authority from local communities, while some of their sovereignty should be yielded to the global community, because the nation-state is too large for effective local community management and too small for effective global management.[15]

Environmental rights must include not just the right to a clean and productive environment, which is the concern of the rich, but more importantly the right of survival and subsistence with dignity for all persons and communities, which is the preoccupation of the poor.[16] Further, ecological duties and citizenship responsibilities also must include community obligations at the local, national, and global levels. Legal conventions among nations not founded on human rights and civic duties at more local levels only legalize injustice and institutionalize ecological degradation, which already is creating environmental refugees and soon perhaps may spawn ecological terrorists out of desperation. So also does administrative control that is insensitive to the needs of the underprivileged and the powerless in a country. Indeed, the question of legal liability and/or administrative regulation with regard to environmental issues remains very problematic, especially at the global level.[17]

A discussion of consumption patterns in the context of environmental rights and ecological duties poses other problems, two of which I mention but briefly. One is that consumption patterns are a problem that transcends national boundaries. Even if it were possible to achieve sustainable development in one nation at the cost of unsustainability in another, as happens all too often in exchange relations between developed and developing nations, this would do little to mitigate the problem of present consumption patterns, because many of their environmental and human health effects are transboundary problems. Unfortunately, national sovereignty is often used to thwart remedial action, infringe upon environmental rights, and negate ecological concerns and duties.[18] Using national sovereignty to obfuscate ecological concerns or human rights is not, of course, the prerogative of any single nation, whether developed or developing. But when the more powerful nations, who are the least in danger of having their sovereignty threatened, indulge in such obscurantism, it is all the more galling. Thus, when then-President Bush of the United States said at UNCED that nothing would make him compromise his nation's way of life, when that lifestyle threatens the global environment, such a statement may be good domestic politics, but it is from an international perspective grossly unethical.

The other problem is that it is also ethically unacceptable that our concern for nature be allowed to negate fundamental human rights. Indeed, a true concern for nature cannot set humans and nature in opposition. Rather, humans must be perceived as a part of nature that preserves, protects, and restores ecological integrity. In fact, only when human and nonhuman nature are in harmony can both be protected.

Ecologically based thinking necessarily leads to an awareness of interdependent communities in ever increasing and inclusive circles to include the human and the biotic. Of course, there is a danger that humans will become too anthropocentric in their thinking. Yet, ways must be found to accommodate the needs of both human and nonhuman nature.

Summary

Agenda 21 contains numerous recommendations to change patterns of consumption from those that are unsustainable to those that are sustainable. I argue that their successful implementation requires a shift in the scientific and legal burdens of proof required for the demonstration of harm due to consumption patterns, and that a failure to do so carries with it ethical implications because the harmful consequences resulting from present patterns of consumption likely will continue.

I also argue that the implementation of Agenda 21's recommendations to change patterns of consumption requires that industrialized countries assume responsibility for historical and present consumption patterns, both of which have been and are comparatively high. Further, this responsibility would seem to be required not solely for pragmatic reasons, but for ethical ones as well. To date, industrialized countries have refused to assume responsibility, undoubtedly for fear of having to assume the costs of reparations.

The adoption of a precautionary approach as suggested by Agenda 21 would seem to be most consistent with reducing human health and environmental risks that result from consumption patterns, would be based upon ethical reasoning as opposed to economic considerations and political power among countries, and would favor protecting developing countries that are least able to bear the costs of climate change. If the precautionary approach is adopted, especially by the developed countries, governmental, corporate, and personal behaviors regarding consumption would have to change in order to lessen the risk of its harmful consequences. From the perspective of developing countries based upon ethical reasoning as opposed to decision making based upon traditional economic analysis and political power, developed countries would be required to pay a so-called environmental debt caused by their historical consumption patterns in the name of their economic development to developing countries in the form of technology transfer and debt relief in order that the latter countries would be able to provide for an appropriate quality of life for their people on a sustainable basis. This approach also would require a reduction in the per capita consumption by developed countries as well as limits on population growth in the most heavily populated and affluent countries, respectively.

Notes

1. S. P. Johnson, *The Earth Summit, The United Nations Conference on Environment and Development (UNCED)* (London: Graham and Trotman/Martinus Nijhoff, 1993).

2. John Lemons, ed. *Scientific Uncertainty and Environmental Problem Solving* (Cambridge, MA: Blackwell Science, Inc., 1996).

3. John Lemons and D. A. Brown, eds., *Sustainable Development: Science, Ethics, and Public Policy* (Dordrecht, Netherlands: Kluwer, 1995).

4. *Daubert v. United States*, 113 S.Ct. 2786 (1993).

5. Kristin Shrader-Frechette, *Ethics of Scientific Research* (Lanham, MD: Rowman and Littlefield, Inc., 1994).

6. C. L. Spash, "Economics, Ethics and Long-Term Environmental Damages," *Environmental Ethics* 15, no. 2 (1993): 117–32.

7. Robert Goodland, Herman Daly, and S. El Serafy, "The Urgent Need for Rapid Transition to Global Environmental Sustainability," *Environmental Conservation* 20 (1993): 297–309.

8. Lemons and Brown, *Sustainable Development*.

9. A. Agarwal and S. Narain, *Global Warming in an Unequal World* (New Delhi: Centre for Science and Environment, 1991).

10. Ernest Partridge, *Responsibilities for Future Generations* (New York: Prometheus Books, 1981).

11. Johnson, *The Earth Summit*.

12. Goodland, Daly, and El Serafy, "The Urgent Need."

13. D. C. Korten, *Getting to the Twenty-First Century: Voluntary Action and the Global Agenda* (New Delhi: Oxford University Press, 1992).

14. N. T. Uphoff, *Rural Development and Local Organization in Asia, Volume I: Introduction and South Asia* (New Delhi: Macmillan, 1982).

15. A. Agarwal and S. Narain, *Towards a Green World: Should Global Environmental Management Be Built on Legal Conventions or Human Rights?* (New Delhi: Centre for Science and Environment, 1992).

16. R. Guha, "Ideological Trends in Indian Environmentalism," *Economics and Political Weekly* 22, no. 49 (1988): 2578–81.

17. P. Ghosh and A. Jaitly, "Legal Liability versus Administrative Regulation: The Problem of Institutional Design in Global Environmental Policy," in *The Road from Rio*, ed. P. Ghosh and A. Jaitly (New Delhi: Tata Energy Research Institute, 1993).

18. Johnson, *The Earth Summit*.

Part Two

Solutions to Problems of Consumption

8

A Nonanthropocentric Environmental Evaluation of Technology for Public Policy: Why Norton's Approach Is Insufficient for Environmental Policy

Laura Westra

The environment is man's first right
We should not allow it to suffer blight
The air we breathe we must not poison
They who do should be sent to prison
Our streams must remain clean all season
Polluting them is clearly treason
The land is life for man and flora,
Fauna and all: should wear that aura,
Protected from the greed and folly
Of man and companies unholy.

—Ken Saro-Wiwa, "A Walk in the Prison Yard"

The Ecological Point of View and the Canadian "Fish Wars"

On March 10, 1995, the story appeared on the front page of Canada's national newspaper, *The Globe and Mail*: "Four warning bursts of machine gun fire across the bow brought the Spanish trawler Estai to a halt after a four-hour chase through the foggy Atlantic." The problem was overfishing beyond the 200-mile limit on the Grand Bank off the coast of Newfoundland. When increased national quotas and the use of complex modern fishing technologies internationally reduced the availability of fish in the North Atlantic,[1] the Spanish fishers pushed their trawlers beyond the legal 200-mile limit, thus coming too close to the

153

already depleted waters surrounding the Canadian mainland. The use of gunpower in defense of fish stocks is almost unprecedented in Canadian history, but Newfoundland's premier, Clyde Wells, explained his action. He argued that the Canadians in many fishing villages have watched their communities slowly die as European vessels fished large amounts of cod and flounder from 1988 to 1993 and caused the disappearance of the cod in 1992; they have also seen Spanish vessels take as much as 50,000 tons of turbot over the last three years, in spite of their own 16,300-ton limit (and the Spaniards' own legal limit of only 3,400 tons).

Is this simply a controversy between two nations, a dispute to be settled through dialogue, diplomacy, and negotiations? This view misses the major point of the controversy, captured in the wording on a placard waved in a Newfoundland fishing village by one of the six thousand demonstrators against Spain: This is a World Fishery, not a Spanish One.[2] The "turbot battle" was eventually settled through an international deal between Canadian Fisheries Minister Brian Tobin and the European Community's representatives. It was clearly a *world* issue in the eyes of the Newfoundland fishers, who had already seen the collapse of the cod stocks and the resulting disappearance of their economy and traditional lifestyles. Canada and all other countries must learn to curb their overall economic goals, and even reduce them from previous years' expectations, if they are not prepared to face the extinction of specific fish as well as traditional lifestyles.

The quest for increased profits based on increased quotas, even if they are sought to support traditional lifestyles, is not necessarily desirable. For instance, although natives in the Amazon claim to be living harmoniously with nature (and they are indeed less disruptive to natural processes than commercially exploitive foreign practices in the area), their goals and those of conservation biology do not necessarily mesh.[3] The problem is that native hunters, for instance, may pursue a species to extinction, then move on to exploit another "resource" beyond its capacity to recover.

From the scientific perspective of the ecosystem approach (and of complex-systems theory), there is no guaranteed "safe," commercial, sustainable catch, but there is also no clear linear causality showing the connection between the overfishing of a resource such as cod and its extinction.[4] Such factors as climate changes, increases in UVB rays because of ozone depletion, increased pollution and dumping in the oceans, and toxic rain are all contributing causes. Hence it is not acceptable to argue that because some practice was not followed in past years, the same guidelines should be followed in the future based on earlier quotas. Continued increases in fishing quotas cannot be supported on the available scientific evidence. New fishing technologies will need to be abandoned—for example, gill nets, which Carl Walters terms "one of the more destructive and wasteful fishing gears ever invented."[5]

Further, neither Canada nor any other country should simply focus on the economic aspects of a natural resource as its only value. The value of natural ecosystems far transcends this narrow view; plants and animals all play important parts in the ecosystems in which they live, fulfilling specific functions that will cease if they become extinct or even if their numbers decrease too significantly. For instance, in a discussion of ecosystems and sustainability in fisheries, M. Hammer et al. state, "Whereas species diversity is a property at the population level, the *functional diversity*, what the organisms do and the variety of responses to environmental changes, especially the diverse space and time scales to which organisms react to each other and the environment, is a *property of the ecosystem.*"[6] To limit oneself to dealing with the areas where *our* interest lies (areas of ecosystem health, viewed and treated as instrumentally valuable) is to ignore the larger picture and the life-support and benchmark functions of the wild, in landscapes of appropriate geographical size (biomes). Hence, the primary concern must focus on the wild (core) areas, even when sustainability is the issue. Sustainability is here understood as undiminished function capacity, supported by the undiminished structural systems of wild areas of appropriate size.[7] To put it plainly, sustainable agriculture, forestry, and sustainable fisheries make little sense unless sustainability of wild ecosystems is addressed first, and at least in the long term, anticipated and required by most North American and global regulations and treaties, all of which include future generations in their reach. Some will argue that as we lack a precise reference point or baseline for ecosystem integrity, we do not need anything to which we ought to conform or to return environmentally. But we do not need to know the specific composition or the detailed structure of a landscape in order to know when it no longer functions. Because of all-pervasive pollution and environmental degradation, we cannot be assured that any area is "as it should be," meaning that the changes that have occurred (including biodiversity losses) are purely due to its natural trajectory and to nonanthropogenic stresses. But we do know when a system has collapsed, that is, when it has lost its natural capacity to function appropriately for its scale and geographic location. Reed Noss says:

Ecosystems remain viable only when their processes—nutrient cycling, energy flow, hydrology, disturbance-recovery regimes, predator-prey dynamics, etc.—continue to operate within their natural range of variability. . . . Furthermore, the integrity of aquatic ecosystems is directly linked to the condition of the landscape around them.[8]

In a general sense, neither specific systemic processes nor predator/ prey dynamics can remain unaffected when naturally occurring predators or prey are eliminated from a system. We also know that when whole areas or whole countries are so affected, they no longer function in support of humans.

For example, in Holland, a totally "managed" country, the balance, however precarious, between intensive manipulation of land and water systems and production results of such manipulation has been lost. Too much chemical input may render agricultural production and the land itself impotent,[9] although not every episode of manipulative intervention equals system collapse. But Holland is presently suffering from the consequences of its neglect of the wild and taking steps to correct its mistakes by closing roads and imposing penalties for excessive cattle and pig operations, rather than offering subsidies, and allowing environmental authorities veto power over all projects found to be ecologically unsound.

Where and how do we draw the line? How much information do we need in order to enforce policies that are contrary to present and past economic growth trends? These are hard questions; answering them is not an easy task, and we must rely on imprecise and divided science to perform it. Although answers are earnestly sought, the immediate priority is to discontinue, alter, or mitigate all practices currently "on trial" and abide by strong precautionary principles instead.[10] All available information indicates that most of the practices in our present technological lifestyle are not "innocent," and that both "juries" and "legal counsel teams" that defend and support them have strong financial interests in their continued existence, in direct opposition to the real public good, as shown in the fish wars example.

When sustainability is discussed in the context of techno-consumerist lifestyles, it is intended purely as ecological sustainability (ES). This does not mean, however, that either economic sustainability (ECS) or social sustainability (SS) are ignored or deemed unimportant. The thrust of my argument is that ES, although some may view it as potentially inimical to the other two (ECS and SS), in the long term, is not. Although this can be shown to be true, for the most part it is the short-term economic advantage that policymakers most often seek and deliberately contrast with ecological imperatives. Robert Goodland argues that there are three types of sustainability, and that they are "clearest when kept separate."[11]

Because ecological sustainability must remain primary, I argue that (1) as many others have noted, current evaluations of technology (and of the business enterprises that depend on these technologies) are insufficient for public policy if they are based only on cost/benefit analyses,[12] and that (2) even the necessary introduction of traditional moral theories and of respect for democratic institutions and practices is not sufficient to acknowledge the required ecological component of public policy decisions, as the fish wars indicated, despite the free, informed citizens' choices that prevailed at the time. As the case for the ethics of integrity unfolds, this chapter attacks consumerism, anthropocentrism, and the reliance on often untested and unproven technologies as the major sources of problems in affluent northwestern countries. None of these represents the only problem we need to address, because the population question is also a major problem. That discussion occurs in the last chapter of this work, because at that stage I will also have addressed the question of microintegrity, and I will have attempted to reconcile the respect for the integrity of individual organisms and the reality of overpopulation as a basic environmental threat.

In the next section I examine the limits of economic evaluations based purely on human preferences. I then turn to a major stumbling block one encounters when proposing a biocentric, holistic approach, that is, the belief that nonanthropocentric theories fail when they are used in support of environmental choices. Some people view all holistic theories as lacking from both a philosophical and a practical point of view. I argue instead that they are superior on both theoretical and practical grounds, and therefore we need to go far beyond both economic and even traditional (intrahuman) moral evaluations to achieve sound environmental policy.

The Limits of Economic Evaluation and Anthropocentrism

Although the use of firearms to protect the natural world was new to Canada in March 1995, illegal protests and even violence have occurred elsewhere. For example, in 1994, protesters from Canada and the United States made their way to British Columbia, threatened violence, and chained themselves to trees to subvert corporate activities and prevent the logging of old-growth forests in Clayoquot Sound. In taking this action, protesters were appealing to international law and to regulatory bodies beyond those of the countries of the dispute, as happened in the Newfoundland fish wars. This was an unprecedented tactic, as for instance, protests by native groups, whether in Canada or the United States, have been intended to support the right to certain lifestyles (and the beliefs that support them). I have argued this point in detail elsewhere.[13] In essence, although traditional native lifestyles are far less disruptive to the environment (because they are far less technologically "advanced") than today's affluent northwestern lifestyles, the natives' main concerns are ethnic self-preservation and, at least in Canada, sovereignty. The goals of conservation biology and sustainability are important and form an integral part of the self-understanding of traditional Inuit and native peoples,[14] but they may be viewed as secondary to present individual and group development goals.

One wonders whether an appeal to traditional, anthropocentric moral doctrines is sufficient to prevent such problems from developing in the face of increasing environmental degradation and mounting scarcity of resources as populations increase. Many have addressed the need to ensure that cost/benefit analyses and economic evaluations of technology focus prominently on ethical considerations beyond aggregate utilities and majority preferences.[15] I believe that the anthropocentric/nonanthropocentric distinction presents a false dichotomy in several senses and that it is no more than a red herring, advanced by those concerned with defending the status quo. Accordingly, they are led to propose a somewhat modified "greened" revamping of the same hazardous, uncritically accepted practices to which all life on earth has been subjected, as I argue in the next section.

Utilities and preferences are normally understood in philosophical and political theory as reflecting the wishes and maybe the (descriptively) perceived good of a society, as do appeals to rights, justice, fairness, and due process. The question, however, is whether ethical considerations based on moral doctrines designed primarily for intraspecific interaction, that is, designed to guide our interpersonal behavior, are in fact sufficient as well as clearly necessary to ensure that our activities conform to an inclusive and enlightened morality. Recent global changes affecting our resource base everywhere prove the inadequacy of calculations that depend solely on economics, so that evaluations founded on moral doctrines and upholding both natural and civil rights appear indeed mandatory. Would that approach have been sufficient in the case of the Newfoundland fishers and the North Atlantic fish stocks? The fishers' earlier arguments, even before the decline of the cod population, could have been supported from the standpoint of human ethics and anthropocentrism. They were concerned with (1) sustainable development (Newfoundland is probably the poorest province in Canada) and increased financial security for themselves and their families; (2) aggregate utility, not for their "preference wants" but for their basic needs; (3) their local/national "visions" specific to the place they inhabited;[16] and (4) their democratic right to free choice.

Although their grounds appeared prima facie to be unimpeachable and could be defensible morally as well as legally in our present worldwide environmental situation, all the four points listed need reexamination in the light of what Don Scherer terms our "upstream/

downstream" world.[17] The underlying notion of human rights is also questionable, in view of Robert McGinn's argument about "technological maximality" and the hazards that approach engenders. The combination of (1) "absolute" human rights—that is, human rights viewed as primary even when they support nonessential, nonbasic preferences; (2) greatly increased numbers of such "rights-holders," and (3) the well-entrenched drive to newer, bigger, and more—that is, to "technological maximality"—jointly engenders threats that are not present in any separate individual action. As we saw in the previous section, Goodland argues for the primacy of ecological sustainability; McGinn proposes "contextualized" theories of rights;[18] either of these positions would have helped to respond to the mounting environmental problems that eventually led to the Canadian fish wars by demanding that the scientific information be available to both policymakers and the general public, and that the "rights" of fishers to increasing quotas and the access to more complex fishing technologies be jointly evaluated.[19]

While both these arguments focus primarily on human beings, they are anthropocentric in an enlightened and morally sensitive way. This sort of anthropocentrism (at least on the part of McGinn) may be close to what Bryan Norton terms "weak anthropocentrism."[20] However, Goodland's argument hinges also on the basic role of natural systems' integrity, in regard to general life support (for both humankind and nonhuman nature).[21] McGinn acknowledges the existence of the ecological impasse to which we are brought by present individualism and by preference-based, largely unrestricted choices, but he believes that it might be sufficient to shift the emphasis to *community* concerns, hence to contextualize present theories of rights.[22]

Could the communitarian emphasis have prevented the crash of the fisheries, which led to violence in the normally peaceful fishing industry? It seems that this would not have been enough. Returning for a moment to the arguments to which the fishers might have appealed, we see that at least one of the strongest is already a communitarian one. One of their concerns was the support of communitarian values and traditional lifestyles. Yet in this typical case, even subordinating *individual* rights to aggregate community or national ones was not enough, unless the community that would have been accepted as primary could have been, minimally, the international global community, or—as I argue in the next section—the community of life.

In contrast, neither the Canadian nor the Spanish fishing communities would have raised the question of other international community rights or the need to reexamine or contextualize their own, as McGinn suggests. Even Mark Sagoff's position in *The Economy of the Earth*, if adopted, might have been insufficient to prevent the violent conflict that arose. He would suggest that the Canadian government should have supported its *citizens'* values, incorporating their local beliefs and practices, rather than the consumers' (and producers') values of increased availability of reasonably priced fish and profit maximization. But Newfoundlanders are a proud people who love both their land and their traditional lifestyles. In their case, their continued dependence on successful local fisheries represents far more than either a consumer's or a producer's preference. It is instead the embodiment of a national or specifically place-based vision of what a traditional good life should be. Therefore, one could argue that it was citizens' values, rather than consumers' values, that motivated their continued quest for increased quotas for cod and eventually turbot.

The same argument could be applied to the Spanish fishers and their traditional village values, on the other side of the ocean. Thus, even if the motive of *all* fishers was not purely economic, the problem of the commons, or of the "common pool" as Eric Freyfogle has it, persists. He says, "According to many economists, the solution to the tragedy of the common pool is to divide the common asset and distribute shares or parts to individual users."[23]

Yet while such privatization emphasizes the need to recognize our limits, and might ensure that "we do not exceed our fair share," it also "divides the haves from the have nots."[24] Hence, it would conflict with traditional moral principles by running counter to both human rights and justice considerations. Privatization also would not offer a solution to the problems raised in the fundamental question posed here about the necessity for additional, but primary, environmental value considerations. As a general prescription, it does nothing to help us limit our overconsumption or to find appropriate locations to dispose of the waste generated. For the latter, we must "stop producing the wastes to begin with, or to break them down into harmless component parts," which is not always possible. We tend to view the earth as a giant pool of resources, unchanging and always there, a stable value where the only question is the allotment of its bounty and the most efficient way of extracting it. "Depletion accounting" also normally fosters this illusion, by depreciating buildings, equipment, and machinery, but not land. Yet the land, too, is vulnerable: through "our pollution and land use practices [we] poison the soil and drain its fertility."[25] The same, mutatis mutandis, could be said about the sea and its fisheries. The basic problem remains our unsustainable lifestyle, particularly in the urban Northwest. Conventional economic rationality rejects the notion that "carrying capacity imposes serious constraints on material growth."[26] The position of those who disagree with the necessity for limits is based on the belief that unlimited substitutions will make ecological critiques and appeals to scarcity obsolete.[27] This optimistic, protechnology attitude, however, appears unjustified.

Returning to the fish wars, if we were to continue our present practices without restraints other than a different allocation of the quotas, and all the North Atlantic fish stocks crashed, we might be able to develop some alternative source of protein, but this would do nothing to restore the fishers' communities or lifestyles. Conversely, we might instead turn to aquaculture as a comparable source of food and a socially adequate source of comparable employment. Nevertheless, aquaculture is also environmentally hazardous, as it releases nutrients and wastes into ecosystems, disrupting their natural processes. The introduction of transgenic fish also affects natural populations, thus biodiversity, and often releases antibiotics into the system and into the food chain.[28] Questions may be raised about the reasons for viewing these results as irrevocably bad. What is wrong, it may be asked, with changes in the species presently existing in various locations? William Broad's *New York Times* article "Creatures of the Deep Find Their Way to the Table" cites the examples of the orange roughy, the rattail, the royal red shrimp, and others as newfound delicacies harvested and marketed in substitution of other, more familiar fish species.[29]

But even though we may change our tastes, and so could future persons, the other side of this particular issue is also brought out in the same article, as Broad asks, "eat it first, study it later?" and in essence admits that "nobody knows how harvesting will affect deep-sea fish species." We are now harvesting more than orange roughies; we are living with the results of our exploitive practices in too many areas. Perhaps the uncertainty, and the possibility of additional future species disappearances, will prompt us to rethink and retrench rather than forge ahead with misplaced hubris and optimism.

The basic problem anywhere, not just for Canadian fisheries, is sustainability. William Rees, for instance, proposes adopting an "ecological worldview," in contrast with the prevailing established "expansionist worldview," which represents "the dominant social paradigm."[30] As Aldo Leopold did before him, Rees recognizes that we are not independent of an "environment," but, as we also saw earlier in Goodland's work, ecological sustainability is foundational, so it makes perfectly good sense to abandon our present unsustainable and indefensible worldview. Rees and Wackernagel say, "By contrast, an ecological economic perspective would see the human economy as an inextricably integrated, completely contained, and wholly dependent sub-system of the ecosphere."[31]

This position is supported by Rees's research in the Vancouver–Lower Fraser Valley region of British Columbia, but it can be easily generalized for all urban, affluent northwestern centers. His findings show that "assuming an average Canadian diet and current management practices," the local regional population supports its consumers' lifestyles by importing "the productive capacity of at least 22 times as much land as it occupies." To put this in a more general way, "the ecological footprints of individual regions are much larger than the land areas they physically occupy."[32]

When we continue to import others' carrying capacity, we are "running an unaccounted ecological deficit," and "our populations are appropriating carrying capacity from elsewhere or from future generations."[33] The same can be said about sinks for our wastes: for both resource appropriation and waste disposal, our northwestern approach has been one of neocolonialism in regard to less-developed countries and ruthless exploitation (through environmental racism) toward minorities and the disempowered in our own countries.[34]

Environmental racism is a concern about humans, but for all other concerns and problems mentioned here it is easy to find arguments that might give a spurious legitimacy to the maintenance of the status quo, perhaps with minor "cosmetic" green changes to put public anxiety to rest, but without actually effecting the radical reorganization of our own and our society's priorities, which are warranted by the present environmental situation.[35] In fact, despite its imprecise language and its undercurrent of inconsistencies, the principles of *Agenda 21* (and the Rio declaration following the 1992 Rio de Janeiro Earth Summit) also demand such a radical review of all national and international laws and regulations.[36]

The fish wars example is even more useful in assessing what sorts of principles we need to resolve such potentially volatile situations. It may be possible to use anthropocentric moral doctrines concerned with human issues at this point in the dispute in order to adjudicate fairly among the various affected parties. But what of the original practices— that is, technologically enhanced fishing—that led to the fish wars?[37] Over time, these practices, along with nonpoint pollution, the steady rise of toxic wastes in the oceans, anthropogenically induced climate changes, and careless overuse through constantly increasing fishing quotas, led to the crash of the fish stocks. This crisis could have been avoided only through policies and practices consistent with an "ecological worldview," one going beyond competing aggregate preferences of various human groups.

In the next section I discuss what such a worldview might require and argue that the radical change called for by the current emergencies can be supported only through an ecocentric or biocentric viewpoint, whether or not our concern is primarily directed toward human beings.

It follows that in an actual situation, such as the fish wars, the contributing factors leading to the problems in the North Atlantic could all be traced back to the exercise of human and civil rights, not all of which can be indicted as supporting only consumers' preferences. Waste, pollution, and the proliferation of hazardous processes and products can all be identified as the result of fast-spreading, untested (or inadequately tested) technologies. It might be argued that some of these technologies (such as time-saving devices, automobiles, and even all-terrain vehicles in some areas) could be viewed as supporting citizens' values: the individual's right to self-fulfillment and actualization could be supported by household time-saving devices; the so-called right to the freedom of mobility, by all kinds of transportation vehicles. Producers' economic interests in growth, development, and successful competition with other producers are also fostered by the same practices. What about equity and the rights of those who are not benefited but are forced to bear the burdens of these technologies? The question raised earlier returns. It is absolutely necessary to consider and reconsider human rights and equity questions. But these questions raise primarily distributive problems. They are not foundational questions like those raised by biocentric concerns: that is, why is it necessary to have these "advanced" fishing technologies and a lifestyle dependent on them?

We may want to modify the way the corporate/technological enterprise operates from the moral point of view by raising some of the questions suggested above. However, we are still not attempting to alter it in a radical way, and this would be a mistake since a partial imposition of restraints is not sufficient. Kristin Shrader-Frechette recounts the example of a fungicide, ethylene dibromide (EDB), which was proven to be carcinogenic in 1973. The procedures necessary for its regulation required another ten years and during that period, "EDB began showing up in bread, flour and cereal products in such quantities that risk assessors predicted that, based on lifetime consumption, EDB would cause up to 200,000 cases of cancer per year in the United States."[38] Even more chilling is that the substitute the industry eventually used, methyl bromide, is a very close chemical relative of the banned EDB and probably equally carcinogenic. To this day, methyl bromide is still not regulated.

A lesson can be learned from such cases. First, it is absolutely necessary to start by introducing moral considerations into the risk assessment of all technologies; second, it seems that even faster, more ethically sensitive assessments may be insufficient to prevent the perpetration of ecoviolence (that is, violence perpetrated in and through the environment). What is required is a radically changed approach, starting from ecocentrism, and a major shift in burden of proof theories and standards. Robert Ulanowicz argues that even in highly funded, uncontroversial research, such as research into cancer causes, a holistic approach would be far more fruitful than the present reductionist method, with exclusive focus on genes or viruses.[39] Holism can make a large difference in issues concerned with the interface between humans and the environment. In addition, an ecocentric perspective would regard all untried and potentially hazardous substances as guilty until proven innocent beyond a doubt. It would suggest that, even then, given the uncertainties endemic to the scientific method, the precautionary principle still needs to be applied.[40]

The shift in the burden of proof suggested here is already part of the language of the Great Lakes Water Quality Agreement (of 1978, ratified in 1987), through its emphasis on "zero discharge" and on "sunset" and "sunrise" chemical controls.[41] These substances can be viewed minimally as not contributing to the natural evolutionary processes of ecosystems, thus as naturally inimical to the mandated respect for ecosystem integrity. In essence, I have argued that an ecosystem can be said to possess integrity (I_a) when it is an unmanaged ecosystem, although not necessarily a pristine one. This aspect of integrity is the most significant one; it is the aspect that differentiates I_a from ecosystem health (I_b), which is compatible with support/manipulation instead.[42] Hence, exotic, potentially hazardous substances and processes would be judged inappropriate, and their introduction into natural systems would not be permitted. As McGinn argues, meaningful changes in our evaluation of technology cannot occur unless we are willing to question our assumptions about rights and the role of democracy.[43]

Beyond the Anthropocentrism/Nonanthropocentrism Debate

The conclusion reached in the previous section indicates that to ameliorate presently accepted technology-dependent lifestyles or redress present inequities, it would be preferable to change our approach and accept the primacy of ecological integrity, as many national and international laws and regulations already do, at least in their language, rather than expect real change from end-of-pipe solutions. Insofar as ecocentrism is akin to deep ecology's platform, however, such a position is in direct conflict with a position such as Norton's: "As academics, spokespersons for deep ecology have been able to avoid adopting policies on difficult, real world cases such as elk destroying their wolf-free ranges, feral goats destroying indigenous vegetation on fragile lands, or park facilities overwhelmed by human visitors."[44]

On the contrary, a truly holistic position such as the one supporting the primacy of integrity has clear-cut answers for all such questions, though not necessarily popular ones, as can be seen from our approach to the fish wars. In every case, when there is human interference giving rise to problems in the wild, it is not only acceptable but mandatory to interfere again to redress the difficulty, temporarily, and with the clear goal to withdraw when the system's evolutionary path has been restored, according to the best scientific information available and under the guidance of the precautionary principle.[45] The goal in this case is one of restoration, as the area affected is wild. That is to say, although the immediate goal is to restore natural function and systemic health, the ultimate goal is to withdraw all support and manipulation, so that some restored systems can return to a state of integrity or unmanaged evolutionary processes once again; hence the present call for the establishment of marine fisheries reserves.[46]

This does not mean that we must altogether discontinue human practices that utilize nature everywhere. It simply indicates that we must recognize the necessity of (1) leaving appropriately sized areas on both land and seas wild and unmanipulated (the required sizes need to be established in dialogue with conservation biology and aquatic ecosystem science) and (2) limiting our intrusive practices upon the rest of the earth to whatever will not have an adverse impact on core/wild areas.[47] Conservation biology, entomology, ecology, and biology will all contribute to the necessary dialogue to establish the scales appropriate to either one or the other of these approaches in different landscapes, globally. As I have argued elsewhere,[48] the ultimate goal of the principle of integrity is to protect and restore both structural and functional aspects of ecological integrity, and this requires that large areas be kept wild.[49] It also demands that we be prepared to "embrace the challenge of complexity," as James Kay and Earl Schneider argue, and thus to abandon the misconception that all systems can and should be managed.[50] Instead, management and controls should be confined to human individuals and societies, except briefly for restoration purposes in core and buffer areas.

By way of contrast, we noted in the case of Canadian fisheries the dismal failure of the presumption to manage nature. Educated guesses about how far we can push the safety factor with our quotas, particularly when these are manipulated by economic and political interests (both of which are notoriously shortsighted) and supported by uneducated democratic preferences and values, are simply insufficient to protect either the fish species or the local survival needs of affected humans. Norton has argued that "long-sighted anthropocentrists and ecocentrists tend to adopt more and more similar policies as scientific evidence is gathered because both value systems—and several others as well—point toward the common-denominator objective of protecting ecological contexts."[51]

Norton is not alone in this belief. Gary Varner, for instance, appears to concur.[52] But in his effort to continue his ongoing campaign against the supporters of intrinsic natural value, Norton appeals to two concepts that as we shall see, are also problematic, either practically or theoretically. He refers to a rare if not nonexistent ethic—that of the long-sighted anthropocentrist. Where does one find such a position? Not among politicians and policymakers, to be sure: the hard pressure of political correctness with regard to other issues tends to relegate green concerns to the back burner, although some examples can be cited, such as the Endangered Species Act and some policies on radioactive waste disposal, both of which take a longsighted approach. What about large multinational corporations? These are somewhat vulnerable to public opinion, but even more vulnerable to shareholders' displeasure and internal and external competition. It will be hard to find much longsightedness in those boardrooms, beyond public relations campaigns to calm the public's "irrationality" and their fears. And if one were to encounter that *rara avis,* a longsighted anthropocentrist, how would one distinguish her from her ecocentrist counterpart?

Norton describes her salient characteristics: she would appreciate "scientific evidence," and thus be disposed to share with the ecocentrist the "objective of protecting ecological contexts."[53] But this is only superficially true. That is, she would be willing to follow that path only if she were convinced that no other path would support her interests equally well. Such beliefs and sentiments are indeed shared by politicians, industry giants, and many others; they are easy to voice because they remain vague and unspecific. Serious questions can be raised: for instance, how far would the weak/longsighted anthropocentrist (WLSA) go to protect such systems? Another question is, For what would she understand that protection to be necessary? For the WLSA, continued exploitation, variously defined, might be a convincing candidate. But, given science's imprecision and the "challenge of complexity," and thus the impossibility of finding a guaranteed "safe" degree of pollution/exploitation, particularly in the face of cumulative and synergistic stresses, how easy would it be to convince the WLSA that her interest would be amply served by an ecologically untenable position? Newfoundland's fishers had every interest in the continued thriving of the fish species upon which they depended, in a far more immediate and vital way than any politician, yet they could not make the connection, even in their own interest.

One could object that scientific uncertainty would also work against the ecocentrist's approach. The differences between the two approaches are significant instead, and they can be captured in two main points.

First, the ecocentrist would start from the primacy and value of wilderness and thus begin by questioning any intrusive or risky practices, shifting the burden of proof to the would-be risk imposers. Her criteria would become progressively more stringent as the proposed technology and economic activity would be intended for human settlements and cities, or for areas of ecosystem health (sustainable agriculture of forestry areas, for instance). Most technological intrusion would be excluded from wild, core areas as required in order to protect their role and function.[54]

Second, given the primary value of preserving or restoring natural, evolutionary function in certain designated areas, and the necessity of ensuring this function through human activities compatible with this goal, the nonanthropocentric holist would use the precautionary principle to decide on all economic and technological issues. The precautionary principle (Principle 15 of the Rio Declaration on Environment and Development) states:

> In order to protect the environment, the precautionary approach shall be widely applied by States, according to their capabilities. Where there are threats of serious or irreversible damage, lack of full scientific certainty shall not be used as a reason for postponing cost-effective measures to prevent environmental damage.[55]

Finally, how will the WLSA vote and act when environmental protection conflicts with local jobs or other legitimate human aspirations, without relying entirely on the example I have proposed? This, it seems to me, is the litmus test for the convergence of ends Norton envisions between his WLSA and the ecocentrist, despite Norton's assertion that his position "recognizes the crucial role of creative, self-organizing systems in support of economic, recreational, aesthetic and spiritual values."[56] As we saw in the fish wars example, even all this may not be enough.

Yet, in some sense, Norton is right: there is a commonality between the two positions, but this commonality emerges only when we subordinate "human economic, recreational, aesthetic and spiritual values," whatever these might be, to the imperative of survival. This imperative represents the common denominator we share with the rest of life. And when we recognize the primacy of that commonality and the ways in which ecological integrity supports it for all, globally, then we are ecocentrists, or biocentric holists (the term I have chosen), because our anthropocentrism has been so weakened as to be nonexistent, dissolved into the reality of our presence first and foremost, as part of the biota of natural systems.[57]

But, some will argue, perhaps it is sufficient merely to recognize that we are a part of the biota of natural systems and that we share our habitat with the rest of life; in that case, it is not necessary to argue for the intrinsic value of nonhuman animals and other individuals and wholes. Those who support this position will view the WLSA as theoretically and philosophically defensible; all other positions, based on ecocentrism or biocentrism, will not be acceptable. This has certainly been Norton's position through the years.[58] The polarization of the two positions is well documented in the environmental ethics literature.[59] But this polarization remains—to say the least—misguided.

The weaker anthropocentrism becomes, the less defensible it is as such, that is, as a variant of anthropocentrism. But why should we weaken anthropocentrism in the first place? Norton's answer, if I understand him correctly, is because humankind has more than economic interests. These other interests represent values that mitigate the crassest forms of purely economic anthropocentrism, thus making the position more acceptable. Norton defines his position as follows:

> A value theory is weakly anthropocentric if all value countenanced by it is explained by reference to some felt preferences of a human individual or by reference to its bearing upon the ideals which exist as elements in a world view essential to determinations of considered preferences.[60]

This position is therefore weak from the standpoint of moral theory as well: it is open to all the charges to which utilitarianism is open in its weakest formulation. Based upon Norton's position, all we can offer to any group, individual, or policymaker intent on advancing her common interests, which might be strongly anthropocentric, is our plea for the support of "values," explained by reference to some "felt or considered preferences of a human individual."[61] Whether these are aggregate rather than individual preferences, and whether they even embody some ideal, the answer is still the same: the result can be purely utilitarian in a time-limited sense (although John Rawls's position might mitigate it to some extent). Choices based on preference satisfaction are often blind to other individual rights and to justice considerations. They can also be culturally relative (for example, in some cultures female genital mutilation is part of a "moral" family-oriented ideal); thus many such preferences may not be universally defensible from a moral standpoint.

The case of the fish wars shows how useless such a position would have been from the standpoint of reaching an environmentally fair and ecologically sound solution. Any position that presents a choice between "considered preference A" and "considered preference B" offers no grounds, other than a counting of heads, efficiency, or (for a policymaker) perhaps political expediency, for the ultimate result. Hence, the proponents of such a position must bear the responsibility for their stance even if, in their individual case, their choice might have been just as sound and prudent as one reached on ecocentric grounds.

The problem is one envisioned by Plato: knowing the road to Larissa without knowing why. In other words, even reaching a right decision on wrong principles may not be sufficient if the principles would permit a morally bad decision on another occasion. This is not based exclusively on a quest for personal moral purity but on the responsibility for consequences to which others, even human innocents now and in the future, may be subjected through our choices, and our choice of principles.

Norton rejects all defenses of intrinsic value in nonhuman nature, whether holistic or individualistic,[62] although he aims his attack primarily at Baird Callicott's own position and his interpretation of the land ethic of Aldo Leopold.[63] Leaving aside for the moment individual grounds for intrinsic value in nonhuman animals, a holistic perspective supports respect for all parts of natural systems, as well as the wholes within which they function. We ourselves are parts, at least physically, of these structures. They also respect system functions—that is, the processes they engender, which involve their biotic and abiotic parts—a necessity when we wish to defend the survival of any species.[64]

An ecocentric position such as the biocentric holism recommended by the principle of integrity (PI) recognizes (1) the interrelationship between human and nonhuman nature and their "connaturality"[65] and kinship;[66] hence (2) the intrinsic value of natural/evolutionary processes;[67] and (3) the foundational value of life-support systems for ecological sustainability.[68] It also acknowledges that (4) ecological sustainability is primary, as it alone supports economic and social sustainability.[69] Therefore (5) at the most basic—that is, at the *life* level—the dichotomy between anthropocentrism and nonanthropocentrism is a false one. I believe that this is true not because anthropocentrism is the only defensible theory but because "preferences" sometimes address want-interests, as well as need-interests, but at the basic level of survival only, we have no interests that are completely separate from those of all other life, so that their "values" and our "values" coincide.[70]

Hence, the argument proposed here is not that humans have interests that are defensible because they are intrinsically valuable beings, unlike any other, but because humans and nonhumans share an interest, a need for a safe habitat, and—whether or not this is consciously acknowledged—the value of survival conditions persists, and it includes the valuable contributions of all participants in ecosystemic processes. This does not render all life equal, but it shows all living things are possessed of value singly and collectively, for themselves and for all else. Rather than relying on preference-satisfaction indicators, a position that has been found morally lacking in risk assessment and technology assessment,[71] my approach defends the general (human and nonhuman) value of integrity and health for various habitats in appropriate proportions.[72]

Norton prefers to isolate another common regulatory and legislative strand, which, like the appeals to ecological integrity, can also be found in many documents: the issue and rights of future generations (of humans, if I understand him correctly). If he is looking for a publicly accepted legislative priority, he is correct. If, however, Norton is seeking a moral basis that is less hard to defend, or less controversial than intrinsic value for nonhumans, then the future-generations emphasis he has chosen is both controversial and debated, and even less easy to sell to the person in the street as a possible preference than ecological life support, with all its prudential implications.[73]

In conclusion, *pace* Norton, there is no clear, obvious, and philosophically defensible difference between the concepts and values that sustain the argument of the WLSA and those that support the intrinsic-value beliefs of the ecocentrist, nor is ecocentrism as vacuous and "exotic" as Norton claims.[74] In practice, Norton claims that holistic/intrinsic-value arguments are impotent. But when dealing with agencies and government bodies (such as Environment Canada or the Great Lakes International Joint Commission) or major organizations like the International Union for the Conservation of Nature (IUCN), it would be no easier to attempt to support environmental action by appealing to the details of philosophical debates regarding future generations than by appealing to intrinsic-value arguments. At the level of scientific evidence and with the support of ecology, the intrinsic-value arguments are not only easier to use, particularly for wholes and processes (though admittedly less so for individual animals, unless endangered), but also by the very same arguments culled from ecology, they are a necessary and integral part of the future-generations arguments Norton prefers. In order to accept a determinant role for duties to future generations, we must understand why we need to respect the life-support function of systemic processes. In other words, if the consequences of unrestrained technological and economic activities were simply various changes in the natural environment requiring changes in preferences and the exercise of our ingenuity and our technological abilities, we would have little or no reason to moderate our activities out of respect for the future, as some argue.[75]

It is only because of the mounting evidence showing the life-support function of systemic processes and the role of their component parts that we must accept that it is not the deprivation of this or that resource that we may inflict on the future but the limitation of the very basis for any life at all. It goes without saying that neither ecology nor biology could make absolute pronouncements about these issues. But the evidence (mentioned in our discussion of agricultural and fishing practices) appears to be on the side of the defense of naturally evolving entities. We affect, severely, the health of all human and nonhuman animals through anthropogenic stress to ecosystems leading to nonevolutionary changes.[76]

Some of the most obvious changes are caused by climate changes, as many have argued. Most of these changes deal with effects on living species and habitats. Yet there are effects that are even more insidious. Cor Van der Weele shows why our present exclusive preoccupation with reductionist causal connections in genes and genetic traits, with the combined impact of our methodological bias toward positivism, blinds us to the reality that "causal choices cannot be avoided."[77] In brief, developmental biology shows the strong effect of environmental conditions, and the time scale for these changes begins before birth: "The ecological environment can be seen as a set of nested structures, beginning with the immediate setting of the developing person, the micro-environment, up to the macro-environment which refers to the cultural or sub-cultural level."[78] The "micro-environment" is the womb or its equivalent in nonmammalian animals. Even small temperature changes (occurring abruptly because of anthropogenic stresses) affect various embryonic traits, including gender, in a number of nonhuman animals. This is similar to the negative impact on reproduction caused by chemicals such as pesticides and herbicides. Temperature changes translate into various effects, one of which, the occurrence of sexual/gender changes, would lead, albeit unintentionally, to the extinction of many species that are documented to be sensitive to such temperature changes.

These effects represent not just the imposition of some substitutions or minor changes that we might impose on future generations, but an almost complete overturning of the most basic support, that of life. It is not only internal factors that affect a fertilized egg or embryo: "when a few pinches of simple salts . . . are added to the water in which a fish (Fundulus) is developing, that fish will undergo a modified process of development and have not two eyes, but one."[79] Hence, internal, reductionist study will yield only a partial cause of development, whereas the external environmental factors are at least codeterminant of future consequences. Without Frankenstein's motivation and determination, we are nevertheless preparing the way for "monsters" for whom we are unwilling to accept responsibility.

Warming trends represent *indirect* global changes that affect reproduction, and thereby individuals as well as species. Recent research has shown that direct effects extending to reproductive function and well beyond it can be traced to certain features of our technological lifestyles and the corporate activities that foster and support them. The groundbreaking research of Theo Colborn and others has shown how manmade chemicals, long known to be hazardous and carcinogenic, and also many others thought to be biologically inert, affect the reproductive organs and related capacities of most species, from fish to birds to mammals, including humans.

As "hormone mimics" they also significantly alter our behavior, intellectual capacities, and parenting abilities.[80] The results of Colborn's research present a clear indictment of the way we interact with corporations and industry. After cataloging a litany of horrors resulting from even minute exposures to polychlorinated biphenyl compounds (PCBs) affecting women of reproductive age, infants, fetuses, and children, Colborn says of the move to produce PCBs:

> Confident of their safety as well as their utility, the Swann Chemical Company, which would soon become part of Monsanto Chemical Company in 1935, quickly moved them into production and onto the market.[81]

It is the corporations who have the resources to research, test, and market these complex and novel products. Even in democratic nations, however, we have no institutional mechanism to oversee, acquire information on (because of trade secrets laws), or debate, let alone impose limits on, these industrial giants. But even the tiniest molecule of a PCB compound is not biodegradable; it is durable, it travels and persists, and thus it has a range of negative effects:

> Researchers studying declining seal populations have found that seventy parts per million of PCBs is enough to cause serious problems for females, including suppressed immune systems and deformities of the uterus and of the fallopian tubes.[82]

Nor are PCBs the only chemicals with far-reaching transgenerational effects. DDT, "PCBs (209 compounds), . . . 75 dioxins, and . . . 135 furans were invented by chemists" in laboratories "to kill insects threatening crops and to give manufacturers new materials such as plastics."[83]

> Inadvertently, however, the chemical engineers had also created chemicals that jeopardize fertility and the unborn. Even worse, we have unknowingly spread them far and wide across the face of the Earth.[84]

These chemicals disrupt the endocrine system, mimic estrogen and other hormones, and block the pathways through which hormones signal normal development of all animals, including humans:

> This is like jamming the line on a cellular phone so it is always as busy and the intended messages are blocked. Without these testosterone signals,

male development gets derailed and boys don't become boys. Instead they become stranded in an ambiguous state where they cannot function as either males or females.[85]

In addition, fungicides "inhibit the body's ability to produce steroids hormones, so vital messages are never sent," whereas long-lasting DDE "depletes hormones by accelerating their breakdown and elimination leaving the body short, not just of estrogen, but of testosterone and the other steroid hormones."[86]

As long as our quietism permits the continuation of present practices, and because governments do not appear to be eager to mandate controls in much of the Western world, here and in Europe emphasis is on deregulation rather than on tighter controls.

In that case, although Colborn and her collaborators propose principles of mitigation and change based on the Wingspread Consensus Statement (July 1991), within the present political and institutional system it is hard to envision acceptance of and compliance with her suggestions. The tobacco industry resisted regulation and controls for a long time, although there were unambiguous links between their products and deaths.[87]

It is my argument that we need to understand and accept this responsibility and recognize our obligation to respect life-support systems from a biocentric standpoint in order to support the changes indicated by these hazards. From Norton's point of view, in order to introduce arguments about future generations, we also need to understand the many ways we may negatively affect them. For this task, simple interhuman considerations will not suffice; we will need to expand our consciousness, our understanding, and our respect as required to include these processes and causal links. The holistic position would thus extend Norton's argument to all future generations of both human and nonhuman life.

A Question of Responsibility

For Hans Jonas responsibility was the "key word for the ethics of human conduct in dealing with technology."[88] Our moral responsibility is supported by the grave consequences of many of our choices. Another example of the *interface* between human activities and ecological sustainability may be taken from an area where scientific uncertainty has been manipulated to discourage radical change: global warming and climate changes.[89] Climate changes have been engendered primarily by human-induced stress to natural systems. Their effects, now increasingly documented in scientific journals, show that they give rise to grave problems for human health, wildlife health and species survival, agricultural productivity and land capacity, ocean habitat degradation, and social upheavals due to severe weather conditions and turbulence (including floods and other catastrophes).[90]

At the outset it seems that no aggregate human preference could or would have supported policies intended to curtail the fast spread of the technologies that were eventually banned through the Montreal and the Copenhagen protocols. Only principles of noninterference and general respect for natural systems, land, air, and water might have made a difference. Dale Jamieson and others argue that "a stable climate, unlike standard commodities, is irreplaceable."[91] Thus, the basic needs of all life are at stake and, correspondingly, our responsibility should extend that far.

If the argument of this chapter can be accepted at least as a reasonable one, then certain consequences will follow, in regard to the evaluation of technology. A reevaluation of the limits of moral theory suggests, as I have argued, that the *primary* criterion for the evaluation of technology should be environmental and, specifically, ecological integrity. If this is accepted, then certain questions about our shared habitat must be raised in our evaluative assessments. They might include some of the following:

1. Has the uncertainty of post-normal science been incorporated in our assessment? Have we applied the precautionary principle?
2. Has the question of the sustainability of natural capital used by the proposed technology been asked and answered within the parameter suggested in (1)?
3. Does the technology to be evaluated exhibit any possible aspects suggesting a negative impact on life-support systems, that is, on the services they provide to all life?
4. Are there obvious or hidden possible threats to biodiversity within the proposed technology?
5. Have the technology's possible synergistic effects with other processes or technologies been evaluated together with its own separate impact?

These questions would be followed by the necessary questions based on traditional theories and values mentioned earlier and are therefore not intended as substitutes but as additional and, in fact, primary questions, followed by still other moral questions. We need to ask ourselves, in regard to each envisioned technology, whether it permits the preservation of sustainable, biodiverse life, *before* we ask whether it also permits moral interspecies dealings among humankind. In light of the arguments of the previous two sections, it seems to me these questions may provide a starting point and stimulate additional thought and research.

Notes

1. Carl Walters, "Fish on the Line," monograph published by the David Suzuki Corporation and the Fisheries Centre, University of British Columbia, Vancouver, BC, 1995.

2. *The Globe and Mail* (Toronto) (March 13, 1995), p. A1.

3. K. Redford and A. Stearman, "Forest Dwelling Native Amazonians and the Conservation of Biodiversity: Interests in Common or in Collision?" *Conservation Biology* 7, 2 (June 1993).

4. Robert Ulanowicz, "Ecosystem Integrity: A Causal Necessity," in *Perspectives on Ecological Integrity*, ed. L. Westra and J. Lemons (Dordrecht, The Netherlands: Kluwer, 1995), pp. 77–87.

5. Walters, "Fish on the Line," pp. 50–52.

6. M. Hammer, A. M. Jansson, and B. O. Jansson, "Diversity, Change and Sustainability: Implications for Fisheries," *Ambio* 22, 2–3 (May 1993).

7. L. Westra, *An Environmental Proposal for Ethics: The Principle of Integrity* (Lanham, MD: Rowman & Littlefield, 1994); see L. Westra "Ecosystem Integrity and Sustainability: The Foundational Value of the Wild," in *Perspectives on Ecological Integrity*, ed. L. Westra and J. Lemons.

8. Reed F. Noss, "What Should Endangered Ecosystems Mean to the Wildlands Project?" *Wild Earth* 5, 4 (Winter 1995/96): 21.

9. RIVM, *National Environmental Outlook, 1990–2010* (Bilthoven, The Netherlands: Rijksinstituut voor Volksgezondheid en Milieuhygiene, 1986).

10. D. A. Brown, "The Role of Law in Sustainable Development and Environmental Protection Decision Making," in *Sustainable Development: Science, Ethics and Public Policy* (Dordrecht, The Netherlands: Kluwer, 1995), pp. 64–76.

11. Robert Goodland, "Environmental Sustainability and the Power Sector—Part I: The Concept of Sustainability," *Impact Assessment* 12, 3 (1994): 276.

12. K. Shrader-Frechette, *Risk and Rationality* (Berkeley: University of California Press, 1991); see Alistair MacIntyre, "Corporate Modernity and Moral Judgment: Are They Mutually Exclusive?" in *Ethics and Problems of the 21st Century*, ed. K. Goodpaster and K. Sayre (Notre Dame, IN: University of Notre Dame Press, 1979), pp. 122–38; Kurt Baier, "Technology and the Sanctity of Life," in *Ethics and Problems of the 21st Century*, ed, K. Goodpaster and K. Sayre, pp. 160–74.

13. L. Westra, "Biotechnology and Transgenics in Agriculture and Aquaculture: The Perspective from Ecosystem Integrity," in *Environmental Values* (Lancaster, England: Lancaster University, White Horse Press, 1996).

14. J. B. Callicott, *In Defense of the Land Ethic* (Albany, NY: State of New York

University Press, 1989), especially "Traditional American Indian and Western European Attitudes Toward Nature: An Overview," pp. 177–201.

15. M. Sagoff, *The Economy of the Earth: Philosophy, Law and the Environment* (Cambridge, England: Cambridge University Press, 1988); see Robert Goodland and Herman Daly, "Why Northern Income Growth Is Not the Solution to Southern Poverty," World Bank Environment Department Divisional Working Paper, No. 1993–43, May 1993.

16. Sagoff, *The Economy of the Earth.*

17. D. Scherer and T. Attig, *Upstream/Downstream* (Philadelphia: Temple University Press, 1990).

18. Robert E. McGinn, "Technology, Demography, and the Anachronism of Traditional Rights," *Journal of Applied Philosophy* 11, 1 (1994): 57–70.

19. Walters, "Fish on the Line."

20. Bryan Norton, "Why I Am Not a Nonanthropocentrist: Callicott and the Failure of Monistic Inherentism," *Environmental Ethics* 17, 4 (Winter 1995): 341–58; see Bryan Norton, "Environmental Ethics and Weak Anthropocentris," *Environmental Ethics* 6, 2 (Summer 1984): 131–36, 138–48.

21. Goodland, "Environmental Sustainability and the Power Sector—Part I: The Concept of Sustainability," pp. 275–304.

22. McGinn, "Technology, Demography, and the Anachronism of Traditional Rights."

23. Eric T. Freyfogle, *Justice and the Earth: Images for Our Planetary Survival* (New York: Free Press, Macmillan, 1993), p. 27.

24. Freyfogle, *Justice and the Earth,* p. 29.

25. Freyfogle, *Justice and the Earth,* pp. 24–27.

26. W. E. Rees and M. Wackernagel, *Our Ecological Footprint* (Gabriola Island, BC: New Society, 1996).

27. M. Sagoff, "Carrying Capacity and Ecological Economics," *Bioscience* 45, 9 (October 1995): 610–20.

28. J. A. Hutchings and R. A. Myers, "What Can Be Learned from the Collapse of a Renewable Resource? Atlantic Cod, *Gadus Morhua,* of Newfoundland, Labrador," *Canadian Journal of Fisheries and Aquatic Science* 51 (1994): 2126–46; see Hammer, et al., "Diversity, Change and Sustainability: Implications for Fisheries"; M. C. Beveridge, M. Lindsay, G. Ross, and L. A. Kelly, "Aquaculture and Biodiversity," *Ambio* 23, 8 (December 1994): 497–502.

29. William Broad, "Creatures of the Deep Find Their Way to the Table," *New York Times* (December 26, 1995).

30. Rees and Wackernagel, *Our Ecological Footprint,* p. 16.

31. Rees and Wackernagel, *Our Ecological Footprint,* p. 4.

32. Rees and Wackernagel, *Our Ecological Footprint,* pp. 14–16.

33. Rees and Wackernagel, *Our Ecological Footprint,* pp. 55–57.

34. L. Westra and P. Wenz, *The Faces of Environmental Racism: The Global Equity Issues* (Lanham, MD: Rowman & Littlefield, 1995).

35. Westra, *An Environmental Proposal for Ethics*; see Freyfogle, *Justice and the Earth.*

36. Brown, "The Role of Law in Sustainable Development and Environmental Protection Decision Making."

37. Walters, "Fish on the Line."

38. Shrader-Frechette, *Risk and Rationality*.

39. R. Ulanowicz, *Ecology, The Ascendent Perspective* (New York: Columbia University Press, in press).

40. Brown, "The Role of Law in Sustainable Development and Environmental Protection Decision Making."

41. Thomas Muir and Anne Sudar, "Toxic Chemicals in the Great Lakes Basin Ecosystem," Environmental Canada, Burlington, Ontario, *Science Advisory Board Report to the International Joint Commission* 15–41 (1987), p. 18.

42. L. Westra, "Ecosystem Integrity and Sustainability: The Foundational Value of the Wild," in *Perspectives on Ecological Integrity*, ed. L. Westra and J. Lemons, pp. 12–13; Westra, *An Environmental Proposal for Ethics*, pp. 24–27, 41.

43. McGinn, "Technology, Demography, and the Anachronism of Traditional Rights."

44. Bryan Norton, *Toward Unity among Environmentalists* (New York: Oxford University Press, 1991), p. 222.

45. Brown, "The Role of Law in Sustainable Development and Environmental Protection Decision Making."

46. D. Pauly, "Principles of Marine Ecology Applied to the Establishment of Marine Fisheries Reserves." 125th Meeting of the American Fishery Society, Tampa (1995).

47. Westra, *An Environmental Proposal for Ethics*; Westra, "Ecosystem Integrity and Sustainability"; James Karr and Ellen Chu, "Ecological Integrity: Reclaiming Lost Connections," in *Perspectives on Ecological Integrity*, ed. L. Westra and J. Lemons, pp. 34–48.

48. Westra, *An Environmental Proposal for Ethics*.

49. Reed F. Noss, "The Wildlands Project: Land Conservation Strategy," *Wild Earth*, special issue (1992): 10–25; Reed F. Noss and A. Y. Cooperrider, *Saving Nature's Legacy* (Washington, DC: Island Press, 1994).

50. James J. Kay and E. Schneider, "The Challenge of the Ecosystem Approach," *Alternatives* 20, 3 (1994): 1–6; reprinted in *Perspectives on Ecological Integrity*, ed. L. Westra and J. Lemons, pp. 49–59.

51. Norton, *Toward Unity among Environmentalists*, p. 246.

52. Gary E. Varner, "Can Animal Rights Activists Be Environmentalists?" in *People, Penguins and Plastic Trees*, 2d ed. (Belmont, CA: Wadsworth, 1995), pp. 254–73.

53. Norton, *Toward Unity among Environmentalists*, p. 246.

54. Karr and Chu, "Ecological Integrity"; See Noss and Cooperrider, *Saving Nature's Legacy*; R. Noss, *Maintaining Ecological Integrity in Representative Reserve Networks*, A World Wildlife Fund Canada/World Wildlife Fund/United States Discussion Paper (January 1995).

55. Brown, "The Role of Law in Sustainable Development and Environmental Protection Decision Making," p. 67.

56. B. G. Norton, "A New Paradigm for Environmental Management," in *Ecosystem Health*, ed. R. Costanza, B. G. Norton, and B. D. Haskell (Washington, DC: Island Press, 1992), p. 24.

57. Hans Lenk, "Ecology and Ethics: Notes about Technology and Economic Consequences," with Matthias Maring, in *Research in Philosophy and Technology*, vol. 12 (Greenwich, CT: JAI Press, 1992), p. 210.

58. Norton, "Environmental Ethics and Weak Anthropocentris"; Norton, "Why I Am Not a Nonanthropocentrist: Callicott and the Failure of Monistic Inherentism."

59. See, for instance, W. Aiken, "Ethical Issues in Agriculture," in *Earthbound: New Introductory Essays in Environmental Ethics*, ed. Tom Regan (New York: Random House, 1984), pp. 247–88; T. Regan, *The Case for Animal Rights* (Berkeley: University of California Press, 1983), to mention but two other opponents of arguments for holism of the ecocentric/biocentric variety.

60. Norton, "Environmental Ethics and Weak Anthropocentris."

61. Norton, "Environmental Ethics and Weak Anthropocentris."

62. Regan, *The Case for Animal Rights*, p. 50; H. Rolston, *Environmental Ethics: Duties to and Values in the Natural World* (Philadelphia: Temple University Press, 1988); K. Goodpaster, "On Being Morally Considerable," *Journal of Philosophy* 75 (1978): 308–25; P. Taylor, *Respect for Nature: A Theory of Environmental Ethics* (Princeton: Princeton University Press, 1986).

63. Norton, "Why I Am Not a Nonanthropocentrist: Callicott and the Failure of Monistic Inherentism."

64. Noss, *Maintaining Ecological Integrity in Representative Reserve Networks*.

65. Klaus Meyer-Abich, *Revolution for Nature*, trans. M. Armstrong (Cambridge, England: White Horse Press, 1993).

66. A. Leopold, *A Sand County Almanac and Sketches Here and There* (New York: Oxford University Press, 1949).

67. Karr and Chu, "Ecological Integrity"; Kay and Schneider, "The Challenge of the Ecosystem Approach"; Ulanowicz, *Ecology, The Ascendent Perspective*.

68. Robert Goodland and Herman Daly, "Universal Environmental Sustainability and the Principle of Integrity," in *Perspectives on Ecological Integrity*, ed. L. Westra and J. Lemons (Dordrecht, The Netherlands: Kluwer, 1995), pp. 102–24.

69. Goodland, "Environmental Sustainability and the Power Sector—Part I: The Concept of Sustainability"; Westra, "Ecosystem Integrity and Sustainability: The Foundational Value of the Wild."

70. Lenk, "Ecology and Ethics: Notes about Technology and Economic Consequences."

71. K. Shrader-Frechette, *Nuclear Power and Public Policy* (Dordrecht, The Netherlands: Kluwer, 1982); Shrader-Frechette, *Risk and Rationality*; McGinn, "Technology, Demography, and the Anachronism of Traditional Rights."

72. Noss and Cooperrider, *Saving Nature's Legacy*; Lenk, "Ecology and Ethics: Notes about Technology and Economic Consequences."

73. E. Partridge, "On the Rights of Future Generations," in *Upstream/Downstream*, ed. D. Scherer and T. Attig (Philadelphia: Temple University Press, 1990), pp. 40–66; Richard De George, "The Environment, Rights and Future Generations," in *Ethics and Problems of the 21st Century*, ed. K. E. Goodpaster and K. M. Sayre, pp. 93–105; Ruth Macklin, "Can Future Generations Correctly Be Said To Have Rights?" in *Responsibilities to Future Generations*, ed. E. Partridge

(Buffalo, NY: Prometheus Books, 1981); Gregory Kavka, "The Paradox of Future Individuals," *Philosophy and Public Affairs* 2, 2 (Spring 1982): 92–112; Derek Parfit, *Reasons and Persons* (Oxford, England: Oxford University Press, 1984).

74. Norton, "Why I Am Not a Nonanthropocentrist: Callicott and the Failure of Monistic Inherentism."

75. De George, "The Environment, Rights and Future Generations."

76. L. Westra, "Integrity, Health and Sustainability: Environmentalism without Racism," in *The Science of the Total Environment,* for the World Health Organization (Oxford, England: Elsevier, 1990); Rita Colwell, "Global Change: Emerging Diseases and New Epidemics," President's Lecture, February 10, 1996, American Association for the Advancement of Science; Janice D. Longstretch, et al., "Effects of Increased Solar Ultraviolet Radiation on Human Health," *Ambio* 24, 3 (May 1995): 153–65.

77. C. Van der Weele, *Images of Development—Environmental Causes in Ontogeny* (Amsterdam: Free University of Amsterdam Press, 1995).

78. Van der Weele, *Images of Development,* p. 8.

79. Van der Weele, *Images of Development,* p. 9.

80. Theo Colborn, Dianne Dumanoski, John Peterson Myers, *Our Stolen Future* (New York: Dutton, 1996), p. 186.

81. Colborn, Dumanoski, and Myers, *Our Stolen Future,* p. 89.

82. Colborn, Dumanoski, and Myers, *Our Stolen Future,* pp. 88–89.

83. Colborn, Dumanoski, and Myers, *Our Stolen Future,* p. 81.

84. Colborn, Dumanoski, and Myers, *Our Stolen Future,* p. 83.

85. Colborn, Dumanoski, and Myers, *Our Stolen Future,* pp. 85–86.

86. Colborn, Dumanoski, and Myers, *Our Stolen Future,* pp. 251–60.

87. Jon Cohen, "Tobacco Money Lights Up a Debate," *Science* 272, "Special News Report" (April 26, 1996): 488–94.

88. Hans Jonas, *The Imperative of Responsibility* (Chicago: University of Chicago Press, 1984).

89. Dale Jamieson, "Managing the Future: Public Policy, Scientific Uncertainty, and Global Warming," in *Upstream/Downstream,* ed. D. Scherer and T. Attig, pp. 67–89; Dale Jamieson, "Ethics, Public Policy and Global Warming," *Science, Technology and Human Values* 17 (1992): 139–53.

90. Westra, "Integrity, Health and Sustainability: Environmentalism without Racism."

91. John Lemons, R. Heredia, D. Jamieson, and C. Spash, "Climate Change and Sustainable Development," in *Sustainable Development: Science, Ethics and Public Policy,* ed. John Lemons and D. Brown (Dordrecht, The Netherlands: Kluwer, 1995), 167.

9

Consumption and the Practice of Land Health

Eric T. Freyfogle

Any inquiry into the ethics of consumption is likely to focus on obvious matters of personal virtue and interpersonal equity. In the case of natural-resource consumption, however, there is an initial, foundational issue having to do with the land itself, with the source from which the natural resources come. In some manner a sound ethic of consumption needs to build upon an ethical orientation toward the land. How that might come about is the subject of this chapter.

The chief aim of most environmental ethics is the promotion of land health. An ethical consumption pattern, then, would be one that (among other traits) is consistent with the achievement of land health. I use the term *land health* largely for the same reasons others do— because of its shorthand convenience and its useful overtones; because it encompasses, howbeit vaguely, the kind of durable, flourishing, self-recreating communal life that is the mark of a lasting link between people and place. The difficulty here, both with the term and with any endeavor to achieve it, is that land health is not an easy matter to come to grips with, particularly when land is understood as the entire ecological community in a place, including the human members. Land health is not a precise scientific concept, capable of exact definition; it is an elusive vision as much as it is a technical measure. This imprecision, however, does not give cause to abandon land health as a foundational limit on consumption and other human conduct. It gives reason instead to develop more practical ways of describing and fostering land health— ways that take into account human ignorance, ways that can better promote, in real human communities, the very virtues and community self-reflection upon which land health ultimately depends.

The poet Gary Snyder offered an observation some years back that provides a useful beginning point for this inquiry. Philosophy, Snyder claimed, is essentially a "place-based exercise."[1] It sounds like an old idea—I hope it is an old idea—although I do not know where Snyder got it. A second starting text is an admonition made by Alexander Pope, often quoted by farm researcher Wes Jackson: "Let nature never be forgot," Pope said, and "consult the genius of the Place in all."[2] Land health, I want to suggest, is most likely to arise in places and among people who develop a "place-based" ethic toward the land, informed by science but guided as much by humble virtue. And this kind of ethic is most likely to emerge among a people who "consult the genius" of their local land, who listen to the land and actively seek out its wisdom even while they pursue their own human aspirations. Land health, in short, is best understood in practical terms, as a way of residing responsibly on the land over the long term, as a practical means by which a community elevates and puts into place its shared vision of right living.

In any ethic of natural-resource consumption, land health ought to supply an important foundational limit. Beyond that and just as important, consumption needs to respect the community-based mechanisms by which land health is fostered: Consumption needs to occur in such a way that local people everywhere have the power and opportunity to develop an ethic of place and translate that ethic into local action—without undue pressures for ethical compromise. As I note briefly in the concluding section, the reasoning that leads to these conclusions also offers insight on matters closely related to consumption, including issues of private land ownership and free trade.

Environmentalism and Community

Social thought in the Western world has long displayed a tension between the individual and the community, whether the community is a two-person married couple, or a larger family, or a tribe or village or religious congregation or something larger still. Environmentalism comes down strongly on the side of the community; it is, or if better understood would be, one of the dominant strands today of communitarian thought. Ecology's first lesson, endlessly repeated, is the lesson of interconnection and interdependence. Although the individual organism does exist in ecological thought and it makes sense at times to study the discrete individual, no individual being exists in isolation. The links among organisms are many, some easily noted, some impossible to trace. Indeed, so extensive and vital are these links that it is more apt to describe an organism not as a separate being but as the sum of its interactions with its physical and biological surroundings: as process, as much or more than substance.

There are two important implications to this ecological reality of interconnection. One implication is that, in the natural order, the whole is far more than its parts. There *is* such a thing as a natural community, however much trouble we might have in describing it, and humans are part of that community, as dependent on the functioning and productivity of the community as any other organism. The second implication is that more or less every human activity, however private and individual, has public repercussions to it. Any activity undertaken on the land is in important part a public activity, even when the land is privately owned.[3] A landowner cannot cut trees, or drain a field, or mow weeds without altering the community of life that includes her land. Given this inevitable interconnection, it is easy to see why communities have a legitimate interest in the use of land. If a human community is to thrive, it has to have the ability, and faces the practical obligation, to promote the health of the land around it. For people to be healthy, the land needs to be healthy. As a prudential matter at least, land health is a worthy goal.

One of the central challenges of environmental ethics, when it deals with matters of community action or community health, is to give content to the idea of community, to figure out the criteria of membership.[4] Who is included in the category of organisms or entities whose well-being is the chief aim of an environmental ethic? Here we have the extensive literature on future generations, animal welfare, the moral worth of species and ecological communities, and the like. We also have the questions about the human role in recognizing value, and whether value can exist without a subjective valuer. The more immediate and practical challenge is to figure out who participates in the decision-making process—who gets to help decide how the community will conduct its affairs? We might want to recognize moral worth in future generations, but we cannot expect unborn people to show up at public hearings. We might let spotted owls have standing in the courtroom, but a human advocate must do the talking. The reality, plainly, is that only adult humans living today are going to decide how the community will behave. The humans who live in a place, and whose lives are intertwined with the place, are going to be the ones who participate in the conversation about land health. These people, or some subset of them, are going to need to get together and talk about the matter, sharing their wisdom, offering their ethical perspectives, and muddling along as best they can.

In practical terms, then, we know *who* is going to decide how best to promote the community's well-being—the people who make up the community, acting directly or indirectly, alone or together. And although we do not know exactly whose moral worth is going to be taken into account, it is hard to imagine a sound environmental ethic that does not adopt a relatively holistic perspective on this issue of value, that does not seek to promote the well-being of the whole, as either an intrinsic or an instrumental good. There will always be debates about how much of nature needs protecting and preserving for the land to remain a fruitful place for human life. There will be debates too about what it means to live a virtuous life and what we need to do in order to fulfill our duties, if any, to future generations and other species. But I want to set all of this aside and concentrate here on the overlaps among the many ethical schemes. To one degree or another, all of them place value on what is variously termed the land or the ecosystem or the biotic community. All of them recognize the ecological principle of interdependence, and thus see the need to promote the well-being of the collective whole, whether as an end result or as a means of promoting the health of certain parts.

The Challenges of Unruly Nature

Land health would be an easier goal to achieve, and indeed easier even to recognize as the primary goal that it is, if it were not such a messy matter. Ideally we could simply haul in the ecologists as expert witnesses, and have them explain what it means for a land community to be healthy. Ecology, though, has no such simple answers, as useful and indispensable as it nonetheless is. Ecology no longer embraces, if it ever really did, the stable, climax community as a guiding paradigm of community well-being, and it rarely refers any longer to the land as organism except in metaphorical terms.[5] Nature is more variable than the old climax-community and organismic models suggested, and its modes and methods are not so easily learned.[6] In fact, modern ecology might seem to cast doubt on the entire idea that there is such a thing as an identifiable natural community that can be more or less healthy, as opposed to just a fluctuating collection of competing organisms, some succeeding better than others.[7] Native communities shift over time; not just individual organisms, but species and groups of species come and go in a given place. The composition of a given biological community can depend on many factors, including the order in which species first appear on a site, which means there is often more than one mature community possible in a given place.[8] When organismic ideas held greatest sway, researchers tended to downplay the importance of factors that disrupted the community, such as fire, storm, disease, pests, and alien species. A fuller ecological understanding includes these disturbance regimes; once they are added back, vegetative climaxes appear more transient and less central. A fire-cleared forest in early stages of vegetative succession is no less "natural" than a mature forest that experiences little observable short-term change.

Aside from this new emphasis on disequilibrium, ecology today also challenges the general notion of land health by showing more clearly how frequently individual species alter their environments. As particular communities evolve they not only affect the species that compose them but they are themselves influenced by their constituent species, sometimes dramatically so. This heightened scholarly attention to species-ecosystem interactions raises an inevitable and seemingly awkward question: if other dominant species can alter their environments—if they do not, and apparently need not, leave their environments unchanged—is it not equally natural for humans to alter their home environments? If oaks and pines, if elephants and gorillas, affect the mix of plants and animals around them, cannot humans do the same? For a species to act in accordance with nature and with the humility expected of such a species, is it in fact necessary to minimize disruption?

Despite these new emphases in ecology—on disequilibrium and on the interpenetration of individual species and community—it remains clear today that natural communities do exist and that they have features and functions that are susceptible to identification. Even ecologists who firmly embrace the idea of disequilibrium are well aware that the natural elements that exist in a given place are more than just a collection of parts, randomly bouncing about.[9] They fit together more snugly than this, in an interdependent way that does create a collective whole and does possess definable characteristics, even if that whole lacks the stability and other attributes of a single organism. As biological and physical elements interact in a given place they give rise to ever-larger levels of biological complexity, and to emergent properties that were not present at the lower levels of organization.[10] Hydrogen and oxygen come together as water, which has properties not present in the two elements separately. Individual bees in isolation do not show the social order and social functioning that are present when they form a hive. Prairie plants fix nitrogen and produce carbohydrates better when acting together than any organism does acting alone. Moving up the level of organization, step by step, emergent properties arise that were not present in, and often not even predictable in, lower levels of organization.

Aiding our understanding on this matter of community are the relatively new disciplines of conservation and population biology, which are slowly deciphering how species fluctuate in numbers and what it takes for particular species to survive.[11] The usual answer is that populations and species need more than just food and shelter: They need particular kinds of habitat, often with particular kinds of hydrological cycles and disturbance regimes, which in turn means, given the pervasiveness of human disruption, that many species can survive today only when a large landscape is actively managed to mimic the natural features with which they evolved. Many species play specialty roles in a community—a reality that provides further evidence of community structure—and they depend for their existence on the continuation of part or much or all of that community.

The new ecology, then, does not so much reject the ideas of land community and land health as render the ideas more difficult to comprehend. It gives reason not to halt community-level study but to work harder at it. One group of scholars at the forefront of this endeavor is seeking to bring meaning to the unruly subject of ecosystem health, and a new journal now focuses entirely on the subject.[12] Other scholars continue to explore the matter of ecological integrity, as a scientific as well as an ethical guideline.[13] Conservation biologists typically work at the species or population level, rather than at the community level, but their lessons have great value in understanding community functioning. Restoration ecologists have gained perhaps the most experience in manipulating communities, as they have sought to replace wetlands and otherwise to reconstruct damaged ecological communities, usually with the aim of improving the health and functioning of larger landscapes.[14]

In brief form, what scientists have learned is that a healthy natural community has a capacity to resist and recover from stress.[15] It typically uses energy and nutrients with high degrees of efficiency, and loses its efficiency, sometimes dramatically so, when materially disturbed. A healthy community has a capacity for self-renewal; it is, in important ways, self-organizing and self-recreating. What is also clear from this scientific work is that humans and many other species depend for their survival not just on particular other species and physical processes, but on the complexities and emergent properties that arise within the community structure. We could not live if we disassembled the natural community around us into its billions of individual parts, and then lined up the parts on the shelves of a huge resource storeroom, taking them down as needed. Too much would be lost in the disassembly.

Despite the progress made in understanding ecosystem health and community functioning, it remains clear that our ignorance of the natural order is vast. Endeavor as we will, our ignorance is not diminishing by much in comparative terms, and nature will long exceed our intellectual grasp. We need to admit this reality. We need to find ways of making decisions that take it into account, ways of deciding that do not look solely to what we know. We need to prepare ourselves to deal with the mistakes that will inevitably happen, leaving room for second chances.

This ignorance about nature does not mean simply that our science is incomplete, and that we cannot know exactly what it means for the land to be healthy. It means that our ethical schemes are incomplete as well. Whether we think in consequentialist terms, or in rights-based terms, or find moral worth in future generations or other species, our ethical calculations are essentially knowledge based. If it matters to us, for example, whether animals have a particular level of mental functioning, we need to know whether they do or do not possess it. If we want to promote the best overall consequences for humans or some other gathering of organisms, we need to be able to trace the consequences of alternative courses of action, and sort out the useful from the harmful, and then add everything up in an overall calculation of utility. The problem with all of these approaches is that they do not tell us what to do when the knowledge runs out. They do not tell us how to fill in gaps in the calculation when we simply do not have the needed data. At some point, moving down almost any ethical course, the knowledge runs out and the darkness begins. We need guidance on peering into that dark; we need guidance on extrapolating from the known to the unknown.

It is at this point that a practical orientation, one that ranks good results about theoretical purity, can lend a useful hand. Practically speaking we have reason to wonder whether the principal contending ethical schemes are really pointing us in noticeably different directions.[16] The points of beginning are far different, to be sure, and the respective paths cover different terrain. But when the knowledge in each case runs out, when we extrapolate from where we end up, peering through the darkness to the end of the path, one wonders really how different the end places are. Readers of Aldo Leopold's land ethic have argued for years whether Leopold did or did not embrace a biocentric world view, or whether he was decidedly anthropocentric and instrumental in his thought. There are traces of many ethical views in Leopold's writing—biocentric, utilitarian, and sentiment- or virtue-based—and yet Leopold had no trouble drawing them together into his land ethic. We can balk at this, of course, and complain that Leopold was simply not sensitive enough to the differences among the various lines of ethical thought. Leopold has already faced similar criticism, for mixing metaphors—depicting nature sometimes in mechanical terms, sometimes in organic ones. But perhaps Leopold was right to assume implicitly that the various ethical strands led to the same general place, to the health of the larger community of which humans and everything else are parts. He could not prove it, to be sure. He could not prove that, in the long run, humans will thrive better in a healthy biotic community. He could not prove that the community would be healthier if humans acted to promote its integrity, stability, and beauty. But he was well aware of his own ignorance and the ignorance of his scientific profession, and he understood the need to extrapolate from the known to the unknown. His land ethic was the way he ultimately proposed for dealing with the darkness, a practical guide for right living on the land.[17]

Given these evident similarities among environmental ethics, and given too what we know about natural communities, it seems expedient if not morally obligatory for us to put a high premium on the well-being of natural communities. We are, in short, wise if not duty-bound to promote land health.[18] As we confront this task, however, we need to understand that land health does not arise from any particular theory of ecosystem functioning, nor is it an idea that will ever have much precision to it. The goal is an elusive one, and we can aim only at a rough approximation of it. Indeed, it might prove more useful, particularly for nonscientists working on the land, to think of land health as more of an ethic than a state of existence, as a practical orientation, as an attitude of caring and humility toward that land that respects the land as an older partner and tries to work with it and learn from it. Land health is best pursued by trial and error, by a community of people working together to learn about the land and trying in good faith to foster its well-being. Using this kind of adaptive management, local people need to organize themselves by watershed or in some other way that makes sense in nature's terms. They need to share their knowledge and values and suggestions. They need to coordinate their efforts, remaining watchful as they do so, paying attention to what they have done and adjusting their behavior when the consequences seem misguided.

Probing Nature's Wisdom

The practical question, the one faced every day by ordinary people in ways little and big, is how to use the land without diminishing the health of the surrounding natural community. As a matter of politics and power, it makes good sense for people to discuss land use as a community concern, and not just make decisions in isolation. When people gather as a community they are more likely to think of the overall good and give weight to the long term.[19] This is not to claim that individuals acting alone will never follow an ethical path, but individual decision making tends to be more self-centered and present-oriented. We have plenty of empirical evidence on that point, as well as evidence that decisions made by people as citizens can differ widely from their decisions as individual consumers. Even in the United States, with its pronounced focus on the liberated individual, there remains a reasonably vibrant strand of civic republican thought in which leaders are expected to rise above self-interest and consider the long-term good of the whole. Some of the most promising practical work going on today in the environmental field is precisely of this type—people coming together, as a community, to consider the well-being of their watershed or ecosystem, and trying to find ways to improve it.

Although the matter cannot be explored here at length, there is good reason to believe that large-scale land use is best undertaken by allowing nonhuman nature to stand as a rough measure of how land ought to be used in a given place. In deciding how to use the land, we ought to make nature our measure, as Wendell Berry so often says.[20] We ought to consult the genius of the place in all, to borrow Alexander Pope's line. We ought to act on the assumption that nature has evolved solutions to fit the climate, terrain, soils, and hydrology of a place, so that life can thrive there.[21]

Using nature as a measure, it needs stating, is far different from viewing wilderness as an ideal for land health, with any human alteration of the land viewed as degradation. Indeed, it is not to suggest even that there still is such a thing as true wilderness, completely unaffected by human life. Substantially wild areas do possess special value, both as places to study and as vital elements in sustaining the well-being of the larger landscape. But much can be learned about ecological processes and community structure, even in places where humans have lived for millennia. The wisdom embedded in nature can be teased out through practical work almost everywhere. Far from exalting wilderness as the one and true healthy landscape, nature-as-measure proposes a way of drawing upon nature for guidance that nonetheless allows humans to make alterations on the land. It features a way of learning from nature that leaves room for humans to play a role in directing the continuing evolution of the natural communities that they help form. It deserves mention too that nature-as-measure does not require the retention of all species that are native to a place. Many species play important community roles, and the community would be diminished by their loss. Moreover, to the extent that land health transcends the scientific and instrumental and becomes an ethical or aesthetic ideal, the preservation of all native species can be part of that ideal—a part that a given human community might well value highly. But community health does not depend on the continued presence of each and every constituent species. Nature is more flexible and resilient than this; so long as they act cautiously and humbly, humans have room in which to maneuver.

It is possible to cite many examples of how humans can benefit by tailoring their practices so as to draw on nature's wisdom. It is becoming

clear, for instance, that nature's ways of dealing with rainfall are worth
studying and following, far more closely than we have in the past. Problems with flooding, soil loss, sedimentation, stream-bank erosion and
the like are all related to human practices that have defied nature's ways
of controlling the flow of water and retaining vital topsoil. One of the
best ongoing efforts to use nature as a measure or model is being undertaken at the Land Institute, in central Kansas, where Wes Jackson and
his team of researchers are developing a form of agriculture modeled
on the local tallgrass prairie, a form of agriculture that, like the prairie,
features perennial polycultures rather than annual monocultures.[22] His
work and the complex thought that gives rise to it deserve careful study,
even by people whose concerns are far removed from the well-being of
Midwestern farmlands. Jackson is not out to duplicate the prairie: He is
out to learn from it. Native prairies do a far better job than Kansas
wheatfields in retaining and using moisture, in preserving and building
soil, and in using nutrients efficiently. The native prairie is not much
bothered by insect pests and generates its own fertility. Perhaps the
closer our agriculture mimics the tallgrass prairie, the more likely it too
can possess these desirable features. Jackson's project is a long-term one,
for it is far from easy to figure out what makes a natural community
work as it does. What is clear is that a community is more than its parts,
and that a community cannot be understood simply by studying its individual parts. The issue, when studying a plant, is not principally what it
can do in isolation, but how it performs and participates in its community.

The approach taken by Wes Jackson and others like him entails a process of asking questions and looking for answers, a process that has come
to be called adaptive management.[23] As John Cobb explains, "We cannot
learn from [nature] except as we ask questions, and we have to be ready
to have the questions revised by the answers."[24] Wendell Berry offers
the same observation in his call for an agriculture centered around a
conversation with the land, a form of interaction that treats nature as
equal subject, not mere object:

> An agriculture using nature, including human nature, as its measure
> would approach the world in the manner of a conversationalist. It would
> not impose its vision and its demands upon a world that it conceives of as
> a stockpile of raw material, inert and indifferent to any use that may be
> made of it. It would not proceed directly or soon to some supposedly ideal
> state of things. It *would* proceed directly and soon to serious thought about
> our condition and our predicament. The use of a place would necessarily
> change, and the response of the place to that use would necessarily change
> the user. The conversation itself would thus assume a kind of creaturely

life, binding the place and its inhabitants together, changing and growing to no end, no final accomplishment, that can be conceived or foreseen.[25]

This kind of attitude toward the land appears to fit well with the lessons of contemporary ecology. It also fits well with, and helps carry forth, certain older ways of dealing with the land, what historian Carolyn Merchant terms the mimetic tradition.[26] Mimesis, the process of imitation, features a more experiential, intuitive approach toward the land, an attitude in which people participate with and in the land and are less detached from it.

Like the mimetic tradition described by Professor Merchant, like the nature-as-measure work of Wes Jackson, like the farming-as-conversation ethic of Wendell Berry, the practice of land health that I describe takes seriously the idea of natural community, not to the exclusion of seeing individual organisms and species but as a vital complement to it. It counsels an internal perspective, in which users of the land see themselves as community members, as parts of something much larger than themselves.[27] They are, as Merchant summarizes, "neither helpless victims nor arrogant dominators of nature but active participants in the destiny of the systems of which they are a part."[28]

Just as the idea of land health will remain vague due to our ignorance of nature, so too we cannot expect the practice of land health to occur as a predictable process, recurring regularly and following worn paths. It will be messier than this, and yet perhaps become more flexible and vibrant because of its messiness. Even to call the practice of land health a process is to give it an undue aura of rules and formality. In successful operation it would become a way of communal life, an acted-out expression of communal being and hope, a shared attempt to chart a course for human life that sustains the long-term functioning of natural systems. Out of this practice would emerge a place-based philosophy of the type that Gary Snyder commended, an ethic of care based on the local land and arising out of the people who live on that land. Good science is essential to this endeavor, as are attentive eyes and a willingness to work, but local practice will give rise to land health only if it calls forth the highest ethical aspirations of a gathered people. Regardless of place, an ethic of care will need a liberal dose of humility and restraint—a willingness to accept limits while relishing the diverse life that flourishes within and because of those limits.

Many local communities, of course, do not display this kind of ethical humility, nor do they typically have available the kind of good science that land health needs. For the practice of land health to succeed, many changes will be needed in terms of community functioning and the dissemination of technical expertise, and much of that change will not come easily.[29] Americans value their liberties highly, particularly their independence as landowners, and they lack many of the community traditions that exist elsewhere in the world.[30] They retain, in particular, no tradition of the locally managed commons, a tradition that, if it existed, could serve as an excellent point of beginning.[31] Nonetheless, Americans are accustomed to dealing with problems through local, democratic action, and they do have a sense that land-use issues are best addressed by and through local government units.[32] What they need are stimulants to get together, to study the condition of their local land and become more familiar with its problems.[33] Without an awareness of local problems, they are unlikely to see any need for change. Without opportunities to talk and exchange ideas and hopes, they are unlikely to take a longer perspective and otherwise elevate their ethical goals.

Where no settled communities exist to begin this kind of conversation, or in the case of communities that are so weakened by economic declines or so pushed by outside forces that they can hardly look beyond the next dollar, more significant changes will plainly be needed. But the reality seems to be that land health simply will not come about unless local people want it to and are prepared to work for it.[34] The practice of land health in some way must engage their energies and visions. If local people are not involved, if they do not understand the problems and play a role in finding the answers, they are likely to subvert the project, either politically or by living in ways that cut against the long-term goals. Getting local people involved, then, is a necessary element in the practice of land health, although far from a sufficient one. In any event, land health is a vision that requires tailoring to a given place, and it leaves room for humans living in that place to make choices about their lives and the kind of landscape they want. If only to help make these choices and to acknowledge the moral dignity of local residents, land health must be primarily a locally based endeavor. Whatever the weaknesses of local communities and the challenges of coaxing them to act, the alternative solutions all seem even less promising. Top-down decision making, the detailed regulatory approach that tells people exactly how to live, is unlikely to make much headway against sustained local resistance. No amount of regulation can turn a devoted land abuser into an attentive, sensitive steward. Only caring, community, science, experience, and good luck can do that.

Aside from the challenges posed by local communities that are ill-equipped or indisposed to promote land health, there are the related problems that arise when even well-focused communities lack the power to control their destiny. In a world of big business, free trade, and mobile capital and labor, local economies are regularly buffeted by external forces. Local producers must often compete in the market with outsiders who are beyond the reach of local norms and rules, which means that local power faces limits. For land health to come about, work is needed at all levels of government, from the most local to the global. Or to put the matter in other terms, citizens must come together in communities of varying sizes, the more local the better, but in all cases at a level that is sufficiently large and potent to perform successfully the needed work of developing and enforcing land-sustaining norms. A given citizen will not be part of just one community; he will be part of many communities of varying size. Although the main practice of land heath will typically occur locally, local efforts will commonly need high-level support and guidance, aimed not just at disseminating good science and prompting local action but at enhancing local autonomy and protecting local efforts from external disruption.

The Ethics of Resource Consumption

A discussion of ethics and resource consumption must address land health and conservation, limits on free trade, nonrenewable resources, and private property rights.

Land Health and Conservation

This line of thinking about land health, as idea and as local practice, provides useful guidance on the subject of resource consumption. In the case of renewable natural resources, overall consumption should be limited by the maximum productivity of the land consistent with the continued health of that land, with the land's maximum yield determined and redetermined from time to time by the local practice I describe. This approach has obvious similarities with the idea of conservation, as embraced and popularized in the United States during the Progressive Era.[35] But there are important differences.

First, as compared with conservation the practice of land health includes a far greater appreciation of human ignorance, a greater sense that nature is sufficiently complex as to require more restrained decision-making practices, principally ones that draw extensively and more humbly upon the genius of the place.

Second, there is a greater appreciation for the parts of nature that were once considered worthless, the pieces that have no market value and that play no obvious role in the production of marketable products. We tended to view these parts as worthless because we thought about them and valued them as discrete items, detached from their ecological homes. Once we start thinking about overall land health, once we embrace a community perspective and admit our limited knowledge of how that community functions, it becomes clear that we need to take a more humble and inclusive view. We need to see that many elements of nature are important because of their community roles, because they help give rise to the higher levels of biological complexity, the emergent properties, that characterize a healthy biological community. We need to realize, importantly, that when we consume natural resources and manipulate the land to produce those resources, we are not just harvesting particular individual species: We are interfering with a community, and while we have no choice but to do so, we can act more wisely than we have done in the past.

A third and related difference is that the approach I advocate counsels us to return more of the land's produce back to the land, to reduce our consumption in a place so as to allow the natural community to function in a healthy manner. Given the importance of community functioning, given the importance within the community of many parts that were once thought dispensable, we need to allow the community of nature to have its own internal needs met first.[36] We need to respect hydrological cycles; we need to leave room for the plants and other species that help the community build and retain its valuable soil; we need to leave room for the many forms of wildlife that help the community resist stress and maintain its ability to recreate. Much of the land's yield needs to stay with the land to promote its health; we cannot assume that all of nature's production is ours for the taking.

Aside from these factors that set limits on how much we take from the land, we have the constraints that arise from the need to promote and protect local decision making—an even bigger difference between the practice here proposed and the central strand of conservation thought. The practice of land health requires people to come together to talk about their natural home and help chart its future. Consumption rates would be subject to this political process. Consumption would be limited by the maximum yield of the land as that land is managed by the adaptive-management decisions of the local community. Local people need to have the power to live ethically, and outsiders should face an obligation to allow them to do so. Outsiders must respect these local activities and allow them to continue without material interference—economic, legal, political, or otherwise—except perhaps in the rare case in which a local community unfairly limits the production of resources (e.g., foodstuffs) that are desperately needed by outsiders.

Limits on Free Trade

This general principle—allowing local people to act responsibly in their dealings with the land—is one that does not fit well with prevailing ideas of free trade. The conflict, very briefly, has to do chiefly with whether outsiders have a right to enter a local market with their goods if by doing so they disrupt local efforts to care for the land. There are two related possibilities here, one more objectionable than the other but both with troubling ripples. The outside producer could simply have an economic advantage, and by producing a good more cheaply render the local producer unable to compete, thereby forcing the local producer either to leave the business or, worse, to lower production costs by disrupting the local land's health—by becoming, that is, an irresponsible community member. The second, more objectionable and perhaps more likely possibility is that the outside producer would gain an advantage over the local producer by misusing distant land in some way, thereby again encouraging the local producer to do the same locally to stay competitive, thus disrupting the local autonomy on which land health depends. In either case, local efforts to promote land health are endangered by outside producers: Trade limits may be needed to allow local communities to act responsibly.

Aside from free trade's impacts on local autonomy, there are the related effects of long-distance trade on popular consciousness. When local people consume what they have locally produced, they are likely to have a greater attachment to the land, a greater sense of how their lives affect the land and how far they can push the land without diminishing its yields. When goods travel around the world, consumers have no such senses. They care about the good itself, chiefly if not solely, and not how and where it was produced or what impacts its production had on its place of origin. In this sense, trade promotes irresponsibility, not by design but as a typical side effect. When people produce for the market, they are more tempted to ignore the land's limits and extract what they can, particularly when the managers in charge are not local community members and when they employ discount rates that reduce the long-term future into insignificance. Their problems are not insurmountable, but they make responsible local action all the more difficult.

Nonrenewable Resources

Most of the resources that we draw from nature are taken from functioning biological communities, but there are some resources that are not. These other resources, nonbiological and largely drawn from below the land's surface, require separate consideration on ethical grounds. When a resource is not part of a functioning ecosystem—like copper, or gold, or petroleum, or gravel—its removal does not raise directly the same issue of land health. Whether a vein of copper does or does not remain in the ground presumably has little effect on the functioning of the biotic community on the overlying surface. In the case of such re-sources, the relevant environmental concerns arise, not from the fact of their consumption, but from the methods of extracting the resources from the ground and from the side effects of their consumption. Mining can be terrifically damaging to the environment and raises important concerns of land health. In addition, when a resource is consumed—petroleum is a good example—the byproducts are often pollutants, and the emission of those pollutants raises further environmental concerns.

The consumption of these resources needs to be set by the land's ability to absorb the ill effects of this extraction and this consumption, rather than by any need to retain in place a stockpile of these re-sources.[37] And decisions about that, about where and how mining might be done and how resources might be consumed to minimize pollution, need to be set as part of the practice of promoting land health. These decisions, then, are also ones in which the human community needs to have an important say. Issues of land health, then, also affect the consumption of nonrenewable natural resources.

Consuming Nonlocal Resources

The comments so far about consumption have all been based on the premise that a community's consumption of nature is drawn entirely from the yield of the local land. This premise is faulty, plainly, for it ignores the common situation in which a community consumes natural resources produced elsewhere. The practice of land health described here would set the limits of the land's yield in a given place. If land health were practiced in every place, we would then have an overall (albeit changing) limit on planetary consumption. Are there limits, how-ever, on consumption in one locale if communities elsewhere are willing to export their produce to that locale?

The answer to this question depends on the matter of local power and autonomy, as well as on issues of interpersonal fairness. It would plainly be wrong for people of great wealth to purchase so much food in a distant community—to outbid, that is, local purchasers—that the people of that community were left starving. A greater likelihood is that mem-bers of a community might forgo the production of food and other ne-cessities, concentrate their work on a single commodity for export, and earn so little cash from their export that they cannot satisfy their mini-mal needs. Situations like these implicate issues of land health when local people lose meaningful control of their land due to economic con-ditions. The good practice of land health requires a minimum level of local autonomy, enough independence so that local people can live sen-sibly without sapping the vigor of the surrounding natural community.

When market forces undercut this ability, when they drive a community to choose between land health and a decent life, the market becomes ethically problematic, and so does the conduct of distant consumers whose wants fuel the market.

Much more needs saying on this issue, but local autonomy and the successful practice of land health must be critical components of that discussion.

Private Property Rights

The issue of consumption often arises in the context of questions of production, which in turn implicates the matter of private property rights in land. How much is consumed is directly linked to the supply, which depends very much on choices made by individual landowners, exercising their private rights.

Environmentalism in general, and the practice of land health described here, propose important limits on private rights.[38] They also propose particular obligations on landowners in terms of helping to make and carry out local decisions.[39] Given the reality of ecological interdependence and the need for joint action to promote land health, it is simply not possible to think about private land as an isolated enclave, operated by an autonomous, unrestrained owner. To the contrary, land ownership ought to entail membership in something larger, in the surrounding human community and in the larger natural community that the land, and the land's owner, help compose. Land ownership ought to mean belonging; it ought to entail a willingness to share in the burdens of sustaining the health and well-being of these communities.

Private property, to be sure, serves important economic and other instrumental goals. It has also long performed certain civic functions, acting as a counterbalance to excessive state power and as a means of dividing economic and political power so as to promote a stable, representative government. But these functions can all be performed fully without sacrificing the community's need to promote the health of local land. Owners can retain sufficient economic autonomy and personal privacy on their lands without any need to insulate them from the community's insistence that they select land-use options that promote the overall well-being. Perhaps the key point to be made here is that a local community can practice land health only if it has a sizeable degree of control over the use of local lands. It must exercise that control fairly, but fairness does not mean treating all land parcels alike. Indeed, a sensitive effort to promote land health will be based on more or less the opposite idea—on the idea that land parcels are presumptively unequal,

that they play differing roles in the natural community and are not ecologically fungible.

The local practice of land health can succeed only if local landowners
participate in it, learning in the process about the conditions and needs
of their landscape, sharing and revising their own values and hopes, and
helping to find ways to improve local health.[40] Ownership, then, will
entail a civic duty of participation, an obligation that accompanies ownership rights. It will include a call to rise above self-interest, to recognize
the common unity and work to promote it.[41]

Although the ecological principle of interconnection is widely understood and accepted, there is less recognition of its corresponding implication—the inevitable reality of individual irresponsibility, particularly
the inevitable irresponsibility of landowners. If a landowner cannot act
without ripple effects that spread beyond property boundaries, it is simply not possible for the owner to contain her conduct, to use her land
so as not to interfere with surrounding lands. That interference could
be modest, it could be overwhelming, but it will always exist. Interference like this is accepted today, but only when and because it fits within
limits set by the community. Landowners can affect neighboring lands,
but not if the impact rises to the level of substantial harm. But what is
harm, and how significant must it be before neighbors can complain?
The answer, really the only possible answer, is that harm becomes legally
and ethically significant when the community says it does, when it sur-
passes some baseline set by consensus. The common law of nuisance is
based on this idea, and so are many modern environmental laws.

The upshot of interconnection and irresponsibility is this: A landowner is justified in imposing impacts on the lands and people around
her if and only if she is willing to submit to similar claims by others—
only if, that is, she is willing to recognize the community's right to set
binding norms. A landowner whose spillover impacts are challenged by
neighbors can only defend by pointing to these norms and claiming that
her conduct fits within these communally set norms. But if the norms
are binding on her neighbors, if they give the landowner license to impose impacts despite her neighbor's complaints, then the owner too
must recognize their validity. She must admit that the community has
the power to set norms, and she must abide by them, just like her neighbors, when they are properly set.

We can conclude by returning to the point of beginning, to Gary Snyder's claim that philosophy is a place-based exercise. If this is true, or
ought to be true, then its truth should nowhere be more evident than
in our dealings with the land, with the broad subject of nature and culture and the ethical norms that guide our interactions with the nonhuman natural realms. How nature functions is very much a place-based

exercise. The plants and animals and soils and waters are all keyed to a given place, even while they transform the place and make it something more and different than it was. Humans, one should think, ought to act the same. We ought to gear our lives to a given place, becoming responsible members of our chosen natural communities, even while we transform them into something new. To do that wisely, we ought to follow Alexander Pope's adage and consult the genius of the place in all, setting our consumption, as well as the other aspects of our interactions with the land, by way of a practical process that promotes land health, a sensitive, humble process that embraces our ignorance and that draws upon, even while it elevates, our highest ethical yearnings.

Notes

1. Gary Snyder, *The Practice of the Wild* (San Francisco: North Point Press, 1990), 64.
2. Alexander Pope, *The Complete Poetical Works of Alexander Pope* (Boston: Houghton Mifflin, 1931), "Epistle to Burlington," line 50, 57.
3. Eric T. Freyfogle, "The Owning and Taking of Sensitive Lands," *UCLA Law Review* 43, no. 77 (1995): 77–138.
4. Roderick Nash offers a survey in Roderick Frazier Nash, *The Rights of Nature: A History of Environmental Ethics* (Madison: University of Wisconsin Press, 1989).
5. Donald Worster, *Nature's Economy: A History of Ecological Ideas*, 2d ed. (New York: Cambridge University Press, 1994).
6. K. S. Shrader-Frechette and E. D. McCoy, *Method in Ecology: Strategies for Conservation* (New York: Cambridge University Press, 1993).
7. Daniel B. Botkin, *Discordant Harmonies: A New Ecology for the Twenty-First Century* (New York: Oxford University Press, 1990).
8. Stuart L. Pimm, *The Balance of Nature? Ecological Issues in the Conservation of Species and Communities* (Chicago: University of Chicago Press, 1991).
9. Michael Barbour, "Ecological Fragmentation in the Fifties," in *Uncommon Ground: Toward Reinventing Nature*, ed. William Cronon (New York: W. W. Norton, 1995).
10. Judith D. Soule and Jon K. Piper, *Farming in Nature's Image: An Ecological Approach to Agriculture* (Washington, D.C.: Island Press, 1992).
11. Reed F. Noss and Allen Y. Cooperrider, *Saving Nature's Legacy: Protecting and Restoring Biodiversity* (Washington, D.C.: Island Press, 1994).
12. Robert Costanza, Bryan G. Norton, and Benjamin D. Haskell, *Ecosystem Health: New Goals for Environmental Management* (Washington, D.C.: Island Press, 1992).
13. Laura Westra, *The Principle of Integrity: An Environment Proposal for Ethics* (Lanham, MD: Rowman and Littlefield, 1994).

14. Stephanie Mills, *In the Service of the Wild: Restoring and Reinhabiting Damaged Land* (Boston: Beacon Press, 1995).

15. Costanza et al., *Ecosystem Health,* 1992.

16. Bryan G. Norton, *Toward Unity Among Environmentalists* (New York: Oxford University Press, 1991).

17. Eric T. Freyfogle, "The Land Ethic and Pilgrim Leopold," *University of Colorado Law Review* 61 (1990): 217.

18. For a similar conclusion, see Westra, *The Principle of Integrity* (1994).

19. Mark Sagoff, *The Economy of the Earth* (New York: Cambridge University Press, 1988).

20. Wendell Berry, *What Are People For?* (San Francisco: North Point Press, 1990).

21. Soule and Piper, *Farming in Nature's Image.*

22. Soule and Piper, *Farming in Nature's Image.*

23. Kai Lee, *Compass and Gyroscope: Integrating Science and Politics for the Environment* (Washington, D.C.: Island Press, 1993).

24. Herman Daly and John B. Cobb Jr., *For the Common Good* (Boston: Beacon Press, 1994).

25. Berry, *What Are People For?* 208–09.

26. Carolyn Merchant, "Restoration and Reunion with Nature," in *Learning to Listen to the Land,* Bill Willers, ed. (Washington, D.C.: Island Press, 1991).

27. Kirkpatrick Sale, *Dwellers in the Land: The Bioregional Vision* (San Francisco: Sierra Club Books, 1985).

28. Merchant, "Restoration and Reunion with Nature," 210.

29. Wes Jackson, *Becoming Native to This Place* (Lexington: University of Kentucky Press, 1994).

30. Willard Gaylin and Bruce Jennings, *The Perversion of Autonomy: The Proper Uses of Coercion and Constraints in Liberal Society* (New York: Free Press, 1996).

31. Wendell Berry, "Preserving Forest Communities," in *Another Turn of the Crank* (Washington, D.C.: Counterpoint Press, 1995).

32. John DeWitt, *Civic Environmentalism: Alternatives to Regulation in States and Communities* (Washington, D.C.: Congressional Quarterly Press, 1994).

33. For one example, see Timothy Beatley, *Habitat Conservation Planning: Endangered Species and Urban Growth* (Austin: University of Texas Press, 1994).

34. Daniel Kemmis, *Community and the Politics of Place* (Norman: University of Oklahoma Press, 1990); *Rebuilding Communities: Experiences and Experiments in Europe,* ed. Vital Rajan (Foxhole, Darington: Green Books, 1993).

35. On conservation, see Samuel P. Hays, *Conservation and the Gospel of Efficiency: The Progressive Conservation Movement 1890–1920* (Cambridge: Harvard University Press, 1959).

36. Soule and Piper, *Farming in Nature's Image.*

37. I ignore here issues of interpersonal and intergenerational equity, that would need to be taken into account.

38. Eric T. Freyfogle, "Ownership and Ecology," *Case Western Reserve Law Review* 43 (1993): 1269.

39. Eric T. Freyfogle, "Ethics, Community and Private Land," *Ecology Law Quarterly* 23 (1996): 631–61.

40. Kemmis, *Community and the Politics of Place.*

41. Freyfogle, "Ethics, Community and Private Land," 631–61.

10

Environmental Sustainability: Eat Better and Kill Less

R. Goodland

Introduction: Environmental Sustainability

This chapter argues that diet matters for environmental sustainability and is addressed to all concerned with accelerating the transition to sustainability in agriculture. Of all the important changes needed in order to approach environmental sustainability in agriculture, I choose to focus on diet for five reasons.

- First, there is little agreement that diet matters for agricultural sustainability or even that it is a legitimate issue for agricultural policy or economic development. Current global trends are moving away from sustainability. An increasing number of analysts report that we are moving toward the limits of global food production.
- Second, diet is a poverty and equity issue. The poor are mainly concerned with the quantity of their diet; the rich with the quality. The rich will always be able to buy what diets they want; but the consumption patterns of the rich may affect the poor.
- Third, much agriculture is not sustainable.[1] Worldwide topsoil loss, salination, waterlogging, depleting aquifers, overgrazing, deforestation, species extinctions, and agrochemical pollution exemplify lack of sustainability in the agriculture sector.
- Fourth, the adverse impact of the agriculture sector on the environment probably exceeds the impacts of all other sectors, even manufacturing and industry, in many countries. Agriculture has degraded more natural capital and caused more extinctions of species than any other sector, and agriculture uses more water than other

203

R. Goodland

sectors of the economy in many nations. Many agricultural practices—such as feedlot runoff, abattoirs, effluent from oilpalm, rubber, and coffee processing—pollute. The energy consumption of
agriculture is substantial in industrial countries and proportionately
even higher in developing countries, considering the diesel used in
tractors and pumps, the energy contents of fertilizers and biocides,
and the fuel consumed in transport.[2]

• Fifth, within agriculture, the case against cattle is strong and intensifying. Cattle have arguably caused or are related to the most environmental damage to the globe of any nonhuman species through
overgrazing, soil erosion, desertification, and tropical deforestation
for ranches. Cattle numbers have increased 100 percent over the
past forty years. Livestock now outnumber humans three to one.

These five reasons form a compelling argument to promote environmental sustainability in the agriculture sector through diet changes. De-
mand-side management, population control, and loss reduction also will
be essential. As a quarter million more people must be fed each day,
sustainability must be approached as a matter of great urgency. But
there are also, as I shall show, health reasons for promoting environmental sustainability by adjusting diet.[3]

We have let the world become so full that there is, unfortunately, already a trade-off between human numbers and diet. H. W. Kendall and
David Pimentel estimate that a world population of 7 billion could be
supported at current levels of nutrition on a vegetarian diet, assuming
ideal distribution and no grain for livestock, but without alleviating current hunger levels.[4] Joel E. Cohen writes that about 2,500 kilocalories
of food are needed for a vegetarian diet, but this figure soars to 9,250
kilocalories if 30 percent of our diet is from animals.[5] If people eat some
meat, only about 2.5 billion could be provided for; this excludes nearly
two out of three people alive today. This is why it is so important for the
world to remain low on the food chain, for those high to descend, and
for us to discourage people from moving up.

The Global Food Crisis

Several factors are contributing to our current global food crisis, including rising grain prices, reductions in food aid, and undernourishment.

Grain Prices

There was no growth in the grain harvest during the first five years of
the 1990s. At the end of 1995, grain carryover reserves dropped to 231

million tons, enough to feed the world for only forty-eight days, an all-time low. As a consequence, the price started to rise. For example, in 1995 wheat and maize prices hit fifteen-year and twelve-year highs respectively. Rice prices started to rise in 1987 and have maintained higher levels in the 1990s, with sharp upward volatility in 1993 and 1995 as carryover stocks fell to twenty-year lows.[6]

Food Aid

Reductions in food aid in 1995—25 percent less than in 1994 and far below the 1993 level—coincide with the increase in cereal prices, reduced availability of grain exports at concessional prices, and adverse conditions in food-importing nations. Low-income food-deficit countries would have needed to raise an additional $3 billion in 1996 for their food imports. Twenty-six countries face exceptional food shortages.[7]

Undernourishment

Between eight hundred million[8] and one billion people lack sufficient food to function minimally. About two hundred million children under five suffer from protein and energy deficiencies.[9] If adequate nutrients such as vitamins, iron, and iodine are considered, the number of malnourished may exceed two billion. Half of these people live in South Asia, one-quarter live in sub-Saharan Africa, and about one-tenth are in China (though China is rich enough to buy grain). The world's population may jump 50 percent to 8.3 billion by 2025. World food consumption also will have to jump by 50 percent by 2025 just to keep up with population increases, without reducing current hunger levels.

Ways to Increase the Availability of Food

Apart from reducing population or changing eating patterns, there are only three choices to increase the availability of food: extensification, intensification, and changing to grain-based diets. None of these choices is encouraging.

Extensification

Extensification is the expansion of cultivated area. There is substantial farmland lying idle in the countries of the Organization for Economic Cooperation and Development (OECD) either because such land has been taken out of cultivation through government policy, is uneconomic, or is fallowing. Possibly 25 percent of current cropland should not be cropped because it is degrading fast. The rate of land abandonment or degradation increases and may exceed the rate of cultivation of new land.[10] As most accessible and fertile soil already has been cultivated at some stage, thus destroying much of its original biodiversity value, practically all of what is not yet cultivated is less suitable or unsuitable for agriculture because it will be lower in quality and more prone to degradation. Much biodiversity will be lost by converting such land to agriculture if conventional management practices are used. It is not by accident that the remaining wildlands, especially tropical forests, are not cultivated. There are compelling environmental reasons why they were left in their natural state until now. These reasons differ from place to place—biodiversity values, habitat, erosion proneness, oligotrophy, inaccessibility, aridity. There may be up to 500 million hectares of potentially arable land; but its productivity will be well below today's average.

Abandonment of highly eroded or otherwise damaged land and the conversion of cropland to nonfarm uses are accelerating, thus further reducing the potential to increase cropped area. Some degraded lands can be fallowed, providing time for rehabilitation. But not much such land can be rehabilitated. Rehabilitation usually takes at least several decades, and such sites remain fragile after rehabilitation.

Thus there is little scope for expansion of agricultural area as a whole, although there is much regional variation. Expansion of cultivated area would probably impose too high an environmental cost for the meager increase in the amount of food produced.

Intensification

The second choice to increase food production is intensifying use of existing cultivated area. Here the outlook is not quite as bleak as for extensification. But the rise in grain yields per hectare during the late 1980s and early 1990s has slowed dramatically. From 1990 through 1993, worldwide grain yield per hectare declined. Japan's rice yields have ceased rising despite unlimited money and top-quality management. Although the International Rice Research Center's prototype rice variety, announced in 1994, may boost yields by 10 percent under field conditions in about five years, its own rice yields have plateaued or are falling, even under the world's most careful scientific management. There is little optimism in agricultural research centers.

Much of the Green Revolution's productivity increases came from increasing energy intensiveness—one hundred fold in some cases.[11] Fossil energy has now become too expensive for that to be repeated. Part of the Green Revolution's success stemmed from using vastly more water, but water is an increasingly scarce resource.

Overgrazing is increasing on every continent. Rangeland beef and mutton production seems unlikely to increase much, leading to a steady decline in per capita supply. The cumulative effects of soil erosion has reduced the potential of perhaps one-third of the world's remaining cropland.

Most major ocean and freshwater fisheries are in decline. Unsustainable catch sizes have exceeded regeneration rates for so long that the fish resource itself is damaged. Pollution and destruction of estuaries, mangroves, wetlands, and other fish habitats intensify these trends. Per capita production of seafood probably peaked in 1989.

However, fish and other aquatic protein provide less than 1 percent of the world's food today and less than 5 percent of the world's protein. While this makes a big difference to many of the world's poor, it is much less significant for global food supplies. Moreover, in the next couple of decades, fish consumption seems likely to decline from 19 kilograms per person to about half that amount. Fish used to be cheap because their food source—plankton—is very widely spread and feeds on sunlight and water. Due to increasing depletion of fish stocks, however, fish prices are now much higher and often not affordable by the poor.

It is true that aquaculture—the "farming" of fish, mollusks, crustaceans, and aquatic plants such as seaweed—could substitute for some natural seafood and river fish. Although aquaculture is unlikely to produce anything like former tonnages of ocean fish catch, today's global aquaculture of 16 million tons could meet 40 percent of world fish demand within fifteen years.[12] In addition, aquaculture can also recycle sewage into protein.

Aquaculture, however, has two extremes. On the one hand, low-tech aquaculture depends for nutrients on autotrophs, such as green plants, plankton, and algae, and it is characterized by both low productivity and low environmental impact. No nutrients are added; harvests are low in amount and effects on the environment. On the other hand, modern aquaculture increasingly depends on high inputs of diesel and feed, such as grain, agricultural residues, and by-catch fish meal. Even so, fish farming is more productive than beef production, for fish need only 2 kilograms of feed per kilogram of liveweight gain, compared with 7 kilograms for beef. Aquaculture, then, merits more attention in the world food effort than does cattle raising.

Aquaculture protein is critical in many diets today—especially for the poor. Expanded aquacultural protein production could decrease the consumption of mammalian protein and reduce the financial and environmental costs that accompany the production and consumption of mammalian protein. Substituting plant protein for aquaculture and mammalian protein, however, would have even more beneficial human and environmental consequences.

The case is similar for irrigation: there is restricted scope for expansion of irrigated area, although much scope for improving current irrigation efficiencies—some 40 percent of water abstracted for irrigation never reaches the farmer's fields. Water is the main limiting factor for world agricultural production.[13] But irrigated area per capita has been falling since 1978.[14] Aquifer extractions in major food-production areas exceed replenishment rates; levels are falling, as much as 1 to 5 meters annually in major croplands of China and India. Irrigation water thus becomes more expensive and is also diverted from agriculture to cities: the world's cities are growing at the rate of one million people each week.

Grain-Based Diets

After extensification and intensification, the third choice to increase the availability of food is to feed grain and vegetables to people rather than to livestock. This could increase food consumption by humans without any increase in production. For a given quantity of grain, many more people could be fed well on grain-based diets, and become healthier, at much lower environmental and social costs than on meat-based diets. Most meat now comes from grain-fed animals. When farm animals were fed largely on surpluses and farm wastes, they acted as valuable buffers, evening out fluctuations in food supply, providing labor, and producing manure. But animals are increasingly the main consumers of grain that was formerly eaten directly by humans. Just as there is a hierarchy of efficiency in meat production (grain-fed beef at the top; krill or sustainably harvested mussels at the bottom), there is also a hierarchy in vegetable foods, with saprophytes (mushrooms and other fungi) above autotrophs (green plants). One could extend this ranking among categories of autotrophs too.

Only 17 percent of China's grain went to livestock in 1985; by 1994 this figure had risen to 23 percent. This compares with the 68 percent of grain fed to livestock in the United States. Because cattle convert grain to meat inefficiently, trends to carnivory exacerbate food deficiencies. This is not yet accepted in sustainability or development debates.

The prospects for increasing the supply of food by expansion of cultivated area are not promising. The prospects for intensification are somewhat more promising, and merit great attention. But we must also look at the demand side. Of course there is much recognized scope for reducing losses. But one underrecognized area for major gains is eating lower down the food chain. Vast amounts of food are wasted by inefficiently converting grains into meat. Eating lower down the food chain would improve health and food supply.

Why We Need to Eat More Sustainably

Every year, affluent people in OECD countries consume about 800 kilograms of grain indirectly,[15] much of it inefficiently converted into animal flesh, with the balance as milk, cheese, eggs, ice cream, and yogurt. Such diets are high in fat and animal protein and low in starch. In contrast, in low-consuming countries, annual consumption of grains averages 200 kilograms per person, practically all of it directly, with high efficiencies in conversion. Such diets are rich in starch and low in fat and animal protein; most protein in these diets comes from beans and grain. The grain consumption ratio between rich and poor countries is about four to one.[16]

The Food and Agriculture Organization (FAO) calculates that almost 50 percent of global grains are fed to livestock.[17] The two countries converting the most grain into meat are the United States and China—160 and about 100 million tons respectively.[18] Feedlot cattle consume 7 kilograms of grain to produce 1 kilogram of liveweight. Pork takes nearly 4 kilograms of grain per kilogram of liveweight. Poultry and fish are more efficient converters, needing about 2 kilograms of grain for each kilogram of liveweight produced. Cheese and egg production are in between, consuming 3 and 2.6 kilograms of grain per kilogram of product respectively.[19]

There are some encouraging as well as discouraging dietary changes. For example, annual U.S. beef consumption peaked in 1976 at 95 pounds per person; in the 1990s, it has stagnated around 66 pounds. U.S. beef consumption grew at only 1 percent between 1990 and 1995. European, especially U.K., beef consumption never reached those levels, but it is falling faster than in the United States. European Union (EU) consumption of beef and veal fell 6 percent between 1990 and 1995.

Developing countries' elites, in contrast, are eating increasingly high up the food chain. Such dietary shifts have long been regarded as an indicator of development; this view must change if sustainability is to be approached. Developing countries' animal consumption between 1960 and 1990 far outstripped human population increases, soaring 48 percent for large ruminants, 53 percent for small ruminants, 200 percent for hogs and 280 percent for poultry. Little of this increased consumption was by the poor. There is an additional undesirable feature in these

TABLE 10.1
Annual Per Capita Grain Use and Consumption of Livestock Products

[kg rounded to the nearest 100 kg]

Country

	U.S.	Italy	China	India
Grain Use	800	400	300	200
Beef	42	16	1	–
Pork	28	20	21	0.4
Poultry	44	19	3	0.4
Mutton	1	1	1	0.2
Milk	271	182	4	31
Cheese	12	12	–	–
Eggs	16	12	7	13

Source: Data from Lester R. Brown, *Full House: Reassessing the Earth's Population Carrying Capacity* (New York: W. W. Norton, 1994).

countries: FAO calculates that increased grain importation into developing countries is to feed animals that are consumed by the minority higher-income sectors of society.[20]

Not only are mammals inefficient converters, but also their production is environmentally costly in terms of water used and greenhouse gas generated. The production of one pound of beef consumes more than 2700 gallons of water, whereas grain production consumes less than 200 gallons, and vegetables about half that. FAO points out that methane from cattle contributes 2.5 percent of global greenhouse gas (GHG) production.[21] Cattle contribute about 60 million tons of GHG per year, slightly less than rice paddies (70 million tons) but more than is caused by burning vegetation (55 million tons), gas drilling (45 million tons), termites (40 million tons), and landfills (40 million tons). As rice production is basically the same as rice consumption within months of harvest, the total rice cycle more or less balances its own GHG production (from soil bacteria) and consumption (from photosynthetic fixing of carbon dioxide).

Increased greenhouse gases—primarily from burning fossil fuel—have increased climatic instability. This reduces the prospects for a sustained series of good harvests and threatens the plankton fish food chain.

Milk consumption also has unfortunate consequences. In affluent countries such as the United States and Italy, milk consumption in its various forms exceeds meat consumption by weight (table 6.1). Its conversion efficiency is low, almost as low as grain-fed beef and much lower than poultry. There is a role for dairy products when they are produced mainly from the family draft cow. When a calf has been fed, there is not much surplus milk left over if its mother is working in the fields; so dairy would decline to low levels if environmental impact and efficiency were internalized. In addition, milk is not the healthiest of foods for adults. Cheese is dubbed "solid cholesterol" by health conscious physicians. Skim milk is more healthful, but it is still less efficient than foods lower down the food chain (fig. 6.1).

The solution is to avoid animal products as much as possible. One acre of cereals can produce two to ten times as much protein as an acre devoted to beef production. One acre of legumes can produce ten to

FIGURE 10.1
Environmental and Bioethical Food Chain Ranking

▲ WORST
Most Impact/Least Efficient/Least Healthy
—To be taxed highest—

1. Mammals:	Swine/Cattle/Goats/Sheep
	Rodents/Lagomorphs/Camelids/Deer
	[Eggs/Cheese/Milk/Butter]
2. Birds:	Chickens/Geese/Ducks/Pigeons/Turkeys

Homeotherms (warm-blooded)
_____
Poikilotherms (cold-blooded)

3. Other vertebrates:	Fish/Reptiles/Amphibians
4. Invertebrates:	Crustaceans/Insects/[Honey/Propolis]/Annelids/
	Mollusks

Heterotrophs   Carnivory
_____
Vegan

5. Saprophytes:	Fungi/Yeasts/Other Microbes
6. Autotrophs:	Legumes/Grains/Vegetables/Starch Crops/Fruits/
	Nuts/Algae

▼ BEST
Least Impact/Most Efficient/Healthiest
—Zero Tax—

twenty times more protein than an acre in beef production. As some cattle graze on semi-arid range, one cannot say that a specific acre used for beef production can be reallocated to grow cereals or legumes instead. But the UN World Food Council calculates that "ten to fifteen percent of cereals now fed to livestock is enough to raise the world food supply to adequate levels."[22]

Grain-Based Diet

Human diets vary enormously between and within countries. I do not advocate that certain diets be legally prohibited. However, we do need to produce food more sustainably and at lower environmental, social, and economic cost. People should always be allowed to choose the diets they want; but the full costs of their choices should be reflected in the price.

When people get richer, they tend to eat higher on the food chain and, more specifically, eat more meat. This partly explains why the world is moving away from sustainability. To achieve sustainability and help avoid hunger or starvation, in poorer societies, we need incentives to descend the food chain, eat less meat, and move toward a grain-based diet. The most-needed transition is toward eating mainly autotrophs (green plants) and saprophytes (mushrooms and other fungi), and consuming fewer products from heterotrophs (animals that cannot manufacture their own food), especially homeotherms (warm-blooded animals).

Eating lower on the food chain reduces the environmental damage and suffering caused by overconsumption and excessive population. This is a lifestyle change that society can adopt if it wants to consume less of the earth's carrying capacity or reduce its "ecological footprint." Both our health and that of the planet would improve. Hunger, starvation, and malnutrition could be alleviated by such trends. Like voluntary population control, better diets are preferable to starvation, disease, and deteriorating environments.

Food and Agricultural Policy

This essay does not advocate immediate, universal adoption of grain-based diets. Instead, I seek an increased awareness of the importance of diet for deferring a solution to the global food crisis and meeting the challenge of sustainable development. A range of remedies will be needed, including education, improved advertising, incentives, internalization of the full costs of grain-fed meat production, and food conversion efficiency taxes.

Educational campaigns already emphasizing the health argument for eating more grains have begun but need to be intensified. Many incentives—for example, school feeding programs, education, improving maternal and child nutrition, and ration shops selling coarse grain—are available and have been tried on smaller scales than will be necessary to foster lifestyle changes. Removal of subsidies for livestock, both direct and indirect, should be an early step. Clearly, international development organizations and any groups seeking to reduce poverty should phase out of livestock production and should leave it to the private sector. Such groups should ensure that good economics prevail: full environmental and social costs should be used in calculating the prices of foods.

The changes I propose are incremental and relatively modest. The main change is the internalization of the costs of dietary preferences. People should continue to be able to choose to eat what they want. But if they choose to eat food with a large negative impact on the environment, they should pay the full costs of such a choice.

In calculating the best ways to promote efficiency in diet and to reduce environmental impact, we should look at direct and indirect subsidies currently enjoyed by the livestock sector. Such subsidies include full social and environmental costs of topsoil loss, erosion, siltation, biodiversity loss, and deforestation due to cattle; water prices (removal of water subsidies, it is said, would increase the cost of one pound of protein from steak to $89); sewage disposal from feedlots; medical costs associated with diets rich in animal products; the evolution of antibiotic-resistant infections caused by routine antibiotic feeding to cattle; transport costs; and internalization of GHG costs in transport, diesel, and fertilizers used for cattle feed production.

I leave the precise methodological nature of the incentives to economists. Taxes have to be shifted away from things we want more of—employment, payrolls, value added—and onto things we want to discourage—throughput, inefficiency, waste, pollution, overuse of renewable resources, such as overharvesting fish, and severance taxes on minerals and coal. Sumptuary taxes or ecotaxes are detailed by Daly and Cobb,[23] and von Weizsäcker and Jesinghaus.[24] Education campaigns and reallocation of research and development investments away from cattle and toward grains, starches, fruits, and legumes should be the start. Presumably the inputs to meat production, such as water, diesel, and grain, could be taxed.

Beef sales are the United States' largest revenue source in the agriculture sector. Just four meatpackers in the United States hold 82 percent of the market, suggesting a low-cost place to tax. Incentive methodology could address taxing feedlots, ranchers, or slaughter houses. The United States' 104 million-head cattle herd is the largest single user of grain, mainly in the form of winter feed cakes or pellets. Possibly that could be taxed. In some counties, livestock account for half the tax base. Presumably this could be raised. Or a land-use intensity tax could be designed to foster intensification, where appropriate, and demote extensification, such as ranching.

Presumably one could carry the argument further, as soon as the food/population outlook worsens, and tax crops based on how inefficiently they use water and fertilizer. If grain is taxed, it would be difficult to discriminate input for cattle from human food use. If taxing grain becomes necessary in the future in order to foster only its most efficient uses, such a regressive tax should be balanced by reducing income taxes and payroll taxes commensurately. Higher-priced grain would then automatically go to the more efficient uses, namely, feeding people.

The aim would be as follows: first, most people of the world, those already at the efficient, low-impact end of the food chain, would remain as they are. Second, affluent people now consuming much meat would consume more efficiently lower down the food chain. Third, people starting to move up the food chain, such as those in China and India, would be encouraged to stay where they are.

If such sustainability and poverty-alleviating measures become widely adopted, mammalian flesh consumption would decline and would consist mainly of males not needed for draft and females when they have finished producing milk. Hogs and poultry would be kept mainly to recycle wastes; their meat would be an occasional by-product. Ruminants would be restricted to natural range unusable for more intensive production. Aquaculture fish would become more widespread.

This conversion-efficiency sliding-scale tax should be refined by adding the "polluter pays" principle. Cattle feedlots and meatpackers would be taxed at the highest rate; domestically fed rodents and lagomorphs at the lowest. If biodiversity and habitat destruction is included in environmental damage, then cattle raised from pastures created from rainforest would be taxed the highest and natural range cattle would incur a lower tax.

No taxes would be paid on grains such as rice, maize, wheat, and buckwheat, starches such as potatoes and cassava, and legumes such as soy, pulses, beans, peas, and peanuts. Modest subsidies on coarse grains such as millet, pearl millet, and sorghum would alleviate hunger and are unlikely to be abused because the rich do not eat these grains. West African elites have abandoned indigenous grains like millet and sorghum, and have substantially converted to imported wheat and rice.

It would become far too complicated to tax crops differentially at the outset. No tax on plant foods and modest subsidy on coarse grains is enough differentiation. The main differentiation should be to tax consumption of mammals and other homeotherms.

Nonfood Agriculture

The same principles could be applied to nonfood agriculture. Alcoholic beverages divert much grain; they also should be taxed on conversion efficiency. Possibly zero tax on beer brewed from grain unsuitable for food; a low tax on beer brewed from excess grain; a higher tax on grain alcohols, such as gin and whisky, and starch alcohols, such as vodka. Grapes grown on rocky hillsides and not displacing food crops would be exempt, so some wine, brandy, and chacha (grape vodka) might escape taxation. Molasses, as a by-product of cane-sugar production, often is released into rivers where it is highly polluting. Therefore, one also might exempt potable spirits distilled from molasses like Cachaça, and rum which otherwise would be a pollutant.

Governmental and public research and development investments should be restricted to the zero-tax foods. Practically all such research and development should be focused on grains, especially coarse grains, starches, legumes, and vegetable oils. There are useful returns to research on fruits, nuts, seasonings, micronutrients and vitamins.

The environmental impact of obtaining cooking fuel can approach the impact of food harvesting, so substantial attention should be given to the environmental sustainability of cooking methods and its fuels. Using solar cookers, fuelwood hedges, efficient stoves, and pressure cookers would decrease the environmental impact of gathering fuelwood and burning agricultural residues. Recycling wastes merits higher attention too. Mulch, manure, agricultural residues, nightsoil, and carcasses are concentrated forms of nutrients. Their recycling decreases the need for fertilizer.

Other Dangers in a Meat Diet

OECD's wasteful and dangerous trend to convert herbivorous livestock to carnivory and even to necrophagy or cannibalism has backfired. Many dead animals are now ground up for livestock feed. In July 1996, the EU banned the sale of brain, spinal cord, and spleen tissue from sheep, because cows develop bovine spongiform encephalopathy (BSE) if fed with brain tissue from BSE-infected sheep. BSE can also be transmitted from cows to sheep. No human is recorded to have contracted scrapie, which has been endemic in U.K. sheep for two hundred years, but few Britons eat sheep brains. BSE may eventually cost U.K. £5 billion sterling. As of mid-1996, 160,000 BSE cases in cows have been reported in the United Kingdom. Now many U.K. cattle are being incinerated. It is not easy to get rid of one million cattle. Burial is not an option because adequate landfill sites have run out. There are too few incinerators for immediate burning. Most of the destroyed cattle are disposed of by rendering the carcasses into tallow (formerly sold to soap powder and cosmetics industries) and grieves (meat and bone meal formerly sold for animal feed). Now such uses are banned; these wastes may be disposed of in power stations, but because this may clog the stations and the smoke will be smelly or unhealthy, mountains of tallow and grieves are piling up.

The Impact of Reduced Meat Consumption on the Grain Market

Any decrease in the consumption of grain-fed flesh would not automatically free for human consumption the millions of tons of grain now fed to cattle, pigs, and poultry every year. Decreasing consumption of grain-fed flesh would cut the profits of grain farmers, who might then grow less grain. This trend is likely to be balanced to a certain extent by the countervailing trend of rising demand for grain and other plant products by people eating less flesh. While farmers would lose the higher profits from selling grain to feedlots, they might still produce grain or other vegetable products for direct consumption at increased efficiencies and with reduced environmental impacts.

With a decrease in the consumption of grain-fed meat, feedlots and slaughterhouses would decline, reducing water pollution substantially. So the world would be more sustainable and healthier. Marginal farmers would go out of business. Less marginal land would be cultivated, bringing immediate benefits to biodiversity. Less pasture and range grazed would free them for more sustainable uses, such as growing olives, many species of nut trees, and orchards. Raising buffalo and other less-risky animals could increase on natural dry range that has no alternative use, preferably at a stocking density well below carrying capacity.

Currently rising grain prices show demand is outstripping supply. This is partly a short-term phenomenon resulting from a series of poor harvests but is also in part a long-term trend propelled by burgeoning populations, environmental degradation, increasing water scarcities, and rising incomes of some of the world's poor (e.g., in China). Grain diverted for meat intensifies this demand. Poor grain consumers will be increasingly unable to meet higher prices.

Will higher grain prices induce greater supply? A trend to more grain and less non-grain food may result, with costs for the poor. Increasing production and diversion of grains to feed tends to expand land allocated to grain and decrease land available for other crops whose prices are not rising as fast as those of grain. This will exert upward pressure on the prices of non-grain crops too. Increasing carnivory, as incomes rise, pressures agricultural prices in general. Since grain will command similar prices whether used for food or feed, it is the poor consumers of grain who are likely to suffer.

Reducing demand for meat will tend to lower grain prices or slow their rise. The precise effect on the grain markets will of course depend on the balance of the complex forces of supply and demand. But it seems reasonable to conclude that net decrease in carnivory would tend to moderate grain prices. Consider the likely effects in China, a grain-importing country. The decrease in grain-fed meat production could depress domestic grain prices, but demand for all foods is strong and likely to remain so because 14 million extra consumers are added each year, while arable land per person is scant, about 0.07 hectares, and decreasing. With a decrease in meat consumption, grain importers would allocate grain more efficiently and, hence, tend to import less. The money saved by importing less grain could be reallocated to domestic food production.

The Health Argument

The fact is that if energy needs are obtained from grain-based diets, then protein requirements are met. Cereals supply 50 percent of dietary protein and calories globally, and up to 70 percent in developing nations.[25] As most poor people worldwide are forced to eat grain-based diets and survive, there should be no argument that eating lower on the food chain risks health. Now even orthodox Western health authorities cannot muster arguments strong enough to satisfy meat lobbies. Italians eat less than half the amount of beef and poultry that Americans eat (table 10.1) and have a higher life expectancy. Part of this is related to diet: "Eat light and live longer" is supported by firm scientific evidence.

Problems arise when energy requirements are not met by grain-based diets, but by low-protein staples such as roots, tubers, bananas, and sweet potatoes. This highlights the importance of legumes and proteinaceous seeds (sunflower, sesame), particularly for vulnerable groups, such as infants. Many studies of extreme or vulnerable groups (such as pregnant women, infants, macrobiotics, athletes, the elderly, the wounded, and Trappists) reconfirm the adequacy of eating low on the food chain.[26] The other side of the argument is increasingly clear. Western carnivory kills or maims increasing numbers of people. The links between serious health conditions—such as stroke, heart disease, cancer, obesity, hypertension, diabetes and food-borne illness—and high-meat diets are now inescapable. The message is clear: eating high on the food chain severely damages one's health. Heart disease in the United States alone costs $66 billion in 1996, according to the American Heart Association. Much of this can be attributed to high-meat diets. Cardiovascular disease need not be a consequence of living if one reduces carnivory. A low-fat grain-based diet has now become the main therapy for the 1.25 million annual preventable U.S. heart attacks. Heart disease can be reversed partly by moving lower on the food chain.

Conclusion

A change in diet is one of the measures urgently needed to approach environmental sustainability in the agricultural sector. Improving diets by moving down the food chain, eating less meat and more grains, would vastly improve food efficiency and reduce waste and environmental impact. Improving diet also improves health. Ethicists advocate diet shifts because equity is more likely to be improved, while pain and killing of animals are reduced. These are compelling arguments to move down the food chain.

Notes

Warm appreciation is offered for all the generous comments on earlier drafts and support received from Lester Brown, Cutler Cleveland, John Cobb, Herman Daly, and David Pimentel.

1. R. Sansoucy, "Livestock: A Driving Force for Food Security and Sustainable Development," *World Animal Review,* vol. 84/85 (1995): 5–17; and "Integration of Sustainable Agriculture and Rural Development Issues in Agricultural Policy," *FAO 1995 Rome Workshop,* ed. S. Breth (Morrilton, Ark.: Winrock, 1995).

2. C. J. Cleveland, "Resource Degradation, Technical Change, and the Productivity of Energy Use in U.S. Agriculture," *Ecological Economics* 13 (1995): 185–201; "The Direct and Indirect Use of Fossil Fuels and Electricity in U.S. Agriculture," *Agriculture, Ecosystems and Environment* 55 (1995): 111–21.

3. That diet has become a major opportunity to improve development is being recognized. See, for example, H. W. Kendall and David Pimentel, "Constraints on the Expansion of the Global Food Supply," *Ambio* 23, no. 3 (1994):

198–216; Lester R. Brown, *Full House: Reassessing the Earth's Population Carrying Capacity* (New York: W. W. Norton, 1994), and *Who Will Feed China?: Wake-Up Call for a Small Planet* (New York: W. W. Norton, 1995); Joel E. Cohen, *How Many People Can the Earth Support?* (New York: W. W. Norton, 1995); Paul R. Ehrlich, Anne H. Ehrlich, and Gretchen C. Daily, *The Stork and the Plow: The Equity Answer to the Human Dilemma* (New York: Putnam, 1995); and Robert Goodland, Catherine Watson, and George Ledec, *Environmental Management in Tropical Agriculture* (Boulder, Colo.: Westview Press, 1984).

4. Kendall and Pimentel, "Constraints on the Expansion of the Global Food Supply," 199.

5. Cohen, *How Many People?* 170.

6. J. M. Harris, "World Agricultural Futures: Regional Sustainability and Ecological Limits," *Ecological Economics* 17, no. 2 (1996): 95–116.

7. J. Diouf, Guest Editorial, *United Nations Non-Governmental Liaison Service*, 57 (April/May 1996): 16.

8. Sansoucy, "Livestock: a Driving Force," 5–17.

9. J. Diouf, Guest Editorial, 16.

10. David Pimentel, "Natural Resources and an Optimum Human Population," *Population and Environment* 15, no. 5 (1994): 347–70; and Kendall and Pimentel, "Constraints on the Expansion of the Global Food Supply," 199–200.

11. Kendall and Pimentel, "Constraints on the Expansion of the Global Food Supply."

12. Lester R. Brown, *Tough Choices: Facing the Challenge of Food Scarcity* (Washington, D.C.: Worldwatch Institute, 1996).

13. Kendall and Pimentel, "Constraints on the Expansion of the Global Food Supply," 200.

14. Sandra Postel, *Last Oasis: Facing Water Scarcity* (New York: W. W. Norton, 1992), 239.

15. Brown, *Full House;* Alan Thein Durning and Holly B. Brough, *Taking Stock: Animal Farming and the Environment* (Washington, D.C.: Worldwatch Institute Paper 103, 1991).

16. Brown, *Full House.*

17. Sansoucy, "Livestock: A Driving Force," 9.

18. Brown, *Who Will Feed China?* 163.

19. Brown, *Full House.*

20. Sansoucy, "Livestock: A Driving Force," 9.

21. Sansoucy, "Livestock: A Driving Force," 13.

22. Goodland et al., *Environmental Management*, 237.

23. Herman E. Daly and John B. Cobb, Jr., *For the Common Good: Redirecting the Economy toward Community, the Environment, and a Sustainable Future*, 2d ed. (Boston: Beacon Press, 1994).

24. Ernst U. von Weizsäcker and Jochen Jesinghaus, *Ecological Tax Reform: A Policy Proposal for Sustainable Development* (London and Atlantic Highlands, N.J.: Zed Books, 1992).

25. Harris, "World Agricultural Futures."

26. See S. I. Barr, K. C. Janell, and J. C. Prior, "Vegetarian vs Nonvegetarian

Diets, Dietary Restraint, and Subclinical Ovulatory Disturbances: Prospective 6-mo Study," *American Journal of Clinical Nutrition* 60, no. 6 (1994): 887–94; A. D. Beardsworth and E. T. Keil, "Contemporary Vegetarianism in the U.K.: Challenge and Incorporation?" *Appetite* 20, no. 3 (1993): 229–34; J. Dwyer and F. M. Loew, "Nutritional Risks of Vegan Diets to Women and Children: Are They Preventable?" *Journal of Agriculture and Environmental Ethics* 7 (1994): 87–110; B. F. Harland, S. A. Smith, M. P. Howard, R. Ellis, and J. C. Smith, Jr., "Nutritional Status and Phytate: Zinc and Pmonks: 10 Years Later," *Journal of the American Dietetic Association* 88, no. 12 (1988): 1562–66; M. C. Herens, P. C. Dagnelie, R. J. Kleber, M. C. J. Mol, and W. A. Van Staveren, "Nutrition and Mental Development of 4–5-Year-Old Children on Macrobiotic Diets," *Journal of Human Nutrition and Dietetics* 5, no. 1 (1992): 1–9; K. C. Janelle and S. I. Barr, "Nutrient Intakes and Eating Behavior Scores of Vegetarian and Nonvegetarian Women," *Journal of the American Dietetic Association* 95, no. 2 (1995): 180–86; A. A. Jensen, S. A. Slorach, and A. Astrup-Jensen, "Factors Affecting the Levels of Residues in Human Milk," in *Chemical Contaminants in Human Milk*, ed. A. Jensen, S. A. Slorach, and A. Astrup-Jensen (Boca Raton, Fla.: CRC Press, 1991), 199–207; A. R. Mangels and S. Havala, "Vegan Diets for Women, Infants, and Children," *Journal of Agricultural and Environmental Ethics* 7, no. 1 (1994): 111–23; V. Sharma and A. Sharma, "Serum Cholesterol Levels in Carcinoma Breast," *Indian Journal of Medical Research* 94 (1991): 193–96; Gary E. Varner, "In Defense of the Vegan Ideal: Rhetoric and Bias in the Nutrition Literature," *Journal of Agricultural and Environmental Ethics* 7, no. 1 (1994): 29–40; and D. S. Weinstein, R. E. Austic, and R. Schwartz, "Cation Excess of Selected Omnivore and Vegetarian Diets," *Ecology of Food and Nutrition* 28, no. 1–2 (1992): 33–43.

11

Toward an Ethics of Consumption: Rethinking the Nature of Growth

Rogene A. Buchholz and Sandra B. Rosenthal

While there has been a concern about pollution of the environment for several years, talk about limits to growth, or more recently, sustainable growth has also raised concerns about resource availability and limits relative to the ability of the planet to provide everyone with an improved material standard of living. There is good reason to believe that our present industrial societies are not sustainable in that they use too many virgin resources and degrade the environment in too many ways, and that such practices cannot continue much longer. If people all over the world want to increase their standard of living on a par with advanced industrial nations like the United States, resources will be used even faster and environmental degradation will increase. The world simply cannot sustain such activities, and aspirations of this sort will exceed the earth's carrying capacity with respect to resources and all aspects of the environment.[1]

The question being asked ever more frequently by commissions and policy makers all over the world is whether growth on the scale projected over the next one to five decades can be managed on a basis that is sustainable, both economically and ecologically. Continued growth in consumption of goods and services and the continued development of a materialistic lifestyle may not be possible under conditions of sustainable growth. The world is already overconsuming resources, witness the depletion of fish stocks around the world, and cannot continue on the path of more and more production. Thus the challenge of the environment is an important one and whether overconsumption is a legitimate problem and changing patterns of consumption are necessary are questions that need examination, particularly as former socialistic economies

221

are moving toward some form of market system to increase economic growth.

The Protestant Ethic

Perhaps the best place to begin such a discussion is to examine the moral system that existed during the development of market systems and provided a legitimacy for their existence. The primary ethical emphasis behind the development of market systems in Western Europe and the United States has been called the Protestant Ethic, because this ethic had religious origins in the newly emerging industrial societies that developed after the Reformation period. The Protestant Ethic helped to legitimize the capitalist system by providing a moral justification for the pursuit of wealth and the distribution of income that were a result of economic activity within this system.[2]

The self-discipline and moral sense of duty and calling that were at the heart of this ethic were vital to the kind of rational economic behavior that early capitalism demanded (calculation, punctuality, productivity). The Protestant Ethic thus contributed to the spirit of capitalism, a spirit that was supportive of individual human enterprise and accumulation of wealth necessary for the development of capitalism. Within this climate, people were motivated to behave in a manner that proved conducive to rapid economic growth of the capitalistic variety and shared values that were consistent with this kind of development.[3]

This ethic contained two major elements: (1) an insistence on the importance of a person's calling, which meant that one's primary responsibility was to do one's best at whatever station God had assigned them in life, rather than to withdraw from the world and devote oneself entirely to God, as the Catholic Church had taught as a counsel of perfection, and (2) the rationalization of all of life as introduced by Calvin's notion of predestination, whereby work became a means of dispersing religious doubt by demonstrating to oneself and others that one was a member of the elect.[4] One was to work hard, be productive, and accumulate wealth; but that wealth was not to be pursued for its own sake or enjoyed in lavish consumption. The more possessions one had, the greater was the obligation to be an obedient steward and hold these possessions undiminished for the glory of God by increasing them through relentless effort. A worldly asceticism was at the heart of this ethic, which gave a religious sanction to acquisition and the rational use of wealth to create more wealth. "The upshot of it all, was that for the first time in history the two capital producing prescriptions, maximization of production and minimization of consumption became components of the same ethical matrix."[5]

The pursuit of material wealth was given a moral justification in that wealth, which was believed to be the fruits of hard work, was a sign of election—as sure a way as was available to disposing of the fear of damnation. This represented a new approach to acquisitiveness and the pursuit of profit over earlier periods. What had been formally regarded at best as something of a personal inclination and choice, had now also become something of a moral duty.[6]

The Protestant Ethic proved to be consistent with the need for the accumulation of capital that is necessary during the early stages of industrial development. Money was saved and reinvested to build up a capital base. Consumption was curtailed in the interests of creating capital wealth. People dedicated themselves to hard work at disagreeable tasks and justified the rationalization of life that capitalism required. Inequality was morally justified if the money earned on capital was reinvested in further capital accumulation that would benefit society as a whole by increasing production and creating more economic wealth.

Thus the Protestant Ethic was a social and moral counterpart to the early stages of capitalism that emphasized both the human and capital sources of productivity and growth and in this sense was the first supply-side theory. It emphasized the human side of production through hard work and the aspect of the calling. It also advocated that people should not only work hard, but that the money they earn in the process should also be put to work and not spent on lavish consumption.

This notion of the Protestant Ethic became of particular importance in American society as capitalism developed and economic wealth was created. It stood as one of the most important underpinnings of American culture, and thrift and industry were believed to hold the key to material success and spiritual fulfillment.[7] Eventually, the Protestant Ethic was stripped of its religious trappings, but the basic assumptions about work and its importance remained the same in industrial societies.

One topic of interest and concern that appeared frequently in both popular and professional literature during the 1970s was the weakening or disappearance of the Protestant Ethic or work ethic from the American scene. There was a good deal of evidence to suggest that the traditional values regarding work and the acquisition of wealth as expressed by the Protestant Ethic were changing in some fashion. Young people were said to be turning away from their parent's dedication to work for the sake of success and were more concerned about finding work that was satisfying and meaningful in terms other than money.[8]

This change in values was already noted as early as 1957 by Clyde

Kluckhohn who, after an extensive survey of the then-available professional literature, concluded that empirical data gave evidence of a decline of the Protestant Work Ethic as the core of the dominant middle-class value system.[9] Then Daniel Bell argued that the Protestant Ethic has been replaced by hedonism in contemporary society—the idea of pleasure as a way of life. American culture was no longer concerned with how to work and achieve, but with how to spend and enjoy.[10]

Perhaps the crowning blow to the work ethic was provided by Daniel Yankelovich in a more recent publication. Yankelovich states that traditionally, Americans have been a thrifty and productive people adhering to the major tenants of the Protestant Ethic and in the process helping to create an abundant and expanding economy. But in the past two decades, Americans have loosened their attachment to this ethic of self-denial and deferred gratification and are committed in one way or another to the search for self-fulfillment.[11]

Behavioral Changes in American Society

The weakening of the traditional work ethic with its inherent restriction on consumption is consistent with a behavioral change in American society. Prior to the Second World War, people by and large were savings oriented and lived by the ethic of deferred gratification. They would not buy houses with large mortgages and run up huge credit card balances but would save their money until they could buy things outright. Gratification of their desires was deferred until they could afford to satisfy them, and then, and only then, was it proper to buy things to enjoy. In other words, most people lived within their immediate means and did not borrow for purposes of increased consumption.

During the 1950s, however, this ethic changed into one of instant gratification, as a consumption society was created where people were encouraged to satisfy their desires now rather than wait until they had the money in hand. Buying on credit was encouraged and long-term mortgages became the order of the day with regard to housing. Why defer gratification when one could buy and enjoy things immediately and pay for them in the future? Companies helped to create this kind of society by making credit easy to obtain through the use of credit cards and by using more sophisticated forms of advertising to increase consumption of their products.

There were many factors behind this change in behavior of the American people, and no one in particular was responsible for this change but everyone in general helped to create a new approach to consumption where instant gratification became a cultural trait, in contrast to earlier times when saving was emphasized. The implications of this change were profound for lifestyles and habits of people, as society became more wealthy and prosperous. Many people lived more interesting lives and had more choices available to them as never before. They traveled more miles, wore more and different clothes, drove more expensive and sophisticated cars, and in general enjoyed rising standards of living that involved consumption of the latest products.

Implications of Instant Gratification

There were many adverse implications to this change, particularly as far as resource usage and environmental impacts were concerned. In the 1960s, concern about the natural environment began to emerge, and a great deal of legislation related to the environment was passed. These environmental concerns about pollution and resource usage run headlong into cultural values related to increased consumption and immediate gratification. Questions are being raised about the feasibility and morality of our society hooked on an ever-increasing standard of living, using up more and more of the world's resources and causing more and more pollution of the environment.

Do the United States and other advanced industrial societies need to cut back on consumption and share some of their wealth with developing nations? Do developed societies need to save something for future generations if they take the concept of sustainability seriously? There are moral questions thus related to intragenerational and intergenerational equity. Is there a need for some new kind of ethic, perhaps an environmental ethic, that would essentially function like the work ethic did in terms of providing moral limits on consumption?

Alan Durning has written a book appropriately entitled *How Much Is Enough?* in which he argues for the creation of what he calls the culture of permanence—a society that lives within its means by drawing on the interest provided by the earth's resources rather than on its principal, a society that seeks fulfillment in a web of friendship, family, and meaningful work. Yet he recognizes the difficulty of transforming consumption-oriented societies into sustainable ones and the problem that material cravings of developing societies pose for resource usage.[12]

For the past forty years, with some exceptions, the overriding goal of people in advanced industrial societies has been one of buying more goods, acquiring more things, and increasing their stock of material wealth. Companies have profited from this consumer culture by catering to the consumer, making goods more convenient to buy, bombarding them with advertising—in general, promoting a consumer society by creating a certain materialistic conception of the good life. Because of this trend, the world's people have consumed as many goods and services since 1950 as all previous generations put together. Since 1940, according to Durning, the United States alone has used up as large a share of the earth's mineral resources as did everyone before them combined.

Aside from the question as to whether all this consumption has really made people happier and more fulfilled, the environmental impacts have been severe as more and more resources have become depleted and it becomes more and more difficult to dispose of waste material. Consumer society is built on two critical assumptions: one, that the world contains an inexhaustible supply of raw materials, and two, that there are bottomless sinks in which to continue to dispose of waste material. Both of these assumptions are now in question, causing many to take a serious look at the sustainability of consumer culture into the future.

Reduction of consumption in industrial societies, however, can have severe repercussions. Since about two-thirds of gross national product or its equivalent in developed countries consists of consumer purchases, it seems obvious that any severe reduction of consumer expenditures would have serious implications for employment, income, investment, and everything else tied into economic growth. Lowering consumption could be self-destructive to advanced industrial societies. Yet if such measures aren't taken, Durning warns, ecological forces may eventually dismantle advanced societies anyhow, in ways that we can't control and that would be even more destructive.

Are there any ways out of this dilemma? Several things suggest themselves. Corporations could be more responsible in their advertising and promotion activities and consumers in their consumption activities by promoting and buying products that have less adverse impacts on the environment. If this kind of consciousness were to be expanded throughout society, much could be done to mitigate environmental impacts by promoting more ecologically sound products and packaging.

However, the goal of green marketing is to change consumption patterns, not necessarily limit consumption. The effort still sends the message that material acquisition can continue unabated and reinforces the image of self-interested human beings whose mission in life is centered upon the consumption and acquisition of material comforts. It focuses on changing personal styles of consumption rather than reducing those levels, particularly in industrialized countries.[13] Thus it does not seem to offer a long-range solution to the problem of overconsumption and continuation of a materialistic lifestyle.

The notion of sustainability may also be of great importance in developing adequate environmental policies and practices to cope with this situation. However, this notion shares traditional assumptions about growth and development. It is based on the assumption that economic growth can continue to be accomplished as long as it is sustainable. Most definitions of sustainability reflect an anthropocentric bias as the unit of sustainability is the human being even if it refers to future generations. Sustainable development operates within a utilitarian framework seeking the greatest good for the greatest numbers of people, including future generations, by reducing waste and inefficiency in the exploitation and consumption of nonrenewable natural resources. It hopes to ensure sustainable yield of renewable resources; it does not question the wisdom of continued economic growth.[14]

Rethinking growth involves a theoretical position that rejects the long-held assumptions that pervade our approach to the understanding of growth, and this in turn requires a rejection of all vestiges of the atomistic understanding of humans and their relation to the world. This assumption gained its entrenchment in human thinking with the rise of modern science and the Cartesian understanding of the nature of science and of the scientific object. Such a linkage, based largely on the presuppositions of a spectator theory of knowledge, led to a naively realistic philosophic interpretation of scientific content. Scientific knowledge provided the literal description of objective fact and excluded our lived qualitative experience as providing access to the natural universe.

This worldview resulted in a quantitatively characterized nature, and the atomicity of discrete individual units that must be brought together through mechanistic laws or related to each other through a mechanistic process. This in turn led to the alienation of humans from nature and a radical dehumanizing of nature. This view of nature as objectified thus justified nature as a quantifiable object of value-free human manipulation. While this established a radical dualism between humans and nature, yet humans, like nature, were understood in terms of isolatable, independent, or atomic units. Moreover, rejecting dualism did not alleviate the problem, for it resulted in reducing the human in its totality to the value-free, quantifiable, mechanistic, atomistic system that constituted physical nature. Given the quantitative, atomistic modern worldview, the wealth of the society is tied up in the goods and services it produces, and growth is measured by the increase in gross national product, which is the sum total of all the goods and services produced in society, whether these goods and services degrade the environment or enhance it in some fashion.

Pragmatism, in focusing on scientific method as the experimental activity in which the scientist engages rather than on the results the scientist obtains, undercuts the self-defeating frameworks and alternatives

228   *Rogene A. Buchholz and Sandra B. Rosenthal*

resulting from the Cartesian worldview, allowing for a relational and qualitative understanding of humans and the natural universe in which they are embedded and of which they are a part.

The Relational Self and the Qualitative Framework for Growth

The pragmatic view of the self as inherently relational is a new way of understanding the self, which denies the atomistic view that gives rise to the extremes of both an individualism that ignores the whole and a collectivism that trivializes the individual. To have a self is to have a particular type of ability, the ability to be aware of one's behavior as part of the social process of adjustment, to be aware of oneself as a social object, as an acting agent within the context of other acting agents.

In incorporating the perspective of, taking the attitude of, or taking the role of the other, the developing self comes to take the perspective of others as a complex, interrelated whole, and in this way comes to incorporate the standards and authority of the group, the organization or system of attitudes and responses that Mead (1934) terms "the generalized other"; this is the passive dimension of the self, the dimension structured by role taking. Yet, in responding to the perspective of the other, the individual responds as a unique center of creative activity. Any self incorporates, by its very nature, both the conformity of the group perspective or group attitudes and the creativity of its unique individual perspective.

These poles of creativity and conformity, operative within the self, are analogously operative in the structure of community, which is constituted by the ongoing process of adjustment between the individual, creative, novel perspective, and the conforming, group perspective. Thus, the individual can be contrasted with the general other, but not with community; the individual is not an atomic building block of community but represents the creative pole within the ongoing dynamics of adjustment. Because of the inseparable interaction of the two poles of self and other constitutive of community, goals for "the whole" cannot be pursued by ignoring consequences for individuals affected, nor can individual goals be adequately pursued apart from the vision of the functioning of the whole.

Moreover, the adjustment of perspectives through rational reconstruction requires not an imposition from on high but a deepening to a more fundamental level of human rapport. Indeed, while experience arises from specific, concrete contexts shaped by a particular tradition, this is not mere inculcation, for the deepening process offers the openness for breaking through and evaluating one's own stance. It allows us to grasp different contexts, to take the perspective of "the other," to participate in dialogue with "the other." Such a deepening does not negate the use of intelligent inquiry, but rather opens it up, frees it from the products of its past in terms of rigidities and abstractions, and focuses it on the dynamics of concrete human existence in all its contextual complexity and richness.

Thus far the discussion has focused on the emergence of selfhood within the dynamics of the human community. However, the self is not only relational in that it is inherently related to the cultural/human community, but also in that it is inherently related to the body; not the body that I "have," but the body that I "am." The human being is within nature. Neither human activity in general nor human knowledge can be separated from the fact that this being is a natural organism dependent upon a natural environment.

But the human organism and the nature within which it is located are both rich with the qualities and values of our everyday experience. Distinctively human traits such as mind, thinking, and selfhood are emergent characteristics of nature and part and parcel of its richness. They refer to ways in which the lived body behaves. Just as the self is essentially intertwined with other selves, so it is essentially intertwined with the body; it a body-self located, if one speaks of location, throughout the biological organism with its reflexive ability as this emerges from and opens onto the relational contexts in which it functions. Human development is ecologically connected with its biological as well as its cultural world. From the backdrop of the above understanding of self, humans and their entire environment, organic and inorganic, take on an inherently relational aspect. To speak of organism and environment in isolation from each other is never true to the situation, for no organism can exist in isolation from an environment, and an environment is what it is in relation to an organism. The properties attributed to the environment belong to it in the context of that interaction. What we have is interaction as an indivisible whole, and it is only within such an interactional context that experience and its qualities function.

The deepening and expansion of perspective to include ever-widening horizons must extend beyond the cultural to the natural world with which we are inseparably intertwined. This receives its most intense form in John Dewey's understanding of experiencing the world religiously as a way of relating one's self with the universe as the totality of conditions with which the self is connected. This unity can be neither apprehended in knowledge nor realized in reflection, for it involves such a totality not as a literal content of the intellect, but as an imaginative extension of the self, not an intellectual grasp but a deepened attunement. This is the reason poets get at nature so well.[15] This would seem to provide a concrete sense of the "holistic approach for the common good, understood beyond Plato's model, as both a communitarian and a universal but nonanthropocentric goal," which Laura Westra considers a requirement for establishing "guidelines of ecosystem integrity."[16]

Such an experience brings about not a change in the intellect alone, but a change in moral consciousness. It allows one to rise above the divisiveness we impose through arbitrary and illusory ingroup/outgroup distinctions by delving beneath to the sense of deep-seated harmonizing of the self with the totality of the conditions to which it relates. And, for all the pragmatists, this involves the entire universe, for their emphasis on continuity reveals that at no time can we separate our developing selves from any part of the universe and claim that it is irrelevant. Indeed, while one may seek to describe objective relationships among interacting individuals—human, nonhuman, organic, and inorganic—that make up the biosphere, yet the properties attributed to the individuals are not possessed by them independently of the interactions in which they exhibit themselves. Nature cannot be dehumanized, nor can humans be denaturalized.

Humans exist within and are part of nature, and any part of nature provides a conceivable relational context for the emergence of value. The sense of value is an immediately experienced quality of our ongoing concrete existence but can be located neither "in" us, nor "out there" in an independently ordered universe. Rather, value is a relational, emergent quality of concrete contexts, and our abstract "oughts" are not rules handed down from on high but rather are experimental hypotheses for the organization of valuing experiences that lead to the enhancement of value for all. The conflict of value, like all conflicts, requires a deepening to a more fundamental level of rapport, to a sense that the concrete richness of humans and the diversity of valuings that must be harmonized, to a sense of one's openness onto a deeper community and the possibilities contained therein.

Our normative claims are about the experience of value, and unless one is attuned to the sense of concrete existence and the value qualities contained therein, our normative claims become sterile and empty. The consumerism of today is partially the product of concrete human striving for ongoing growth. Moreover, when the fragmentary roles of individuals are substituted for the concrete human being, then the holistic skills needed for the reconstruction and expansion of value-laden self-community growth cannot occur.

The Pragmatic Rethinking of Growth

Given the above framework, growth cannot be understood in terms of mere accumulation or mere increase. Rather, growth involves the ongoing reconstruction of experience to bring about the integration and expansion of contexts with which selfhood is intertwined. The growth of the self is a process by which it achieves fuller, richer, more inclusive, and more complex interactions with its environment. It cannot be understood only in terms of the organization of one's own person, the artificiality of oneself in isolation, but rather requires growth of context as well. Growth incorporates an encompassing sympathetic understanding of varied and diverse interests, thus leading to tolerance not as a sacrifice but as an enlargement of self; not as something totally other but as something sympathetically incorporated as an expansion of one's self.[17]

The development of the ability both to create and to respond constructively to the creation of novel and/or other perspectives, as well as to incorporate the perspective of the other, not as something totally alien but as something sympathetically understood, is at once growth of the self. The pragmatic understanding of growth involves reintegration of problematic situations in ways that lead to expansion of self, of community, and of the relation between the two. Moreover, though not independent of intelligent inquiry, growth is not merely a change in an intellectual perspective but rather is a change that affects and is affected by the individual in its total concreteness, allowing one to become more attuned to the fullness of existence in its concreteness and hence more appreciative of its qualitative richness and value-laden contexts. In this way, growth is best understood as an increase in the moral-esthetic richness of experience.

Mark Sagoff takes note of the distinction ecological economists make between "economic growth" or the increase in quantity that cannot be sustainable indefinitely, and "economic development" or improvement in quality of life that may be so sustainable, and argues that neither ecological nor mainstream economists can provide utilitarian or instrumental "sustainable growth problem" support for the cause of environmentalism. The ultimate defense of the environment, he holds, must be moral rather than economic.[18]

The ultimate defense of the environment must indeed be moral, but so must the defense of economic growth. It was stressed earlier that the Protestant Work Ethic provided a moral framework for early stages of industrialization. However, the moral vision itself eventually became production/consumption. There is needed a new moral vision in which to place production and consumption, and the vision offered by pragmatism is that of concrete growth as inherently moral and qualitative. The moral defense of the environment and of economic growth stem from the same soil—the nature of growth in its concrete fullness. Economic growth is an abstraction from a concrete situation, and when it stifles rather than furthers concrete growth, it is an abstraction that forgets the concrete reality it is intended to serve, a fallacy similar to that operative in the modern world-view understanding of the quantification of nature. Moreover, to separate economic growth from its moral soil is a remnant of the fact-value distinction rooted in the dichotomies of that era.

The distinction between economic growth as increase in quantity and economic development as improvement in quality of life does not, as Sagoff well argues, provide for the defense of the environment.[19] This is because quality of life is itself understood as enhanced through economic production rather than through ongoing concrete growth. For ongoing concrete growth as inherently moral requires integration of ever-widening contexts of the environments of which we are culturally and naturally a part. To speak of economic development as enhancing quality of life while destroying the environments within which ongoing growth is achieved shows the abstract and non-relational understanding of quality of life incorporated in the concept of economic development.

As has been noted, "Once material sufficiency is secured," there is no longer a correlation of quality of life "with national or personal income,"[20] and the thought that there is involves a misguided understanding of quality of life. The protection of the environment and the enhancement of quality of life are inextricably joined through their dependency on the moral nature of concrete growth as involving the ongoing integration and expansion of concrete contexts in their qualitative richness in workable ways.

This leads directly to the issue of workability. First, workability cannot be taken in the sense of workable for oneself only, for the entire discussion has stressed that the self is inextricably tied to the community of which it is a part. Second, workability cannot be taken in terms of the short-range expedient, for actions and their consequences extend into an indefinite future and determine the possibilities available in that future. Finally, workability cannot be taken in terms of some abstract aspect of life, such as economic workability, for workability as normative involves the ongoing development of the concrete richness of human experience in its entirety. It was seen above that community life in general involves the functioning of humans in their concrete fullness, and this functioning embodies moral dimensions throughout. Workability within community in general, then, must ultimately concern the enrichment of concrete human existence in its entirety. Workability in the ongoing dynamics of community life has, like growth, an inherently moral quality.

The significance of workable consequences involved in the choice among values is encapsulated in Dewey's assertion that, "In short, the thing actually at stake in any serious deliberation is not a difference of quantity, but what kind of person one is to become, what sort of self is in the making, what kind of a world is in the making."[21] What is needed for responsibility in directing the course of growth in the most workable ways is the development of the reorganizing and ordering capabilities of creative intelligence, the imaginative grasp of authentic possibilities, the vitality of motivation and, undergirding it all, a deepened attunement to the sense of concrete human existence in its richness, diversity, and multiple types of interrelatedness with the social, cultural, political, and natural environments of which it is a part. It is this attunement that will give vitality to the diverse and changing experimental courses of action we develop to guide the direction of ongoing growth for individuals, corporations, and the totality of environments in which they are relationally embedded.

Notes

1. J. McNeill, "Strategies for Sustainable Economic Development," *Scientific American* 261, no. 3 (1989): 155–65; R. A. Forsch and N. E. Gallopoulos, "Strategies for Manufacturing," *Scientific American* 261, no. 3 (1989): 144–52.

2. M. Weber, *The Protestant Ethic and the Spirit of Capitalism* (New York: Charles Scribner's Sons, 1958).

3. R. LaPiere, *The Freudian Ethic* (New York: Duell, Sloan, and Pearce, 1959).

4. D. C. McClelland, *The Achieving Society* (New York: Vanguard, 1944).

5. G. W. Ditz, "The Protestant Ethic and the Market Economy," *Kyklos* 33, no. 4 (1980): 626–27.

6. R. B. Perry, *Puritanism and Democracy* (New York: Vanguard, 1944).

7. C. Lasch, *The Culture of Narcissism: American Life in an Age of Diminishing Expectations* (New York: Norton, 1978).

8. H. L. Sheppard and N. Q. Herrick, *Where Have All the Robots Gone* (New York: Free Press, 1972); Special Task Force to the Secretary of HEW, *Work in America* (Cambridge: MIT Press, 1973); and J. Gooding, *The Job Revolution* (New York: Walker and Co., 1972).

9. C. Kluckhohn, "Have There Been Discernible Shifts in American Values During the Past Generation?" *The American Style: Essays in Value and Performance*, ed. E. E. Morrison (New York: Harper and Brothers, 158), 201–24.

10. D. Bell, *The Cultural Contradictions of Capitalism* (New York: Basic Books, 1976).

11. D. Yankelovich, *New Rules: The Search for Self-Fulfillment in a World Turned Upside Down* (New York: Random House, 1981).

12. A. Durning, *How Much is Enough?* (New York: W. W. Norton, 1992).

13. R. E. Purser, C. Park, and A. Montuori, "Limits to Anthropocentrism: Toward an Ecocentric Organization Paradigm?" *Academy of Management Review* 20, no. 4 (1995): 1053–89.

14. Purser, Park, and Montuori, "Limits to Anthropocentrism."

15. J. Dewey, *Ethics: The Middle Works, Volume 5*, ed. Jo Ann Boydston (Carbondale: University of Southern Illinois Press, 1978).

16. L. Westra, "Ecosystem Integrity and Sustainability: The Foundational Values of the Wild," *Perspectives on Ecological Integrity*, ed. L. Westra and J. Lemons (Dordrecht, Netherlands: Kluwer, 1995), 20.

17. G. H. Mead, *Mind, Self, and Society*, ed. Charles Morris (Chicago: University of Chicago Press, 1934).

18. M. Sagoff, "Carrying Capacity and Ecological Economics," *BioScience* 45, no. 9 (1995): 610–24.

19. Sagoff, "Carrying Capacity."

20. M. Wackernagel and W. E. Rees, *Our Ecological Footprint: Reducing Human Impact on the Earth* (Gabriola Island, B.C., and Philadelphia: New Society Publishers, 1996), 135–6.

21. J. Dewey, *Human Nature and Conduct: The Middle Works, Volume 14*, ed. Jo Ann Boydston (Carbondale: University of Southern Illinois Press, 1983), 216–17.

Part Three

Consumption and Cornucopia

12

Scarcity or Abundance?

Julian L. Simon

My central proposition here is simply stated: Almost every trend that affects human welfare points in a positive direction, as long as we consider a reasonably long period of time and hence grasp the overall trend.

I will first review some important absolute trends in human welfare. To repeat, my thesis is that just about every important measure of human welfare shows improvement over the decade and centuries.

Let's start with some trends and conclusions that have long represented the uncontroversial settled wisdom of the economists and other experts who work in these fields, except for the case of population growth. On that latter subject, what you read below was a minority viewpoint until sometime in the 1980s, at which point the mainstream scientific opinion shifted almost all the way to the position set forth here.

Length of Life

The most important and amazing demographic fact—the greatest human achievement in history—is the decrease in the world's death rate. We see that it took thousands of years for life expectancy at birth to increase from just over twenty years to the high 20s. Then, in just the past two centuries, the length of life you could expect for your newborn child in the advanced countries jumped from perhaps thirty years to about seventy-five years. It is this decrease in the death rate that is the cause of there being a larger world population nowadays than in former times. Is this not the greatest change that humankind has ever experienced?

Then, starting well after World War II, the length of life one could expect in the *poor* countries leaped upward by perhaps fifteen or even twenty years, caused by advances in agriculture, sanitation, and medicine. Are not these trends remarkably benign?

Agricultural Labor Force

The best simple measure of a country's standard of living is the proportion of the labor force that works in agriculture. If almost everyone works at farming, there can be little production of non-agricultural goods. We see the astonishing decline over the centuries in the proportion of the population working in agriculture in Great Britain to only about one person in fifty, and the same story describes the United States. This has enabled us to increase our consumption per person by a factor perhaps of 20 or 40 over the centuries.

Raw Materials

During all of human existence, people have worried about running out of natural resources—flint, game animals, what have you. Amazingly, all the evidence shows that exactly the opposite has been true. Raw materials—all of them—are becoming more available rather than more scarce. [Data] clearly shows that natural resource scarcity—as measured by the economically meaningful indicator of cost or price for copper, which is representative of all raw materials—has been decreasing rather than increasing in the long run, with only temporary exceptions from time to time. In the case of copper, we have evidence that the trend of falling prices has been going on for a very long time. In the eighteenth century BCE in Babylonia under Hammurabi—almost 4,000 years ago—the price of copper was about 1,000 times its price in the United States now, relative to wages. And there is no reason why this downward trend might not continue forever.

The trend toward greater availability includes the most counterintuitive case of all—oil. The price rises in crude oil since the 1970s did not stem from increases in the cost of world supply, but rather cartel political action. The production cost in the Persian Gulf still is perhaps 25–75 cents per barrel (1993 dollars). Concerning energy in general, there is no reason to believe that the supply of energy is finite, or that the price of energy will not continue its long-run decrease forever. I realize that it seems strange that the supply of energy is not finite or limited, but if you want a full discussion of the subject, I hope that you will consult another of my books.[1]

Food

Food is an especially important resource. The evidence is particularly strong for food that we are on a benign trend despite rising population. The long-run price of wheat relative to wages, and even relative to consumer products, is down, due to increased productivity.

Famine deaths have decreased during the past century even in absolute terms, let alone relative to population, which pertains particularly to the poor countries. Food consumption per person is up over the last thirty years. Africa's food production per person is down, but by 1993 few people still believe that Africa's suffering has anything to do with a shortage of land or water or sun. Hunger in Africa clearly stems from civil wars and the collectivization of agriculture, which periodic droughts have made more murderous.

Human Life and Labor

There is only one important resource which has shown a trend of increasing scarcity rather than increasing abundance—human beings. Yes, there are more people on Earth now than ever before. But if we measure the scarcity of people the same way that we measure the scarcity of other economic goods—by how much we must pay to obtain their services—we see that wages and salaries have been going up all over the world, in poor as well as rich countries. The amount that you must pay to obtain the services of a manager or a cook has risen in India, just as the price of a cook or a manager has risen in the United States over the decades. The increases in the prices of people's services are a clear indication that people are becoming more scarce economically even though there are more of us.

Cleanliness of the Environment

Ask an average roomful of people if our environment is becoming dirtier or cleaner, and most will say "dirtier." The irrefutable facts are that the air in the United States (and in other rich countries) is safer to breathe now than in decades past. The quantities of pollutants have been declining, especially particulates which are the main pollutant.

The proportion of sites monitoring water of good drinkability in the United States has increased since the data began in 1961. Our environment is increasingly healthy, with every prospect that this trend will continue.

The Vanishing Farmland Crisis

The supposed problem of farmland being urbanized has now been entirely discredited, out-and-out disavowed by those who created the scare. This saga serves to illuminate many similar environmental issues. What about the greenhouse effect? The ozone layer? Acid rain? I'm not a technical expert on the atmosphere. I can say with confidence, however, that on all of these issues there is major scientific controversy about what has happened until now, why it happened, and what might happen in the future. All of these scares are recent, and there has not yet been time for complete research to be done and for the intellectual dust to settle. There may be hard problems here, or there may not.

Even more important for people is that no threatening trend in *human welfare* has been connected to those phenomena. There has been no increase in skin cancers from ozone, no damage to agriculture from a greenhouse effect, and at most slight damage to lakes from acid rain. It may even be that a greenhouse effect would benefit us on balance by warming some areas we'd like warmer, and by increasing the carbon dioxide to agriculture.

Perhaps the most important aspect of the greenhouse–ozone–acid rain complex, and of their as-yet unknown cousin scares which will surely be brought before the public in the future, is that we now have large and ever-increasing capabilities to reverse such trends if they are proven to be dangerous, and at costs that are manageable. Dealing with greenhouse–ozone–acid rain would not place an insuperable constraint upon growth, and would not constitute an ultimate limit upon the increase of productive output or of population. So we can look these issues squarely in the eye and move on.

Are These Predictions Sure Enough to Bet On?

I am so sure of all these upbeat statements that I offer to bet on them, my winnings going to fund new research. Here is the offer: You pick (a) any measure of human welfare—such as life expectancy, infant mortality, the price of aluminum or gasoline, the amount of education per cohort of young people, the rate of ownership of television sets, you name it; (b) a country (or a region such as the developing countries, or the world as a whole); (c) any future year, and I'll bet a week's or a month's pay that that indicator shows improvement relative to the present while you bet that it shows deterioration.

Here is the overarching theory that I offer you to explain why things happen exactly the opposite of the way Malthus and the contemporary Malthusians predict—and why I offer to bet that any measure of human welfare that you choose will show improvement rather than deterioration.

In 1951, Theodore Schultz published an article called "The Declining Economic Importance of Land." He showed that because of technological change, two related things were happening: Food production per person was going up, and the need for agricultural land was going down—even as population was growing very fast. In 1963, Harold Barnett and Chandler Morse showed that despite all the theory about limited quantities of raw materials, and reducing richness of the lodes that are mined, all the raw materials they studied had become less expensive and more available for the decades since the 1870s.

A general process underlies these specific findings: Human beings create more than they use, on average. It had to be so, or we would be an extinct species. And this process is, as the physicists say, an invariance. It applies to all metals, all fuels, all foods, and all other measures of human welfare, and it applies in all countries, and at all times. In other words, this is a theory of "everything economic," or really, a theory of economic history.

Consider this example of the process by which people wind up with increasing availability rather than decreasing availability of resources. England was full of alarm in the 1600s at an impending shortage of energy due to the deforestation of the country for firewood. People feared a scarcity of fuel for both heating and the iron industry. This impending scarcity led to the development of coal.

Then in the mid-1800s, the English came to worry about an impending coal crisis. The great English economist W. S. Jevons calculated that a shortage of coal would bring England's industry to a standstill by 1900; he carefully assessed that oil could never make a decisive difference. Triggered by the impending scarcity of coal (and of whale oil, whose story comes next), ingenious profit-minded people developed oil into a more desirable fuel than coal ever was. And in 1993, we find England exporting both coal and oil.

Another element in the story: Because of increased demand due to population growth and increased income, the price of whale oil for lamps jumped in the 1840s, and the U.S. Civil War pushed it even higher, leading to a whale oil "crisis." This provided incentive for enterprising people to discover and produce substitutes. First came oil from rapeseed, olives, linseed, and camphene oil from pine trees. Then inventors learned how to get coal oil from coal. Other ingenious persons produced kerosene from the rock oil that seeped to the surface, a product so desirable that its price then rose from $0.75 a gallon to $2.00. This high price stimulated enterprisers to focus on the supply of oil, and finally Edwin L. Drake brought in his famous well in Titusville, Pennsylvania. Learning how to refine the oil took a while. But in a few years there were hundreds of small refiners in the United States, and soon the bottom fell out of the whale oil market, the price falling from $2.50 or more at its peak around 1866 to well below $1.00.

We should note that it was not the English or American governments that developed coal or oil, because governments are not effective developers of new technology. Rather, it was individual entrepreneurs who sensed the need, saw opportunity, used all kinds of available information and ideas, made lots of false starts which were very costly to many of these individuals but not to others, and eventually arrived at coal as a viable fuel—because there were enough independent individuals investigating the matter for at least some of them to arrive at sound ideas and methods. And this happened in the context of a competitive enterprise system that worked to produce what was needed by the public. And the entire process of impending shortage and new solution left us better off than if the shortage problem had never arisen.

Here we must address another crucial element in the economics of resources and population—the extent to which the political–social–economic system provides personal freedom from government coercion. Skilled persons require an appropriate social and economic framework that provides incentives for working hard and taking risks, enabling their talents to flower and come to fruition. The key elements of such a framework are economic liberty, respect for property, and fair and sensible rules of the market that are enforced equally for all.

The world's problem is not too many people, but lack of political and economic freedom. Powerful evidence comes from pairs of countries that have the same culture and history, and had much the same standard of living when they split apart after World War II—East and West Germany, North and South Korea, Taiwan and China. In each case the centrally planned communist country began with less population "pressure," as measured by density per square kilometer, than did the market-directed economy. And the communist and non-communist countries also started with much the same birth rates. But the market-directed economies have performed much better economically than the centrally planned economies. This powerful explanation of economic development cuts the ground from under population growth as a likely explanation.

In 1993, there is an important new element not present twenty years ago. The scientific community now agrees with almost all of what you have just heard. My comments do not represent a single lone voice, but rather the scientific consensus.

In 1986, the National Research Council and the National Academy of Sciences published a book on population growth and economic development prepared by a prestigious scholarly group. This "official" report reversed almost completely the frightening conclusions of the previous 1971 NAS report. "Population growth is at *most* a minor factor. . . . The scarcity of exhaustible resources is at most a minor constraint on economic growth,"[2] it now says. It found benefits of additional people as well as costs.

A host of review articles by distinguished economic demographers in the last three or four years have confirmed that this "revisionist" view is indeed consistent with the scientific evidence, though not all the writers would go as far as I do in pointing out the positive long-run effects of population growth. The consensus is more toward a "neutral" judgment. But this is a huge change from the earlier judgment that population growth is economically detrimental.

By 1993, anyone who asserts that population growth damages the economy must either be unaware of the recent economic literature on the subject, or turn a blind eye to the scientific evidence.

These are some of the elements of bad thinking that predispose people to doomsday thinking: (a) Lack of understanding of statistical variability and of the consequent need for looking at a large and representative sample and not just a few casual observations; (b) Lack of historical perspective and the need for looking at long-time series and not just a few recent observations; (c) Lack of proportion in judgments; (d) Lack of understanding of the Hume–Hayek idea of spontaneously evolving cooperative social systems—Adam Smith's "invisible hand"; (e) Seduction by exponential growth and the rest of Malthusian thinking; (f) Lack of understanding of Frederic Bastiat's and Henry Hazlitt's one key lesson of policy economics—that we must consider not just the short-run effects of an action that we might take but also the effects well into the future, and not just the local effect but also the effect on faraway communities. That is, we must take into account not just the immediate and obvious impacts, but also the slow-responding adjustments which diffuse far from the point of initial contact and which often have the opposite result from the short-run localized effects.

In response to questions about species extinction, the World Conservation Union (IUCN) commissioned a book edited by Whitmore and

Sayer[3] to inquire into the extent of extinctions that appeared after the first draft of this book. The results of that project must be considered amazing. All the authors are ecologists who express concern about the rate of extinction. Nevertheless, they all agree that the rate of *known* extinctions has been and continues to be very low. This is a sampling of quotations (with emphasis supplied), first on the subject of the estimated rates:

> . . . IUCN, together with the World Conservation Monitoring Centre, has amassed large volumes of data from specialists around the world relating to species decline, and it would seem sensible to compare these more empirical data with the global extinction estimates. In fact, these and other data indicate *that the number of recorded extinctions for both plants and animals is very small. . . .*[4]
>
> *Known extinction rates are very low.* Reasonably good data exist only for mammals and birds, and the current rate of extinction is about one species per year.[5] If other taxa were to exhibit the same liability to extinction as mammals and birds (as some authors suggest, although others would dispute this), then, if the total number of species in the world is, say, 30 million, the annual rate of extinction would be some 2300 species per year. This is a very significant and disturbing number, but it is much less than most estimates given over the last decade.[6]
>
> . . . [I]f we assume that today's tropical forests occupy only about 80% of the area they did in the 1830s, *it must be assumed that during this contraction, very large numbers of species have been lost in some areas. Yet surprisingly there is no clear-cut evidence for this.* . . . Despite extensive enquiries we have been unable to obtain conclusive evidence to support the suggestion that massive extinctions have taken place in recent times as Norman Myers and others have suggested. On the contrary, work on projects such as Flora Meso-Americana has, at least in some cases, revealed an increase in abundance in many species.[7]
>
> . . . *[A]ctual extinctions remain low.* . . . "Many endangered species appear to have either an almost miraculous capacity for survival, or a guardian angel is watching over their destiny! This means that it is not too late to attempt to protect the Mediterranean flora as a whole, while still identifying appropriate priorities with regard to the goals and means of conservation."[8]
>
> While better knowledge of extinction rates can clearly improve the design of public policies, it is equally apparent that *estimates of global extinction rates are fraught with imprecision. We do not yet know how many species exist, even to within an order of magnitude.*[9]

The most important difference between my and the doomsters' approach to environmental issues is that I base my conclusions on the historical record of the past rather than Malthusian speculation that is inconsistent with the historical statistical record . . . [S]ome striking examples of data show that human welfare has been improving rather than deteriorating, while (and because) population has been growing.

Notes

The phrase *scarcity or abundance* is from Norman Myers and Julian L. Simon, *Scarcity or Abundance?* (New York: W. W. Norton, 1994), pp. 6–21; 196–203; 207. Reprinted by permission of the publisher.

1. See Julian Simon, *The Ultimate Resource* (Princeton: Princeton University Press, 1981), chapters 1–3. See also Julian Simon, *The State of Humanity* (Boston and Oxford: Basil Blackwell, 1994).

2. National Research Council, Committee on Population, and Working Group on Population Growth and Economic Development, *Population Growth and Economic Development: Policy Questions* (Washington D.C.: National Academy Press, 1986).

3. T. C. Whitmore and J. A. Sayers, eds., *Tropical Deforestation and Species Extinction* (New York: Chapman and Hall, 1992).

4. V. H. Heywood and S. N. Stuart, "Species Extinctions in Tropical Forests," in *Tropical Deforestation and Species Extinction*, Whitmore and Sayers, eds. 93.

5. W. V. Reid, "How Many Species Will There Be?" in *Tropical Deforestation and Species Extinction*, Whitmore and Sayers, eds., 55.

6. Heywood and Stuart, 94.

7. Blackmore, personal communication, 1991.

8. Heywood and Stuart, 102.

9. Reid, 56.

13

Holes in the Cornucopia

Ernest Partridge

Introduction

Why take Julian Simon seriously?

This economist has asked us to believe such things as the following:

- The supply of natural resources [is] really infinite![1]
- There is no reason to believe that at any given moment in the future the available quantity of any natural resource or service at present prices will be much smaller than it is now, or nonexistent.[2]
- "We now have in our hands—in our libraries, really—the technology to feed, clothe, and supply energy to an ever-growing population for the next 7 billion years. . . . We [are] able to go on increasing forever."[3]
- "Even the total weight of the earth is not a theoretical limit to the amount of copper that might be available to earthlings in the future. Only the total weight of the universe. . . ."[4] [After all, alchemy is said to be] "preposterous because it is impractical now. But . . . so was electricity considered impractical a century ago."[5] "In the end, copper and oil come out of our minds. That's really where they are."[6]
- "Population density does not damage health or psychological and social well-being."[7]
- "There is no statistical evidence for rapid loss of species in next two decades."
- "The climate does not show signs of unusual and threatening changes."[8]

With such assertions flatly refuted by the preponderance of informed scientific evidence and opinion, why should we take Julian Simon seriously?

247

Because so many do. For instance, Simon's cornucopism is believed to deserve a hearing by such prestigious publications as *Science*, which published one of his papers, in 1980,[9] and also the *Bulletin of the Atomic Scientists* (1984),[10] and *New Scientist* (1986).[11] And his influential book, *The Ultimate Resource*, was considered significant enough to be published by Princeton University Press.

Moreover, among those who take Simon's views seriously are national and international leaders and legislators who are determining our environmental policy. In fact, "business as usual" in political economy treats cornucopism as an "as if" presupposition, that is, established private and political institutions in the world economy are acting "as if" they accepted cornucopism.

Few if any individuals who are well-informed about ecology, the atmospheric sciences, or thermodynamics can be much impressed by the cornucopian arguments. Nonetheless, it is very important that we understand these ideas and identify the presuppositions upon which they stand, and then set down a clearly articulated refutation thereof. For not only has Professor Simon received a respectful hearing among audiences of educated individuals who should know better; still worse, the general tenets of his view are, like it or not, the unarticulated assumptions behind the theory and practice of international commerce and politics.

Accordingly, we should take Julian Simon very seriously.

What is interesting about Simon's position is that the data that he cites are, in all probability, for the most part correct. The trouble is that these data are either irrelevant or partial, and as a result, do not sustain his cheerful worldview.[12] However, that worldview is supported by several presuppositions that are occasionally stated or hinted at but more often unacknowledged. And some of the more salient of these presuppositions can be inferred, not by the pattern of evidence that he cites, but by the patterns of significant information that he disregards.

The superficial plausibility of Simon's position is gained much more through his *exclusion* than through his citing of data. As we shall see, missing from Simon's cheerful prognoses is any acknowledgment or apparent comprehension of such fundamental ecological principles as nutrient cycling, feedback mechanisms, and limiting factors, or even that very foundation of physical science: *thermodynamics* and *entropy*. His perspective is confined to his own field of market economics. Herein is the trap that caught no less of a bioscientist than Paul Ehrlich, who, in 1980, carelessly consented to "wager" Simon that pending shortages in five designated metals would cause a rise in their prices during the next decade. Simon won that wager. Ehrlich's mistake was to consent to "play the game" according to the rules of Simon's discipline of economics.

Recently, Ehrlich and his colleague, Stephen Schneider, challenged Simon to a new wager, this time utilizing indexes derived from atmospheric and soil science and also involving supplies of rice, wheat, and firewood, and additional factors such as AIDS mortality, ocean fisheries, male sperm counts, and species extinctions. Simon refused the offer, on the grounds that these indicators, based upon the biological and physical conditions, "have only indirect effects on people."[13]

I do not attempt in this essay to refute Simon's "cornucopism" point by point—a task that has been ably undertaken by individuals far more scientifically qualified than myself. Instead, this is an exercise in excavative analysis: that is, an attempt to search out the presuppositions of cornucopism—the axioms that must be assumed for Julian Simon's reassurances to stand up. If, as I hope to prove, at least a few of these presuppositions can be shown to be untenable, then so too are Professor Simon's reassurances.

If this analysis succeeds in overturning cornucopism, I cannot be entirely pleased with the accomplishment. I would like to believe that we can grow forever and that all environmental problems can be solved in short order by human ingenuity. It is a cheerful universe that Professor Simon describes for us. Unfortunately, as Richard Feynman used to remind his students, it is not the universe that we happen to live in, and for reasons that physicists like Feynman are especially well qualified to demonstrate.

Very well, then just what kind of universe *does* Simon describe?

The Essentials of Cornucopism

The fundamental tenets of Julian Simon's position appear to be the following:

- The supply of natural resources is infinite.
- Almost all trends in environmental quality are positive.
- History is a reliable guide to future possibilities.
- There is only one scarcity: Human brain power—"The Ultimate Resource."
- Accordingly, population growth rates are not a problem, except possibly in the sense of being too slow.

Let us spell out these claims in order.

The supply of natural resources is infinite.

Closer inspection shows that Simon means by this that "the supply of natural resources is not finite in any economic sense."[14] If shortages appear and prices begin to rise, "human ingenuity" gets to work and finds cheaper ways to extract or recycle the resource or else find alternative resources that provide the same "service"—for example, coal for whale oil, then petroleum for coal.[15] In the future, there is no practical limit to what human brain power will provide, not even, as we noted above, *alchemy:* the transmutation of elements.

Not content with this rather straightforward explanation of "nonfinitude," Simon boldly ventures beyond the fringe. "Finitude," he reminds us, is a concept that "originates in mathematics." He then proceeds with an argument so strange that it must be quoted at some length, if we are to believe that he really means what he is saying:

> The length of a one-inch line is finite in the sense that it is bounded at both ends. But the line within the endpoints contains an infinite number of points; these points cannot be counted, because they have no defined size. Therefore, the number of points in a one-inch segment [of a line] is not finite. *Similarly,* the quantity of copper that will ever be available to us is not finite, because there is no method (even in principle) of making an appropriate count of it.[16] (my italics)

Note that word *similarly.* Clearly, Simon wishes to draw an inference from mathematics to the "real world." Unfortunately, such an inference is invalid, since:

> in the context of mathematics . . . all propositions are tautologous definitions. . . . But scientific subjects are empirical rather than definitional. . . . [Thus] mathematics is not a science in the ordinary sense because it does not deal with facts other than the stuff of mathematics itself, and hence such terms as "finite" do not have the same meaning elsewhere that they do in mathematics.[17]

This quotation is wholly consistent with the view of mathematics that is generally accepted by scientists, mathematicians, and philosophers today—as well as by Julian Simon, who is the author. In fact, of the two quotations just cited, the second appears just one page after the first. Remarkably, Simon seems quite unaware that he has thus totally demolished the conclusion that he painstakingly attempted to establish just three paragraphs previous.

But there is worse to come. In that same "points in a line" example, Simon equates (without supporting argument) the concepts of "indeterminate" and "not finite" (which he is willing to treat as "infinite"). Continuing: "The quantity of a natural resource that might be available to us . . . can never be known even in principle, just as the number of points in a one-inch line can never be counted even in principle. . . . Hence resources are not 'finite' in any meaningful sense."

I should find this very reassuring: for if the day of my death is indeterminate, then by Simon's reckoning I can assume that I am immortal. And since that drill hole on my property, left from a failed attempt at oil exploration, is of indeterminate depth, I can assume that it is infinitely deep. Absurd? Of course! But what else could he mean by his inference from "indeterminate" to "infinite"?

The remaining tenets of Simon's cornucopism can be stated briefly.

Almost all trends in environmental quality are positive.

This is the essential message of Simon's book, *The Ultimate Resource*, of his 1980 paper in *Science*, and indeed of most of his writings. In the anthology, *The Resourceful Earth*, coedited with Herman Kahn, he writes:

> If present trends continue, the world in 2000 will be *less* crowded (though more populated), *less* polluted, *more* stable ecologically, and *less* vulnerable to resource-supply disruption than the world we live in now. Stresses involving population, resources, and environment will be *less in the future than now*.[18]

History is a reliable guide to future possibilities.

To the objection that "history is not a good guide" to understanding the future, because "we are at a turning point in history," Simon replies:

> All throughout history people have felt that they are at a turning point, and it has not turned out to be so. . . . If we cannot base our judgments about the future largely on past experience, in conjunction with reasonable theoretical explanations of that experience, then all our experience and all our science are without value.[19]

As we shall see, it is just those "theoretical explanations of experience," provided by informed scientists, that are the undoing of Simon's optimism.

There is only one scarcity: Human brain power—"The Ultimate Resource."

Simon writes: "The main fuel to speed the world's progress is the stock of human knowledge. And the ultimate resource is skilled, spirited, hopeful people, exerting their wills and imaginations to provide for themselves and their families, thereby inevitably contributing to the benefit of everyone."[20] It then follows that

Population growth rates are not a problem.

Except possibly in the sense of being too slow. The ultimate constraint upon our capacity to enjoy unlimited raw materials at acceptable prices is knowledge. And the source of knowledge is the human mind. Ultimately, then, the key constraint is human imagination and the exercise of educated skills. Hence an increase of human beings constitutes an addition to the crucial stock of resources, along with causing additional consumption of resources.[21]

Some Presuppositions of Cornucopism

This remarkable collection of assertions describes a worldview radically at odds with that of most biological and physical scientists. It is a view that, if true, would seem to rest upon a number of presuppositions equally at odds with "establishment science." In this section, I sketch what appear to me to be the presuppositions that are both most crucial to the cornucopian worldview and most vulnerable to scientific and conceptual criticism. The task of refuting these assumptions will occupy us throughout the remainder of this essay.

Many or most of these assumptions would be rejected by Simon and the cornucopians. But if I have done my work effectively, that rejection is so much the worse for cornucopism, since a rejection of these presuppositions entails a rejection of their worldview. So the challenge of this analysis is simply this: can the cornucopists carry forth their cheerful view of the world without the baggage of the seemingly absurd assumptions on which they rest? I submit that they cannot.

History assures us that human progress is perpetual. The essential parameters of historical development are invariable, and thus there are no essential discontinuities in history. Accordingly, since history discloses that human ingenuity has always eventually triumphed over environmental adversity in the past, there is no reason to doubt that it will do so in the future.

The question of what, if any, meaning and lessons might be drawn from history is one of the most profound and intractable issues in both philosophy and history. And that very fact undermines much of the cornucopian argument, which requires a naive and simplistic belief that history is a *reliable* predictor of the future.

The cornucopian argument rests, not only upon a false reading of history, but also on an over-simplistic notion of induction: namely, that the long history of successful human "coping" with nature gives us inductive warrant to assume more of the same in the future.

By way of refutation, environmental alarmists like to tell the story of the optimist who falls off a high building and who reflects, two-thirds of the way down, "well, so far, so good!" I prefer another tale told by Bertrand Russell, which concerns a certain farmer and his turkey. From the point of view of the reflective turkey, the farmer will *always* greet him in the morning with a bucket of grain. Why? Because, by simple inductive reasoning, it follows that the more often this happens, the more secure he is in the belief that it will happen again—until, one morning, the farmer appears with an axe. Now from the farmer's better informed point of view, he knows that the more often the turkey gets the grain, the *less* likely it is that he will survive another day. Similarly, life underwriters adopt the farmer's point of view.

Eco-scientists, like the farmer, have the better informed point of view. They understand all too well that "business as usual," celebrated by the cornucopians, is undermining the physical-biotic structure that supports that "business," and that the more our industrial "business as usual" continues as it has, the less likely it is that we will be able to continue. We are, as eco-scientists like to put it, living off our biotic capital. All this is so, due to conditions in the real world well known to, and exhaustively studied by, these scientists—conditions systematically discounted and ignored by the cornucopians.

Nature is just inert "stuff," a warehouse of resources, on which we act and from which we take, but about which we need not give special notice. If nature causes us problems, we simply assemble our "best minds" and they will take care of it.

Professor Simon's "nature" is a very strange place—almost a caricature of George Berkeley's subjective idealism; it exists only when we take note of it. "To be is to be a commodity." (More fairly: "To be of any concern to us, is to be a commodity.") Complete your transaction, turn your attention elsewhere, and nature will, for all practical purposes, just disappear until you next find need of it—infinitely and perpetually available. Moreover, nature is also an infinite "sink." When we throw something "away," it is really "away"—it never comes back. The chain of causation, which is very useful to us when we want resources from nature, somehow just stops when we cease taking note of it.

The Berkeleyan worldview goes even further: "to be is to be intended." It then follows that there are no "unintended consequences." In other words, after we enjoy the desired effect, there are no further causes. Pesticide residues "go away," never to appear again. The CO_2 produced by the burning of fossil fuels is of no further concern to us. Nor are the pesticides after they kill the pests and are thus miraculously rendered innocuous to songbirds.

Of course, the cornucopians will retort that this is an unfair caricature—and of course they are right. And yet, they act as if this were so. Cornucopians pay almost no attention to the complications and costs of unintended consequences, and they are quite unimpressed by the findings, even less the warnings, of scientists who study ongoing phenomena in uncommodified nature. And if they admit that causation continues unnoticed, they will then claim, "well never mind, we can fix all that—don't underestimate the power of human ingenuity, especially when motivated by the profit motive."

In short, cornucopians seem to be totally unconcerned by Commoner's law: *You can't do just one thing.* And they rarely bother to ask Hardin's query: *And then what?* All this is surpassingly strange since, despite their allegiance to free market theory, the cornucopians thus conveniently ignore that most fundamental of economic maxims: there is no such thing as a free lunch.

Nature (and, in particular the biosphere) is a mechanical order, not a systemic order.

This axiom of the cornucopian worldview is challenged by the late economist, Nicholas Georgescu-Roegen, who writes:

> the founders of the neoclassical school set out to erect an economic science after the pattern of mechanics [and thus], analytic pieces that adorn the standard economic literature reduce the economic process to a self-sustained mechanical analogue. The patent fact that between the economic process and the material environment there exists a continuous mutual influence which is history making carries no weight with the standard economist.[22]

But while the "pattern of mechanics" is implicit in neoclassical economic theory, it is contrary to the principles of thermodynamics: "The opposition between the entropy law—with its unidirectional qualitative change—and mechanics—where everything can move either forward or backward while remaining self-identical—is accepted without reservation by every physicist and philosopher of science."[23] Georgescu-Roegen's enduring legacy is his demonstration that *entropy*, the cornerstone of physical science, challenges the very foundations of classical economic theory—even more, the reassurances of the cornucopians. We have much more to say about *entropy* shortly.

Simon's mechanistic view of physical reality is nowhere more evident than in his dismissal of concerns about global warming:

> no threatening trend in *human welfare* has been connected to [global warming]. . . . It may even be that a greenhouse effect would benefit us on balance by warming some areas we'd like warmer, and by increasing the carbon dioxide to agriculture. . . . [Moreover], we now have large and ever-increasing capabilities to reverse such trends if they are proven to be dangerous, and at costs that are manageable.[24] (Simon's italics)

Unfortunately, Simon offers not a word to identify these putative "means" to unscramble the atmospheric omelet.

Simon's view here of global atmospheric processes is astonishingly ill-informed. Brushing aside whole libraries of scientific data, he chooses to regard "global warming" as "global warming—*period.*" He acknowledges no changes in "warehouse Earth" except that everywhere things are a bit warmer. To Simon, "warming" the Earth is essentially no different than turning up the thermostat and warming up the house. He thus fails to recognize that the global climate is a *system.* Accordingly, global warming *in toto* would mean that some regions might in fact be cooler, some much hotter, some dryer, some wetter, some subject to more violent tropical storms, and so on, far beyond our reckoning. Ocean currents would likely change with dramatic consequences; for example, just a slight change of direction in the Gulf Stream could condemn Great Britain to a climate comparable to its latitudinal opposite, Labrador. (Of course, as we have seen, if scientists tell us that "we don't know the full effects" of something, Simon routinely interprets this to mean "there are no effects.") Also, Simon typically fails to comprehend the sensitivity of established ecosystems to such sudden climatic changes. For example, whole forest ecosystems, unable to migrate to more favorable climates, would collapse.

Because elementary matter cannot be destroyed, we'll never run out of resources. The dumps and sinks of today are the mines of tomorrow.

This seems to make superficial sense to the mechanist mind-set of reversible processes favored by the cornucopians. However, elemental resources that are scattered as garbage are often woefully beyond recovery. This is so due to some fundamental thermodynamic principles, to which we will return.

In particular, nature can be successfully managed. So-called biological services are fully replicable if not dispensable, once we put our engineering skills to the task.

Biological services, like so many basic concepts of the life and physical sciences, are totally ignored in Julian Simon's writings. Small wonder. To acknowledge these services is to admit that it just might be possible that the natural order that created and nurtured our species might be forever beyond our managerial capabilities. Yet such capabilities are implicit in Simon's cavalier assumption that any problems that might arise can be handled by human ingenuity.

Very well, cornucopians, manage *this!*

The biotic services that we can cite are endless: I will settle for two. First, the phytoplankton, whose production of atmospheric oxygen rivals that of the tropical rain forests. Next, consider permanent removal of CO_2 from the atmosphere by zooplankton, coral, and mollusks (which convert it into carbonates and eventually into limestone). And plankton, of course, is the base of the oceanic ecosystem and is thus utterly necessary if we are to be fed from the seas. And yet, the plankton are threatened by ultraviolet radiation from ozone depletion. Not to worry, Simon reassures us, since that increased UV radiation might improve our vitamin C intake, and the harmful effects might be overcome by wearing hats and sunglasses—and anyway, "if human interaction is causing the change, then human intervention can reverse it."[25]

Unfortunately, neither hats nor sunglasses are of much use to the plankton.

Then there are micro-invertebrates—what E. O. Wilson calls "the little things that run the world," including the mites, worms, and bacteria that transform "dirt" into *soil* and that transform the waste of completed life into nutrients for new life. Of these "little things," Wilson notes:

> we need invertebrates but they don't need us. . . . If invertebrates were to disappear, I doubt that the human species could last more than a few months. . . . The earth would rot. As dead vegetation piled up and dried out, narrowing and closing the channels of the nutrient cycles, other complex forms of vegetation would die off, and with them the last remnants of the vertebrates. The remaining fungi, after enjoying a population explosion of stupendous proportions, would also perish. Within a few decades, the world would return to the state of a billion years ago, composed primarily of bacteria, algae, and a few other very simple multicellular plants.[26]

There is literally no end to an accounting of our debt to the other life forms that maintain the physical-chemical-biotic nexus that is the ecosphere—*Gaia*. But in Julian Simon's writings, there is scarcely a beginning of an acknowledgment of that debt.

In fact, we cannot manage the Earth, precisely because the planet is not an "inert warehouse"; rather, it is a lively place, more complex and wonderful (literally, full of wonders) than we can ever know or even imagine. It is all this, because it is, first and foremost, *systemic*, and thus it displays these features:

- *Energy* that *flows* and *nutrients* that *cycle* through the life forms of the trophic pyramids.
- Biotic and atmospheric action is *synergistic*, in ways that constantly surprise us and thus are out of our control. For example, photochemical smog, we have found, is more than just a soup of component air pollutants. It is a substance cooked into existence by those substances, through the catalytic action of sunlight.
- the biosphere displays numerous *feedback effects*: positive feedbacks that initiate runaway sequences, such as red tides or possibly, for that matter, the greenhouse effects; and negative feedbacks that are characteristic of stable ecosystems.
- We must also cope with *time-lag effects*, such as reforestation, or the so-called geological storage of toxic materials, or the slow spread of pollutants through aquifers.
- We are constantly surprised by *threshold effects* or "tipping effects," such as when a forest or a lake appears capable of absorbing pollutants without harm, until eventually a slight increase causes massive die-offs or eutrophication. (In popular parlance, this phenomenon is known as "the straw that breaks the back.")

Because of these mechanisms, and many more, the biosphere is, to paraphrase J. D. S. Haldane, not only more mysterious than we suppose, but more mysterious than we can suppose. Accordingly, the biosphere is *not* reliably "manageable."

Whatever problems may appear, human ingenuity will be equal to it. We've always solved our problems in the past, and we'll continue to do so long into the future.

Of course, most of this essay is an attempt to answer this cheerful reassurance, and our most systematic rejoinder will appear in the discussion of entropy, below. However, an epistemological note might be appropriate here, prefaced by a personal recollection.

Several years ago, I was engaged in a debate with a fundamentalist preacher. To his claims of the virtual existence of a heaven and hell, I protested that he was offering no evidence to support his claim. He replied, "just you wait—you are eventually going to encounter plenty of evidence, when you meet your Maker!"

His retort was not particularly useful at the time.

I submit that this oft-reiterated claim, "human ingenuity will be equal to the task," is superempirical hand-waving of the same type. It is simply a secular eschatology—a kind of cargo cultism, which attempts to answer scientifically validated challenges with unverifiable promises.

In the meantime, human ingenuity *has* been at work—and in the very biotic, atmospheric, and other sciences that the cornucopians summarily dismiss. Their confidence in "gray matter" thus appears to be curiously selective. Never mind, they tell us, what ingenious humans in the sciences are telling us now, and kindly disregard the weight of evidence and the strength of inference amassed through this applied ingenuity. The cornucopians have faith that somehow, sometime, some other ingenious humans will eventually come along to prove that they are right. "Just you wait!"

"The facts speak for themselves."

To the anticipated criticism, "but what about the other side's data?" Simon boldly replies, "there are no other data." He continues, "I invite you to test for yourself this assertion that the conditions of humanity have gotten better." And he then refers the readers to the Census Bureau's *Statistical Abstract of the United States*. He concludes, "every single measure shows a trend of improvement rather than the deterioration that the doomsayers claim has occurred."[27]

No data? Perhaps he just has not bothered to look. Simon claims that "There is no documentation of further data produced by biologists since 1979 to demonstrate what Norman Myers was saying" about mass extinctions. Myers replies, "during those thirteen years, the number of papers published on the mass extinction crisis is over three hundred. . . . No documentation, no data, Professor Simon?"[28]

Simply put, Simon counts as data what he wants to use as data. The rest he simply disregards. As we stated at the outset, the problem with Simon's argument is not that the data he cites is not factual, but that it is partial or irrelevant. And it is that vast body of unacknowledged fact and theory that demolishes the cornucopian view.

"The facts speak for themselves" is the first refuge of the huckster posing as a scientist.[29] But as anyone even casually familiar with the philosophy of science knows full well, facts only speak to us *in context* of other facts, and guided by theory. This is what distinguishes sound scientific theory and ad hoc caricatures such as creation science and, I submit, cornucopism. In the case of science, theory arises out of observation of facts, effectively classified and organized. In caricature science, the imposed theory selects facts and predetermines what is to count as a fact and as evidence. And finally, sound science is vulnerable to Karl Popper's "falsifiability principle"; that is, the principle that scientific theories must yield implications that can clearly and unequivocally be shown to be otherwise, if the world is *not* what the theory describes it to be. Political and religious apologists do not submit to such a test. Nor does Simon's worldview, for recall his stock-in-trade, unverifiable, super-empirical plea: "human ingenuity will come up with an answer, some-time."

Facts do *not* speak for themselves. Give someone a carte blanche li-cense both to pick any facts that he chooses and to disregard any others that he may find inconvenient, and he will be able to claim a demonstra-tion of virtually anything under the sun. However, by violating the falsi-fiability rule, this self-concocted ability to prove anything whatever amounts to a capacity to prove nothing at all.

The preponderance of scientific opinion and theory, in the relevant disciplines of ecology, atmospherics, soils, demographics, and even physics, is simply wrong. Julian Simon and his friends know better. Furthermore, the well-known pessimism of envi-ronmental scientists is suspiciously motivated.

With this claim the cornucopians, quite frankly, display colossal *chutz-pah*. For they contend, in effect, that the consensus opinion of entire fields of established sciences—ecology, atmospheric chemistry and cli-matology, demographics, agronomy, and so on—are fundamentally in error. All this scientific investigation and expertise is casually brushed aside in favor of historical analogies ("trends"), selected anecdotes, and abstract economic modeling. Still worse, at the close of his *Science* and *Bulletin of the Atomic Scientists* articles, and throughout the two books ex-amined herein, Professor Simon practices unlicensed psychotherapy as he claims that the pessimism of "established science" is a conspiracy, motivated by careerism, competitive grantsmanship, a public fascination with bad news, and willingness to exaggerate in order to mobilize public activism.[30]

The Entropy Trap

The most fundamental error of the cornucopian worldview is that it takes no account of the laws of thermodynamics, and particularly of the condition known as *entropy*.[31] And since these laws are at the foundation of modern physics and thus "no exception to [the thermodynamic laws] has ever been observed,"[32] it follows that the cornucopians must be dealing with a different physical universe than the one we happen to reside in.

While thermodynamics can be one of the most devilishly difficult branches of physics (and far beyond the comprehension of this writer), in its general, nonquantitative formulation, the second law is quite simple: "the free ['useful'] heat-energy of a closed system continuously and irrevocably degrades itself into bound ['useless'] energy . . . Entropy (i.e., the amount of bound energy) of a closed system continuously increases or . . . the order of such a system steadily turns into disorder."[33]

Ehrlich, Ehrlich and Holdren express the second thermodynamic law as follows: "all physical processes, natural and technological, proceed in such a way that the availability of the energy involved decreases. . . . What is consumed when we use energy . . . is not energy itself but its availability for doing useful work." They then spell out five significant implications of the second law:

1. In any transformation of energy, some of the energy is degraded.
2. No process is possible whose sole result is the conversion of a given quantity of heat (thermal energy) into an equal amount of useful work.
3. No process is possible whose sole result is the flow of heat from a colder body to a hotter one.
4. The availability of a given quantity of energy can only be used once; that is, the property of convertibility into useful work cannot be "recycled."
5. In spontaneous processes, concentrations (of anything) tend to disperse, structure tends to disappear, order becomes disorder.[34]

This final formulation, linking *work and heat* to *structure, order, and probability*, is the most puzzling implication of the second law, and the implication that bears most heavily on the cornucopian worldview. An elaboration is in order.

The most memorable explanation, to my mind, comes from Isaac Asimov.[35] Consider a typical child's bedroom. When clean, it is orderly and improbable. Then entropy sets in, and it becomes disorderly and probable. Why probable? Because, for example, dirty socks belong in just one place—the laundry basket—but instead end up anywhere else, which is a more "probable" location than the basket. A made-up bed is just one improbable condition of numerous states of the bed; "unmade" is all the others.

Then Mother sees the entropic mess and says, "No dinner for you, young man, until you clean this up!" So what does it take to reverse entropy and achieve the improbably neat condition? Knowledge of where things belong (information) and *energy*.

Next, consider dispersion and probability." The tea in the tea bag disperses into the cup of hot water. Never does the tea in the cup return to the tea bag. Every pool game begins with a "break" of a racked triangle of fifteen balls. No game has ever succeeded in returning the scattered balls to a triangle. For that you need outside information and energy—a player racking them up. You will never shuffle a deck of cards into the order of suits. (Conceivably possible but virtually impossible.) "You can not unscramble an egg" (C. P. Snow). Once again, "all physical processes proceed in such a way that the entropy of the universe increases." "We can't win, we can't break even, and we can't get out of the game."[36]

In the realm of deliberate action, this means that *order, concentration, and useful energy is purchased at the expense of more disorder, dispersion, and lost potential.* You can't strike a match twice; water pressure having turned a turbine cannot turn it again, until solar energy has evaporated it, turned into rain again, and dropped it on the upstream watershed.

But if a local reversal of entropy ("negative entropy," or *negentropy*) must result in a net increase in systemic entropy, how then does life evolve toward greater complexity—from probable to improbable states? Simply because the entropy that drives the negentropy that is life and evolution comes to us from an external source: the sun. In short: the biosphere and human culture are entropy pumps powered by solar energy (in the case of human culture, solar energy stored in biomass and fossil fuels).

The implication for environmental policy and management is stark: *all our environmental "problems" are the result of prior "solutions"!* Think about it! The solution to premature death has resulted in the population explosion. The solution to mass transportation has led to air pollution. The solution of intensive agriculture has caused nitrate pollution of groundwater and the eutrophication of streams.

This undoing of our good intentions has received popular notice in Edward Tenner's new book, *Why Things Bite Back: Technology and the Revenge of Unintended Consequences.*[37] In his review of the book in *Science,* Langdon Winner cites some of these unintended consequences:

> Antibiotics marshaled against disease have spawned new varieties of highly virulent drug-resistant bacteria that pose new threats to human health. Methods for preventing forest fires have been so effective in preserving the dry underbrush that wildfires are now enormous conflagrations. . . . Cleverly engineered structures that have altered the contours of rivers and beaches have unwittingly contributed to the lethal force of "natural disaster" that now vex civilization.[38]

Herein lies the fatal flaw in the cornucopians' attempt to extrapolate into the future favorable trends (i.e., increased wealth and resources) from the past. While, in the past, we have exported our entropy cost to the environment as pollution, we have managed to get away with it. For, true to the traditional pioneer spirit, we have been able to use it up, then move on. But now, with the expanding population, there is no more "on" to move to, and still worse, the pollution sink that is the environment is nearing saturation, whereby the synergisms, feedbacks, and threshold effects begin to kick in. In fact, this has already happened in the Grand Banks fisheries and is likely happening in the atmosphere with ozone depletion and global warming. But don't expect the cornu-copians to recognize any of this. *Entropy* and *thermodynamics* (along with *synergism, threshold,* and *feedback*) are missing from the indexes of the two Simon books on my desk, and I cannot recall encountering any of these concepts anywhere in Simon's writings.[39]

Finally, the principle that "order (negentropy) is purchased at the price of greater disorder (entropy)" may be the undoing of Simon's secular eschatology, that is, the faith that we'll think of something— don't underestimate the ingenuity of human beings. It is the irreparable hole in the cornucopia, since however we might manage to "fix" (re-verse the entropy of) developing environmental problems, these fixes are destined to create still more problems (entropy). (Remember: every environmental problem we now have is the result of a prior solution.) Thus we are running a race with our shadow, with the light source for-ever behind our backs. It won't do just to run faster. The rules of that game forbid ultimate success: we can't win, we can't break even, we can't leave the game. Perhaps the only acceptable option is to cherish and preserve the system that brought us here in the first place, namely, the ecosystem. If so, we might once again charge the entropy bill to the sun's account.

A Beautiful Theory and an Inscrutable World

An analysis of far-out examples is a useful and favorite trick of econ-omists

—Julian Simon[40]

The Theory is Beautiful; It's Reality that Has Me Baffled.

—Source unknown

How can intelligent and well-educated individuals such as Julian Simon arrive at such bizarre conclusions? John Ruggie, the moderator of Julian Simon's debate with Norman Myers, offers an intriguing suggestion:

The underlying ontology of [Myers' and Simon's] worlds . . . differs. Si-mon's world is made up of palpable and infinitely divisible units, existing within a field of discrete events. In contrast, Myers' world is made up of indivisible wholes, linked together by cycles and conjunctures that are subject to butterfly effects. If Simon's dominant metaphor is mechanical, Myers's is organic.[41]

As we have seen, the Simon worldview is an ontology in a Kantian sense: it is a priori, and thus not the product of empirical investigation of the world, but rather a theoretical construct that imposes his view upon the world, thus dictating what will and what will not count as evidence as to the nature of the world. And since that worldview is presupposed, and refuting evidence is excluded a priori, this is an ontology that violates the most fundamental requirement of scientific inquiry, *falsifiability*; namely, the requirement that all scientific hypotheses clearly indicate the type of evidence that would prove it false. In simple terms, nothing will budge Simon's worldview, since he declares, at the outset, that nothing will be allowed to do so.

Clearly, Simon's ontology is derived from a dominant paradigm of his discipline of economics: *the perfect market*. In theory, the perfect market has these qualities:

An infinite (or very large) pool of potential buyers and sellers ("agents")
Radical autonomy: i.e., no collusion among the potential agents
All relevant information available to the agents
No transaction costs
No externalities, positive or negative, resulting from the transactions
Transactions, once completed, are final
All transactions are completely voluntary
"Pareto Optimality:" no transactions that leave a party worse off
All agents are solely motivated to maximize their personal utility, or "preference satisfaction" (i.e., all parties are so-called "economic men"[42])

The perfect market thus aggregates autonomous agents, prepared to exchange discrete items such as cash, goods, services, resources. It is this theoretical construct that describes the mechanistic and atomistic world of Simon's ontology. It is also, let us note, a world wherein market incentives activate the human ingenuity that, Simon believes, can in principle overcome all obstacles—be they ecological or even thermodynamic.

As all economists (including Simon) would readily agree, the theoretical perfect market composed of economic agents is an ideal type, nowhere found in the real world. However, like ideal types in physics such as a frictionless machine, absolute zero, and perfect vacuum (also nowhere exemplified in nature), the perfect market and economic man are essential to the abstract quantified modeling that characterizes modern economic theory.[43]

This abstract worldview of autonomous, utility-maximizing rational agents is replicated in the political ideology of *libertarianism*, with its fundamental and inviolable rights to *life*, *liberty*, and *property*, and its concomitant denial of welfare rights and social duties. Accordingly, to the libertarian, the only legitimate functions of government are the protection of life, liberty, and property from external threats (the military), internal threat (the police), and civil disputes (the courts). To the libertarian, all else—education, welfare, promotion of the arts, protection of the environment, and so on—are solely the concern of private individuals, and no business of the government. Thus the libertarian repeats in his political theory what the classical economist describes in his central paradigm: an aggregate of discrete, autonomous individuals, each owning items and parcels of property, totally encapsulated by title and well-defined boundary lines. To both, society is like a swap meet, composed of self-serving economic persons, all mutual strangers meeting on inert Newtonian space (which, *qua* inert, is totally unaffected by what transpires upon it).[44]

Classical, free-market economic theory, then, appears to be the foundation of Simon's atomistic worldview of autonomous individuals, inviolable property lines, and discrete events. From this *idée fixe* of the perfect market he moves outward to a theory of politics, libertarianism, and thence to a theory of physical reality—a view of a world of infinite resources, infinite possibilities, infinite growth, all this unhampered by such limitations and complications as feedbacks, synergisms, time lapses, and above all, *entropy*. In this Simonized world, nature is a passive theater whereupon we seek to maximize our individual utilities, all the while absorbing our assaults without consequences. By this account, in nature, just as in the market, when a transaction is agreed to and the exchange is made, then that's the end of it. All acts are disconnected. You *can* do just one thing! No need to ask Hardin's query: "and then what?" To Julian Simon, then, *economics* is the queen of sciences, according to which human endeavor and even physical reality is best interpreted. This point of view is not unique to Simon: for example, A. Myrick Freeman writes that " to the economist, the environment is a scarce resource which contributes to human welfare."[45] And William Baxter:

All our environmental problems are, in essence, specific instances of a problem of great familiarity: how can we arrange our society so as to make the most effective use of our resources. . . . To assert that there is . . . an environmental problem is to assert, at least implicitly, that one or more resources is not being used so as to maximize human satisfactions. . . . Environmental problems are economic problems, and better insight can be gained by economic analysis.[46]

In short, in an audacious reversal of Copernicus, these economists are proposing to place humanity back at the center of the physical universe. In contradistinction, the economist Georgescu-Roegen insists that "the economic process is solidly anchored to a material base which is subject to definite constraints."[47] Gaylord Nelson puts the matter more bluntly: "the economy is a wholly owned subsidiary of the environment."[48]

Unfortunately, Julian Simon's ontology simply does not describe the world that we live in, since it is articulated with a fundamental disregard of basic ecological (which is to say natural) laws—not to mention the findings of behavioral science and the insights of moral philosophy (which we cannot elaborate in this space).[49] The surveyor can plot a property line within the inch, but that line has no meaning or significance to the conditions of nature that give that property its value—and that, for that matter, sustain our very lives. The atmosphere, the ocean, cycling nutrients, migrating birds, insects and spores, global pollution sinks and heat sinks—none of these are the least aware of property lines. None can be meaningfully contained within the confines, and thus within the concept, of "inviolable private property."

While Julian Simon's ontology selects, a priori, what is to count as data and evidence, it does not enjoy a priori immunity from the challenge of scientific facts. Nature, as discovered and articulated in the body of modern bioscience, talks back to Simon's ontology. Simon's reductive, atomistic worldview entails claims that are empirically falsifiable (thus scientifically meaningful), and furthermore, demonstrably false (thus scientifically refuted). Simply put, human ingenuity, exemplified by modern science, has persuasively demonstrated that in the real world, energy flows up trophic pyramids, nutrients recycle through and back into ecosystems, and entropy reigns supreme, and thus each solution generates new problems. Furthermore, science has taught us that the atmosphere, the oceans, and the soil, which support our lives, are in fact *systems* and not infinitely large and inert dumps. In short, life (including human life) and its supporting mechanisms are simply not what Julian Simon claimed them to be. Commoner's law—"you can't do just one thing"—is more than a slogan: it is a demonstrable fact.

Conclusions

Why, then, is Julian Simon taken seriously?

The dominant paradigm in the industrialized world requires constant growth. One might call this the shark economy since, like the shark, it has to move constantly in order to stay alive. Quiescence means death. The engine of the modern economy is return on investment, that is, growth. Steady-state and the end of growth (the sigmoid curve) are equally axiomatic in natural ecosystems. So the two economies, *natural* and *industrial*, are based upon logically contrary axioms.

Thus the economists' choice is simple and stark: either devise and defend a new economic theory that accommodates itself to the basic conditions of life as articulated by the life and physical sciences, or else simply elect to ignore these facts and deal instead with a fanciful world. Clearly, Simon chose the latter course and, in the face of both common sense and scientific evidence, posited, as he had to, a world of infinite resources that is supportive of perpetual growth.

I once heard Paul Ehrlich remark that if an engineer proposed a design for an aircraft with a constantly expanding crew, we would think him mad. And yet, when an economist defends a theory that posits a perpetually growing global economy, he is awarded a Nobel Prize. Notwithstanding that, perpetual growth is unknown in the natural world.

While I argue that there are severe limitations to the applicability of economic theory to the natural world, economic theory might nonetheless help to explain the successful promulgation of Professor Simon's ideas: There is a demand, lavishly rewarded, for an apologia for classical economic practice, for a justification of global industrial business as usual, and thus for a dismissal of the eco-scientists' warnings. Julian Simon has met that demand with extraordinary wit and cleverness.

In short, if there had been no Julian Simon he would have to be invented.

But Simon posits a worldview and proposes a policy that can only lead to ruin. To paraphrase the wise and much-lamented physicist, Richard Feynman, "For a successful environmental policy, reality must take precedence over wishful thinking, for nature cannot be fooled."[50]

Notes

1. I take this to be a fair paraphrase, since it is taken from the title of chapter 3 of Simon's book, *The Ultimate Resource*, "Can the Supply of Natural Resources Really Be Infinite? Yes!" (Princeton: Princeton University Press, 1981).

2. *The Ultimate Resource*, 48.

3. Norman Myers and Julian Simon, *Scarcity or Abundance* (New York: Norton, 1994), 65.

4. Julian Simon, "Resources, Population, Environment: An Oversupply of False Bad News," *Science* 208 (June 1980): 1435–36.

5. Julian Simon, "Reply to Critics, Letters Section," *Science* 208 (December 19, 1980): 1306.

6. Myers and Simon, *Scarcity or Abundance*, 100. Norman Myers is here quoting Simon in *The Ultimate Resource*. Unfortunately, there is no page reference for Myers's citation.

7. Another chapter title (chapter 18) in Simon, *The Ultimate Resource*.

8. These last two from Julian Simon, "Bright Global Future," *Bulletin of the Atomic Scientists* (November 1984): 14.

9. Simon, "Resources, Population, Environment: An Oversupply of False Bad News," 1431–37. This is not to say that this esteemed publication erred in choosing to publish Simon's paper. The paper is valuable for the significant policies that it supports and for its display of fallacies assembled in support of what, to many, are plausible conclusions. Equally valuable as the paper were the abundant criticisms that were to follow in the "Letters" section of *Science*.

10. Simon, "Bright Global Future," (November 1984): 14–18. This article has its origin in a symposium at the 1984 annual meeting of the American Association for the Advancement of Science, "Knockdown-Dragout on the Global Future," which featured Prof. Simon.

11. "Disappearing Species, Deforestation and Data," *New Scientist* 110 (May 15, 1986): 60–63.

12. As an example of a non sequitur, consider Simon's dismissal of governmental concern about soil erosion, which he charges is a "fraud." On the contrary, he says (perhaps correctly) that soil loss has decreased by all of 6 percent (from 5.1 tons/acre to 4.8 tons/acre). But it does not follow from this that it is of no concern. Quite the contrary, he cites and does not contest Al Gore's observation that "eight acres of prime topsoil floats past Memphis every hour" and that half of the topsoil of Iowa has been lost to erosion. So the question he should ask, and doesn't, is whether this allegedly "reduced" loss still constitutes a problem. If so, then what is the "fraud"? (Myers and Simon, *Scarcity or Abundance*, 53). (Analogously, the FBI reports a 15 percent drop in murder rates last year. According to Prof. Simon's logic, it then follows that murder is no longer a problem in the United States.)

13. Charles Petit, "Two Stanford Scholars Take on Rosy Economist," *San Francisco Chronicle*, May 18, 1995, 15(A). The final quotation is from Petit, not Simon.

14. Simon, *The Ultimate Resource*, [42.]

15. Simon, "Bright Global Future," 15.

16. Simon, "Bright Global Future," 47.

17. Simon, "Bright Global Future," 48.

18. Quoted by Simon in "Bright Global Future," 14.

19. Simon, "Bright Global Future," 16.

20. Myers and Simon, *Scarcity or Abundance*, 33. Philosopher Jan Narveson fully concurs: "Sustainability has become the buzz-word, the implication being that life as we currently know it and enjoy it is not sustainable. . . . Should we be impressed by that? . . . [T]he answer is no. Future generations will consist, after all, of rational animals, resourceful people like our ancestors and (I hope!) our-

selves. They will be able to cope. The human species has made a decent or better than decent life for itself in an incredible variety of "ecologies." . . . It is astonishing how contemporary humans can overlook the resourcefulness of their fellows in all of this recent cant about ecology. . . . There is . . . no resource problem of consequence for the globe." (Jan Narveson, "Humanism for Humans," *Free Inquiry* (Spring 1993): 24.

21. Simon, "Resources, Population," 1435–36.

22. Nicholas Georgescu-Roegen, "The Entropy Law and the Economic Problem," in *Valuing the Earth: Economics, Ecology, Ethics*, ed. Herman E. Daly and Kenneth N. Townsend (Boston: MIT Press, 1993), 75.

23. Georgescu-Roegen, "Entropy, Economic Problem," 87–88.

24. Myers and Simon, *Scarcity or Abundance*, 18–19. Simon is referring here to acid rain and ozone depletion as well as the greenhouse effect. However, our focus of concern here is on global warming. About the ozone layer, Simon reports "there has been no increase in skin cancers from ozone." I doubt that he would be able to convince the Australians of this.

25. Myers and Simon, *Scarcity or Abundance*, 63.

26. Edward O. Wilson, "The Little Things That Run the World," *Conservation Biology* 1, no. 4 (December 1987): 344.

27. Myers and Simon, *Scarcity or Abundance*, 64.

28. Myers and Simon, *Scarcity or Abundance*, 129.

29. As an example, consider the recent NBC program on "The Mysterious Origins of Man," which has attracted the ire of *Science* magazine and the AAAS. In this strange compendium of kookery, we were told that dinosaurs and humans coexisted, that the sphinx was built 25,000 years ago, and that the site of Atlantis is now under a mile of Antarctic ice. At the close, the "host," Charlton Heston, urged us to "keep an open mind" and reminded us that "the facts speak for themselves."

30. Simon, "Resources, Population," 1436–37. See also, Simon, "Bright Global Future," 16. "The conspiracy of establishment science" is a recurrent theme among creationists, UFO-logists, and other pseudoscientific groups. The charge of "establishment conspiracy" was particularly prominent in the NBC-TV program, "The Mysterious Origins of Man," cited in the preceding note.

31. The title *The Entropy Trap* is "borrowed" from Kenneth Boulding, *The Meaning of the Twentieth Century* (New York: Harper Colophon, 1965), chap. 7. I can think of no better way to describe the significance of the concept of entropy to environmental policy.

32. Paul R. Ehrlich, and Anne H. Ehrlich, and John Holdren, "Availability, Entropy and the Laws of Thermodynamics," in Georgescu-Roegen, "Entropy, Economic Problem," 69.

33. The source of this formulation is Nicholas Georgescu-Roegen who, along with Herman Daly and Kenneth Boulding, is one of the few economists to take entropy seriously. Georgescu-Roegen, "Entropy, Economic Problem," 78.

34. Ehrlich, Ehrlich, and Holdren, "Availability," 71.

35. I have long since forgotten just where I read this. However, I am quite (though not totally) certain, that the source of this example is Isaac Asimov.

36. Ehrlich, Ehrlich, and Holdren, *Availability,* 72.

37. New York: Knopf, 1966.

38. *Science* 224, (August 23, 1996): 1052.

39. The contrast between the economists' and the physicists' treatment of *heat* is instructive. In the taxonomy of classical economics, heat is a subset of *energy,* which in turn is a subset of the category of *economic resources;* that is, *heat* is just one of many economic *goods.* To the physicist studying the potentiality of all physical activity, heat is virtually everything. All work proceeds from heat differential (free energy), and the end product of all useful activity is useless or bound heat. In other words, according to the second law of thermodynamics, without heat differential, nothing happens.

40. Simon, *The Ultimate Resource,* 43.

41. John Ruggie, "Forward" to Myers and Simon, *Scarcity or Abundance,* xiv.

42. While I would prefer the politically correct *economic person,* the term *man* is used here to reflect an historically established gender preference: economic man (*homo economicus*).

43. If the physicist uses ideal types to advantage, then why not the economist? Because the difference between the disciplines is crucial: In physics, these ideal types are derived, one at a time, from carefully conducted experiments and measurements, and they are asymptomatic extrapolations from near perfect laboratory conditions end points of precisely measured empirical functions. And finally, in physics, unlike economics, these ideal types, when employed in the hypothetical-deductive methodology of physical science, yield falsifiable predictions and thence experimental verifications. None of this is true of the economists' ideal types. They are not extrapolated to zero, they are not the single controlled variables of experiments, but rather are bundled together in theoretical constructs. Furthermore, they posit, irrelevant to their theory, conditions which are in fact inalienable to human motives and economic activity: such things as transaction costs, externalities, collusion, restricted access, imperfect information, distributive injustice, self-transcending motivation, and communal loyalty.

44. For a more developed critique of libertarianism, see my "Environmental Justice and Shared Fate," *Human Ecology Review* 2, no. 2 (Winter/Spring 1996): 138–47.

45. "The Ethical Basis of the Economic View of the Environment," Center for the Study of Value and Social Policy (Boulder: University of Colorado Press, 1983).

46. *People or Penguins: The Case for Optimal Pollution* (New York: Columbia University Press, 1974), 15–17.

47. Georgescu-Roegen, "Entropy, Economic Problem," 81.

48. "The Bankruptcy Files," *Wilderness* 58 (Summer 1994), 3.

49. But let this much suffice: First of all, human beings are in fact inalienably *social animals* and not the egoistic autonomous agents of the classical economic paradigm. Well-ordered societies can only exist and endure if the members thereof have concerns that transcend their personal "utility maximization." (I develop this notion at length in my essay, "Why Care About the Future?" in

Responsibilities to Future Generations, ed. Ernest Partridge (Buffalo, NY: Prometheus Books, 1981). See also Mark Sagoff, *The Economy of the Earth* (Cambridge: Cambridge University Press, 1988), chaps. 2 and 3. Furthermore, perfect free-market transactions, far from being exemplars of rational decision-making, often have little to do with rationality. We do not regard willingness to pay as relevant in the criminal or civil justice systems. Nor is this relevant in national defense or in education. Scientific and scholarly papers are not evaluated by pricing at the margin, nor are mathematical proofs or even economic theories. And moral issues are not properly settled by the free market, otherwise, we would still condone slavery. Clearly, the life of *homo economicus* is neither healthy, nor moral, nor even, in the final analysis, rational.

50. Originally, "for a successful technology, reality must take precedence over public relations, for nature cannot be fooled." This remark appeared at the close of Feynman's dissent from the report of the Challenger Committee.

14

Do We Consume Too Much?

Mark Sagoff

In 1994, when delegates from around the world gathered in Cairo for
the International Conference on Population and Development, representatives from developing countries protested that a baby born in the
United States will consume during its lifetime twenty times as much of
the world's resources as an African or an Indian baby.[1] The problem for
the world's environment, they argued, is overconsumption in the North,
not overpopulation in the South. Consumption in industrialized nations
"has led to overexploitation of the resources of developing countries,"
a speaker from Kenya declared. A delegate from Antigua reproached
the wealthiest 20 percent of the world's population for consuming 80
percent of the goods and services produced from the earth's resources.[2]

Do we consume too much? To some, the answer is self-evident. If
there is only so much food, timber, petroleum, and other material to go
around, the more we consume, the less must be available for others. The
global economy cannot grow indefinitely on a finite planet. As populations increase and economies expand, natural resources must be depleted; prices will rise, and humanity—especially the poor and future
generations at all income levels—will suffer as a result.[3]

Other reasons to suppose we consume too much are less often stated
though also widely believed. Of these the simplest—a lesson we learn
from our parents and from literature since the Old Testament—may be
the best: although we must satisfy basic needs, a good life is not one
devoted to amassing material possessions; what we own comes to own
us, keeping us from fulfilling commitments that give meaning to life,
such as those to family, friends, and faith. The appreciation of nature
also deepens our lives. As we consume more, however, we are more likely

271

to transform the natural world, so that less of it will remain for us to appreciate.

Today those who wish to protect the natural environment rarely offer ethical or spiritual reasons for the policies they favor. Instead they say we are running out of resources or causing the collapse of ecosystems on which we depend. Predictions of resource scarcity appear objective and scientific, whereas pronouncements that nature is sacred or that greed is bad appear judgmental or even embarrassing in a secular society. Prudential and economic arguments, moreover, have succeeded better than moral or spiritual ones in swaying public policy.

These prudential and economic arguments are not likely to succeed much longer. It is simply wrong to believe that nature sets physical limits to economic growth—that is, to prosperity and the production and consumption of goods and services on which it is based. The idea that increasing consumption will inevitably lead to depletion and scarcity, as plausible as it may seem, is mistaken both in principle and in fact. It is based on four misconceptions.

Misconception No. 1: We Are Running Out of Raw Materials

In the 1970s Paul Ehrlich, a biologist at Stanford University, predicted that global shortages would soon send prices for food, fresh water, energy, metals, paper, and other materials sharply higher. "It seems certain," Paul and Anne Ehrlich wrote in *The End of Affluence* (1974), "that energy shortages will be with us for the rest of the century, and that before 1985 mankind will enter a genuine age of scarcity in which many things besides energy will be in short supply." Crucial materials would near depletion during the 1980s, Ehrlich predicted, pushing prices out of reach. "Starvation among people will be accompanied by starvation of industries for the materials they require."[4]

Things have not turned out as Ehrlich expected. In the early 1990s real prices for food overall fell.[5] Raw materials—including energy resources—are generally more abundant and less expensive today than they were twenty years ago. When Ehrlich wrote, economically recoverable world reserves of petroleum stood at 640 billion barrels.[6] Since that time reserves have increased by more than 50 percent, reaching more than 1,000 billion barrels in 1989.[7] They have held steady in spite of rising consumption. The pre-tax real price of gasoline was lower during this decade than at any other time since 1947.[8] The World Energy Council announced in 1992 that "fears of imminent [resource] exhaustion that were widely held 20 years ago are now considered to have been unfounded."[9]

The World Resources Institute, in a 1994–1995 report, referred to "the frequently expressed concern that high levels of consumption will lead to resource depletion and to physical shortages that might limit growth or development opportunity."[10] Examining the evidence, however, the institute said that "the world is not yet running out of most nonrenewable resources and is not likely to, at least in the next few decades."[11] A 1988 report from the Office of Technology Assessment concluded, "The nation's future has probably never been less constrained by the cost of natural resources."[12]

It is reasonable to expect that as raw materials become less expensive, they will be more rapidly depleted. This expectation is also mistaken. From 1980 to 1990, for example, while the prices of resource-based commodities declined (the price of rubber by 40 percent, cement by 40 percent, and coal by almost 50 percent), reserves of most raw materials increased.[13] Economists offer three explanations.

First, with regard to subsoil resources, the world becomes ever more adept at discovering new reserves and exploiting old ones. Exploring for oil, for example, used to be a hit-or-miss proposition, resulting in a lot of dry holes. Today oil companies can use seismic waves to help them create precise computer images of the earth.[14] New methods of extraction—for example, using bacteria to leach metals from low-grade ores—greatly increase resource recovery. Reserves of resources "are actually functions of technology," one analyst has written. "The more advanced the technology, the more reserves become known and recoverable."[15]

Second, plentiful resources can be used in place of those that become scarce. Analysts speak of an Age of Substitutability and point, for example, to nanotubes, tiny cylinders of carbon whose molecular structure forms fibers a hundred times as strong as steel, at one-sixth the weight.[16] As technologies that use more-abundant resources substitute for those needing less-abundant ones—for example, ceramics in place of tungsten, fiber optics in place of copper wire, aluminum cans in place of tin ones—the demand for and the price of the less-abundant resources decline.

Third, the more we learn about materials, the more efficiently we use them. The progress from candles to carbon-filament to tungsten incandescent lamps, for example, decreased the energy required for and the cost of a unit of household lighting by many times. Compact fluorescent lights are four times as efficient as today's incandescent bulbs and last ten to twenty times as long.[17] Comparable energy savings are available in other appliances: for example, refrigerators sold in 1993 were 23 percent more efficient than those sold in 1990 and 65 percent more efficient than those sold in 1980, saving consumers billions in electric bills.[18]

Amory Lovins, the director of the Rocky Mountain Institute, has described a new generation of ultralight automobiles that could deliver the safety and muscle of today's cars but with far better mileage—four times as much in prototypes and ten times as much in projected models.[19] Since in today's cars only 15 to 20 percent of the fuel's energy reaches the wheels (the rest is lost in the engine and the transmission), and since materials lighter and stronger than steel are available or on the way, no expert questions the feasibility of the high-mileage vehicles Lovins describes.

As lighter materials replace heavier ones, the U.S. economy continues to shed weight. Our per capita consumption of raw materials such as forestry products and metals has, measured by weight, declined steadily over the past twenty years. A recent World Resources Institute study measured the "materials intensity" of our economy—that is, "the total material input and the hidden or indirect material flows, including deliberate landscape alterations" required for each dollar's worth of economic output. "The result shows a clearly declining pattern of materials intensity, supporting the conclusion that economic activity is growing somewhat more rapidly than natural resource use."[20] Of course, we should do better. The Organization for Economic Cooperation and Development, an association of the world's industrialized nations, has proposed that its members strive as a long-range goal to decrease their materials intensity by a factor of ten.[21]

Communications also illustrates the trend toward lighter, smaller, less materials-intensive technology. Just as telegraph cables replaced frigates in transmitting messages across the Atlantic and carried more information faster, glass fibers and microwaves have replaced cables—each new technology using less materials but providing greater capacity for sending and receiving information. Areas not yet wired for telephones (in the former Soviet Union, for example) are expected to leapfrog directly into cellular communications.[22] Robert Solow, a Nobel laureate in economics, says that if the future is like the past, "there will be prolonged and substantial reductions in natural-resource requirements per unit of real output." He asks, "Why shouldn't the productivity of most natural resources rise more or less steadily through time, like the productivity of labor?"[23]

Misconception No. 2: We Are Running Out of Food and Timber

The United Nations projects that the global population, currently 5.7 billion, will peak at about 10 billion in the next century and then stabilize or even decline.[24] Can the earth feed that many people? Even if food crops increase sufficiently, other renewable resources, including many fisheries and forests, are already under pressure. Should we expect fish stocks to collapse or forests to disappear?

The world already produces enough cereals and oilseeds to feed 10 billion people a vegetarian diet adequate in protein and calories. If, however, the idea is to feed 10 billion people not healthful vegetarian diets but the kind of meat-laden meals that Americans eat, the production of grains and oilseeds may have to triple—primarily to feed livestock.[25] Is anything like this kind of productivity in the cards?

Maybe. From 1961 to 1994 global production of food doubled. Global output of grain rose from about 630 million tons in 1950 to about 1.8 billion tons in 1992, largely as a result of greater yields.[26] Developing countries from 1974 to 1994 increased wheat yields per acre by almost 100 percent, corn yields by 72 percent, and rice yields by 52 percent.[27] "The generation of farmers on the land in 1950 was the first in history to double the production of food," the Worldwatch Institute has reported. "By 1984, they had outstripped population growth enough to raise per capita grain output an unprecedented 40 percent."[28] From a two-year period ending in 1981 to a two-year period ending in 1990 the real prices of basic foods fell 38 percent on world markets, according to a 1992 United Nations report.[29] Prices for food have continually decreased since the end of the eighteenth century, when Thomas Malthus argued that rapid population growth must lead to mass starvation by exceeding the carrying capacity of the earth.

Farmers worldwide could double the acreage in production, but this should not be necessary.[30] Better seeds, more irrigation, multi-cropping, and additional use of fertilizer could greatly increase agricultural yields in the developing world, which are now generally only half those in the industrialized countries. It is biologically possible to raise yields of rice to about seven tons per acre—about four times the current average in the developing world.[31] Super strains of cassava, a potato-like root crop eaten by millions of Africans, promise to increase yields tenfold.[32] American farmers can also do better. In a good year, such as 1994, Iowa corn growers average about 3.5 tons per acre, but farmers more than double that yield in National Corn Growers Association competitions.[33]

In drier parts of the world the scarcity of fresh water presents the greatest challenge to agriculture. But the problem is regional, not global. Fortunately, as Lester Brown, of the Worldwatch Institute, points out, "there are vast opportunities for increasing water efficiency" in arid regions, ranging from installing better water-delivery systems to planting drought-resistant crops.[34] He adds, "Scientists can help push back the physical frontiers of cropping by developing varieties that are more drought resistant, salt tolerant, and early maturing. The payoff on the first two could be particularly high."[35]

As if in response, Novartis Seeds has announced a program to develop water-efficient and salt-tolerant crops, including genetically engineered varieties of wheat.[36] Researchers in Mexico have announced the development of drought-resistant corn that can boost yields by a third. Biotechnologists are converting annual crops into perennial ones, eliminating the need for yearly planting. They also hope to enable cereal crops to fix their own nitrogen, as legumes do, minimizing the need for fertilizer (genetically engineered nitrogen-fixing bacteria have already been test-marketed to farmers). Commercial varieties of crops such as corn, tomatoes, and potatoes that have been genetically engineered to be resistant to pests and diseases have been approved for field testing in the United States; several are now being sold and planted.[37]A new breed of rice, 25 percent more productive than any currently in use, suggests that the Gene Revolution can take over where the Green Revolution left off.[38] Biotechnology, as the historian Paul Kennedy has written, introduces "an entirely new stage in humankind's attempts to produce more crops and plants."[39]

Biotechnology cannot, however, address the major causes of famine: poverty, trade barriers, corruption, mismanagement, ethnic antagonism, anarchy, war, and male-dominated societies that deprive women of food. Local land depletion, itself a consequence of poverty and institutional failure, is also a factor.[40] Those who are too poor to use sound farming practices are compelled to overexploit the resources on which they depend. As the economist Partha Dasgupta has written, "Population growth, poverty and degradation of local resources often fuel one another."[41] The amount of food in world trade is constrained less by the resource base than by the maldistribution of wealth.

Analysts who believe that the world is running out of resources often argue that famines occur not as a result of political or economic conditions but because there are "too many people." Unfortunately, as the economist Amartya Sen has pointed out, public officials who think in Malthusian terms assume that when absolute levels of food supplies are adequate, famine will not occur. This conviction diverts attention from the actual causes of famine, which has occurred in places where food output kept pace with population growth but people were too destitute to buy it.[42]

We would have run out of food long ago had we tried to supply ourselves entirely by hunting and gathering. Likewise, if we depend on nature's gifts, we will exhaust many of the world's important fisheries. Fortunately, we are learning to cultivate fish as we do other crops. Genetic engineers have designed fish for better flavor and color as well as for faster growth, improved disease resistance, and other traits. Two farmed species—Silver Carp and Grass Carp—already rank among the ten most-consumed fish worldwide.[43] A specially bred tilapia, known as the "aquatic chicken," takes six months to grow to a harvestable size of about one and a half pounds.[44]

Aquaculture produced more than 16 million tons of fish in 1993; capacity has expanded over the past decade at an annual rate of 10 percent by quantity and 14 percent by value. In 1993 fish farms produced 22 percent of all food fish consumed in the world and 90 percent of all oysters sold.[45] The World Bank reports that aquaculture could provide 40 percent of all fish consumed and more than half the value of fish harvested within the next fifteen years.[46]

For those who lament the decline of natural fisheries and the human communities that grew up with them, the successes of aquaculture may offer no consolation. In the Pacific Northwest, for example, overfishing in combination with dams and habitat destruction has reduced the wild salmon population by 80 percent. Wild salmon—but not their bioengineered aquacultural cousins—contribute to the cultural identity and sense of place of the Northwest. When wild salmon disappear, so will some of the region's history, character, and pride. What is true of wild salmon is also true of whales, dolphins, and other magnificent creatures—as they lose their economic importance, their aesthetic and moral worth becomes all the more evident. Economic considerations pull in one direction, moral considerations in the other. This conflict colors all our battles over the environment.

The transition from hunting and gathering to farming, which is changing the fishing industry, has taken place more slowly in forestry. Still there is no sign of a timber famine. In the United States forests now provide the largest harvests in history, and there is more forested U.S. area today than there was in 1920.[47] Bill McKibben has observed that the eastern United States, which loggers and farmers in the eighteenth and nineteenth centuries nearly denuded of trees, has become reforested during this century.[48] One reason is that farms reverted to woods. Another is that machinery replaced animals; each draft animal required two or three cleared acres for pasture.

Natural reforestation is likely to continue as biotechnology makes areas used for logging more productive. According to Roger Sedjo, a respected forestry expert, advances in tree farming, if implemented widely, would permit the world to meet its entire demand for industrial wood using just 200 million acres of plantations—an area equal to only five percent of current forest land. As less land is required for commercial tree production, more natural forests may be protected—as they should be, for aesthetic, ethical, and spiritual reasons.[49]

Often natural resources are so plentiful and therefore inexpensive that they undercut the necessary transition to technological alternatives.

If the U.S. government did not protect wild forests from commercial exploitation, the timber industry would have little incentive to invest in tree plantations, where it can multiply yields by a factor of ten and take advantage of the results of genetic research. Only by investing in plantation silviculture can North American forestry fend off price competition from rapidly developing tree plantations in the Southern Hemisphere.[50] Biotechnology-based silviculture can in the near future be expected to underprice "extractive" forestry worldwide. In this decade China will plant about 150 million acres of trees; India now plants four times the area it harvests commercially.[51]

The expansion of fish and tree farming confirms the belief held by Peter Drucker and other management experts that our economy depends far more on the progress of technology than on the exploitation of nature. Although raw materials will always be necessary, knowledge has become the essential factor in the production of goods and services. In other words, the limits to knowledge are the only limits to growth. "Where there is effective management," Drucker has written, "that is, application of knowledge to knowledge, we can always obtain the other resources."[52] The reasons to preserve nature are ethical more often than they are economic. Indeed, if we assume, along with Drucker and others, that resource scarcities do not exist or are easily averted, it is hard to see how economic theory, which after all concerns scarcity, can even provide a conceptual basis for valuing the environment.

Misconception No. 3: We Are Running Out of Energy

Probably the most persistent worries about resource scarcity concern energy. "The supply of fuels and other natural resources is becoming the limiting factor constraining the rate of economic growth," a group of experts proclaimed in 1986. They predicted the exhaustion of domestic oil and gas supplies by 2020 and, within a few decades, "major energy shortages as well as food shortages in the world."[53]

Contrary to these expectations, no global shortages of hydrocarbon fuels are in sight. "One sees no immediate danger of 'running out' of energy in a global sense," writes John P. Holdren, a professor of environmental policy at Harvard University. According to Holdren, reserves of oil and natural gas will last seventy to a hundred years if exploited at 1990 rates. (This does not take into account huge deposits of oil shale, heavy oils, and gas from unconventional sources.) He concludes that "running out of energy resources in any global sense is not what the energy problem is all about."[54]

The global energy problem has less to do with depleting resources than with controlling pollutants. Scientists generally agree that gases, principally carbon dioxide, emitted in the combustion of hydrocarbon fuels can build up in and warm the atmosphere by trapping sunlight. Since carbon dioxide enhances photosynthetic activity, plants to some extent absorb the carbon dioxide we produce. In 1995 researchers reported in *Science* that vegetation in the Northern Hemisphere in 1992 and 1993 converted into trees and other plant tissue 3.5 billion tons of carbon—more than half the carbon produced by the burning of hydrocarbon fuels worldwide.[55]

However successful this and other feedback mechanisms may be in slowing the processes of global warming, a broad scientific consensus, reflected in a 1992 international treaty, has emerged for stabilizing and then decreasing emissions of carbon dioxide and other "greenhouse" gases. This goal is well within the technological reach of the United States and other industrialized countries.[56] Amory Lovins, among others, has described commercially available technologies that can "support present or greatly expanded worldwide economic activity while stabilizing global climate—and saving money." He observes that "even very large expansions in population and industrial activity need not be energy-constrained."[57]

Lovins and other environmentalists contend that pollution-free energy from largely untapped sources is available in amounts exceeding our needs. Geothermal energy—which makes use of heat from the earth's core—is theoretically accessible through drilling technology in the United States in amounts thousands of times as great as the amount of energy contained in domestic coal reserves. Tidal energy is also promising.[58] Analysts who study solar power generally agree with Lester Brown, of the Worldwatch Institute, that "technologies are ready to begin building a world energy system largely powered by solar resources."[59] In the future these and other renewable energy sources may be harnessed to the nation's system of storing and delivering electricity.

Joseph Romm and Charles Curtis have described advances in photovoltaic cells (which convert sunlight into electricity), fuel cells (which convert the hydrogen in fuels directly to electricity and heat, producing virtually no pollution), and wind power. According to these authors, genetically engineered organisms used to ferment organic matter could, with further research and development, bring down the costs of ethanol and other environmentally friendly "biofuels" to make them competitive with gasoline.[60]

Environmentalists who, like Amory Lovins, believe that our economy can grow and still reduce greenhouse gases emphasize not only that we should be able to move to renewable forms of energy but also that we can use fossil fuels more efficiently. Some improvements are already evident. In developed countries the energy intensity of production—the amount of fuel burned per dollar of economic output—has been decreasing by about 2 percent a year.[61]

From 1973 to 1986, for example, energy consumption in the United States remained virtually flat while economic production grew by almost 40 percent. Compared with Germany or Japan, this is a poor showing.[62] The Japanese, who tax fuel more heavily than we do, use only half as much energy as the United States per unit of economic output. (Japanese environmental regulations are also generally stricter than ours; if anything, this has improved the competitiveness of Japanese industry.) The United States still wastes hundreds of billions of dollars annually in energy inefficiency. By becoming as energy-efficient as Japan, the United States could expand its economy and become more competitive internationally.[63]

Technology transfer can hasten sound economic development worldwide. Many environmentalists, however, argue that economies cannot expand without exceeding the physical limits nature sets—for example, with respect to energy. These environmentalists, who regard increasing affluence as a principal cause of environmental degradation, call for economic retrenchment and retraction—a small economy for a small earth. With Paul Ehrlich, they reject "the hope that development can greatly increase the size of the economic pie and pull many more people out of poverty." This hope is "basically a humane idea," Ehrlich has written, "made insane by the constraints nature places on human activity."[64]

In developing countries, however, a no-growth economy "will deprive entire populations of access to better living conditions and lead to even more deforestation and land degradation," as Goldemberg warns.[65] Moreover, citizens of developed countries are likely to resist an energy policy that they associate with poverty, discomfort, sacrifice, and pain. Technological pessimism, then, may not be the best option for environmentalists. It is certainly not the only one.

Misconception No. 4: The North Exploits the South

William Reilly, when he served as administrator of the Environmental Protection Agency in the Bush Administration, encountered a persistent criticism at international meetings on the environment. "The problem for the world's environment is your consumption, not our population," delegates from the developing world told him. Some of these delegates later took Reilly aside. "The North buys too little from the South," they confided. "The real problem is too little demand for our exports."[66]

The delegates who told Reilly that the North consumes too little of what the South produces have a point. "With a few exceptions (notably petroleum)," a report from the World Resources Institute observes, "most of the natural resources consumed in the United States are from domestic sources."[67] Throughout the 1980s the United States and Canada were the world's leading exporters of raw materials.[68] The United States consistently leads the world in farm exports, running huge agricultural trade surpluses. The share of raw materials used in the North that it buys from the South stands at a thirty-year low and continues to decline; industrialized nations trade largely among themselves.[69] The World Resources Institute has reported that "the United States is largely self-sufficient in natural resources."[70] Again, excepting petroleum, bauxite (from which aluminum is made), "and a few other industrial minerals, its material flows are almost entirely internal."[71]

Sugar provides an instructive example of how the North excludes—rather than exploits—the resources of the South. Since 1796 the United States has protected domestic sugar against imports.[72] American sugar growers, in part as a reward for large contributions to political campaigns, have long enjoyed a system of quotas and prohibitive tariffs against foreign competition.[73] American consumers paid about three times world prices for sugar in the 1980s, enriching a small cartel of U.S. growers. *Forbes* magazine has estimated that a single family, the Fanjuls, of Palm Beach, reaps more than $65 million a year as a result of quotas for sugar.[74]

About 100,000 Kenyans make a living on small plots of land growing pyrethrum flowers, the source of a comparatively environmentally safe insecticide of which the United States has been the largest importer. The U.S. Department of Commerce, however, awarded $1.2 million to a biotechnology firm to engineer pyrethrum genetically. Industrial countries will soon be able to synthesize all the pyrethrum they need and undersell Kenyan farmers.[75]

An article in *Foreign Policy* in December 1995 observed that the biotechnological innovations that create "substitutes for everything from vanilla to cocoa and coffee threaten to eliminate the livelihood of millions of Third World agricultural workers."[76] Vanilla cultured in laboratories costs a fifth as much as vanilla extracted from beans and thus jeopardizes the livelihood of tens of thousands of vanilla farmers in Madagascar.[77] In the past, farms produced agricultural commodities and factories processed them. In the future, factories may "grow" as well as process many of the most valuable commodities—or the two functions will become one. As one plant scientist has said, "We have to stop thinking of these things as plant cells, and start thinking of them as new microorganisms, with all the potential that implies"—meaning, for instance, that the cells could be made to grow in commercially feasible quantities in laboratories, not fields.[78]

The North not only balks at buying sugar and other crops from developing countries; it also dumps its excess agricultural commodities, especially grain, on them. After the Second World War, American farmers, using price supports left over from the New Deal, produced vast wheat surpluses, which the United States exported at concessionary prices to Europe and then the Third World. These enormous transfers of cereals to the South, institutionalized during the 1950s and 1960s by U.S. food aid, continued during the 1970s and 1980s, as the United States and the European Community vied for markets, each outdoing the other in subsidizing agricultural exports.[79]

Grain imports from the United States "created food dependence within two decades in countries which had been mostly self-sufficient in food at the end of World War II," the sociologist Harriet Friedmann has written. Tropical countries soon matched the grain gluts of the North with their own surpluses of cocoa, coffee, tea, bananas, and other export commodities. Accordingly, prices for these commodities collapsed as early as 1970, catching developing nations in a scissors. As Friedmann describes it, "One blade was food import dependency. The other blade was declining revenues for traditional exports of tropical crops."[80]

It might be better for the environment if the North exchanged the crops for which it is ecologically suited—wheat, for example—for crops easily grown in the South, such as coffee, cocoa, palm oil, and tea. Contrary to common belief, these tropical export crops—which grow on trees and bushes, providing canopy and continuous root structures to protect the soil—are less damaging to the soil than are traditional staples such as cereals and root crops.[81] Better markets for tropical crops could help developing nations to employ their rural populations and to protect their natural resources. Allen Hammond, of the World Resources Institute, points out that "if poor nations cannot export anything else, they will export their misery—in the form of drugs, diseases, terrorism, migration, and environmental degradation."[82]

Peasants in less-developed nations often confront intractable poverty, an entrenched land-tenure system, and a lack of infrastructure; they have little access to markets, education, or employment. Many of the rural poor, according to the environmental consultant Norman Myers, "have no option but to over-exploit environmental resource stocks in order to survive"—for example, by "increasingly encroaching onto tropical forests among other low-potential lands."[83] Myers observes that the principal agents of tropical deforestation are refugees from civil war and rural poverty, who are forced to eke out a living on marginal lands. According to Myers, slash-and-burn farming by displaced peasants accounts for far more deforestation than all commercial uses of forests combined. Most of the wood from trees harvested in tropical forests— that is, those not cleared for farms—is used locally for fuel. The likeliest path to protecting the rain forest is through economic development that enables peasants to farm efficiently, on land better suited to farming than to forest, and to puchase kerosene and other fuels.[84]

These poorest of the poor, Myers has written, "are causing as much natural-resource depletion as the other three billion developing-world people put together."[85] Peasants who try to scratch a living from an inhospitable environment, according to Myers, "are often the principal cause of deforestation, desertification, and soil erosion" as well as of the "mass extinction of species."[86] These people "can be helped primarily by being brought into the mainstream of sustainable development, with all the basic needs benefits that would supply."[87]

Many have argued that economic activity, affluence, and growth automatically lead to resource depletion, environmental deterioration, and ecological collapse. Yet greater productivity and prosperity—which is what economists mean by growth—have become prerequisite for controlling urban pollution and protecting sensitive ecological systems such as rain forests. Otherwise, destitute people who are unable to acquire food and fuel will create pollution and destroy forests. Without economic growth, which also correlates with lower fertility, the environmental and population problems of the South will only get worse. For impoverished countries facing environmental disaster, economic growth may be the one thing that is sustainable.

What Is Wrong With Consumption?

Any of us who attended college in the 1960s and 1970s took pride in how little we owned. We celebrated our freedom when we could fit all our possessions—mostly a stereo—into the back of a Beetle. Decades later, middle aged and middle class, many of us have accumulated an appalling amount of stuff. Piled high with gas grills, lawn mowers, excess furniture, bicycles, children's toys, garden implements, lumber, cinder blocks, ladders, lawn and leaf bags stuffed with memorabilia, and boxes yet to be unpacked from the last move, the two-car garages beside our suburban homes are too full to accommodate the family minivan. The quantity of resources, particularly energy, we waste and the quantity of trash we throw away (recycling somewhat eases our conscience) add to our consternation.

Even if predictions of resource depletion and ecological collapse are mistaken, it seems that they should be true, to punish us for our sins.

We are distressed by the suffering of others, the erosion of the ties of community, family, and friendship, and the loss of the beauty and spontaneity of the natural world. These concerns reflect the most traditional and fundamental of American religious and cultural values. Simple compassion instructs us to give to relieve the misery of others. There is a lot of misery worldwide to relieve. But as bad as the situation is, it is improving. In 1960 nearly 70 percent of the people in the world lived at or below the subsistence level. Today less than a third do, and the number enjoying fairly satisfactory conditions (as measured by the United Nations Human Development Index) rose from 25 percent in 1960 to 60 percent in 1992.[88] Over the twenty-five years before 1992, average per capita consumption in developing countries increased 75 percent in real terms.[89] The pace of improvements is also increasing. In developing countries in that period, for example, power generation and the number of telephone lines per capita doubled, while the number of households with access to clean water grew by half.[90]

What is worsening is the discrepancy in income between the wealthy and the poor. Although world income measured in real terms has increased by 700 percent since the Second World War, the wealthiest people have absorbed most of the gains. Since 1960 the richest fifth of the world's people have seen their share of the world's income increase from 70 to 85 percent. Thus one-fifth of the world's population possesses much more than four-fifths of the world's wealth, while the share held by all others has correspondingly fallen; that of the world's poorest 20 percent has declined from 2.3 to 1.4 percent.[91]

Benjamin Barber has described market forces that "mesmerize the world with fast music, fast computers, and fast food—with MTV, Macintosh, and McDonald's, pressing nations into one commercially homogeneous global network: one McWorld tied together by technology, ecology, communications, and commerce."[92] Affluent citizens of South Korea, Thailand, India, Brazil, Mexico, and many other rapidly developing nations have joined with Americans, Europeans, Japanese, and others to form an urban and cosmopolitan international society. Those who participate in this global network are less and less beholden to local customs and traditions. Meanwhile, ethnic, tribal, and other cultural groups that do not dissolve into McWorld often define themselves in opposition to it—fiercely asserting their ethnic, religious, and territorial identities.

The imposition of a market economy on traditional cultures in the name of development—for example, the insistence that everyone produce and consume more—can dissolve the ties to family, land, community, and place on which indigenous peoples traditionally rely for their security. Thus development projects intended to relieve the poverty of indigenous peoples may, by causing the loss of cultural identity, engender the very powerlessness they aim to remedy. Pope Paul VI, in the encyclical "Populorum Progressio" (1967), described the tragic dilemma confronting indigenous peoples: "either to preserve traditional beliefs and structures and reject social progress; or to embrace foreign technology and foreign culture, and reject ancestral traditions with their wealth of humanism."[93]

Economists in earlier times predicted that wealth would not matter to people once they attained a comfortable standard of living. "In ease of body and peace of mind, all the different ranks of life are nearly upon a level," wrote Adam Smith, the eighteenth-century English advocate of the free market.[94] In the 1930s the British economist John Maynard Keynes argued that after a period of great expansion further accumulation of wealth would no longer improve personal well-being.[95] Subsequent economists, however, found that even after much of the industrial world had attained the levels of wealth Keynes thought were sufficient, people still wanted more. From this they inferred that wants are insatiable.[96]

Perhaps this is true. But the insatiability of wants and desires poses a difficulty for standard economic theory, which posits that humanity's single goal is to increase or maximize wealth. If wants increase as fast as income grows, what purpose can wealth serve?[97]

Critics often attack standard economic theory on the ground that economic growth is "unsustainable." We are running out of resources, they say; we court ecological disaster. Whether or not growth is sustainable, there is little reason to think that once people attain a decent standard of living, continued growth is desirable. The economist Robert H. Nelson recently wrote that it is no longer possible for most people to believe that economic progress will "solve all the problems of mankind, spiritual as well as material."[98] As long as the debate over sustainability is framed in terms of the physical limits to growth rather than the moral purpose of it, mainstream economic theory will have the better of the argument. If the debate were framed in moral or social terms, the result might well be otherwise.

Making a Place for Nature

According to Thoreau, "a man's relation to Nature must come very near to a personal one."[99] For environmentalists in the tradition of Thoreau and John Muir, stewardship is a form of fellowship; although we must use nature, we do not value it primarily for the economic purposes it serves. We take our bearings from the natural world—our sense of time from its days and seasons, our sense of place from the character of a landscape and the particular plants and animals native to it. An intimacy with nature ends our isolation in the world. We know where we belong, and we can find the way home.

In defending old-growth forests, wetlands, or species we make our best arguments when we think of nature chiefly in aesthetic and moral terms.[100] Rather than having the courage of our moral and cultural convictions, however, we too often rely on economic arguments for protecting nature, in the process attributing to natural objects more instrumental value than they have. By claiming that a threatened species may harbor lifesaving drugs, for example, we impute to that species an economic value or a price much greater than it fetches in a market. When we make the prices come out right, we rescue economic theory but not necessarily the environment.

There is no credible argument, moreover, that all or even most of the species we are concerned to protect are essential to the functioning of the ecological systems on which we depend. (If whales went extinct, for example, the seas would not fill up with krill.) David Ehrenfeld, a biologist at Rutgers University, makes this point in relation to the vast ecological changes we have already survived. "Even a mighty dominant like the American chestnut," Ehrenfeld has written, "extending over half a continent, all but disappeared without bringing the eastern deciduous forest down with it." Ehrenfeld points out that the species most likely to be endangered are those the biosphere is least likely to miss. "Many of these species were never common or ecologically influential; by no stretch of the imagination can we make them out to be vital cogs in the ecological machine."[101]

Species may be profoundly important for cultural and spiritual reasons, however. Consider again the example of the wild salmon, whose habitat is being destroyed by hydroelectric dams along the Columbia River. Although this loss is unimportant to the economy overall (there is no shortage of salmon), it is of the greatest significance to the Amerindian tribes that have traditionally subsisted on wild salmon, and to the region as a whole. By viewing local flora and fauna as a sacred heritage—by recognizing their intrinsic value—we discover who we are rather than what we want. On moral and cultural grounds society might be justified in making great economic sacrifices—removing hydro dams, for example—to protect remnant populations of the Snake River sockeye, even if, as critics complain, hundreds or thousands of dollars are spent for every fish that is saved.

Even those plants and animals that do not define places possess enormous intrinsic value and are worth preserving for their own sake. What gives these creatures value lies in their histories, wonderful in themselves, rather than in any use to which they can be put. The biologist E. O. Wilson elegantly takes up this theme: "Every kind of organism has reached this moment in time by threading one needle after another, throwing up brilliant artifices to survive and reproduce against nearly impossible odds."[102] Every plant or animal evokes not just sympathy but also reverence and wonder in those who know it.

In *Earth in the Balance* (1992), Al Gore, then a senator, wrote, "We have become so successful at controlling nature that we have lost our connection to it."[103] It is all too easy, Gore wrote, "to regard the earth as a collection of 'resources' having an intrinsic value no larger than their usefulness at the moment."[104] The question before us is not whether we are going to run out of resources. It is whether economics is the appropriate context for thinking about environmental policy.

Even John Stuart Mill, one of the principal authors of utilitarian philosophy, recognized that the natural world has great intrinsic and not just instrumental value. More than a century ago, as England lost its last truly wild places, Mill condemned a world

> with nothing left to the spontaneous activity of nature; with every rood of land brought into cultivation, which is capable of growing food for human beings; every flowery waste or natural pasture ploughed up; all quadrupeds or birds which are not domesticated for man's use exterminated as his rivals for food, every hedgerow or superfluous tree rooted out, and scarcely a place left where a wild shrub or flower could grow without being eradicated as a weed in the name of improved agriculture.[105]

The world has the wealth and the resources to provide everyone the opportunity to live a decent life. We consume too much when market relationships displace the bonds of community, compassion, culture, and place. We consume too much when consumption becomes an end in itself and makes us lose affection and reverence for the natural world.

Notes

1. Copyright 1997 Mark Sagoff, as first published in the *Atlantic Monthly*. The author gratefully acknowledges support under a grant from the Global Stewardship Initiative of the Pew Charitable Trusts to the Institute for Philosophy and Public Policy. The views expressed are those of the author, not necessarily of any grant-making agency.

2. See Doug Struck, "Rich Nations Challenged on Resource Consumption," *Baltimore Sun*, 9 September 1994. Struck quotes Assumpta Rego, a Kenyan delegate and geography professor in Nairobi. "The industrial countries have consumption that has led to overexploitation of the resources of developing

countries," Rego said. The same article quotes Gus Speth, former director of the Council on Environmental Quality and now administrator of the United Nations Development Programme. "Population growth in the developing world isn't the main threat to the planet's sustainability. The biggest threat comes from . . . resource consumption in the industrialized world," Speth said. See also, statement by the Honorable Timothy E. Wirth at the Preparatory Meeting, May 11, 1993, for the International Conference on Population and Development: "Industrialized nations have a disproportionate impact on the global environment. Representing less than one quarter of the world's population, developed nations consume 75 percent of all raw material and create a similar percentage of all solid waste." The United States Mission to the United Nations, USUN Press Release #63–(93).

3. See, for example, Herman E. Daly, "From Empty-world Economics to Full-world Economics: Recognizing an Historical Turning Point in Economic Development," in *Population, Ecology, and Lifestyle*, ed. Robert Goodland, Herman E. Daly, and Salah El Serafy (Washington, D.C.: Island Press, 1992), 23–37.

4. Paul R. Ehrlich and Anne H. Ehrlich, *The End of Affluence* (New York: Ballantine Books, 1974), 33.

5. "Over the course of the twentieth century, according to a careful study conducted by the World Bank and published in 1988, the relative price of food grains dropped by over 40 percent." For this and other supporting evidence, see Nicholas Eberstadt, "Population, Food, and Income: Global Trends in the Twentieth Century," in *The True State of the Planet*, ed. Ronald Baily (New York: Free Press, for the Competitive Enterprise Institute, 1995), 7–47.

6. Paul and Anne Ehrlich give this estimate in *The End of Affluence*, 48.

7. The World Resources Institute, the United Nations Environment Programme, The United Nations Development Programme, and the World Bank, *World Resources 1996–97* (New York: Oxford University Press, 1996), 275 (observing that estimates of global petroleum reserves have increased by 43 percent between 1984 and 1994). Since 1989, "new discoveries, additions, and recisions have broadly matched the world's production, leaving total reserves basically unchanged."

8. Stephen Moore, "The Coming Age of Abundance," in *The True State of the Planet*, ed. Ronald Bailey (New York: Free Press, 1995), 110–39.

9. World Resources Institute, *World Resources 1994–95* (New York: Oxford University Press, 1994), 9 (quoting the World Energy Council's 16th *Survey of Energy Resources*).

10. World Resources Institute, *World Resources 1994–95*, 5.

11. World Resources Institute, *World Resources 1994–95*, 5.

12. Quoted and cited in Moore, "The Coming Age of Abundance," 137.

13. See Moore, "The Coming Age of Abundance," ed. 126–27.

14. See Michael Gianturco, "Seeing Into the Earth," *Forbes*, 20 June 1994, 120.

15. Thomas H. Lee, "Advanced Fossil Fuel Systems and Beyond," in *Technology and Environment*, ed. Jesse H. Ausubel and Hedy E. Sladovich (Washington, D.C.: National Academy Press, 1989), 114–36.

16. H. E. Goeller and Alvin M. Weinberg, "The Age of Substitutability," *Science* 191 (February 20, 1976): 683–89. Curt Suplee, "Infinitesimal Carbon Structures May Hold Gigantic Potential," *Washington Post*, 2 December 1996, 3 (A).

17. See Jesse Ausubel, "Can Technology Spare the Earth?" *American Scientist* 84 (March–April 1996): 166–78. For further information, see Solstice: Internet Information Service of the Center for Renewable Energy and Sustainable Technology, *http://www.crest.org*.

18. See "Appliance Standards are Getting Results," *Energy Conservation News* 18, no. 2 (September 1, 1995).

19. Amory B. Lovins and L. Hunter Lovins, "Reinventing the Wheels," *Atlantic Monthly*, January 1995; available at *http://www.theAtlantic.com/atlantic/issues/96apr/oil/wheels.htm.*

20. See World Resources Institute, *World Resources 1994–1995*, 15; see also Albert Adriannse et al., *Resource Flows: The Material Basis of Industrial Economies* (Washington, D.C.: World Resources Institute, Wuppertal Institute, and others, 1997), 2.

21. Adriannse et al., *Resource Flows*, 2.

22. See Peter Blomquist, "Fighting Poverty in the Information Age," *Seattle Times*, October 18, 1995, 5 (B).

23. Robert M. Solow, "Is the End of the World at Hand?" in *The Economic Growth Controversy*, ed. Andrew Weintraub, Eli Schwartz, and J. Richard Aronson (White Plains, NY: Institute of Arts and Sciences Press, 1973), 49.

24. See World Resources Institute et al., *World Resources 1996–97*, 173–74.

25. See Paul Waggoner, *How Much Land Can 10 Billion People Spare for Nature? Task Force Report 121* (Ames, IA: Council for Agricultural Science and Technology, February 1994), esp. chap. 5. See also World Resources Institute, *World Resources 1994–95*, chap. 6, 107–8.

26. See Lester R. Brown, Christopher Flavin, and Hal Kane, *Vital Signs 1996* (New York: W. W. Norton, 1996), 25; see also Ronald Bailey, ed., *The True State of the Planet*, (New York: Free Press, 1995), 409.

27. "Feeding a Hungrier World," *Washington Post*, 13 February 1995, 3 (A).

28. Lester Brown et al., *State of the World 1995*, ed. Linda Starke (New York: W. W. Norton, 1995), 7; Amartya Sen, "Population: Delusion and Reality," *New York Review of Books*, 22 September 1994, 62–67; Amartya Sen discusses these and similar statistics in "Population and Reasoned Agency: Food, Fertility and Economic Development" in *Population, Economic Development, and the Environment*, ed. Kerstin Lindahl-Kiessling and Hans Landberg (New York: Oxford University Press, 1994).

29. UNCTAD VIII, Analytical Report by the UNCTAD Secretariat the Conference (New York: United Nations, 1992), Table V-S, 235.

30. See Vaclav Smil, *Global Ecology* (London: Routledge, 1993), 46.

31. "Feeding a Hungrier World," *Washington Post*, 13 February 1995, 3 (A).

32. David Briscoe, "Can the World Feed 8 Billion More People by 2025?" *Charleston Gazette*, 28 October 1996, 1 (A).

33. Waggoner, *How Much Land Can Ten Billion People Spare for Nature?* 26–27, citing National Corngrowers Association 1993 Tabulation of the 1992 Maize

Yield Contest. Annual yields of biomass up to 550 tons per hectare are theoretically possible for algal cultures; yields half as great have been achieved. See Richard Radmer and Bessel Kok, "Photosynthesis: Limited Yields, Unlimited Dreams," *BioScience* 27, no. 9 (Sept. 1977): 599–604. See also, Paul Waggoner, "How Much Land Can Ten Billion People Spare for Nature?" in *The Liberation of the Environment, Daedalus,* ed. Jesse Ausubel (Summer 1996): 73–94.

34. Lester R. Brown, Christopher Flavin, and Sandra Postel, *Saving the Planet* (New York: Norton, 1991), 87.

35. Lester R. Brown, "The Grain Drain," *The Futurist* 23, no. 4 (July–August 1989): 17–18.

36. Nuala Moran, "Scientists Engineer a Fruitful Harvest," *The Independent,* 24 July 1994, 4 (describing field trials of genetically engineered wheat). For a useful survey of developments in agricultural biotechnology, see Sheldon Krimsky and Roger Wrubel, *Agricultural Biotechnology and the Environment: Science, Policy, and Social Issues* (Urbana: University of Illinois Press, 1996).

37. Robert Cooke, "Aw Shucks, This Here's Great Corn," *Newsday,* 9 August 1994, 25 (describing corn genetically engineered to be 40 percent more productive and to withstand drought and poor soil conditions); Rebecca Goldberg, "Novel Crops and Other Transgenics: How Green Are They?" in *Agricultural Biotechnology: Novel Products and New Partnerships, NABC Report 3,* ed. Ralph W. F. Hardy and Jane Baker Segelken (Ithaca, NH: National Agricultural Biotechnology Council, 1996); and World Resources Institute, *World Resources 1994–95,* 118–21.

38. Royce Rensberger, "New 'Super Rice' Nearing Fruition," *Washington Post,* 24 October 1994, 1 (A). For a thorough study of the prospects of improvement in rice yields in Asia and Latin America, see James Lang, *Feeding a Hungry Planet: Rice, Research and Development in Asia and Latin America* (Chapel Hill: University of North Carolina Press, 1996).

39. Paul Kennedy, *Preparing for the Twenty-First Century* (New York: Vintage Books, 1993), 70.

40. World Bank, *World Development Report 1992* (New York: Oxford University Press, 1992), 30–33. The Bank states (30): "Land-hungry farmers resort to cultivating unsuitable areas—steeply sloped, erosion-prone hillsides; semiarid land where soil degradation is rapid; and tropical forests where crop yields on cleared fields frequently drop sharply after just a few years. . . . Poor families often lack the resources to avoid degrading their environment."

41. Partha S. Dasgupta, "Population, Poverty and the Local Environment," *Scientific American,* February 1995, 41. Dasgupta also explores the power relations that led to starvation, e.g., "In poor households in the Indian subcontinent, for example, men and boys usually get more sustenance than do women and girls, and the elderly get less than the young."

42. Sen among other scholars points out that insistence on the Malthusian belief that overpopulation and global food scarcity are the causes of famine, by diverting attention from the real causes of malnutrition, namely, poverty and powerlessness, that have caused the deaths of many millions of people. "First, by focusing on such misleading variables as food output per unit of population,

the Malthusian approach profoundly misspecifies the problems facing the poor of the world." Since global food supplies are more than adequate to meet human needs, the Malthusian is then led to complacency. "It is often overlooked that what may be called 'Malthusian optimism' has actually killed millions of people." Amartya Sen, *Resources, Values and Development* (Cambridge: Harvard University Press, 1984), 524; see also, Jean Dreze and Amartya Sen, *Hunger and Public Action* (Oxford: Clarendon Press, 1989), 26–28.

43. Lester Brown et al., *State of the World 1995*, 30.

44. Christopher Dinsmore, "Tilapia Fish Farm, New in Suffolk, Aims Toward a Growing Market, *Virginian-Pilot*, 8 September 1995, 2 (D).

45. Lester R. Brown, Hal Hane, and David M. Roodman, *Vital Signs 1994* (New York: Norton, 1994), 34; Lester Brown et al., *Vital Signs 1996*, 32.

46. James Harding, "World Bank Sees Big Future of Fish Farming," *Financial Times*, 15 May 1995, 4.

47. Roger A. Sedjo, "Forest Resources: Resilient and Serviceable," in *America's Renewable Resources*, ed. Kenneth Frederick and Roger Sedjo (Washington, D.C.: Resources for the Future, 1991), 81–120.

48. Bill McKibben, "An Explosion of Green," *Atlantic Monthly* 275, no. 4: 61–83. Available at *http://www.theatlantic.com/election/connection/environ/green.htm.*

49. Roger A. Sedjo, "Forests: Conflicting Signals," in *The True State of the Planet*, ed. Ronald Bailey (New York: Free Press, 1995), 180.

50. See Sedjo, "Forest Resources: Resilient and Serviceable," 111.

51. World Resources Institute, *World Resources 1994–95*, 79, 134.

52. Peter Drucker, *Post Capitalist Society* (New York: Harper Business, 1993), 45.

53. John Gever, Robert Kaufmann, David Skole, Charles Vorosmarty, *Beyond Oil: The Threat to Food and Fuel in the Coming Decades*, a project of Carrying Capacity, Inc. (Cambridge, MA: Ballinger, 1986), 9, xxix, and xxx. These authors announced that "the supply of fuels and other natural resources is becoming the limiting factor constraining the rate of economic growth" (9, italics removed).

54. John Holdren, "The Energy Predicament in Perspective," in *Confronting Climate Change: Risks, Implications and Responses*, ed. Irving M. Mintzer (New York: Cambridge University Press, 1992), 163–69; quotation at 165.

55. P. Ciais et al., "A Large Northern Hemisphere Terrestrial CO_2," *Science* 269 (August 25, 1995): 1098–1100.

56. For a discussion of the extent to which industrialized nations are developing non-carbon-based sources of energy (thus moving to a hydrogen economy), see Nebojsa Nakicenovic, "Freeing Energy from Carbon," in Jesse Ausubel, "The Liberation of the Environment," *Daedalus* 125, no. 3 (Summer 1996): 95–112.A.

57. Amory B. Lovins, "Energy, People, and Industrialization," in *Resources, Environment, and Population: Present Knowledge, Future Options*, ed. Kingsley Davis and Nikhail S. Bernstam (New York: Oxford University Press, 1991), 95–124; quotation at p. 95. For further evidence and testimony to this effect, see Thomas B. Johnsson et al., eds., *Renewable Energy: Sources for Fuels and Electricity* (Washington, D.C.: Island Press, 1993).

58. For discussion of the promise of geothermal, tidal, and other alternative forms of energy, see Johnsson et al., eds., *Renewable Energy*; and see Michael Brower, *Cool Energy: Renewable Solutions to Environmental Problems* (Cambridge: MIT Press, 1992); Robert H. Williams, "Powering the Future: Efficient Use and Renewable Supplies Are Key," *EPA Journal* 18, no. 4: 15–19; and "Positive Energy," *Sierra* (March/April 1991): 37–47.

59. Brown, Flavin, and Postel, *Saving the Planet, 10.*

60. Joseph J. Romm and Charles B. Curtis, "Mideast Oil Forever?" *Atlantic Monthly* 277, no. 4 (April 1996): 57–74. Available at *http://www.theatlantic.com/atlantic/issues/96apr/oil/oil.htm* .

61. See A. Denny Ellerman, "Energy Policies, R&D, and Public Policy," in *The Energy Crisis: Unresolved Issues and Enduring Legacies*, ed. Davis Lewis Feldman (Baltimore: Johns Hopkins University Press, 1996), 62–69.

62. See Michael Brower, *Cool Energy*, 13–15.

63. For data comparing energy efficiency in the United States with that of its trading partners and relevant analysis and recommendations, see Joseph J. Romm and Amory B. Lovins, "Fueling a Competitive Economy: Profiting from Energy," *Foreign Affairs* (Winter 1992): 46–60. For further evidence and argument, see Michael E. Porter and Claas Van der Linder, "Green and Competitive: Ending the Stalemate," *Harvard Business Review* (September–October 1995): 120–30.

64. Paul R. Ehrlich and Anne H. Ehrlich, *The Population Explosion* (New York: Simon and Schuster, 1990), 269 n. 29.

65. Jose Goldemberg, "Energy Needs in Developing Countries and Sustainability," *Science* 269, no. 5227 (August 25, 1995), 1058–59.

66. In a phone interview, December 21, 1994, Mr. Reilly vouched for these remarks, noting that this incident happened more than once.

67. World Resources Institute, *World Resources 1994–95*, 16.

68. World Resources Institute, *World Resources 1994–95*, 291.

69. World Resources Institute, *World Resources 1994–95.*

70. World Resources Institute, *World Resources 1994–95*, 13–16.

71. Albert Adriannse et al., *Resource Flows*, 13.

72. See "America's Farm Subsidies," *Economist*, June 27, 1992.

73. Sean Holton, "Sugar Growers Reap Bonanza in Glades," *Orlando Sentinel Tribune*, 18 September 1990, 1 (A).

74. Phyllis Berman and Alexandra Alger, "The Set-aside Charade," *Forbes* (March 13, 1995): 78.

75. For this and other examples, see Kate de Selincourt, "Future Shock: Effects of Biotechnology on Developing Countries," *New Statesman & Society* 6, no. 281 (December 3, 1993). De Selincourt's larger study, "Genetic Engineering Targets Third World Crops," is available from the Panos Institute, 9 White Lion Street, London N1 ORP. The *Washington Post* reports that Agridyne is spending $3 million on getting genetically engineered microbes to express pyrethrum. (See Sally Lehrman, "Splicing Genes or Slicing Exports? U.S. Firms' Bioengineered Tropical Plants May Threaten Third World Farmers," *Washington Post*, September 27, 1992, 1 (H).

76. Robin Broad and John Cavanaugh, "Don't Neglect the Impoverished South's Developing Countries," *Foreign Policy* (December 22, 1995: 18–27.

77. Lehrman, "Splicing Genes, or Slicing Exports?"

78. Quoted in Mary Ellen Curtin, "Harvesting Profitable Products from Plant Tissue Culture," *Bio/Technology* 1 (1983): 657. See also, R. S. Chaleff, "Isolation of Agronomically Useful Mutants from Plant Cell Cultures," *Science* 219 (1983): 676–82. ("With recognition of the similarities between cultured plant cells and microorganisms came the expectation that all the extraordinary feats of genetic experimentation accomplished with microbes would soon be realized with plants." Also, at 679, Chaleff enumerates the difficulties that must be resolved before this expectation may be fulfilled.)

79. For documentation and further analysis, see Bruce L. Gardner, "The Political Economy of U.S. Export Subsidies for Wheat," in *The Political Economy of American Trade Policy*, ed. Anne Krueger (Chicago: University of Chicago Press, 1996), 291–331. See also Derek Biyearly, "The Political Economy of Third World Food Imports: The Case of Wheat," *Economic Development and Cultural Change* 35 (1987): 307–28.

80. Harriet Friedmann, "The International Relations of Food: The Unfolding Crisis of National Regulation," in *Food: Multidisciplinary Perspectives*, ed. Barbara Harriss-White and Sir Raymond Hoffendberg (Oxford: Blackwell, 1994), 102–3.

81. Partha Dasgupta, Carl Folke, and Karl-Goren Maler, "The Environmental Resource Base of Human Welfare," *Population, Economic Development, and the Environment* (New York: Oxford University Press, 1994), 31.

82. Personal communication, April 2, 1997.

83. Norman Myers, "Population and Biodiversity" in *Population: The Complex Reality*, ed. Sir Francis Graham-Smith (Golden, CO: North American Press, 1994), 117–36; quotation at 129.

84. "The World's Forests and Human Populations: Their Environmental Interconnections," in *Resources, Environment, and Population: Present Knowledge, Future Options*, ed. Kingsley Davis and Nikhail S. Bernstam (New York: Oxford University Press, 1991): 237–51, especially 243.

85. Norman Myers, "The Question of Linkages in Environment and Development," *BioScience* 43, no. 5 (May 1993): 306.

86. Myers, "The Question of Linkages in Environment and Development," 306.

87. Myers, "The Question of Linkages in Environment and Development," 306. See also, Norman Myers, "Population, Environment, Development," *Environmental Conservation* 20, no. 3 (Autumn 1993): 205.

88. United Nations Development Programme (UNDP), *Human Development Report 1994* (New York: Oxford University Press, 1994), 2.

89. World Bank, *World Development Report: 1992* (New York: Oxford University Press, 1992), 29.

90. World Bank, *World Development Report: 1994* (New York: Oxford University Press, 1994), 1.

91. UNDP, *Human Development Report 1994*, 35.

92. Benjamin R. Barber, "Jihad vs. McWorld," *Atlantic Monthly* 269, no. 3 (1992): 53–65; quotation at 53.

93. Pope Paul VI, "Populorum Progressio," Encyclical of Pope Paul VI on the Development of Peoples, March 26, 1967, in *The Papal Encyclicals 1958–1981*, ed. Claudia C. Ihm (Wilmington, NC: McGrath Publishing, 1981), 183–85; quotation at 184.

94. Adam Smith, *The Theory of the Moral Sentiments*, ed. D. D. Raphael and A. L. Macfie (Oxford: Clarendon Press, 1976), bk. 4, pp. 1, 11, 185.

95. See John Maynard Keynes, "Economic Possibilities for Our Grandchildren" (1930), in Keynes, *Essays in Persuasion* (New York: Norton, 1963), 366, 369–70, 372.

96. For discussion, see Robert H. Nelson, *Reaching for Heaven on Earth: The Theological Meaning of Economics* (Lanham, MD: Rowman and Littlefield, 1991), chap. 6.

97. See Herbert Stein, "The Washington Economist: The End of Economics as We Know It," *The American Enterprise*, publication of the American Enterprise Institute (September–October 1994): 6–9.

98. Robert H. Nelson, "In Memoriam: On the Death of the 'Market Mechanism,' " *Ecological Economics* 20 (1997): 187–97; quotation at 188.

99. H. D. Thoreau, *The Journal of Henry David Thoreau* 10, ed. Bradford Torrey and Francis H. Allen (Boston: Houghton Mifflin Company, 1949), 252.

100. Aesthetic, cultural, and moral terms, of course, may also have economic and prudential significance. For an insightful discussion of normative terms such as *health* and *integrity* as applied to ecological communities and systems, see Laura Westra, *An Environmental Proposal for Ethics: The Principle of Integrity* (Lanham, MD: Rowman and Littlefield, 1994).

101. David Ehrenfeld, "Why Put a Value on Biodiversity?" in *Biodiversity*, ed. E. O. Wilson (Washington, D.C.: National Academy Press, 1988), 212–16; quotation at 215.

102. Edward O. Wilson, *The Diversity of Life* (Cambridge: Harvard University Press, 1992), 345.

103. Senator Al Gore, *Earth in the Balance: Ecology and the Human Spirit* (Boston: Houghton Mifflin Company, 1992), 225.

104. Gore, Earth in the Balance, 1.

105. John Stuart Mill, *Principles of Political Economy with Some of Their Applications to Social Philosophy* (1848) (Fairfield, NJ: Augustus M. Kelley Publishers, 1987), book 4, chap. 6, section 2, 750.

Part Four

Consumption and Sustainable Business

15

A Boat for Thoreau: A Discourse on Ecology, Ethics, and the Making of Things

William McDonough

One of the great leaders of the United States, Thomas Jefferson, saw himself primarily as a designer. This is evident from his tombstone, which he designed, and on which we can read three things: *"Thomas Jefferson, author of the Declaration of American Independence, author of the Statute of Virginia for Religious Freedom, and Father of the University of Virginia."* These were the three things Jefferson thought were worth mentioning on his tombstone. He did not record his various activities—that he had been president of the United States, minister to France, an architect. He recorded only what he had left behind for future generations: his creative legacy to the world, his lasting contributions to prosperity. Consider looking at the world as a series of design assignments. How would we present the design assignment of the Declaration of Independence? Perhaps it could be framed like this: please prepare a document that provides us with the concept of "life, liberty and the pursuit of happiness free from remote tyranny." That would be the retroactive design assignment of the Declaration of Independence.

In Mr. Jefferson's case, "remote tyranny" referred to the King of England, George III: someone who ruled from a distant place, who was not sensitive to local needs and circumstance. Now, seven generations later, I believe we need to look at the concept of many Declarations of Interdependence, because we realize that some of the remote tyranny future generations will suffer is us. Right now, we—as a culture—are imposing what I call intergenerational remote tyranny. I would like to focus on this tyrannizing effect from a design perspective and consider how we can design it out.

Thomas Jefferson clearly understood the idea of intergenerational remote tyranny. In 1789, he wrote a letter to James Madison, which I paraphrase here:

> The earth belongs to the living. No man may by natural right oblige the lands he owns or occupies to debts greater than those that may be paid during his own lifetime. Because if he could, then the world would belong to the dead and not to the living.[1]

In *Silent Spring*, Rachel Carson stated that the founding fathers who wrote the Bill of Rights—despite their intellectual gifts and foresight—could not have imagined that corporations, governments, and individuals would poison children downstream.[2] They did not protect us from this kind of tyranny in the Bill of Rights because they could not even conceive of such a problem. We have to remember that Jefferson and Madison were living in a world that was effectively solar-powered. Their homes, the original grounds of the University of Virginia, were built with local materials: local clay, local fuel sources, solar-driven fuel sources. These people inhabited a world of natural energy flows. At that time, you could look out to the West and see a vast expanse of natural resources. Petrochemicals had not yet been invented. Yet Jefferson's phrase "The earth belongs to the living" is a powerful commentary on the tyrannies we are now seeing due to poor design.

Regulations are signals of design failure. They can even be seen—in the case of regulated toxic emissions—as licenses to kill. Polluters are basically telling us, "You are going to be poisoned. The question is, how long will it take?" Regulation is a signal of design and ethical failure. So I agree with a lot of the discussion about removing regulations to liberate business, but I would like to do it for all generations, not just this one. And I would like to do it by design, on purpose, with intention.

Jefferson's design legacy still provides for us, his seventh generation, and it continues to offer profound benefits even as the world changes around us. To see the legacy he brought to the Bill of Rights more clearly, we have to consider what it promulgated over time and imagine what it might promulgate in the future.

Jefferson wrote, "No man may by natural right. . . ." "Natural rights" had become a fundamental concept for Jefferson, and he expanded on it often. In *The Rights of Nature*, Roderick Nash pointed out that the concept of rights has been expanding since the Magna Carta gave rights to white noble English males in 1215. In 1776, the Declaration of Independence gave rights to white American land-owning males. In 1864, we had the Emancipation Proclamation. In 1922, female suffrage. In 1964, the Civil Rights Voting Act. And then, in 1973, the Endangered Species Act: the first time in our history that human beings took responsibility for giving other living species the right to exist. We acknowledged the rights of nature itself. From our perspective, "natural rights" has now expanded to include the rights of nature itself.[3]

If we project this pattern out, it is clear that our next discourse must be about endangered ecosystems, because we are finally realizing our interdependent connection to the natural world, and it won't be enough that there's a snail here or a condor there. We now understand that we are all connected to the web of life. Our understanding of rights and responsibilities must expand to include the rights and responsibilities of all living things.

Many people question the use of the word *dominion* in the Book of Genesis, which states that human beings are given dominion over the earth. Some wish the word had been *stewardship*, because of the relationship that might imply. Yet stewardship and dominion are both still anthropocentric concepts and presume we are in charge of everything. The Native American question is really the most relevant: How do we find ourselves in kinship with nature? How do we recognize ourselves as a vital and responsible part of it? To see the world this way, and to begin creating things within that context, is an exciting prospect. We need to understand and design for a world of fecundity, growth, and abundance, not for a world of destruction, loss, and limits.

What is the natural world, and how are humans meant to inhabit it? In 1836, Emerson wrote an essay entitled "Nature" in which he reflected on these questions: If human beings are natural, are all things made by humans natural? For that matter, what is Nature? He concluded that Nature is all those things that are immutable—those "essences" unaffected by man. His examples were the mountains, the oceans, the leaves.[4]

Following Emerson, Thoreau contemplated the mutability of nature and the search for our rightful and meaningful place within it. Unlike Emerson, however, he understood that we can affect the natural world. Today, the notion that nature is immutable, that there are "essences" so powerful they are beyond our ability to affect them, is obsolete.

We used to be able to throw things away. Remember that? Things went "away." Where is "away" now? "Away" is here. "Away" is someone's backyard. There is no place to go from here. We now see that we inhabit a smaller and smaller planet. "Away" has become very close indeed.

In this context, we must again ask ourselves, "What is natural?" and, "What are our intentions as evidenced by our designs?" Early in the

1830s, Ralph Waldo Emerson went to Europe on a sailboat and returned on a steamship. Let me abstract this for effect: He went over on a solar-powered recyclable craft operated by craftspersons practicing ancient arts in the open air. He returned in a steel rust-bucket putting oil on the water and smoke in the sky, operated by people working in the dark shoveling fossil fuels into the mouths of boilers. We are still designing steamships. Most buildings we design are essentially steamships. On any given day, the sun is shining and we're inside with the lights on causing the production of nuclear isotopes, carbon dioxide, nitrous oxides, and sulfur dioxide. Every time you find yourself in a building illuminated by electric light when the sun is shining, you should think, "I am in a steamship. I am in the dark." We need a new design. We need a boat for Thoreau.

Peter Senge, a professor at MIT's Sloan School of Management, works with a Learning Laboratory, a program where he discusses how organizations learn to learn. One of the first questions he asks the CEOs and chairs that attend his leadership program is, "Who is the leader on a ship crossing the ocean?" The responses he gets are *captain, navigator, helmsman.* But Senge tells them no: the leader of that ship is the designer of that ship, because you can be the best captain in the world, but if your ship is not designed to be seaworthy, you're going down.[5] From my perspective as a designer, the ship designed during the First Industrial Revolution is going down. I want to focus on the design of that ship, and I want us to imagine what the boat for Thoreau might be like—how it would work, what it would be made of, and what effects it might have. This boat is my metaphor for the design assignment of the Next Industrial Revolution.

What is the fundamental design principle of a steamship and most modern systems? The only one I can discover is, "If brute force doesn't work, you're not using enough of it." In fact, that's the design principle behind most modern architecture, behind what is known as the "International Style." You can build the same building in Reykjavik as in Rangoon, you simply heat one and cool the other. If you're too hot or too cold, just add more energy. If brute force doesn't work, you're not using enough of it. This principle kills culture. This principle kills society. This principle kills nature. And this principle kills diversity. It kills the richness of experience—the wealth of our relationship to the web of life and place.

I would like to posit the design principles for the Next Industrial Revolution, and I would also like to describe a new design assignment. But first, let me describe the retroactive design assignment of the First Industrial Revolution: Would you design a system of production and a system of commerce that

- produces billions of pounds of highly toxic hazardous material and puts them in your soil, your air, and your water every year?
- measures prosperity by how much of your natural capital you can dig up, burn, deplete, throw into holes in the ground and into the rivers and otherwise destroy?
- measures productivity by how few people are working?
- measures progress by how many smokestacks you have?
- requires thousands of complex regulations to keep you from killing each other too quickly?
- produces a few things so highly dangerous and toxic they will require future generations to maintain constant vigilance while living in terror?

That is the retroactive design assignment of the First Industrial Revolution. Is this an ethical assignment?

I am sure the framers of the Bill of Rights had no idea this could be posited as a design. In fact, I don't think it is a design, because it didn't happen by intention. The First Industrial Revolution happened incrementally, in a series of steps, as designers and engineers responded to single problems with the materials and information at hand. We have now reached the point where we can agree that this is not a design assignment we wish to accept in our time, and it is certainly not one we want to pass on to our children. It is time to look again at the horizon with delight and anticipation, with a new responsibility and a new design legacy in mind.

A magnificent example of true intergenerational responsibility is the great Peacemaker of the Six Nations of the Iroquois, who instructed all chiefs to make decisions on behalf of their seventh generation to come. Those of us here today are Thomas Jefferson's seventh generation: he designed the Declaration of Independence for us. So it's our turn now to make decisions on behalf of our seventh generation. Let's design a system for what I call the Next Industrial Revolution that

- introduces no hazardous material into the soil, the air, and the water every year
- measures prosperity by how much natural capital and how much solar income we can accrue in productive and fecund ways
- measures productivity by how many people are being gainfully and meaningfully employed
- measures progress by how many buildings have no smokestacks, no dangerous effluents, and no pipes

- does not require regulations to stop us from killing one another too quickly
- produces nothing that will require future generations to maintain vigilance and live in terror

I believe we can accomplish great and profitable things within that conceptual framework. But first, we must step out of the framework of guilt. Guilt does not help us. People who feel guilty often tell themselves, "I am guilty, I am guilty," and then they keep doing what they were doing. This is the way they compensate, by saying, "I am bad. I am bad. I am sorry." What we need is a much more productive concept: Negligence starts tomorrow.

If you recognize the tragic consequences of bad design and mindlessly continue to do what you are doing, then you are negligent. But what we want is change, not guilt. Because if you project the tragedy, as Jaime Lerner, the brilliant civic visionary and governor of Parana, Brazil, has pointed out, you have the tragedy. Unless you change immediately, you are unintentionally invested in watching the tragedy occur. As designers with intention, you have then adopted what Governor Lerner would call a "Strategy of Tragedy." As he would say, when you recognize the tragedy you have the tragedy.

The New York City Regional Plan Association just published a report entitled *A Region at Risk*, which indicated that a generation ago the impervious surfaces of the New York metropolitan region—the roads, the buildings, the parking lots—made up 19 percent of the city's surfaces. In 1996, they made up 30 percent. The projection for 2020? 45 percent impervious surfaces. Imagine this pattern continuing until the amount of impervious surfaces[6] rises to 70 or 80 percent. Where are the songbirds? What is the temperature? Where do the children play? What does the water look like? This is a tragedy. How do we deal with this tragedy? The only way to counter a Strategy of Tragedy is to adopt a Strategy of Change.

This Strategy of Change must go beyond what business and government have responded with, which we call "eco-efficiency." A primary response to the Earth Summit by the Business Council for Sustainable Development and the environmental organizations was eco-efficiency—do more with less. Although eco-efficiency is a noble and valuable concept, it is not going to save us for several reasons. First of all, its motivation is guilt. When we adopt eco-efficiency, we are basically telling ourselves, "I am bad. I am bad. I am using too much fuel and too much wood. I'm destroying cultures. I'm creating pollution. I've got to cut my energy consumption. I've got to go through all this tedious stuff because I'm bad."

When I gave the opening address at a conference celebrating the conclusion of the Environmental Protection Agency's 33/50 Voluntary Toxics Reduction Program last year, we found that people there were very excited—and rightly so—because they had achieved toxic reductions of 90 percent. But we have to wonder what we were doing before these reductions. Even more importantly, we have to realize that the 10 percent we have now becomes a new, negative 100 percent, because current scientific studies are telling us that even the smallest trace amounts of certain contaminants can have devastating effects—on our endocrine systems, for example. So this smaller amount of dangerous effluent becomes a new 100 percent to eliminate entirely. This isn't revolutionary; it's still a linear process headed for zero and never getting there, like Zeno's Paradox. What do we tell our children? "You're really bad. Try to feel better by being less bad. And your goal is zero." This is our legacy? I don't know any business person who thinks a goal of zero is very exciting.

From the "Third World's" perspective, eco-efficiency is simply the "First World" figuring out how to use the "Third World's" resources longer. Since our 20 percent of the world is using up 80 percent of the world's resources, they see eco-efficiency as a way for us to steal from the rest of the world for a longer period of time.

That's the problem with eco-efficiency from a designer's perspective: it tells us to leave the way we do things in the world the same—to just get better and more "efficient" at it. It's the same system that got us into trouble in the first place, slowed down. Paradoxically, this may make eco-efficiency even more insidious, because people are lulled into thinking the problem is being solved, when we're really just going in the same direction.

Let me borrow an analogy from Dave Crockett, a city councilor in Chattanooga: if you're driving out of Charlottesville, Virginia, you can go north to Washington, D.C., or you can go south to Lynchburg. If you find yourself going one hundred miles an hour toward Washington when you're supposed to be going to Lynchburg, it isn't going to help you to slow down to twenty miles an hour. We've got to turn around. We've got to be going somewhere else. But where? What principles do we use to get there?

A real Strategy of Change requires a new and inspiring vision of taking, making, using, and consuming in the world. We need massive creative imagination, with the design goal of imagining what perfect looks like. Then we can have a new, *positive*, 100 percent to work on. That's what I'm really interested in: redesign toward that 100 percent, so we can wake up in the morning and say, "I am only 20 percent sustainable. Tomorrow I want to be 21 percent. I'm trying to reach 100 percent sustainability. That's my chart." We've got to chart a new course and begin heading in a different direction. That means we have to start imagining

what the new course looks like, and start framing the conditions required to achieve it.

I have developed some principles that we use in our work:

1) *Waste Equals Food.*[7] In nature, there is no such thing as waste, so the
   first thing we must do is eliminate the concept of waste. I am not
   saying we need to minimize waste; I am saying we need to eliminate the entire concept of waste.
2) *Use Current Solar Income.* Nature does not mine the past; it does not
   borrow from the future. It operates on current income. Most of us
   can't pursue our professional lives working out of capital reserves.
   We have to work with current income, and so should our designs.
3) *Respect Diversity.* One size does not fit all. We are all different. Every
   place in the world is completely different; material flows, spiritual
   flows, character flows, cultural flows, energy flows—all of these
   vary in different places. We should celebrate our differences instead of trying to make us all the same.

These are the fundamental principles. But we also need new design criteria. The traditional design criteria used by designers until now are
three: *cost, performance,* and *aesthetics.* Can I afford it? Does it work? Do I
like it? Now we have to add three more characteristics: Is it ecologically
intelligent? Is it just? Is it fun? How do I apply these principles to find
out what is ecologically intelligent? How do I apply these principles to
find out what is just? (The fun part I'm going to leave to you.)

If *Waste Equals Food,* we eliminate the concept of waste. If we eliminate
the concept of waste, there is no such thing as waste, and everything
becomes a product. So we need some guidelines to help us design these
products. I have been inspired by a chemist named Michael Braungart
from Germany, and he and I have developed a series of protocols that
we use when designing products. We've identified a whole typology of
products.

If *Waste Equals Food* and "food" implies nutrients, then we need to
understand that nutrients work within a metabolism. What are the metabolisms we find in the world? What are the artifacts of human artifice,
and what is their relationship to these metabolisms? Remember that
question of Emerson's: If human beings are natural, are all things made
by humans natural? We now know that many things made by humans
are not "natural." So there are two fundamental metabolisms in the
world: one is biological, the world of biological systems, of which we are
physically a part; the other is the metabolism of human industry that
exists apart from natural systems. We need to design products to go into

each of these metabolisms so that they nourish one metabolism without contaminating the other.

The things we design to go into the biological metabolism should not contain mutagens, carcinogens, heavy metals, persistent toxins, bio-accumulative substances, or endocrine disrupters. The things we design to go into the technical metabolism should circulate in a closed loop forever; they should not unintentionally contaminate the organic metabolism, because many materials we marshal into the technical metabolism can damage or kill the organic metabolism.

We need to design into these two metabolisms, and this will mean products are differentiated into three fundamental types: a *Product of Consumption*, a *Product of Service*, and an *Unmarketable Product*. A *Product of Consumption* is designed to return safely to the organic cycle. It is literally a consumable and goes back to the soil. A *Product of Service* is designed to go back into the technical cycle, into the industrial metabolism from which it came. An *Unmarketable Product* is a product that should not be made because it can't feed either of these two metabolisms; this category includes substances such as radioactive materials and currently indissoluble contaminated materials, like the chromium contained in shoes.

I spent most of my childhood in the Far East, in Hong Kong, and when I moved to America, I was amazed by the fact that we no longer seem to be people with lives; we've become "consumers" with lifestyles. When did we stop being people with lives? We are not "consumers." We are people. The media will tell us how many "consumers" bought television sets, but how do you consume a television set?

Imagine I had a television hidden behind my desk and I said, "I have this amazing thing. It's a *Product of Service* because you want the function, not the thing. You want the service the item provides, but you do not necessarily want the ownership of its complex and potentially hazardous materials. Again, you want the function, not the thing. Before I tell you what the thing does, which will interest you, let me tell you what it is: It is thousands of chemicals, it has toxic heavy metals, it has a potentially implosive glass tube, and we want you to put it at eye level with your children and encourage them to play with it." Do you want this in your house? Why are we selling people hazardous waste? What do you want with this thing? You want to watch television—you don't want to own hazardous waste. When you pay for a television set today you have the right (the "right") to take this combination of valuable heavy metals and miscellaneous toxins and dump it in a trash can. Future generations are going to look back and say, "What were you thinking? What did you do with the mercury? What did you do with the chromium? You lost its quality! You put it in little holes all over the planet where we can never get it back! And it is persistently toxic! What were you thinking?"

Think about the redesign of this product as a *Product of Service*, because what happens is remarkable. When you have finished with the use of the machine, you ask yourself, "Whose food is this?" A television set is obviously food for the electronics and other industries.

My partner and I work with major corporations to redesign these products to be, in effect, leased by the manufacturer to the customer— not *consumer*, customer. Customers purchase the use of a machine, and when they are finished with it they can return it to the manufacturer and say, "Thank you very much for the use of this television. I would like a new one." The system is designed so that the old product goes back into what we call the "technical cycle" and becomes a *Product of Service* again—forever. This design for return we call our Eco-leasing concept.

We talk about recycling, but most of us don't recycle in the full sense of the word; we often do what Michael Braungart and I call "downcycling"—we reduce the quality of a material until its value is practically nonexistent. In other words, we slow its journey to the landfill. For example, when a high quality plastic like PET is "recycled" it may be mixed with other plastics to produce a hybrid of much lower quality, which is then used to make park benches. The original elevated quality can never be retrieved. So what we call recycling is still working with a *Cradle-to-Grave* life cycle.

Michael Braungart points out that the *Cradle-to-Grave* mentality is definitely Northern European. In Sweden, if you throw a banana peel on the ground it is going to be there a long time, because nothing rots quickly. Northern Europeans tended to bury everything. Western culture, then, tends to bury unwanted things. Consequently, our culture developed products in terms of a *Cradle-to-Grave* life cycle concept; once you finish with something you bury it because you don't want to look at it. In the abstract, one might say it's too bad the First Industrial Revolution didn't begin in a place like Mali. As Dr. Braungart notes, if you go to "primitive" places today, you might see a lot of aluminum cans lying on the ground outside a fence and think the people there are inconsiderate and slovenly. But those people once drank out of clay cups or gourds, and when they finished, they would simply toss the vessel over the fence and the goats, ants, or beetles would take it away. Its organic materials would nourish other organisms and go back to the soil. So these people are still doing what they've been doing forever; modern production just hasn't provided them with an intelligent design for a container that turns back into dirt—a design in what I call a *Cradle-to-Cradle* life cycle.

Plastic bottles could easily be redesigned so that they don't contain questionable substances and could safely replenish the soil. Right now they may contain antimony, catalytic residues, UV stabilizers, plasticizers, and antioxidants. What happens when the people in Mali throw that over the fence? Why not design a bottle so that when you finish with it you toss it into the compost or it biodegrades by the roadside, or it can be used as fuel for needy people to cook with? It should be safe fuel. If a clothing manufacturer wants to make clothing out of it, it should not contain potentially toxic substances. Plastic bottles were not originally designed to become clothing; they were designed to hold liquids. We have a fundamental design problem. We need to design things so they go into the biological or the technical cycle, safely, *Cradle-to-Cradle*.

Use Current Solar Income. I think we're going to resolve the energy problem, because we have current solar income. Energy from the sun is the only income the planet has (except for meteorites); all our other materials are already here. If you're in business, you understand that you must work from current income, not savings. Because we have that income from the sun, I think it won't be long before we find elegant solutions to the energy situation.

The University of Virginia's School of Architecture is about to build a building addition project designed to be a net energy exporter, a structure that produces more energy than it consumes. Why would we want to make a building that produces more energy than it needs? The reason is that *sustainability* may just be a shibboleth—the magic word that lets us into the temple of hope. A lot of people use the term *sustainability* as if it's going to save us. But sustainability as it's presently defined may be only the edge between destruction and restoration. Why would we want to simply sustain where we are now? We're in a depletive mode. We need to actually design things that are restorative. Think about the high-tech designs you see around you: airplanes, computers, space age stores. Imagine how much farther we can go, how wonderfully ambitious we can really be.

What is one of the best designs we know of for inspiration? How about a tree? How about a design that can accrue solar income, is fecund, produces habitat for all sorts of living things including people, provides fuel, food, and micro-climate, distills and transpires water, sequesters carbon, and makes oxygen? How many things do you know that do that? How many things have humans designed that make oxygen?

Why not make a building that produces oxygen? Why not make a building that produces energy? We're not very bright or ambitious designers if we can't even emulate a tree, which nature has put right there in front of us as an obvious model. Just compare a tree to most rooms. Right now, I'm in a room that sucks electrical energy from a grid, I'm responsible for the production of nuclear isotopes simply by turning on a light switch, and I'm probably breathing all sorts of chemical experiments I don't even realize I am undertaking. Compared to a tree, this is obviously primitive design. If I'm going to be a sophisticated designer, I had better start thinking more about trees—about buildings that produce more energy than they need and purify their water, and I had better start thinking about designing buildings and sites that absorb water quickly and release it slowly in a pure form like healthy soil. A building could be a restorative thing, a thing that is more fecund than destructive.

Do modern buildings absorb water quickly and release it slowly? Absolutely not. Water coming to human environments has been treated as if it is chemistry, H_2O suffering from physics, and falling, and we have got to get it away as quickly as possible. But water is the flux of life. Human beings are biology; we are where chemistry and physics conjoin. So our designs need to celebrate this flux and celebrate water, not just flush it, contaminated, away as fast as we can. We are now conceptualizing designs "without pipes." We are designing building materials and sites that absorb, filter, and transpire water, that keep buildings cool and provide habitat on site. Just like nature, they will release water slowly and cleanly.

One particular project we are designing right now is a new corporate campus for a large corporation in San Bruno, California, near San Francisco. The roof is a giant, undulating, grass-covered savannah. In the middle of the site there is an open-air courtyard around an established grove of oaks. So from the air a bird looking down might think, "Oh. That looks nice." Where are the songbirds in modern building? This roof is for songbirds. When you're inside the building the ceiling looks like a cloud. The interior is fully daylit, so the sun illumines the work space during the day. Workers spending their day indoors feel as if they've been outdoors. We've put in raised floors, which everyone wants for planning flexibility but no one can afford, and we've put them in because they allow us to run cool evening air from the San Francisco area against the concrete slabs all night long to refresh the air and cool the building down. This design means we don't have to pump foreign energy into the building during the day to cool it, and it also means there's fresh air individually directed into each person's breathing zone. Because of these strategies, we're able to cut energy equipment and energy consumption and pay for the raised floors. The building works just like an old hacienda, but goes even further with new techniques. From the air the roof is the earth. From the interior the roof is the sky. A building that's like a tree. A building that's like a meadow. Why not do this all the time?

We *can* do this all the time, but we need integrative thinking. We need new design principles, new aesthetics, and new engineering. Imagine what might happen if we applied our design principles to various things starting with the molecule and working up the scale to buildings, cities, and regions.

We were asked to design a fabric for a unit of the Steelcase Corporation, the largest office furniture maker in the country, and we told them we were honored to be among the famous designers they'd selected—Richard Meier, Aldo Rossi, Robert Venturi, Denise Scott Brown—these were all impressive architects. But we said we had one stipulation: unlike the others, we would not just design what the fabric looks like, we would design what it is. The company told us they expected we might say that, so they presented us with an option: what about a blend of cotton, which is natural, and PET soda bottles, which are recycled? If you put the two together, they said, you have natural, you have recycled—all the current eco-product buzzwords. You're all set. It's also durable and cheap.

But let's think about this for a minute: Is this blend an organic nutrient? Is this a *Product of Consumption*? Can it go back to soil safely? Not with the PET. Is it a product of service? Can it go back to technical cycles? Not with the cotton. Look again at our criteria: Is it ecologically intelligent? Is it just? Cotton currently occasions over 20 percent of the world's pesticide use, causes hydrological disasters, and has never been associated with social fairness. As I mentioned earlier, recycled fabrics from plastic bottles may contain antioxidants, UV stabilizers, and antimony residues from catalytic reactions. Does this belong next to human skin? Why would we want to help a company make this kind of product?

In this case, we decided to create a fabric that would be an organic nutrient, a Product of Consumption. Our client, Susan Lyons, the design director at DesignTex, arranged for us to work at Rohner Textil, a respected textile mill in Switzerland, with Albin Kälin, a director who had already made many advances at his mill. But when we arrived, Kälin told us that our project was fortuitous, because the trimmings of his bolts of cloth had just been declared hazardous waste by the Swiss government. He could no longer bury or burn it in Switzerland but had to pay to export the trimmings. Haven't you hit the wall of the First Industrial Revolution when the edges of your product are declared hazardous waste but you can still sell what's in the middle? With eco-efficiency, people contend, "My cadmium releases have been reduced and reduced," but if you look carefully, you realize that their new worst emission may be the product itself.

"Wouldn't it be nice," we told Kälin, "if the trimmings of your cloth became mulch for the local garden club?" So we got to work, and the first thing we reviewed was what it means to sit in a cloth-covered chair for extended periods of time. The fabric makers had interviewed people in wheelchairs, since they represent the worst case of extensive sitting, and we found out that they wanted dryness, because the biggest problem they have is moisture buildup. So we used wool, which absorbs water, and ramie, a plant similar to nettles, which provides a strong structural fiber that wicks water. The wool in the fabric absorbs moisture and the ramie wicks it away, so you're cool in the summer, warm in the winter, and comfortable all the time. Is it ecologically intelligent? Is it just? Ramie has been organically grown for thousands of years without any help from the chemical industry. And we hope the sheep in New Zealand are happy—they're free-ranging sheep.

Once we had developed the cloth, we had the finishes, the dyes, and all the rest of the process materials to consider. Remember the smokestack analogy: the filters have to be in our heads, not on the ends of pipes. Design filters. Our design filters told us that if this fabric were going back to the soil safely, it had to be free of mutagens, carcinogens, heavy metals, persistent toxins, bio-accumulatives, endocrine disrupters, and so on. Then we approached sixty chemical companies, and when we asked them to join us and put their products through this review, they summarily declined. Finally, the chairman of Ciba Geigy in Basel agreed to let us in.

Michael Braungart and our scientific colleagues reviewed 8,000 chemicals in the textile industry using this "design filter" and had to eliminate 7,962. This left 38 chemicals. We created the entire fabric line with those 38 chemicals. Everything we needed—dyes, auxiliaries, fixatives, et cetera—came from those 38 chemicals. The fabric has won gold medals and design awards and is a success in the marketplace. It is good business, and it is also creating a new standard for business excellence.

After the fabric was in production at the factory in Switzerland, a strange thing happened. Inspectors came to inspect the water coming out of the factory, and they thought their equipment was broken. They didn't find the things they expected to find. So they went to the front of the factory and checked the inflow pipes. As they expected, the water going in was Swiss drinking water. Their equipment was fine. It turned out that during the manufacturing process the fabrics were further filtering and purifying the water. Consider this concept: when the water coming out of your factory is as clean as the water going into your factory, and the water going into your factory is Swiss drinking water, that means you can cap the pipe. That means you would rather use your effluent than your influent. If you don't have anything bad coming out of the factory, there's nothing to regulate. Isn't that interesting: there are no more regulations implicit in this complete redesign. In fact, there are less! In this case, there may be none at all. This is not eco-efficiency—this mill is not "less" bad. It's not bad, period. We did not say we wanted to cut our cadmium or our mercury as much as we can. We completely redesigned this product based on a new set of principles. Welcome to the Next Industrial Revolution.[8]

What happened within the chemical industry as a result of all these efforts is also interesting. Naturally, your ordinary engineers who were using conventional materials got a little nervous, because implicit in what we were doing was an analysis of what had gone on before. Why were they using this chemical? Why all this cobalt? Why all this antimony? Why all these heavy metals? Why mutagens? Why carcinogens? The chemists told us that because their customers wanted something blue, their job was to figure out how to make it blue, not to solve environmental or health problems—just to make sure to tell customers to be careful handling the stuff and stay within regulatory limits. Is this ethical? Is this intelligent?

Regulatory structures cost a lot of money and require the government to tax their commerce in order to get the money to set up a regulatory structure. Then, the same people the government just taxed have to spend money to set up an *antiregulatory* structure to respond to the regulatory structure. Now, have we made anything yet? How are we doing on competition in world markets? What does it mean when environmental regulation all of a sudden prevents you from being in the marketplace and competing with Taiwan, Korea, and the Philippines, where their environmental regulations are not so stringent and they can make things more cheaply? What ends up happening is that commerce, which is looking for the quickest, cheapest thing, goes to Taiwan, goes to Korea, and buys chemicals and dyes because they are much less expensive than the locally produced ones. But because these cheap materials are not produced as carefully, what customers get from them is what we call "Products Plus": you get the dye, plus, perhaps, PCBs, plus heavy metals, plus carcinogens, plus all of these other things you did not intend to buy but that come with the cheap product. Instead of going to someone who is working hard to be clean and good, commerce goes to companies that have figured out how to compete purely on an economic basis. That's a tough economic situation.

The Dutch realized that if their industries could police themselves, the government would not have to regulate them, and they would not have to place those compliance cost burdens on their industries. They could compete in world markets. So they created the Green Plan, which asks Dutch commerce to figure out the quickest, most effective solution to environmental problems, and if commerce doesn't do that then the government says it will have to step in to regulate. Now that all of this is taking place, imagine what would happen if the textile industry in Holland started to look around and ask, "How do we do this?" And suddenly, because of our redesign, here is Ciba Geigy with a package of thirty-eight chemicals that will make any color safely. To guarantee quality, all you have to do is specify their whole package. But you must use their package exclusively, or other chemicals reviewed with the same "design filter," because in order to guarantee quality you can't contaminate it with materials from some other supplier who has not been reviewed. As a result of using this exclusive protocol, you do not need special storage rooms for hazardous waste. You do not need to file with regulatory agents for handling hazardous material. Your workers are not wearing protective equipment anymore because there is nothing to fear. Within the textile industry this little revolution starts: "Wait a minute! I hear over there they're not exposing their workers to carcinogens. Why can't we do that?" And the chairman of a major chemical company looks pretty smart for having taken the obvious next step in Total Quality Management.

Let's look at the concept of Total Quality Management, at the ideas started by W. Edwards Deming. He began as a statistician who was sent into factories to monitor production during World War II. Since so many men were at war, women had gone in to work in the factories, and he was there to judge the statistical effect. Let's abstract this story for a moment to get the main point of his discovery: a statistician goes into the factory, and he notes that the men who had manufactured artillery shells before the women took over produced, say, approximately a thousand shells a day, with an inspector throwing out "rejects" at the end of the process. The men expected lemons, they expected failure. They anticipated it and planned on it.

After the men had gone to war, the statistician watched the women at work to see what would happen. He watched them make twenty shells in the first week, forty in the next, then eighty, then a hundred, then three hundred, then five hundred, then seven hundred, then nine hundred, then twelve hundred, then fourteen hundred. They leveled off at a thousand, and all the shells were perfect. Production was up, quality was up. The statistician investigated the system more closely to find out what had happened, and guess what he found out? The women talked to each other. They sat in the round and discussed their mutual problems and needs. There was no hierarchy, no inspection. They went about their business and shared the worst work. They also adopted the policy that they would not accept the concept of failure: the idea of making an artillery shell that would blow up in their husbands' faces in the middle of the war was absolutely unacceptable to them. They eliminated the concept of failure. They did not count on failure, and the result was Total Quality Management.

When the men came back after the war, the statistician explained what had happened, but the men told him they had hierarchies, they had quotas, they were inspection-based, and they had just won a major war. So the statistician moved on to a more hospitable audience in Japan, and the rest is history.

The United States eventually profited from his experience. I remember when you used to buy a car and you hoped it wouldn't turn out to be a lemon. No one expects a lemon today, but when I was a kid, you didn't want to be the one who got the lemon. You were expecting one to come off the line. Then "Quality" became "Job One" at Ford after years of being "Job One" in Japan, which captured huge pieces of the auto market. That was literally due to Deming.

The Total Quality Management concept started a revolution in production. Because those women rejected the concept of failure—the concept of a defective product—Total Quality Management can be seen as a working engagement to the concept of zero defects. Just-in-time delivery came along as a result of high interest rates, high handling costs, and expensive inventory, and can be seen as providing the benefits of zero inventory. Zero accidents have always been a noble goal, and now, with total redesign, we can have zero emissions and zero waste (of undesirable materials). As Gunter Pauli likes to say, this is the next step in Total Quality Management.

The organic fabric we designed is a *Product of Consumption*; after its useful life, it goes back into the organic metabolism and feeds the soil. We're also working with Guilford of Maine, a subsidiary of Interface Corporation, to design the *Product of Service* version of fabrics, and we're working with partners in the chemical industry to develop and redesign polyester products that eliminate concerns for heavy metal residues from catalytic reactions, so people will no longer be exposed to them. Then, if we actually do recycle these materials back into the human environment, we will not be recycling heavy metals. We're also designing new dye protocols. In fact, we've recently identified a whole new line of dyes to go with polyesters based on our "design filters." The resulting fabrics will be safe and recyclable forever. They will never need to go into a landfill.

Interface Corporation is a major U.S. carpet and textile manufacturer that wants to lead the way in the Next Industrial Revolution. Ray Anderson, Interface Inc.'s founder and chairman, read about our concepts in Paul Hawken's *Ecology of Commerce*,[9] and was moved by this important book to transform his business.

Interface Corporation is also adopting our *Product of Service* concept and the eco-leasing concept that goes with it for their large carpet business. They are calling it their Evergreen Lease™. One way to understand how this concept has revolutionary economic implications is to think of it this way: If you buy a conventional carpet you buy a liability, not an asset. When you finish with it you're going to have to pay to get it re-moved. What does that mean to American business, to natural flows and materials, to prosperity? The chairman of Interface understood the problems of such a system. By adopting the *Product of Service* concept, his company will continue to own the material but will effectively lease it and maintain it for the customer that wants the use of it. When the customer has finished with the service of the carpet, Interface will take back their *technical nutrient.*

However, it's not enough to take a carpet back if it's not designed properly. The average carpet is nylon embedded in fiberglass and PVC. It was never designed to be recycled. You can really only "downcycle" it: you shave off some of the nylon material, and then you're left with a material "soup" that you can't use effectively. We've redesigned the ac-tual carpet and its entire delivery system so a customer can say, "I don't like red anymore. I want blue," without feeling guilty. Right now, when you order a carpet you're contributing to the destruction of natural sys-tems, because you're basically taking a bunch of petrochemicals the manufacturer compiled to make the product and then throwing them "away" in a landfill. Under the new protocol, your carpet order would create jobs and the negative material flows would go down or be elimi-nated. Consequently, when you want to change your carpet color you can have fun instead of feeling guilty. The old design process requires virgin or imperfect recycled material; the new design employs people to recirculate technical nutrients. So you can trade throwing away petro-chemicals for jobs.

What else does this new protocol mean to commerce? If our compa-nies and countries expect to be wealthy in the future, why would they put the valuable nutrients of their industry into a landfill? The essence of our argument to Ray Anderson was simply this: If you'd been using this concept from day one, you would have four billion pounds of tech-nical nutrients designed for use in your industry. That's how much car-pet you've made since you started the company. *Four billion pounds*, and where is it? It's in holes in the ground, or on its way there. The street value of this? Over one billion dollars. This is how you could accrue capital over time and accrue assets: by designing carpet to constantly become technical nutrients for your own company. Michael Braungart and I can apply this thinking to almost any industry with similar results.

On the regional level, we helped create the concept of Zero Emissions Zoning for Chattanooga, "the Pittsburgh of the South." Chattanooga had what Dave Crockett called a "civic heart attack" in 1968. The city was rated as having the worst air quality in the country—even worse than Los Angeles. So the city's civic leaders looked at this problem and de-cided to clean up their own air. They've been doing this for the last thirty years. But when their eco-industrial concept was initially proposed, a lot of industry CEOs said, "Zero Emissions Concept? What are you talking about? No corporation is going to accept it. No one will come here and do business." Then Gunter Pauli, who worked with Ecover in Europe and is now at the United Nations University in Tokyo, arranged an international conference and announced one of the first companies to agree with the Zero Emissions Concept in Chattanooga: DuPont. The chairman of DuPont actually stood up in Chattanooga and declared zero emissions a goal for his entire company. This is not a marginal event. This is big business.

Many industrial leaders claim there is no such thing as a factory without emissions. What we are talking about is zero waste and unwanted emissions. But we did it in Switzerland, so we respond with Amory Lovins's famous phrase, "It exists, therefore it is possible." I think these new design assignments are the most exciting and revolutionary ways of approaching commerce. And I believe that commerce is the primary engine of change, which is why I am involved with and respect the power of commerce so deeply.

Paul Hawken introduced me to the book *Systems of Survival*, in which Jane Jacobs states that humans have developed two fundamental systems for their own survival: the syndrome of the guardian and the syndrome of commerce.[10] A guardian is, for example, the government, a system that is meant to preserve, protect, and maintain. We grow very nervous when our government officials get cozy with commerce, because the guardian is meant to shun commerce. You should not be able to buy a government official. And the guardian's biggest fear is a traitor, someone who has *sold out*—a commercial term. The government will kill a traitor. It will go to war, and it can incarcerate and even kill you if you threaten the state or society. It's the only system that can legally sanction murder and duplicity.

So the guardian is slow, serious, and reserves the exclusive right to kill. Commerce, on the other hand, is meant to be quick, creative, adroit, and honest. If you are dishonest, people will stop doing business with you, because it doesn't take them long to realize that their involvement with you is not profitable if you cheat, lie, or steal. Now, let me restate the characteristics of the guardian versus those of commerce: the guardian is simple, slow, direct and even brutal when it feels the need to be. Commerce is quick, clever, and honest. As Jacobs points out, every time you put the two together you get what she calls a "monstrous hybrid."

When a city or town calls for Zero Emissions Zoning, what are they saying? That's the guardian saying, "Don't try to kill us. We'll do transportation and schools, but don't try to kill us, business." Then business—it would be DuPont in Chattanooga's case—says, "We can do that. With no complex regulations, we can figure out how not to release anything that will kill you. That's our job." The guardian wouldn't need to regulate commerce, and commerce wouldn't have to figure out how to respond to detailed micromanaged regulations, but only if commerce designs comprehensive production systems that don't release toxic emissions. Commerce doesn't need to be in the killing business.

We must, by design, allow commerce to do what commerce does best: be creative, be inventive, be quick, be smart, and be honest. And let government do what government does best—simple, important things like saying, "Don't kill us." Then our arrangements get less confused and complex.

Finally, I believe our primary design assignment, and the question we should ask ourselves in business in the future, come down to this: How do you love all the children? Not some of the children. Not just your own children. All of the children.

Jaime Lerner has been working with the whole city of Curitiba, Brazil, around this precept. He has been developing systems that respect all the children's needs for safe shelter and food, health care, education, transportation, creative opportunity, dignity, and hope. When it was time for the city to build a public library, instead of San Francisco's response—a central 100-million-dollar mausoleum for books—Curitiba's leaders asked themselves how they could provide library services for every single child in the city, including the impoverished ones in the flavelas. They decided that with their limited budget, all they could afford was many tiny libraries, each the size of a small house.

In front of every library they put a "friendly beacon of knowledge," a brightly colored and illuminated lighthouse for visibility and security. A volunteer forester, teacher, or parent sits in a little room behind a window and watches the street, reads a book, and makes sure the children are safe going to and from the library. The library holds the reference books the children need for school, as well as books the poorest children can "buy" in exchange for compostible garbage. Curitiba's goal is to put one of these libraries in each neighborhood, within easy walking distance of every child in the city. The children will have all the books they need for school, and they'll also have access to the World Wide Web. That's how they decided to design a library in Curitiba.

How do you love all the children? Well, for one thing, imagine that your outlet pipes are immediately upstream of your inlet pipes, and you'll begin to understand. We have to take responsibility for all the children, for all the generations. We're all going to have to do this, not just those "in charge." It's going to require massive creativity—*massive creativity*. It's going to require a complete redesign of commerce itself.

Let's get creative and start redesigning a new kind of prosperity for ourselves, but let's make sure this prosperity includes everyone else, including our seventh generation to come. Design for all of our prosperity, not just your own prosperity. We can start by eliminating our destruction masquerading as consumption, and begin to enjoy the search for our rightful and responsible place in the natural world. Get prosperous. Get very prosperous, because then people will want to imitate you. But honor that thing in yourself, that creativity in your spirit and your place that is really the sacred trust for all generations. We need to design a system of production and consumption and a system of commerce that will allow everyone life, liberty, and the pursuit of happiness in their own place, free from remote tyranny—the remote tyranny that is us and our bad design.

Notes

Adapted from a speech given by Mr. McDonough to the Darden Graduate School of Business Administration, December 17, 1996. Copyright 1997 by William A. McDonough. All rights reserved.

1. Thomas Jefferson, *The Political Writings of Thomas Jefferson*, ed. Merrill D. Peterson (Woodlawn: Walk Press, 1993).

2. Rachel Carson, *Silent Spring* (Boston: Houghton Mifflin, 1987).

3. Roderick Nash, *The Rights of Nature: A History of Environmental Ethics* (Madison: University of Wisconsin Press, 1989).

4. Ralph Waldo Emerson, "Nature," *Selections from Ralph Waldo Emerson*, ed. Stephen E. Whicher (Boston: Houghton Mifflin, 1957).

5. Peter Senge, *The Fifth Discipline* (New York: Doubleday, 1991).

6. Tony Hiss and Robert D. Yaro, *A Region at Risk: The Third Regional Plan for the New York-New Jersey-Connecticut Metropolitan Area* (Washington, D.C.: Island Press, 1996).

7. Mr. McDonough has developed and trademarked certain terms to describe his product and systems design protocols. These terms include: *Waste Equals Food, Product of Consumption, Product of Service, Eco-leasing Concept, technical nutrient, downcycling, Cradle-to-Cradle.*

8. See Matthew Mehalik, Michael Gorman, and Patricia Werhane, "Design-Tex, Inc.," *Darden Case Bibliography* (Charlottesville, VA: Colgate-Darden School of Business, 1996), and Matthew Mehalik, Michael Gorman, and Patricia Werhane, "Rohner Textil AG.," *Darden Case Bibliography* (Charlottesville, VA: Colgate-Darden School of Business, 1997).

9. Paul Hawken, *The Ecology of Commerce: A Declaration of Sustainability* (New York: HarperCollins, 1993).

10. Jane Jacobs, *Systems of Survival: A Dialogue on the Moral Foundations of Commerce and Politics* (New York: Vintage Books, 1992).

16

Consuming Oneself: The Dynamics of Consumption

Andrea Larson

Introduction

Entrepreneurial individuals and organizations have well-established reputations for innovation and challenges to established ways of operating. Joseph Schumpter, the early twentieth century economist, identified the entrepreneurial function as the prime source of economic change in society.[1] Schumpter observed that the "creative response" of entrepreneurial forces introduces innovation outside the range of existing practice. He captures this creative response in five categories, alone or in combination: new technologies, new products, new markets, new processes, and new organizational forms. At the millennium, this entrepreneurial sector of the economy is creating jobs and generating innovations at unprecedented rates and consequently accounting for much of the dramatic change in industrialized economics.

Little noticed, however, is a subsegment of this entrepreneurial sector, the individuals and companies operating under sustainability principles. Sustainable businesses integrate consideration of social and ecological components into all aspects of their operations, not as an "add-on" factor after profitability goals have been achieved, but as a consideration necessarily integrated into products, manufacturing operations, sourcing, internal decision making, and strategy design. A growing population of organizations, these firms are putting flesh on the theoretical skeleton of sustainability. With a rich array of innovative approaches, they offer an alternative to the traditional business model that, for the most part, still eschews social and environmental concerns, often positioning them in opposition to corporate profitability and financial health. Although the entrepreneurial firms are diverse, companies that strive toward the ideal of sustainable business share common characteristics. For instance, they embrace an alternative view of consumption. It is in this alternative offering that we see a socially and economically viable window of opportunity. While the obstacles are significant, the human capacity for creativity and innovation gives cause for optimism.

Scenario 1

Sally Fox, founder of Natural Cotton Colours, grows organic cotton plants that yield strong fibers. These are spun and woven into organic cotton fabrics used on furniture and for clothing. Her company is responding to, and generating, the market for organic fabric. Concerned about the heavy application of chemicals on cotton, Fox spent several years developing the cotton using no pesticides, fungicides, or defoliants, breeding strains of naturally colored South American plants from seeds through hand cross-pollination until the right fiber strength and colors had been obtained.

Scenario 2

Stonyfield Farm, Inc., is a yogurt producer in New Hampshire. A major rationale for the company's creation was to preserve small-scale New England family farms that practiced sustainable dairy agriculture. Sustainable agriculture employs practices that avoid the use of toxic chemicals on the land that provides grazing for cows, which in turn produce the milk used in Stonyfield's yogurt. Furthermore, Stonyfield's milk suppliers agree not to use bovine growth hormones, a laboratory-produced synthetic additive injected into cows to artificially increase their milk production.

Scenario 3

At Ecover, a small company based in Belgium, rapidly biodegradable cleaning products are produced in a manufacturing facility that meets a zero pollution emission standard. All process wastewater is cleaned, purified, and reused. The building is made of 100 percent recyclable and biodegradable materials. Ecover also has strong financial incentives to encourage nonpolluting transportation alternatives for employees and offers its building space for community activities.

Scenario 4

The Swedish company IKEA, the world's largest furniture and home furnishings retailer, has adopted a global corporate policy that prohibits the use of old-growth forest wood or tropical wood in its furniture. All timber must come from sustainably managed forests. IKEA has eliminated the use of chlorine in its catalog paper, uses 100 percent recycled paper fibers, and is committed to eliminating waste in its retail stores. The "Trash Is Cash" program has transformed the thinking of retail store workers to see trash as a revenue-generating resource.

Scenario 5

Walden Paddlers, a small company outside of Boston, Massachusetts, makes high performance recreational kayaks out of recycled plastic. Paul Farrow, the founder, was told it was technologically impossible to create such a product, no manufacturer could produce it, and that recycled plastic meeting the performance standards could not be found. Today the company offers three models of 100 percent recycled plastic kayaks. The company is growing and doing well financially. In 1996, the founder opened a second company to make additional consumer products from recycled milk bottles and plastic manufacturing scrap.

The purpose of this essay is to explore an alternative concept of consumption inherent in these accounts. Found in an increasing number of firms, this alternative perspective reflects both practical redefinition of consumption at the company level and a broader reconceptualization of consumption at the societal level.

The Definition of Consumption

The term *consumption* brings to mind a variety of commonly held definitions. Let us explore briefly the nature of consumption tied to individual wants, to waste generation, and to marketplace logic. On the one hand, consumption is the expression of our individual material wants and needs, with attendant guilt and concern for truly defining our needs versus our wants. In other words, if we would only use what we *need*, instead of what we *want*, we would consume far fewer resources. Consumption, from this perspective, has become a familiar topic of media attention and consumer reflection in American society, as individuals increasingly de-link well-being with the accumulation (consumption) of things.

From a second vantage point, the term *consumption* generates images of Western societies (ourselves writ large) consuming an ever-growing volume of goods to sustain economic growth and its attendant "good life." While linked to individual needs/wants, consumption in this case has more macro-level associations, for example, greed and mindless acquisitiveness on a grand scale, landfills at capacity (and subsequent costs passed on to individuals and businesses), the wide-spread pollution of water supplies, barges filled with garbage in search of destinations in less industrialized countries, and health effects of polluted air from burning (consuming) fossil fuels. In this picture, consumption and waste are fused. Thoughtless large-scale consumption has generated massive amounts of waste so that consumption has become a waste disposal problem and waste a public health hazard.

A third view is offered by the average business person. Here accumulation and waste are not the focus; *production* is the focus. The driving logic of production and consumption is not within individuals, or even businesses, but out in the marketplace. Corporations produce goods that the market demands. Inputs are consumed in the process and, necessarily, waste is generated. But, from this view, although companies are becoming more efficient about waste, their primary responsibility is to *produce*. It is the customer who "consumes." The business manager simply responds to market-dictated demands.

The notion of consumption when viewed from these three perspectives reveals itself as a somewhat ambiguous concept in its simultaneous connection to individual values, waste generation and disposal, and market dynamics. The latter, however—market dynamics—appears to be a trump card, muting the others. Why do the market-based ideas of consumption tend to dominate and obscure other approaches? This occurs because markets have taken on a life of their own. As though divorced from human intention, markets are seen to have patterns and create outcomes that are reified such that the legitimacy of other perspectives pales in comparison. Let us examine this assertion more closely. Managers and leaders of businesses make many unspoken assumptions about the consumption of raw materials and about consumers' demand and consumption of finished goods. Foremost among these assumptions is that consumption (equated here with consumer demand) is inherently good, that it positively feeds the economy, that higher consumption of all kinds grows the economy, and that growth is good for everyone. This is the familiar growing pie imagery with the pie made up of more and more goods, preferably new and appealing goods that customers desire, and with the assumption that we all benefit from more volume and more variety of products. Within this mind-set the increasing pie is also the capitalist economy's proxy for individual economic and social well-being. If the pie is growing, then more people get more products and services and are consequently happier and lead better lives. To grow the pie, markets must be left alone and permitted to allocate resources efficiently. Although environmental problems are readily recognized by executives and managers, no special response is needed, except to comply with government/environmental regulations. The implicit assumption is that when associated costs rise sufficiently, the market will adjust prices and consumers will pay for pollution and resource depletion expenses.

Economic Indices

Our economic measurement indices reflect and perpetuate these ideas about consumption. The Gross National Product, the annual market value of a nation's output of goods and services, including government purchases, is the measuring stick for economies and is widely accepted as a representation of the relative wealth and living standard of a population. A larger GNP signals economic success for the country and for individuals when the GNP is allocated across the population on a per capita basis. The assumption is that the faster the economy is growing in these terms, the better off are its people. This logic is an unspoken premise behind the term *consumption*. Economic growth (greater consumption), defined this way, *is* progress. Under this framework costs associated with oil spill cleanups and jobs created to care for people suffering from environmentally created illnesses push economic growth indicators upward and therefore represent social progress.

Internationally, consumption of capital is another proxy for progress. The report in the September 1996 *Business Times* that Asia took US$65 billion of the $100 billion in United States' foreign direct investments absorbed by developing countries is heralded as good news, as an indicator of that region's prospects for near-term growth. China alone accounted for $38 billion of the total investments by the United States in developing economies. Given cropland destruction accompanying China's industrialization process, and the challenge of feeding China's people and creating reasonably healthy urban living standards for the millions that are migrating to cities, do investment statistics really reflect progress and improved human welfare? Despite these contradictions, countries whose investments and per capita GNP figure fall relative to other nations interpret the drop as a competitive failure.

An Alternative View

We now turn back to the company scenarios that introduced this chapter. When held up against the traditional indices and definitions of consumption, these companies offer a pragmatic and conceptual challenge. The entrepreneurial leaders of these organizations recognize that waste is inefficient and that reducing waste, or alternatively using or selling it as a resource for some other process, makes economic sense. But beyond this more obvious shift, seen by many firms in the 1990s as simply green efficiency, are more fundamental ideas. The leaders of these firms see that humans are consuming their own habitat, a habitat consisting of resources essential to species survival. For these business leaders traditional notions of consumption translate into consuming ourselves, as environmental degradation increasingly manifests itself in human health problems, worldwide deforestation and desertification, soil depletion, contamination of fresh water, and overfishing in ocean fisheries. They understand that unless changes are made to society's definition of consumption, people will "consume" the soil, water, and air. While their lives in the next few decades may not be substantially affected, continuing to travel down the current path "consumes" the resources of their children and grandchildren.

Sally Fox, founder of Organic Cotton Colours, the American company that grows organic cotton, cultivated her distinctive perspective on consumption from her Gambian Peace Corps experiences in which she watched the excessive application of pesticides to West African farms. An entomology student in college, she returned to graduate school to study ecologically benign methods of controlling insects. Combining her knowledge of biological pest control with systematic breeding of pest-resistant strains of naturally colored cotton, she created a company that considers consumption differently. First is her challenge to the widespread consumption of chemicals to soil and agricultural products. The presence of these harmful and persistent chemicals in soil, air, and water is ubiquitous worldwide. Sally Fox would agree with the conclusions of the authors of a recent book, *Our Stolen Future*, that we should cease our production and consumption of toxic synthetic chemicals, the deleterious effects of which are only now coming to light. Despite growing evidence of problems, challenging existing consumption patterns is still a radical departure from the norm. As the top users of insecticides in the United States, cotton farmers apply approximately 100 million pounds of agricultural chemicals to their crops each year (worth over $500 million dollars in commerce) in concentrations much higher than for food products, and including pesticides considered unsafe for food application. We wear these cottons against our skin and the chemicals end up in human food. Cotton seed hulls are used as dairy and beef cattle feed. Kernels are processed into cottonseed oil, which is widely used in shortening, margarine, salad oil, potato chips, cookies, and other prepared foods.

Not only does Fox have to reject conventional notions of chemical consumption for cotton production, she also must be an advocate for her customers' consumption of a new product. This requires an understanding of the value chain steps of growers, spinners (who create the fiber), weavers (who produce the cloth), and manufacturers (who apply the cloth to products), and it requires educating consumers so that consumption patterns for cotton products ultimately shift from traditional to organic. For Fox, this is simply the way it must be done. Stewardship requires rethinking the human relationship to land and questioning accepted patterns of consumption.

Gary Hirchberg, president and CEO of Stonyfield Farm, Inc., has built a yogurt product company that incorporates the multiple missions of providing high quality, nutritious natural yogurt products, educating consumers about the value of preserving family farms practicing sustainable agriculture, and serving as a model that environmentally and socially responsible businesses can also be profitable. Consistent with these goals Stonyfield uses all-natural sweeteners, and milk free from artificial bovine growth hormones, and has developed a production process designed to make yogurt with a long shelf life without the use of preservatives and additives. By supporting sustainable agriculture Stonyfield provides a steady market for small-scale New England dairy farmers who decline to use chemicals in their operations. This commitment to the preservation of sustainable agriculture practices is at work through community activity in New Hampshire, where the company is headquartered, and extends nationally through support of science education program development for children.

Acutely aware of the interconnections between a more ecologically sustainable society and the behavior of consumers, the company pursues its educational purpose with a passion and humor. The "Just Say Moo" public awareness campaign informs consumers about the use of growth hormones and has encouraged the regulators to include a list of hormonal additives in product labeling. Other initiatives inform the public of the societal effects of their consumption patterns and the choices they make in the supermarket. The company is a major underwriter of the National Public Radio weekly environmental education series "Living on Earth," runs a "Planet Protectors" program to educate children on conservation, and offers purchasers of its yogurt participation in a "Have a Cow" program that helps them better understand the process of dairy agriculture and the linkages between consumer choice, environmental protection, and public health. Active in initiatives to preserve rain forests, the firm purchases guava and papaya for its yogurt from the Amazon rain forest region and supports international organizations that work to preserve rainforest areas for indigenous populations. For this firm, the company's purchasing (consumption) behavior is seen as an opportunity to achieve objectives of healthy food, sustainable agricul-

tural practices, and habitat preservation domestically and internationally.
Ecover manufactures a wide range of biodegradable cleaning products for household and industrial use. The company operates under the four key objectives of service "to the environment and local community, society, culture, and the economies in which we operate." The formulas for their cleaning products incorporate organic renewable substitute ingredients to achieve 98 percent biodegradability within five days, a standard that far exceeds the industry. By using vegetable oil, starch from potatoes or corn, sugar derivatives, citrus fruit and natural essential oils and avoiding optical brighteners and synthetic perfumes, Ecover offers product formulations that are effective, and the company avoids toxic chemical use. These practices and their continued efforts to make additional gains in environmental protection set them apart from traditional companies in their industry, which continue to use ingredients that degrade slowly and are suspected or known carcinogens or allergens. Ecover's washing powder is ten times less toxic than its nearest competitor and up to 15,000 times less so than the brand leader in the market.

Ecover's 5,300-square-meter facility in Malle, Belgium, was designed as a closed ecological system with zero emissions. The only solid waste coming from the building is the product and packaging. Waste water is purified in a reed meadow next to the manufacturing plant and reused inside the facility as well as applied to the grass roof in the summer to provide evaporative cooling for the building. Sustainably harvested wood and other renewable and recyclable materials were the materials used in construction. Inherent in this design is a radical redefinition of consumption. Resources and materials consumed must be returned to natural systems with minimal adverse effect.

IKEA has gone far down this path of redefining consumption. Under the "Cash for Trash" program, IKEA store managers examine all waste material leaving their stores in garbage trucks (for which they pay increasingly higher costs due to rising landfill dumping fees). The garbage is sorted and analyzed. One store manager in Gothenberg, Sweden, literally had the large trash containers overturned in the parking lot and personally led the process of picking through the contents. When waste was understood in this graphic and tactile way, steps were taken to avoid wasting materials in the first place, and to find alternative markets into which organic material, paper, and plastic waste could be sold. Its top management team has adopted a comprehensive strategy for bringing IKEA's products and activities in line with the scientific principles that govern the earth's ecological systems and biosphere. Adapting ideas from The Natural Step (see appendix), the company works hard internally and through its extensive supplier network worldwide to reduce or eliminate any activity that violates the regenerative capacities of ecosystems. The Natural Step framework offers a model for sustainable business that can guide practical decision making in firms. For example, for IKEA appropriate consumption cannot include endangered tree species or old growth forests. Wood sourcing for IKEA's furniture must conform to this rule. To the extent possible the firm extends its reconceptualization to include avoiding synthetic toxic chemicals in the manufacture of its products and catalog printing. The company searches for every opportunity to reduce waste and avoid pollution, selecting transportation modes and suppliers that understand and embrace this standard. IKEA's responsibility for "consumption" "of natural resources, of chemicals used in manufacturing and printing, of finished consumer products" extends out through its network of relationships with stakeholders including consumers, suppliers, coworkers, governments, and environmental groups. As the largest home furnishing company in the world and one of the largest volume catalog distributors, top executives believe consumption of resources carries with it obligations and the need to apply ecological systems thinking to understanding the global effect of corporate activity."[2]

In the case of Walden Paddlers, the entrepreneurial company that makes kayaks from recycled plastic, the founder was familiar with the landfill crisis in the northeastern United States. The region lacks sufficient space for landfills because of limitations on dumping imposed by fees, landfill regulations, and water and soil contamination from materials that historically have been routinely deposited. Taking a portion of the flow of waste (plastic milk containers and manufacturing process waste) that would ordinarily go into a landfill and converting it into useful and ultimately recyclable new products is evidence of a vision that takes waste generated by traditional consumption and keeps it in a closed loop of recyclable materials. The company founder, Paul Farrow, insists on a conservation ethic that permeates the company's marketing strategy and how it deals with suppliers, distributors, and customers. For example, Farrow worked with a supplier to design re-usable packaging when he found their standard packaging ended up in landfills. His determination to replace a linear sequence "product, to consumer, to landfill" with a cyclical one, demanded the formation of a new network of collaborative partners. Each member designer, recycled plastics wholesaler, manufacturer, retailer, and consumer at some level understands and buys into a new concept of consumption.

What distinguishes the leaders of these firms from more traditional ones? How do these business pioneers view consumption? One shared characteristic is the explicit assumption about the world as a context for human activity. A salient reality for the leaders of these companies is that the planet is a living organism. Most of these managers come from the first generation of people to have understood, in more than abstract terms, that the planet is a unique and delicate creation suspended in space. Growing up with the first space flights and photographs of the earth from space, this generation had the dramatic and visceral realization that we do indeed live on a unique and finite planet. For the first time in human history, large numbers of people saw the earth from a distance. Spinning in space, surrounded only with a thin atmosphere, the earth could be seen as a closed system of chemical and biological interactions that has enabled complex life forms to evolve over billions of years. The earth began to be understood by formally educated populations as an organism with its own metabolism pulsing with changing forces (climate, weather, geothermal disturbances) and processes for renewal (photosynthesis, water cycles).

What distinguishes these firms and leaders? They are reinventing commercial activity so that consumption, as traditionally understood, is an anachronism, an ill-conceived activity that with greater knowledge now must be rejected. What they share is an awareness of economic activity as absolutely dependent on and interdependent with natural ecological systems. As a result they are acutely aware of consumption patterns in the firm and with their network of collaborators (suppliers and customers). Each company has its own strategy for consuming less, changing consumption patterns to reduce adverse effects, and educating others to adopt a more sophisticated systems-based understanding of consumption.

The firms discussed here are less isolated and eclectic than they might have appeared even a few years ago, because incorporation of ecological considerations into companies is on a dramatic increase. However, there are various levels of such adoption. The first level is driven by narrow but compelling economic efficiencies. In other words, it is less costly to use fewer resources and generate minimal waste. A second level of corporate adoption of environmental values is to see the competitive advantage of being or appearing "green." These approaches are important transition phases, but the company cases discussed in this essay illustrate a more comprehensive, longer-term, and values-driven strategy. This strategy has economic efficiency built in, and many use environmental responsibility to competitive advantage. But these firms go further to create a qualitatively different model of the firm, with a fundamentally different definition of consumption inherent in corporate strategy. Furthermore, they do not stop at the traditionally conceived "borders" of their organizations, but extend their strategies and actions out through a collaborative network of suppliers and customers.

In the end, each firm challenges certain current consumption patterns of pesticides and other chemicals, plastics, building materials, wood products, and so on, taking the position (although not necessarily publicly) that historical economic and institutional patterns "consume" and destroy air, soil, and water, the very elements of which we are made.

Rethinking consumption is a significant challenge. The equation of consumption = progress has tremendous staying power. It is only recently that this equation has been challenged by economists who offer alternative and seemingly more accurate representations of a country's economic condition. The Net Economic Welfare (NEW) index calculates economic activity that makes no contribution to human welfare or actually detracts from it ("disamenities") such as the cost of pollution cleanup and medical care costs from pollution-created illnesses. These amounts are subtracted to yield a slower-growing indicator of well-being and dramatically reveal that economic benefits of growth are not commensurate with expanding national output of goods and services. Applying sustainability principles to the indexing of growth, the Index of Sustainable Economic Welfare (ISEW) goes further to incorporate the cost of pollution and land degeneration through pollution, cropland and wetland losses, and other factors that adversely influence human welfare.[3] Due to rapid environmental deterioration, in the 1980s the ISEW declined 0.8 percent in the United States after increasing only about 0.7 percent in the 1970s. This compared with an average of 1.9 percent GNP growth for those two decades, under the traditional measuring stick. For countries depending heavily on natural assets such as forest timber, oil and extractive minerals, and croplands for exports, incorporating the depletion of these assets into the calculation of national welfare results in a more somber assessment of economic growth. Destroying assets and living on the current income they generate is a short-term strategy, and national welfare measurements that deny this reality are powerful obstacles to understanding the true character of national consumption.

Rethinking our definitions of consumption is occurring across the board, and changes will be made. But perhaps the most dramatic changes are already going on in small and large companies in which a small number of leaders understand what needs to be done and are willing to take action. Some say the leading firms are on the cusp of a significant shift in the evolution of capitalist economics. At the millennium it is difficult to gauge their future influence; however, voices calling for a new industrial revolution are on the rise. Essential to that revolution is a conscious rethinking of the purpose and conduct of commercial activity. According to this view, the intent and the behavior of businesses must be examined, questioned, and refashioned to realize a sustainable socioeconomic system. At the core of this reconceptualization is the definition of consumption.

Notes

1. Joseph A. Schumpter in *The Economics and Sociology of Capitalism*, ed. Richard Swedberg (Princeton: Princeton University Press, 1991).
2. Andrea Larson and Joel Reichert, "IKEA and The Natural Step," UVA-G-0501, *Darden Case Bibliography* (Charlottesville, VA: Colgate-Darden School of Business, 1996).
3. ISEW was developed in Herman E. Daly and John B. Cobb Jr., *For the Common Good* (Boston: Beacon Press, 1994), 443–507.

Appendix

The Natural Step (TNS)

The Natural Step is both a framework for understanding environmental problems and a nonprofit institution that offers training and education. The framework evolved from a lengthy process of debate and revision out of which scientists from a wide variety of disciplines achieved consensus on four "system conditions" necessary for a sustainable society. The conditions, in combination with training and education, offer ways to go beyond *understanding* environmental issues to *solving* environmental problems. The scientific basis for TNS enables groups to form a consensus about how to move forward and make decisions that logically integrate environmental issues. Broadly applicable to communities, governments, academic institutions, and other non-profits, TNS principles also can be used by corporations and are being adopted by firms to guide strategy and redesign products and production processes. The system conditions are set out in the table below. Well-known international companies now working with The Natural Step guidelines include Monsanto, IKEA, Interface, Ontario, Hydro, and AB Electrolux.

TABLE 16.1
System Conditions—The Natural Step

System Condition	This means:	Reason:	Question to ask:
1. *Substances from the Earth's crust must not systematically increase in the ecosphere*	Fossil fuels, metals and other minerals must not be extracted at a faster pace than their slow redeposit and reintegration into the Earth's crust	Otherwise the concentration of substances in the ecosphere will increase and eventually reach limits "often unknown" beyond which irreversible changes occur	Does your organization systematically decrease its economic dependence on underground metals, fuels and other minerals?
2. *Substances produced by society must not systematically increase in the ecosphere*	Substances must not be produced at a faster pace than they can be broken down and integrated into the cycles of nature or deposited into the Earth's crust	Otherwise the concentration of substances in the ecosphere will increase and eventually reach limits "often unknown" beyond which irreversible changes occur	Does your organization systematically decrease its economic dependence on persistent unnatural substances?
3. *The physical basis for productivity and diversity of nature must not be systematically diminished*	We cannot harvest or manipulate ecosystems in such a way that productive capacity and diversity systematically diminish	Our health and prosperity depend on the capacity of nature to reconcentrate and restructure wastes into new resources	Does you organization systematically decrease its economic dependence on activities which encroach on productive parts of nature, e.g., over-fishing?
4. *Fair and efficient use of resources with respect to meeting human needs*	Basic human needs must be met with the most resource-efficient methods possible, and their satisfaction must take precedence over provision of luxuries	Humanity must prosper with a resource metabolism meeting system conditions 1-3. This is necessary in order to get the social stability and cooperation for achieving the changes in time	Does your organization systematically decrease its economic dependence on using an unnecessarily large amount of resources in relation to added human value?

Source: TNS NEWS, no. 1, Winter 1996.

17

Toward a Sustainable Tomorrow

Michael E. Gorman, Matthew M. Mehalik,
Scott Sonenshein, and Wendy Warren

Introduction

In his provocative novel *Ishmael,* Daniel Quinn argues that about ten thousand years ago, a new kind of Taker civilization emerged, one based on the idea of dominion over the earth. The Takers developed agricultural technologies that gave them the ability to produce more food than they needed, thereby expanding the population. The alternative hunter-gatherer and herder cultures Quinn refers to as Leavers, indicate the way in which they allow nature to limit their population and guide their choice of food and other resources: "the Takers systematically destroy their competitors' food to make room for their own. Nothing like this occurs in the natural community. The rule there is: Take what you need, and leave the rest alone."[1]

For Quinn, any attempt to promote sustainable development without a change in Taker attitudes would be a failure. What is needed is for human beings to change the fundamental myth or story on which most of the civilized world operates: "The old horror of Man Supreme, wiping out everything on this planet that doesn't serve his needs directly or indirectly."[2]

Quinn believes in creating virtuous people by altering the story most of us live by—once we have internalized a new myth, we will know how to share resources, not just with other human beings but also with other species. Quinn's example suggests the importance of another factor in sustainable development: moral imagination.

According to Patricia Werhane, moral imagination involves "at least four things: (1) that one disengage oneself from one's role, one's particular situation, or context; (2) that one become aware of the kind of scheme one has adopted and/or that is operating in a particular kind of context; (3) that one creatively envision new possibilities, possibilities for fresh ways to frame experiences and new solutions to present dilemmas; and (4) that one evaluate the old context, the scope or range of the conceptual schemes at work, and new possibilities."[3]

Quinn's "story we live by" is equivalent to a higher-order schema that dictates a whole complex of attitudes or actions. Consider someone who operates on Taker assumptions. These views will not seem like assumptions. They will simply appear to be a reflection of reality: "The earth belongs to the human species. We are special, unique—our intelligence and technological process give us the right to expand, grow, multiply and use the Earth in a way that satisfies our needs." The first step in moral imagination is to see that this so-called right is in fact a view, that other views are possible.

Moral imagination needs to be exercised by those who take Leaver assumptions for granted as well:

> The problem is that man's conquest of the world has itself devastated the world. And in spite of the mastery we've attained, we don't have enough mastery to *stop* devastating the world—or to repair the devastation we've already wrought. We've poured our poisons into the world as though it was a bottomless pit—and we *go on* pouring our poisons into the world. We've gobbled up irreplaceable resources as though they could never run out—and we *go on* gobbling them up. . . . Only one thing can save us. We have to *increase* our mastery of the world . . . *go on* conquering it until our rule is *absolute*. Then, when we're in *complete* control, everything will be fine. All the life processes of this planet will be where they belong—where the Gods meant them to be—in our hands. And we'll manipulate them the way a programmer manipulates a computer.[4]

Paul Hawken expresses this "Leaver" philosophy "in terms of an economic golden rule for the restorative economy: Leave the world better than you found it, take no more than you need, try not to harm life or the environment, make amends if you do."[5]

This assumption that control and mastery are always bad is also a view that needs to be analyzed critically. There is substantial evidence that technological progress can reduce pollution[6] and that growth can even be beneficial for the environment, in some situations. One should not hold either a Leaver or Taker position dogmatically. Moral imagination is a tool for combating dogma and for recognizing that there are different ethical perspectives that can be applied to a problem.

One place to begin is the corporation. Government policies should be changed to encourage responsible corporate practices; such changes would include making prices reflect environmental costs, taxes on natural resources, and allowing resource companies to form utilities. But even if such radical changes in our current system of taxation and regulation cannot be implemented, imaginative business leaders can push ahead toward sustainability. Ray Anderson, the CEO of Interface, learned from Hawken that "business and industry, the largest, wealthiest, most pervasive institution on earth, must take the lead in saving the earth from man-made collapse."[7] One option is The Natural Step (TNS), a set of principles first proposed by Dr. Karl-Henrik Robèrt in 1989. The purpose of TNS it to develop and share a framework of scientifically based principles (as the first and second laws of thermodynamics) that can serve as a compass to guide society to a sustainable future. Today, TNS is used by companies like Interface, which became the first company in the United States to commit to TNS principles. TNS and William McDonough share a basic metaphor: the closed-loop cycle. McDonough refers to this in his principle "waste equals food," where he calls for the design of closed-loop systems for eliminating the concept of waste. TNS refers to the closed-loop metaphor by using the first and second laws of thermodynamics.

In chapter 15 of this volume, McDonough describes DesignTex and Rohner Textil,[8] two companies directly influenced by McDonough's principle, "waste equals food." This case demonstrates that it is possible to articulate a philosophy for sustainable development and translate it into a schema that can be used to guide practical solutions. In the case of an environmentally intelligent fabric, the schema was William McDonough's. Albin Kälin and Susan Lyons were prepared to understand and adopt this schema: in the course of developing the product, they had to recruit others into a network of suppliers, backers, and buyers. Part of this recruitment involved creating scripts for accomplishing sustainable goals; however, it was not sufficient to teach scripts—at least some of the other members of the network had to acquire the overall schema and exercise a great deal of moral imagination to "translate" that schema into a sustainable, economically viable, and beautiful product. In what follows we describe a second case that takes us into the developing world and concerns the principle, "work from current solar income."

Solar Electric Light Fund

The Solar Electric Light Fund (SELF) was founded to help provide rural areas in the developing world with photovoltaic power, an energy source that poses minimal environmental threats. Working first in areas of rural China and South Africa, SELF's founder, Neville Williams, understood that it was inevitable that electricity would come to such areas. The important question is not whether the developing world will be electrified, but in what manner. What will the consequences of such electrification be? Will environmental externalities be the norm? Williams notes that "the first person to show up with electricity wins!" Eager for power, the developing world jumps at any opportunity afforded to it. Yet, if the developing world follows the path of the West by extending grid extensions backed by fossil fuels, the environment will be headed toward catastrophe. Williams notes that "even if they [the developing world] could afford to run the wires out from power plants, which is not economically feasible—we would pollute the world beyond imagination." (Currently, the developing world consumes approximately 1,000 million tons of oil equivalent per year, an amount threefold that of the energy of coal mined in Europe and twofold that in the United States.)

Williams set out to demonstrate that technological change, improved standards of living, and environmental respect are realizable and consistent goals, not merely utopian ideals. By using photovoltaic technology (PV), which harnesses the sun's rays and converts them into energy, Williams was attempting to avoid the mistakes that the West encountered from its technological revolution: "If the Third World develops in the way we did," declares Williams, "the world would be a wreck. The biggest threat to global warming and to greenhouse gases in the future is the unbridled development of the Third World because 70 to 80 percent of the people in developing countries don't even have electricity."

SELF's method is simple. It first convinces individuals that photovoltaic power (power generated by solar cells) works by donating some units either to specific families or to local community centers. Then it provides them with financial mechanisms to enable the purchase of their own units—it is no easy task convincing a rural farmer to forgo approximately one-half of his $500 annual income for a solar unit that he has never used before. Not only does SELF endeavor to electrify the developing world in an environmentally safe manner, it requires that individuals who receive that power pay for it themselves.

The typical photovoltaic system that SELF uses supplies between twenty and sixty watts peak of output per unit and is composed of a rechargeable battery for energy storage, a battery charge controller, lights, an outlet for low power-consuming appliances (e.g., television or radio), switches, interconnecting wires, and mounting hardware. Such units have proven to be more than adequate in meeting the needs of users, many of whom are experiencing power for the first time. Unlike coal, batteries, or kerosene, the Department of Energy's National Renewable Energy Laboratory classifies PV as "one of the most benign forms of electricity generation available." PV units pose only a small environmental impact that comes from disposal of the batteries that store energy for the units. Otherwise, PV units provide safe, environmentally clean energy.

The PV units are the perfect matches for rural villagers. The units are relatively cheap, providing twenty years' worth of power for under $500. Additionally, they require little skill in maintaining them and have very few mechanical problems. Of more importance is their relatively low threat to the environment.

SELF is not a charitable organization; they seek only paying customers. SELF promotes individual responsibility for two other important reasons: to both ensure that the units are properly cared for and to give individuals in the developing world a sense of pride that comes from ownership of goods. SELF's efforts have demonstrated that when individuals have to use their own scarce resources to pay for PV units, they use them efficiently. Individuals have too few resources to misuse or not care for such a precious investment. Maintenance of the unit is also performed with responsibility, as the owner takes pride in his investment, enjoying a sense of social prestige.

While SELF does not dole out technology, it does provide assistance. However, that assistance is not financial per se; rather, it comes in the form of helping individuals afford the technology by providing loans using concessionary financing. The process is quite simple but has proven to be remarkably successful. SELF makes an initial contribution to a "solar fund" (usually from a grant) to allow for capital used to provide loans to persons wishing to buy a PV unit. SELF collects a down payment from the purchaser and places the payment into a "solar bank." Monthly payments on the loans are also recycled into a solar bank. The solar bank is then used to lend funds to more individuals wishing to buy their own PV units. Similarly, their down payments and monthly installments are recycled, enabling even more families to receive units. The fund thus becomes revolving, using previous payments to finance future loans.[9]

SELF was not inspired directly by McDonough, but it does illustrate the principle "work from current solar income." It also illustrates how sustainability can be made to work in the developing world, which is now going through an enormous industrial revolution. Integral to SELF's philosophy is getting locals to own and take responsibility for the technology. In this case, they do not have to buy into the sustainable schema—they just have to want power. In the future, as photovoltaics spread into areas where there are alternatives for power, it will become important to persuade others to adopt a sustainable schema. Even more than in the DesignTex and Rohner case, costs will be crucial: most people in the developing world cannot afford to pay a large premium for adopting sustainable ideas. What remains to be seen is whether the fabric created by DesignTex and Rohner Textil will become an international model for the design of other, similar products, and whether SELF can help create larger private enterprises that will spread solar technology throughout rural areas of the developing world. If these and other efforts are successful, it will demonstrate that moral imagination can be translated into schemata and scripts that will make technology a factor in reducing environmental impacts instead of contributing to them.

Notes

1. Daniel Quinn, *Ishmael: An Adventure of the Mind and Spirit* (New York: Bantam/Turner, 1992), 127.

2. Quinn, *Ishmael*, 249.

3. Patricia H. Werhane, " Moral Imagination and Management Decision-Making," *Business Ethics Quarterly*, Ruffin Lecture Series, 8 (1998), forthcoming.

4. Quinn, 80–81.

5. Paul Hawken, *The Ecology of Commerce* (New York: HarperCollins, 1993).

6. J. L. Bast, P. J. Hill, and R. C. Rue, *Eco-Sanity: A Common-Sense Guide to Environmentalism* (Lanham, MD: Madison Books, 1994).

7. R. C. Anderson, *The Journey from There to Here: The Eco-Odyssey of a CEO* (Big Sky, MT: U.S. Green Building Council, 1995).

8. For different perspectives on DesignTex snd Rohner Textil see Matthew Mehalik, M. Gorman and P. Werhane, "DesignTex, Inc. (A) and (B)," UVA-E-0099, *Darden Case Bibliography* (Charlottesville, VA: Colgate-Darden School of Business, 1996); Matthew Mehalik, M. Gorman and P. Werhane, "Rohner Textil AG (A), (B), (C), (D), (E)," UVA-E-0107, *Darden Case Bibliography* (Charlottesville, VA: Colgate-Darden School of Business, 1997); and Michael E. Gorman, *Transforming Nature: Ethics, Invention and Discovery* (Boston: Kluwer Academic Publishers, 1998), 237–75.

9. Scott Sonenshein, Michael Gorman, and Patricia H. Werhane, "Solar Electric Light Fund," UVA-E-0112, *Darden Case Bibliography* (Charlottesville, VA: Colgate-Darden School of Business, 1997).

18

Shades of Green: Business, Ethics, and the Environment

R. Edward Freeman, Jessica Pierce, and Richard Dodd

The Challenge of Business Leadership Today

It is possible for business leaders to make money, do the right thing, and participate in saving the earth. It is possible to fit these ideas together, but it is not easy. We have to warn you here and now that we don't have any quick solutions, magic bullets, or foolproof formulas for success. The issues are too difficult and messy for any such nonsense. Instead we are going to suggest how to begin to understand the concepts of business, ethics, and the environment so that they can work together.

This is an exercise about possibilities. Instead of showing the myriad ways that business, ethics, and the environment conflict and lead to impossible choices, we are going to ask the question, "How is it possible to put these ideas together?"[1] In today's world and the one we are creating for our children, all three are necessary. Our businesses must continue to create value for their financiers and other stakeholders. In an interconnected global economy, we can no longer afford the ethical excesses that many see as characteristic of the last several decades. And, if we are to leave a livable world for our children and their children, we simply must pay attention to environmental matters.

Most of the methods, concepts, ideas, theories, and techniques that we use in business do not put business, ethics, and the environment together. From discounted cash flow to human resources planning, neither ethics nor the environment are central to the way we think about business.

Everyone shares the joke about the very idea of "business ethics" as an oxymoron, two words whose definitions are contradictory. Much of business language is oriented toward seeing a conflict between business and ethics. We routinely juxtapose profits with ethics, as if making an ethical decision costs profits.[2] We sometimes qualify difficult choices that distribute harms and benefits to communities and employees as "business decisions," signaling that business and ethics are not compatible.[3]

The environment fares no better. It is seen as a necessary evil, a cost to be minimized or a regulation with which to comply. We almost never think about the environment as central to the main metaphors of business, its strategic and people management systems, unless, of course, there is some regulation that constrains business strategy, a mess to be cleaned up or a public issue that pits executives against environmentalists. Historically, business people have been neither encouraged nor discouraged to get involved with environmental concerns. Our models and theories of business have traditionally been simply *silent* on the subject of the environment. The world of the 1990s, however, is beginning to make a great deal of noise.

More and more citizens see themselves as environmentalists. Governments are increasing their cooperative actions to address global environmental concerns such as global warming and biodiversity. And interest groups are beginning to propose solutions to problems that involve business decision-making outside of and beyond government regulation.

So, what we desperately need are some new ideas, concepts, and theories that allow us to think about business, ethics, and the environment in one full breath. We need to see these issues as going together rather than in conflict. Today's challenge to business leadership is sustaining profitability, doing the right thing, and being green.

The Environment: It's Everywhere

Early on the morning of March 24, 1989, the super tanker Exxon *Valdez* ran aground on Bligh Reef in Prince William Sound off the coast of Alaska. In the days following the accident, every action or inaction by Exxon executives, government officials and environmentalists was subjected to an unprecedented public scrutiny.

In addition to the damage caused by the release of millions of gallons of oil into the ecosystem, the *Valdez* incident symbolizes an important milestone in business history. The environment is an issue that has come to stay. It is not a fad, passing fancy, or the issue of the day.

There is not a single aspect of our world today that can escape the scrutiny of environmental analysis. Pollution of air, water, and land; the production and disposal of hazardous wastes; solid waste disposal;

chemical and nuclear spills and accidents; global warming and the greenhouse effect; ozone depletion; deforestation and desertification; biodiversity; and overpopulation are a few of the issues that today's executive needs to understand to be environmentally literate.

We are treated to daily doom and gloom press reports about the state of the earth. Scientists have "discovered" that global warming is or is not a problem, is or is not caused by solar storms, is or is not related to the emission of greenhouse gases, and so forth. We want to know the answer, the whole truth, "just the facts," about the environment, and we get disturbed by so many conflicting reports.

The truth is this: there is no one truth about the environment. The truth is also this: we have not lived in a way that respects the environment and preserves it for our children's children.

Our Children's Future: A Wager

Let's assume an optimistic scenario that implies that the gloomy forecasts are all wrong. Maybe there is enough land for landfills for generations to come. Global warming may be elusive. Many chemicals may well be harmless. The destruction of forests may be insignificant and worth the benefits of development. Clean and healthful water may someday be plentiful. And it may be that we can invent the technology we need to compensate for whatever damage we actually have done to the earth.

Are you willing to bet the future of your children on this optimistic scenario? If it is wrong, or even partially wrong, with respect to, say, global warming, then there will be no inhabitable world left for our children. Like Pascal's Wager,[4] we are going to assume that it is reasonable to bet that there is, in fact, an environmental crisis. The consequences of being wrong are too great to bet otherwise.

Yet the great majority of responses to the environmental crisis have been at best ineffective. The main response mode has been to marshal the public policy process to legislate that the air and water be cleaner, and to assign the costs of doing so to states, localities, and businesses. Twenty plus years of environmental regulation in the United States has led to "environmental gridlock." There is disagreement and contention at several important levels.

First of all, as we stated earlier, there isn't any one truth about the state of the environment. Many (but not all) individual scientific "facts" are disputable. There is widespread disagreement about the scientific answers to environmental questions, even about how the questions should be stated.

Second, among those who agree about the science around a particular issue, there is still disagreement about the appropriate public policy. Even if we agree that greenhouse gases lead to global warming, we may well disagree that limiting carbon dioxide emissions to 1990 levels will solve the problem.

Third, there is disagreement about the underlying values. How should we live? By exploiting the earth's resources? By conserving the earth's resources? By living with nature? Should we be vegetarians to improve the ability of advanced societies to feed the hungry and use land efficiently? Should we recycle or should we consume green products or should we build an ethic of "anti-consumption," of saving the earth rather than consuming it?

These three levels of disagreement lead to gridlock, especially in a public policy process that purports to base policy on facts rather than values. Overlay these three levels of disagreement on a litigious system of finding, blaming, and punishing polluters of the past and the result is a conversation about the environment that goes nowhere fast.

We believe that this public policy process needs to change, that we need to have a better conversation about the environment and the role of governments, but we are not willing to wait for these changes to take place. Instead we want to suggest another mode of response to the environmental crisis: business strategy. If we can come to see how business activity can take place, systematically, in environmentally friendly ways, then we can respond to the environmental crisis in lasting and effective ways.[5]

The Basics of Business: What Do You Stand For?

At the thousands of McDonald's franchises around the world one thing is the same: McDonald's values. "QVC" means Quality, Value, and Cleanliness, and the very idea of McDonald's is built around realizing these values. This is why at any McDonald's anywhere you get good quality, fast-food, a clean restaurant, and a good comparative price. The very meaning of McDonald's encompasses these values, and everyone, from CEO to fry cook, has to understand their job in terms of these values.

Strangely enough, a tiny company, only a fraction of the size of McDonald's works the same way. The company is called Johnsonville Sausage in Johnsonville and Sheboygan, Wisconsin. It is highly profitable, fast growing, and is based on different values from McDonald's. At Johnsonville Sausage the operating philosophy is self-improvement. The company exists in order for the individuals in it to realize their goals and to continue to improve themselves.

There is a revolution afoot in business today. And it is a revolution with values at its core. Sparked by Tom Peters and Bob Waterman's best-selling book, *In Search Of Excellence*, the rediscovery of Edward Demming's ideas on the productive workplace and the role of values and quality, and the countless programs for individual and organizational change that have been ignited by an increasingly competitive global marketplace, business today is turning to values.[6]

At one level, this emphasis on values cuts against the traditions of business. It has always been assumed that business promotes only one primary value—profits. Both the academic research and the how-to books on business are full of ideas on how to become more profitable. And profits are important as they are the lifeblood of business. But surely the purpose of life is not simply to breathe or to have our hearts go on beating. As important as these activities are, we humans are capable of more, of standing for some principles, or caring for others, or creating value for ourselves and others. Even those few people who care only for themselves still must be good enough citizens to avoid trampling on the rights and projects of others.

Organizations are no different. Profits are important, necessary—add any words you want—but there is more. Businesses can, and often do, stand for something more than profitability. Some, like IBM, stand for creating value for customers, employees, and shareholders. Others, like Merck, stand for the alleviation of human suffering. Still others, like Mesa Petroleum, may well stand for creating value for shareholders only, but even those companies must do so within the confines of the law and public expectations that could be turned into law.

This concern for values can be summarized in the idea of enterprise strategy, or asking the question, "What do you stand for?" The typical strategy process in a company asks someone to think about these questions: (1) What businesses are we in? (2) What is our competitive advantage in these businesses? (3) How can we sustain competitive advantage? What product/market focus should we take? What needs to change in order to be successful?

Some set of these questions goes into every company architecture of its portfolio of businesses. Even small businesses have to have some business plan, perhaps in the mind of the entrepreneur, which articulates how that small business creates, captures, and sustains value.

But, if this values revolution in business is meaningful, there is a prior question, the question of enterprise strategy: "What do you stand for?" By articulating an answer to this question, thereby setting forth a statement of the core values of the organization, the strategy questions mentioned earlier will have some context in which they can be answered. For instance, if you stand for human dignity and some basic idea of human rights for all, then there are probably some markets that you will not serve, and some products and services that you will not provide. If you stand for quality, cleanliness, and value, then there are certain business opportunities that you will forego because you cannot produce the quality service, or do it in a clean environment, or provide it at a price that gives good value.

Now all of this may sound rather fanciful, but the basic point is that businesses have discovered that articulating some bedrock, some foundation, some basic values has enormous benefits. The business becomes focused around these values. People, from executives to mail clerks, begin to believe in them or are attracted to the firm because of these values. In short, business strategy just makes more sense in the context of values.

It is easy to see how thinking about the environment and about ethics are compatible with the values revolution. By clearly stating and understanding the core beliefs that an organization has or wants to adopt about ethical issues such as honesty, integrity, dignity of individuals, caring about others, and so on, policies that are straightforward and easily implementable can be designed. By clearly thinking through a position on the environment—whether it is just complying with the law or trying to leave the earth better than we found it—we can begin to marshal resources to realize these basic beliefs.

Executives can begin to meet the challenge of leadership we articulated earlier—being profitable, doing the right thing, and helping to save the earth—by understanding and articulating an enterprise strategy, an answer to the question, "What do we stand for?" From huge DuPont to little Ben and Jerry's, from oil and chemical companies to retail boutiques, articulating what you stand for on the environment is step one to a greener world, one that we can pass along to our children.

It's Not Easy Being Green

There are many ways that businesses can adopt strategies that are more friendly toward the environment. None of them are simple. In the words of that great philosopher, Kermit the Frog, "It's not easy being green."

We want to suggest that there are four primary "shades of green," and each has its own logic, and each has many interpretations. Let's call these shades: (1) light green; (2) market green; (3) stakeholder green; and (4) dark green. You can think of these shades as phases of development of a company's strategy, moving from light green to dark green, but keep in mind that each shade has its own logic. It isn't necessary to move from one shade to the next. And each shade offers its own way to create and sustain value, so that business, ethics, and the environment go together. Here's a brief thumbnail sketch of the logic of each shade of green.

Light Green, or Legal Green, is a shade with which most companies are familiar. Being Light Green involves complying with the following principle:

Light Green Principle

Create and sustain competitive advantage by ensuring that your company is in compliance with the law.

The logic of Light Green relies on the public policy process to drive its strategy. But, it is a mistake to think that no competitive advantage is possible for every company has to obey the law—a mistake on two counts.

First, as Michael Porter and his colleagues have argued, countries with strict environmental standards seem to gain an edge in global marketplaces—they become more efficient and have better technology. Secondly, within an industry, companies actively can pursue public policies that fit with their special competitive advantage. By innovating with technology and know-how, a company gains an advantage over a competitor who cannot comply as efficiently. Light Green thinking thus creates the possibility for competitive advantage.

Market Green logic is different. Rather than focus on the public policy process, Market Green logic focuses on customers. The following principle is at work:

Market Green Principle

Create and sustain competitive advantage by paying attention to the environmental preferences of customers.

Market Green strategies are based on the greening of the customer, a fast-growing yet controversial phenomenon. Today's customer-focused, market-driven company cannot afford to miss the fact that customers prefer environmentally friendly products—and without added costs. Again it is easy to see that creating and sustaining competitive advantage is a matter of "better, cheaper, faster." Companies that can meet these environmental needs will be the winners. Customer perceptions about the shade of green of the company will be crucial, but most importantly the products and services have to perform.

McDonald's decision to ban Styrofoam cartons was driven in part by customers' perceptions that polystyrene was bad for the environment. But if the new containers made from treated paper cannot be recycled or biodegraded, customer needs will not have been met, and someone else will produce a more environmentally friendly burger.

Market Green logic just applies good old-fashioned "smell the customer" thinking to the environment. Note that this may or may not be in conjunction with Legal Green. Market Green logic roots competitive advantage in customer needs and the ability of the customer-driven company to deliver on these needs. There is nothing unusual except giving up the costly belief that environmentally friendly products always entail higher costs and competitive disadvantages. Notice that Market Green logic can apply to the industrial sector as well as the consumer sector and to services as well as products.

Stakeholder Green is a shade darker than Market Green. It applies Market Green logic to key stakeholder groups such as customers, suppliers, employees, communities, shareholders, and other financiers. There are many different ways to slice the stakeholder pie. Companies can seek to maximize the benefits of one group, or they can seek to harmonize the interests of all groups. The point is that Stakeholder Green gets its color from responding to the needs of some or all stakeholder groups. It obeys the following principle:

Stakeholder Green Principle

Create and sustain competitive advantage by responding to the environmental preferences of stakeholders.

Stakeholder Green strategies are based on a more thoroughgoing adoption of environmental principles among all aspects of a company's operations. Many companies have adopted a version of Stakeholder Green by requiring suppliers to meet environmental requirements and by setting strict standards for the manufacturing process. Paying attention to recyclable material in consumer packaging, educating employees on environmental issues, participating in community efforts to clean up the environment, and appealing to investors who want to invest in green companies are all a part of Stakeholder Green. This shade is different because it does not require one action or a focused set of actions; rather, it requires anticipating and responding to a whole set of issues regarding the environment. As such it is more complicated than the earlier shades. The logic of Stakeholder Green is similar to the logic of quality processes. Unless quality processes permeate a company at all levels, they are doomed to fail. There are different levels of commitment to Stakeholder Green, just as there are different levels of commitment to quality, but any effective commitment must be pervasive.

Dark Green is a shade for which few companies strive. Being Dark Green commits a company to being a leader in making environmental principles a fundamental basis for doing business. Dark Green suggests the following principle:

Dark Green Principle

Create and sustain value in a way that sustains and cares for the earth. To most business people this principle will sound pretty idealistic or fanciful. Their skepticism only points out how much we have ignored the environment in our ways of thinking about business. Indigenous people know that this principle must be obeyed. We teach our children to care for their things and the things—such as our homes and land—that we share. It is not a large stretch of the imagination to expect that the same values are possible in business.

Dark Green logic is not antibusiness, though many people will believe it is. Humans create value for each other, and *business* is the name we have given that process. Dark Green logic just says that we must respect and care for the earth in this process of value creation.

There are more than four shades of green. Look at these four as anchors that can define what is possible for your company. Dark Green is not for everyone, while Light Green may be more universal. Indeed Dark Green raises more questions than it answers. It reminds us that the very idea of "living with the earth" or "treating the earth with respect" are difficult issues that bring forth deep philosophical questions.

Our argument is not that we should find the optimal shade for everyone, but that variation is good. That is, imagine a world in which there are thousands of enterprises each trying to realize competitive advantage through environmental means. Undoubtedly, many of these innovations will fail, but some will succeed, and many will lead to other, more important innovations. It is only through a large-scale process of many small innovations that real, lasting change can occur. Perhaps while such innovation is emerging, someone, somewhere, will invent a revolutionary "pollution machine" that will cure all of our environmental ills, or some official will "discover" the perfect set of regulations. All well and good if that happens, but we are suggesting a more modest and, we believe, more workable approach.

Tough Questions

Ultimately how we run our companies reflects our commitment to how we want to live. Our values are lived through our behavior. Someone who espouses green values but who does nothing to realize those values lives in bad faith or self-deception. Bad faith means that we say one thing and do another, and self-deception means we are not honest with ourselves about what we truly believe and how we really want to live. Ethics, in life and in business, starts with an assumption of good faith and self-awareness, or at least an acknowledgment of the difficulties involved in being authentic to our true beliefs.

Nowhere do we see these issues more plainly than in environmental values. Talk is cheap, and its price is related to a shared history and culture of not living in a way that guarantees our children a future. We believe there are many ways to live—indeed many ways to live in an environmentally sustainable way—but we also know that our values have not always led us in any sustainable direction.

The point is that we do depend on the natural world and, especially today, the natural world depends on us for its survival. Humans have the capability to destroy life on earth, and such a capability implies a responsibility to live ethically. We argue that any shade of green that you adopt raises important questions about our responsibility to live ethically. We explore three of these philosophical challenges here. Briefly they are conservation, social justice, and ecology.

The conservation challenge tells us to conserve the earth's resources for the future and is a minimal response to Our Children's Future Wager.

The social justice challenge tells us that there are many ways to improve the institutions that we have created. It focuses on those who have been mistreated by those institutions—women, minorities, indigenous peoples—and traces a connection between their mistreatment and the way we view the environment.

The ecological challenge comes in many forms, but it asks us to view the Earth as a living organism and to find a way to talk about the Earth and its creatures in our human-centered moral discourse. We should live in a way that is sustainable and self-renewing, rather than destructive of current resources.

Each of these three philosophies challenges our ways of doing business. It is easiest to integrate conservation with the normal ways we think about business, but we argue that what is necessary to meet Our Children's Future is a conversation that takes all three philosophies into account. We need to understand how we redefine business and make it consistent with each of these three views.

Barriers to a Green Conversation

If we are going to explore how we can rethink business along an environmental dimension, and if the outcome of this conversation is to be not one but many different ways of creating and sustaining value, then we must be on the lookout for barriers that will prevent us from engaging the tough issues. We believe that most of these barriers are our own inabilities to entertain new ideas: our mind-sets. We have identified five mind-sets that all say that our project, the integration of business, ethics, and the environment into new modes of thinking, is impossible.

The Regulatory Mind-set.

This mind-set sees the environment as a part of the business-government relationship to be spelled out in terms of regulation or public policy. The Regulatory Mind-set says that the best way to take care of the environment is through the public policy process that produces laws and rules with which business must comply. It discounts the possibility and the wisdom of voluntary initiatives that stem from deeply held environmental values, or even the desire to respond to environmental preferences. While the recent history of concern with the environment has usually meant the passage of laws and their attendant regulations, the debate today goes far beyond a regulatory mind-set. Regulation lags the real world, and regulation inevitably entails unforeseen consequences. Our question for the Regulatory Mind-set is: Are you confident that government, as it currently works, will create a sustainable future for your children?

The Cost/Benefit Mind-set

The Cost/Benefit Mind-set is sometimes closely related to the Regulatory Mind-set simply because many regulatory regimes use cost/benefit methods to determine "proper" regulations. The Cost/Benefit Mind-set says that cleaning up the environment or making products and services more environmentally friendly has costs and benefits. And we should go only so far as the benefits outweighing the costs.

There are several problems with this view. The first is that if you focus on costs and benefits, you will fail to use "innovation." The argument is similar to the quality approach. By focusing on the cost of quality, managers make wrong decisions. Instead by focusing on quality processes that involve extraordinary customer service or stretch goals such as zero defects, human innovation takes over and drives quality up and costs down. The Cost/Benefit Mind-set says that there is a contradiction between "environmentally friendly" and costs. Many companies are discovering that by adopting one or more of the shades of green that we recommend here, they are making money and becoming more environmentally friendly. By focusing on costs and benefits, managers inevitably are led to ask the wrong questions.

The second problem with the Cost/Benefit Mind-set is that it assumes one particular set of underlying values: economic ones. Many environmentalists, executives, and other thinkers have questioned the priority of our current ways of thinking about economics. All value is not economic value, and anyone who believes that it is, is trying to get us to live in a certain way. Does the last gorilla have just an economic value? What about the beauty of the Grand Tetons? What about the futures of our children? Human life is rich and complex and is not reducible solely to an economic calculation. It is degrading to all of us to think that we only value people and things in economic terms.

The Constraint Mind-set

Still, many will argue that the main purpose of business is to create and sustain economic value, and everything else from ethics to the environment to meaningful work is best viewed as a side constraint. The business of business is business. Anything else should be viewed as not the main objective of business.

There is a nugget of truth here, like there is in all of these prevalent mind-sets. Economic value has been the main focus of business, and other kinds of value have been seen as constraining a kind of unfettered capitalism, driven by the urge to win, succeed, and compete. A more thoughtful analysis of economic value creation, however, shows that it is impossible to separate out economic, political, social, and personal aspects of value. When the employees of Delta buy a jet for the company, when Johnson and Johnson recalls Tylenol, when Body Shop employees volunteer to help the homeless, when Mattel donates money to the part of Los Angeles destroyed by riots, all of these actions imply it is possible for a company to be driven by economics and by ethics. No one is arguing that economics is unimportant, but we are insisting that the reduction of all human value creation and value sustaining activity to economic measures misses the mark. Business does more, as Adam Smith realized, and to reduce capitalism to economics endangers our free society.[7]

The Sustainable Development Mind-set

It may seem strange to lump what is supposed to be a way to save the earth with mind-sets that prevent environmental progress. Obviously not all discussions of sustainable development act as barriers, but one recent discussion simply misses the mark. The Brundtland Report, the basis of

the Rio Earth Summit in 1992, called on governments to redefine economic activity to become sustainable. The problem with this view is that
it calls on governments to have an intrusive role in the process of value
creation, and if we have learned anything from the collapse of state
socialism, it is that governments and centralized approaches do not work
very well. Ultimately, a worldwide regime of environmental cooperation
could become a worldwide hegemony of democratic freedom, especially
if combined with the other mind-sets. Decisions on the future of whole
industries and companies could become a matter just of government's
beliefs about what is sustainable.

Recall our view, that there is no one truth about the environment. We
believe that it is necessary to adopt a radically decentralized approach,
which focuses on shared values, and a conversation about those shared
values. If such an approach is not viable, then we should see the heavy
hand of the state as part and parcel of our failure to integrate business,
ethics, and the environment.

The Greenwashing Mind-set

The Greenwashing Mind-set pervades many discussions of the environment. Characteristic of it is the view that business could never act on
values other than profit maximization. And whenever we see a company
engaged in something that looks like it might be good for the environment, we should be deeply skeptical. Really, if truth be told, the company is probably trying to make money, or avoid some future cost, or
engage in other narrowly self-interested schemes. Many environmental
programs at companies are, on this view, cleverly disguised attempts to
be seen as green, while really continuing in an environmentally destructive mode.

Many times when we have presented these ideas to groups that contained people who were deeply committed to environmental values but
had little real contact with the inner workings of business, there has
been an assumption that "business is bad."[8]

Surely, there are attempts to greenwash—portray trivial changes to
products, services, and processes in grand and glorious environmental
terms. And we should look carefully at such claims. However, the assumption that therefore all business attempts at environmental action
are suspect simply does not follow.

We want to suggest that we be skeptical of all grand environmental
claims, whether they be from business, government, environmental
groups, or scientists. The arena is very uncertain and complex, and the
Greenwashing Mind-set makes our task impossible, so we shall set this
mind-set aside. Of course, businesses want to make money, but it doesn't

follow that the environment must be left out of the equation, or that profit is the only value that counts.

Summary

We have chosen a difficult project—we want to engage you in a conversation about how to think about business, ethics, and the environment together rather than separately. We are optimistic that the fruits of such a conversation can make a difference, to us and to our children. If you are confident that your children have a safe and secure future then you don't need to wrestle with the questions that this conversation raises, and you don't need to examine your values and behavior to see if there needs to be change, but we do not share your confidence.

We do not have confidence that the future is secure, nor do we have confidence that our current institutions, as well meaning as they may be, are doing all that is necessary. We are confident that if we can begin to think about business in environmentally sound ways, we can make real progress.

Notes

1. We have no doubt that there can be and indeed are multiple conflicts. These conflicts are a result of the conceptual schemes we've brought to bear on these issues. Our argument is that we need a new conceptual scheme, one that considers the possibility that these ideas can fit together.

2. That many see "ethics" and "profits" as contradictory is evident from the reading of a great deal of the literature on business theory and business ethics.

3. Of course, these "business decisions" are moral in nature. They distribute harms and benefits to other stakeholders, usually shareholders.

4. Philosopher Blaise Pascal proposed the following wager in the seventeenth century: Suppose Christianity is correct. If you are not a believer you are in for a seriously hot eternity in Hell. So, it is rational to believe in Christianity or to act as if it is correct. Now, Pascal's Wager doesn't work in its original form because it is a tenet of both Christianity and liberalism that individuals can decide for themselves whether to mortgage their own future in eternity for a few temporal moments of pleasure during life on earth. Our Children's Wager doesn't suffer from the same logical defect because the point is that our children will not get to make those choices if we do not begin to live differently. We have used *children* in the sense of future generations, which include, but are not limited to, existing children.

5. Our approach is radical—at least for business theorists and environmentalists. Most writing about the environment acts as if business is evil, and most

writing on business acts as if business is separate from the environment. We want to stake out some new territory.

6. Note that this shift to values is not always in moral terms, even though Freeman and Gilbert argue that it should be. Many executives see these values as instrumental, leading to profits.

7. Adam Smith was primarily concerned about justice.

8. For a more careful analysis of this idea, see R. Edward Freeman, "The Business Sucks Story," The Darden School Working Papers (Charlottesville, VA: University of Virginia, 1996).

Index

About the Contributors

George Brenkert is professor of philosophy at the University of Tennessee, Knoxville, and visiting professor in the School of Business Administration at Georgetown University. He received his Ph.D. from the University of Michigan. He specializes in the areas of business ethics, social and political philosophy, and ethics. His international experience includes two years in India on Fulbright grants and one year in Germany on an Alexander von Humboldt fellowship. He is currently writing a book on the ethics of marketing.

Donald A. Brown is the program manager for United Nations Organizations in the International Environment Policy Section of the Office of International Affairs of the United States Environmental Protection Agency. In this position, Brown acts as the liaison between the U.S. EPA and the United Nations Commission on Sustainable Development, the United Nations Environment Program, and the United Nations Development Program.

Rogene A. Buchholz is the Legendre-Soule Professor of Business Ethics at Loyola University of New Orleans. He has written more than fifty articles and nine books in the areas of business and public policy, business ethics, and the environment. He is on the editorial board of several journals and served as chair of the Social Issues in Management Division of the Academy of Management.

Herman E. Daly is currently senior research scholar at the University of Maryland, School of Public Affairs. From 1988 to 1994 he was senior economist in the Environment Department of the World Bank. He has served as Ford Foundation Visiting Professor at the University of Ceará (Brazil), as a research associate at Yale University, as a visiting fellow at the Australian National University, and as a Senior Fulbright Lecturer in Brazil. He has served on the boards of advisors of numerous environ-

373

mental organizations and is cofounder and associate editor of the *Journal of Ecological Economics*. He is coauthor with theologian John Cobb of *For the Common Good* (Beacon Press, 1991). His latest book, *Beyond Growth: The Economics of Sustainable Development*, was published by Beacon Press in 1996.

Richard Dodd is a manager in AT Kearney's London office, where he works closely with international organizations on major business challenges. Prior to joining AT Kearney, he worked for three years with Arthur D. Little in Brussels, Belgium, where he helped European companies with environmental strategy and management assignments. He has also worked extensively in environmental policy and economics with national governments and the European Commission.

R. Edward Freeman is Elis and Signe Olsson Professor of Business Administration and director of the Olsson Center for Applied Ethics at the Darden Graduate School of Business Administration at the University of Virginia, and professor of religious studies. His books include *Strategic Management: A Stakeholder Approach, Ethics and Agency Theory* (with N. Bowie), *Business Ethics: The State of the Art*, and *Corporate Strategy and the Search for Ethics* (with D. Gilbert Jr.).

Eric T. Freyfogle is the Max L. Rowe Professor of Law at the University of Illinois at Urbana-Champaign. He is the author of *Justice and the Earth: Images for our Planetary Survival* (Free Press, 1993) and more than three dozen scholarly and popular articles on property ownership, natural resources law, and environmental law and policy. A native of central Illinois, he has long been active in state and local environmental organizations.

Robert Goodland is the environmental advisor to the World Bank. He has written extensively on environmental issues, especially in developing countries.

Michael E. Gorman is an associate professor in the Division of Technology, Culture, and Communications at the University of Virginia, where he teaches about technology and ethics, communications, and the psychology of invention and discovery. His research interests include experimental simulations of scientific reasoning, described in his book *Simulating Science* (Indiana University Press, 1992) and case studies of ethics, invention, and discovery.

Andrea Larson is on the faculty at the University of Virginia's Darden Graduate School of Business Administration, teaching in the M.B.A. program and in executive education programs. Andrea's teaching and research focus is in the field of entrepreneurship, alliances and networks, and innovation. Her articles have appeared in leading academic journals including *The Journal of Business Venturing, Entrepreneurship Theory and Practice,* and *Administrative Science Quarterly.* Current work highlights entrepreneurial leadership and innovation in the area of ecologically and socially sustainable business models.

John Lemons is professor of biology in the Department of Life Sciences at the University of New England, Biddeford, Maine. He served as editor in chief of *The Environmental Professional,* the official journal of the National Association of Environmental Professionals (NAEP), from 1990 through 1995. Dr. Lemons has authored approximately one hundred articles and seven books on environmental problem solving, including *Sustainable Development: Science, Ethics and Public Policy* (Kluwer Academic Publishers, 1995) and *Scientific Uncertainty and Environmental Problem-Solving* (Blackwell Science, Inc., 1996).

Don Mayer has been at Oakland University since 1990, primarily teaching legal environment of business, international business law, and business ethics. After graduating from Duke Law School in 1973, he served in the U.S. Air Force as an attorney for the judge advocate general's office, practiced law in Asheville, North Carolina, attended Georgetown University Law Center for an advanced degree in international law, and began teaching at the School of Business at Western Carolina University in 1985. His interest in environmental matters dates back to 1984, when a client asked advice on establishing a nuclear waste facility on an island in the Philippine archipelago.

William A. McDonough, F.A.I.A., authored "The Hannover Principles: Design for Sustainability" for the city of Hannover in preparation for the World's Fair 2000. He has established the Institute for Sustainable Design at the University of Virginia, where he is dean of the School of Architecture. As principal of William McDonough + Partners, he brings architecture and planning design to a wide range of projects worldwide. He is cofounder of McDonough Braungart Design Chemistry, a product design and development firm that partners with industry to design materials and systems for sustainability.

Matthew Mehalik is a doctoral student in the Department of Engineering and at the Darden School, University of Virginia, and the author of several case studies on environmentally sustainable design.

Ernest Partridge is currently research associate in the Department of Philosophy, University of California at Riverside. His areas of interest include environmental ethics, policy analysis, moral philosophy, and applied ethics, with a particular interest in the issue of the responsibility to future generations. In recent and continuing visits to Russia, Dr. Partridge has established productive and ongoing communication and cooperation with international scholars and scientists involved in global environmental issues. He is editor of the anthology *Responsibilities to Future Generations*.

Jessica Pierce works as a bioethicist at the University of Nebraska Medical Center. The central focus of her work is on connections between health and the environment, particularly the relationship between the delivery of health care in the United States and global ecological trends such as global warming and resource scarcity. In addition to research and writing in the area of environmental and medical ethics, she is active in promoting environmental programs at the Medical Center and other Omaha area hospitals.

William E. Rees is currently professor and director of the University of British Columbia's School of Community and Regional Planning. Dr. Rees researches the public policy implications of global environmental trends from the perspective of ecological economics and human carrying capacity. He originated the "ecological footprint" concept, which generates area-based estimates of both the natural capital requirements of the economy and of humanity's ecological deficit.

Joel Reichart is a doctoral candidate in business ethics at the Darden School, University of Virginia. His previous publications have appeared in *Business Ethics Quarterly* and *Perspectives on Ecological Integrity*. His research interests include rational choice theory, the ethics of sustainable development, and the conjunction of environmental and business ethics.

Sandra B. Rosenthal is professor of philosophy at Loyola University of New Orleans. In addition to more than one hundred fifty articles relating to American pragmatism, she has authored or coauthored nine books in the area. She is a member of the editorial board of numerous journals and book series, and has served as president of several major philosophical societies.

Mark Sagoff is senior research scholar at the Institute for Philosophy and Public Policy at the University of Maryland. He has published extensively in journals of philosophy, law, and public policy. He is the author of *The Economy of the Earth: Philosophy, Law and the Environment*.

Julian L. Simon was professor of business administration at the University of Maryland, College Park, and the author of *The Ultimate Resource* and *Population and Development in Poor Countries*, among other books, and coeditor, with Herman Kahn, of *The Resourceful Earth: A Response to the Global 2000 Report.*

Scott Sonenshein is a fourth-year undergraduate at the University of Virginia pursuing a distinguished major degree in business ethics. He has published case studies covering engineering, environmental, and business ethics for rural solar electrification in the development world and is now researching the effects of the introduction of technology on gender roles and social inequalities in South Africa.

Wendy Warren is a graduate student in urban and environmental planning in the School of Architecture at the University of Virginia. She received her B.A. in urban affairs with a minor in music from Virginia Polytechnic Institute and State University. Her research interests include environmental planning, policy analysis, and case studies of sustainable ethics and designs. She has also coauthored with Andrea Larson a technical note on The Natural Step.

Patricia H. Werhane is the Ruffin Professor of Business Ethics at the Darden School, Graduate School of Business Administration, University of Virginia. Her books include *Ethical Issues in Business,* edited with Tom Donaldson, and *Adam Smith and His Legacy for Modern Capitalism.* She is editor in chief of *Business Ethics Quarterly* and is on the editorial board of the *Journal of Business Ethics.*

Laura Westra is professor of philosophy at the University of Windsor and the secretary of the International Society for Environmental Ethics. Her publications include *An Environmental Proposal for Ethics: The Principle of Integrity* and *Living in Integrity.* Coedited books include *Faces of Environmental Racism, The Greeks and the Environment, Technology and Values, Perspectives on Ecological Integrity,* and *Ecological Sustainability and Integrity: Concepts and Approaches.* She has published about sixty articles in such journals as *Environmental Ethics, Environmental Values,* and *Global Bioethics.*